Please remember that t͟ P9-CEM-031
and that it belongs only t͟emporarily to each
person who uses it. Be considerate. Do
not write in this, or any, library book.

Regulating the Lives of Women
(Revised Edition)

WITHDRAWN

Praise for *Regulating the Lives of Women*

"...especially welcome during a period of growing inequalities between rich and poor and partisan efforts to decrease the size and scope of entitlement programs. Along with historical and legislative analyses of income security policies and data on their scope and usage, Abramovitz provides an alternative perspective that focuses on decreasing poverty and exploitation and overcoming gender, race, and class inequalities."
—Roberta Spalter-Roth, Institute for Women's Policy Research

"This new edition deepens, enlarges, and updates the sweep of our understanding at a time when the rights of poor women are more imperiled than ever."
—Rickie Solinger, *Wake Up Little Susie: Single Pregnancy and Race Before Roe vs. Wade*

"A brilliant work. It is refreshing to have a feminist perspective that does not ignore the existence of women of color or leave them at the margins of concern."
—Hubie Jones, Special Assistant to the Chancellor for Urban Affairs, U-Mass, Boston

"Abramovitz's coherent history of women and welfare and her illuminating analysis of the current attack on welfare programs is a major contribution to understanding the dynamics of welfare, gender and race in America. Activists need this book as well as scholars, as we begin re-envisioning and rebuilding social welfare policies that work for women.
—Martha F. Davis, *Brutal Need: Lawyers and the Welfare Rights Movement*

"This book should be required reading for anyone interested in the history of the welfare state."
—Betty Reid Mandell, *New Politics*

"[Mimi Abramovitz] has turned out a book filled with fascinating and useful facts and insights. In bringing together and making sound theoretical use of such a wealth of hitherto scattered information, she has done a great service to the cause of women and social welfare reform."
—Winifred Bell, *Journal of Teaching in Social Work*

158661

VC Lib

Regulating the Lives of Women

Social Welfare Policy from
Colonial Times to the Present
(Revised Edition)

WITHDRAWN

Mimi Abramovitz

South End Press   Boston, MA

Copyright © 1996 by Mimi Abramovitz
First edition originally printed by South End Press in 1988

Any properly footnoted quotation of up to 500 sequential words may be used without permission, as long as the total number of words quoted does not exceed 2,000. For longer quotations or for a greater number of total words, please write for permission to South End Press.
Text design and production by the South End Press collective
Cover design by Deborah Blau

REVISED EDITION

Library of Congress Cataloging-in-Publication Data

Abramovitz, Mimi
Regulating the Lives of Women:social welfare policy from colonial times to the present/Mimi Abramovitz
p. cm.
Includes index.
ISBN 0-89608-551-1: $22.00 (pbk)
ISBN 0-89608-552-x: $40.00 (cloth)

1. Women, Poor—United States—History. 2. Public Welfare—United States—History. 3. Family social work—United States—History. 4. Social Security—United States—History. I. Title.
HV699.A424 1996   96-9172
362.8'3'0973—dc20   CIP

South End Press, 7 Brookline St., Cambridge MA 02139

02 01 00 99 98   3 4 5 6 7

Dedicated to my mother, Lillian Gruber, 1912-1967
a woman ahead of her time

Please remember that this is a library book,
and that it belongs only temporarily to each
person who uses it. Be considerate. Do
not write in this, or any, library book.

Contents

Acknowledgments

Writing a book is both an independent endeavor *and* a product of all that has come before. The values given me by my family, friends, and education clearly influenced the questions that I've asked. The social movements I participated in—Civil Rights, anti-war, and Women's Liberation—all played an enormous role in shaping my worldview.

The subjectivity and isolation involved in writing means that the advice and support of others is crucial. Many colleagues contributed to the development of this book. Harold Lewis, Miriam Dinerman, Dorothy O. Helly, Dorothy Miller, Joel Blau, and Jan Hagan read extensive portions of the manuscript and discussed it with me in depth. Their comments were invaluable in helping me to clarify, modify, develop, and present my ideas. The critiques and perceptive responses offered by Joan Tronto, Barbara Cristy, Sylvia Wenston, and Jo Grellong immensely improved specific chapters. In particular, I want to thank Clarke C. Chambers. The extra time, the attention to detail, the long singlespaced typed letters, and the many drafts he read added enormously to the depth, breadth, and historical accuracy of the book. I shamelessly took advantage of his love for American social welfare history. His enthusiastic encouragement validated my efforts and gave me the courage to proceed.

My intellectual debt to Frances Fox Piven and Richard A. Cloward, authors of *Regulating the Poor: The Functions of Public Welfare,* is acknowledged in the title of the book. As one of the first in my social work education to offer an analytic framework for understanding the origins and functions of public welfare, *Regulating the Poor* suggested the possibility of having a way to think about the welfare state. While my ideas, like the authors' own, have developed since then, the impact of that important work has remained.

Hunter College School of Social Work, where I worked while writing this book, offered a supportive environment. Donna Shalala, President of Hunter College, created an atmosphere in which feminists might thrive. Harold Lewis, Dean of the School of Social Work, regularly encouraged me to pursue my ideas and not to avoid risks. The faculty

Committee on Women's Issues in the Curriculum reinforced the excitement of discovering and teaching about women's lives. Tom Jennings, Head Librarian and the rest of the Social Work Library staff brought relevant materials to my attention and made sure that I had the books that I needed. Students who enrolled in my course on women and social welfare policy provided important feedback on many aspects of the book. Their penetrating questions, willingness to share personal experiences, and creative papers regularly challenged my thinking and helped to keep me going when, after several years of writing, the material felt less fresh to me, but obviously not to them.

The professional forums provided by conferences held by National Association of Social Workers, The Council of Social Work Education, The Society for the Study of Social Problems, and by the professional journals including *Social Work, Social Service Review,* and the *Journal of Social Work Education* were another important source of input and exchange.

Cynthia Peters, the editor of this book, and the other people at South End Press deserve special thanks for tolerating my numerous questions and even more numerous last minute editorial changes. Cynthia's careful reading of the manuscript, her ability to edit my writing while maintaining respect for my ideas, and her overall commitment to the book improved it at every turn.

The patience and good will of my friends and particularly their insistence that I stop and play during the most tedious moments was more than sustaining, it was essential. Ruth Sidel, Susan Schacher, Carol Baker, and Sam, May and Lisa Gruber provided a valuable support, helping me to believe in the book and to trust that others would find it meaningful. But most profoundly, I appreciate the fundamental patience, love, and support given to me by my husband, Bob. While he rarely liked the time that writing the book absorbed, he always was there when I needed him. The intellectual help he gave me along the way and the pleasure he took in the book's development will always have deep meaning for me.

Preface

Much has happened since the first edition of *Regulating the Lives of Women* was published in 1988. When I was writing this book in the mid-1980s, the effect of deindustrialization, globalization, and downsizing; the rightward shift in the political climate, and the mounting attack on the welfare state that have become so familiar were just becoming visible. Unfortunately, since then the American public has felt the full impact of the austerity-driven economic recovery plan that the Reagan administration launched in 1981.

Reaganomics, which was further elaborated by Presidents Bush and Clinton, called for redistributing income upwards from the have-nots to the haves, cheapening the cost of labor, shrinking the welfare state, and weakening the influence of popular movements. To implement this pro-business agenda, the Reagan administration, knowingly created a huge deficit by increasing military spending (although the United States was not at war) and refusing to collect taxes the nation needed to pay its bills. It then used the gap between revenues and expenditures to justify cutting social programs. Instead of opposing this, the New Democrats signaled their support for a smaller federal government and a weaker welfare state by rejecting their party's New Deal and Great Society heritages. The 1994 Republican Contract with America upped the ante by announcing plans to severely limit the role of the federal government so that private enterprise could reign fully and without regulation or restraint.

Meanwhile, the conservatives made "family values" a household word. The Republican Party opposed women's right to abortion, Dan Quayle attacked Murphy Brown—a middle-class TV character who decided to become a single mother—and Charles Murray declared that "illegitimacy" was the nation's number one social problem. Unlike the laissez-faire or economic conservatives who call for less government intervention in the economy, these social conservatives did not hesitate to use state power to impose their agenda—no abortions, no divorce, no immigrants, no affirmative action, no labor laws, no social welfare programs—on everyone else.

Rather than devise new solutions to the nation's underlying social and economic problems, since the early 1980s, the nation's leaders have attacked the average family's standard of living, a wide range of social programs, and the ability of social movements to fight back. The income gap between the rich and the poor has reached record highs, the purchasing power of the average wage has fallen sharply, and the major social movements—labor, civil rights, and women—are on the defensive. The resulting economic insecurity became a breeding ground for a backlash against these groups and immigrants, as well as the entitlement programs serving both the middle class and the poor. The conservative campaign has taken its toll.

The revised edition of *Regulating the Lives of Women* updates the story of women and social welfare to reflect current data, recent trends, and the intensified assault on the programs analyzed in the first edition of the book: Social Security, Unemployment Insurance, and Aid To Families With Dependent Children (AFDC). Also known as "entitlements," these programs represent a governmental commitment to people in need: retirees, jobless workers, and destitute single mothers. Not only have these programs suffered the backlash that developed since 1988, but they have also been its major target for at least three reasons. First, to cheapen the cost of labor it is necessary to press market wages down. Since income support programs provide an alternative to wages, they must be kept below the lowest prevailing wage. Second, as an alternative source of income, these entitlement programs provide women with a way out of abusive relationships and all workers with the wherewithal to avoid exploitative jobs. Thus, they threaten both male domination and business profits. Third, attacking entitlements and other social welfare programs offers a convenient scapegoat for the structural causes of the sagging economy and mounting social problems; if these reasons were fully understood by the wider public, it might turn against business and the state.

Completely rewritten, the last two chapters pick up where the original edition left off. The history and analysis of women and welfare that I laid out before the passage of the 1988 Family Support Act remains valid and relevant today, especially the discussion of the family ethic embedded in social welfare policy, or what now is called, "family values." Indeed, my original argument that social program's came under attack, in part, because they increasingly failed to uphold the work and family ethics turns out to be even more valid than it was before. Since then, the effort to use social policy to enforce the idealized version of women's roles; to maintain a double standard of womanhood; to reward and punish women based on their race, class, and marital status; to reconcile the competing demands for women's low-paid market and unpaid domestic work; and to accommodate other labor market needs has become both stronger and more mean-spirited. Moreover, it also became clear that the attack on AFDC was but the opening round in a wider attack on the entire welfare state.

While I have been very pleased with the widespread interest in the first edition of this book in the fields of social work, U.S. history, sociology, and women's studies, among others, given the changes in the economy and government, I have received many requests for an update. I also wanted to bring new data and analyses to bear on what has happened to all three income support programs since the mid-1980s and to present an alternative interpretation to the current mainstream view that a "culture of entitlements" discourages work and marriage, promotes dependence, and encourages people to challenge authority.

The newly revised chapters discuss how women fared when Congress legislated both cuts and controversial changes in the Social Security, Unemployment Insurance, and AFDC programs. However, most of the attention is focused on AFDC because this book is about regulating women's lives, and, more than the other programs, women turn to AFDC when they need support. In addition, the current efforts to cut social programs began with and made most headway with AFDC, which as a program just for poor single mothers, has always won less political support than the other two programs, which serve the middle class as well as the poor. Finally, although they too have lost ground, to date the Social Security and Unemployment Insurance programs have suffered fewer major changes. However, this may change sooner than we think, given the current drive to build public support for privatizing or otherwise "reforming" them.

Both editions of this book were written during heated debates over welfare and published just before Congress agreed on a final bill. The first edition was completed just before Congress passed the 1988 Family Support Act, which transformed AFDC from a program to help poor single mothers stay home with their children into a mandatory work program. Since the Family Support Act had culminated two decades of efforts to change welfare, it took most of us by surprise when, in 1992, the issue of welfare reappeared on the national political agenda, before the true impact of the 1988 law could be determined. By 1994, it was apparent that the renewed welfare reform drive had less to do with the well-being of poor women and children and more to do with winning votes. The AFDC attack became the leading edge of the backlash against society-wide changes in family structures, the launching pad for the ensuing assault on the entire welfare state, and a key to the effort to discredit the role of the federal government. Politicians also used "welfare reform" to inflame the divisive politics of hate.

The second edition of *Regulating the Lives of Women* was completed before the even more heated debate over welfare resulted in new legislation. Nonetheless, when I was writing the update, it was all too clear what elected officials had in store for poor women. Many governors and state legislatures had already implemented highly punitive welfare reforms designed to modify the behavior of women on welfare. Likewise, while the Democratic Party, the Republican Party, and the National Governor's Association had each proposed to use the strong arm of government to control the work and family life of poor women. These plans received considerable support from the White House and from Congress. Senators and Representatives from both sides of the aisle also endorsed the Republican plan to strip AFDC and other social programs of their entitlement status by converting them into state-administered block grants. The move toward block grants will increase the power of the states over social welfare programs, reduce their accountability, and severely limit the funds available for AFDC. Block grants take us back to the future: they return public assistance programs to the way they were run before the 1935 Social Security Act federalized them and will force opponents of welfare reform to engage in battles in fifty different states.

The new Conclusion of *Regulating the Lives of Women* updates the discussion of the kinds of changes needed to improve the lives of poor women and to make society more just. The brief overview of the mounting fight made by poor women and their supporters against the attack on welfare refutes the idea, promoted by some, that women are passive and apolitical and that resistance and advocacy are dead. While the drive to weaken social movements has certainly placed them on the defensive and made their work much harder, their endurance reminds us that injustice has always politicized some people, fueled social protests, and promoted social change. The re-emergence of a welfare rights movement and the support given it by middle-class women's organizations has been particularly inspiring. This growing activism and my participation in it has kept me going, despite today's hard times and the long road ahead. It has taught me the benefits of having a long-term perspective and the wisdom of Margaret Mead, the well-known anthropologist, who once said, "Never doubt for a single moment that a small group of people can change the world. Indeed, that has been the only way."

Introduction

In 1993, women headed 24 percent of the nation's 36 million families with children, but 53 percent of all poor families with children, a sharp increase from 1960 when 9 percent of the families with children and 28 percent of poor families were headed by a woman.[1] The characterization of this change as the "feminization of poverty" implies that poverty has only recently become a women's issue. History, however, suggests otherwise. indeed, women's impoverishment dates back to colonial America when from one-third to one-half of a town's poor were likely to be female. Despite the historic povertization of women and their ever-rising numbers among social welfare clients and workers, the relationship between American women and the welfare state remains relatively unexplored. The result is an understanding of the welfare state that is grounded in the experience of male recipients and generalized to women as if there were no differences between them; at best it is incomplete, at worst quite distorted.

The lack of attention to poor women in the social welfare literature reflects several things including a preoccupation with the work ethic, an acceptance of the nuclear family as the only viable family unit, and minimal research interest in the well-being of poor women. From the start, social welfare policy has been shaped by the work ethic and the belief that the provision of benefits to able-bodied persons will weaken their motivation to work. As a result, the cash assistance programs including Social Security benefits, Unemployment Insurance, and Aid To Families with Dependent Children (AFDC) enforce the work ethic either by rewarding higher paid workers over those who earn less or by encouraging able-bodied persons to choose paid labor (no matter what the wage levels or working conditions) over government aid. Such policies have kept the labor market supplied with men who are expected to work productively and provide for their families. This portrayal of social welfare policy highlights the problems of male recipients of aid, but it only partially explains, and in fact obscures, the

1

plight of female recipients. They are, after all, the guardians of the domestic sphere, even when they work. If social welfare policy conveys to men the message that they belong in the labor market regardless of prevailing wages and working conditions, it tells women that their primary place is marriage and the home, regardless of *its* safety or security. Work by women tends to go unrewarded, by social programs and frequently it becomes a "punishment" for those who have strayed outside the bounds of "femininity."

Social welfare policy's preoccupation with the nuclear family unit featuring a male breadwinner and an economically dependent female homemaker, reveals the presence of a strong "family ethic"—one that has had a profound influence over the relationship between women and the welfare state. Despite the continued presence of many types of families, social welfare programs have consistently favored the conventional family model that uncritically freezes women and men into rigid gender roles. The rules and regulations of social welfare programs benefit those who live in traditional family structures while penalizing alternative family forms where poor women and women of color tend to predominate. Indeed, as historian Elizabeth Fox-Genovese reminds us, the very model of the family that we now take for granted resulted "directly from the determination of early modern state-builders to provide themselves with the most governable population possible."[1] Rulers have viewed the family as the basis of social cohesion and order in society, the transmitter and reproducer of accepted values and traditions, and the instigator of basic loyalties.

Finally, social welfare scholars from various disciplines have paid little attention to the lives of poor women. Their work frequently lacked gender distinctions and thus excluded the particular experience of the majority of social welfare clients and workers who were female. But even as social science began to focus on women, the voices of poor women and women of color remained unheard. The attention devoted to the lives of working-, middle-, and upper-class women, women of reknown, and the female relatives of famous men, largely ignored the record of poor women, immigrant women, and women of color. Of the scholars who have begun to investigate the lives of poor women, only a few have made the relationship between poor women and the welfare state their target of study. To fill this gap, to deepen our knowledge of the social welfare system, and to make its programs more responsive to women, we need to apply a "gender-lens" to the welfare state. That is, we need to ask questions that bring women into view. To this end, I will focus on a new concept that plays a critical but unexplored role in shaping the relationship between women and the welfare state: the family ethic.

As a dominant social norm, the family ethic articulates the terms of women's work and family roles. According to its rules, proper women marry and have children while being supported by and subordinated to a male breadwinner. Even through major transformations in the political economy, the family ethic has persisted. In colonial America, for example, women's role in the home was expected to be an economically productive one. Since the industrial revolution, however, the family ethic geared the female homemaker's duties toward consuming (rather than producing), maintaining the health and well-being of family members, socializing children to their proper adult roles, caring for the sick and aged, and overseeing the maintenance of the household. Despite changes in the definition of women's economic role, the family ethic has, throughout history, placed women in the home, subordinate to men. It has made them the guardians of family and community morality, expected them to remain pious and chaste and to tame male sexuality, and defined them as weak and in need of male protection and control.

Using the family ethic to re-examine the welfare state has uncovered those assumptions about women's proper roles that are buried in social welfare policies and has revealed how compliance with the family ethic became the basis for distinguishing between deserving and undeserving women. Within a paradigm based on the work ethic and without a gender-lens, social welfare scholars have not been able to locate women's place in the social welfare system with any precision. Why, for example, are widows with young children considered to be among those "deserving" of aid, while other single mothers are treated harshly? How can we explain the long history of channeling destitute mothers into the labor market even though the family ethic supposedly requires them to stay at home? Why do universal programs serving the middle class as well as the poor, such as Social Security, favor married over single persons, homemakers over working wives, and one-earner over two-earner couples? Why do Unemployment Insurance policies make it difficult for women to combine work and family responsibilities?

Since the colonial times, social welfare policies have treated women differently based on the extent to which their lives conformed to the terms of the family ethic. In each historical period, married women, previously married women, or those whose breadwinners provided adequate support received better treatment under social welfare policies than single women, unwed mothers, and women whose breadwinners could not provide enough. Likewise, the rules of social programs have favored full-time homemakers over working wives. In brief, such programs have tended to reward women whose lives include marriage, motherhood, and homemaking but to penalize women who did not or could not choose such pursuits. Denied the "rights of womanhood," this latter group could not expect protection or respectability and instead faced social stigma, economic insecurity, and such penalties as mandatory work requirements, child removal, and strict government supervision of their parenting, sexual, and social life.

The differential impact of welfare state policies on women by class, race, and marital status adversely affected many women but meshed with the needs of the political economy. By setting a strict standard which judged women as "deserving" or "undeserving," the welfare state has upheld a certain view of women's roles and has simultaneously helped to meet the economy's need for women's unpaid labor in the home and their low-paid labor in the market.

Neither the ideology of women's roles nor the social welfare system are static nor do they operate in isolation. Both are part of and reflect changes in the wider social order. Indeed, the structure and content of the book seeks to capture the dynamics of the relationship between ideology (the family ethic), the welfare state, and the changing political economy from the colonial poor laws to the 1935 Social Security Act to Reaganomics. Chapter One, "Towards a Feminist Theory of the Welfare State," presents the conceptual and theoretical frameworks that inform the book. It summarizes the view of the welfare state articulated by classical liberalism and traditional marxism, traces the development of feminist thinking on the welfare state from its roots in these political theories, and suggests that socialist-feminism is most adaptable for a discussion of the welfare state given its analysis of gender and the dynamics of the overall political economy. The long untold story of the female pauper begins with Chapters Two and Three which focus on colonial America. Chapter Two describes how colonial leaders recruited white wives, white indentured servants, and black female slaves to the New World once they realized that commercial profits and economic development depended on the creation of families, a permanent labor force, and stable communities. This chapter also details the colonial family ethic that governed a woman's work and family life and how its impact varied with her race, class, and marital status. Chapter Three, describes the povertization of colonial women, the colonial view of poverty, and the ways in which the codification of the family ethic in colonial poor laws, family law, and slave codes operated to regulate women's productive and reproductive labor.

The next two chapters move into the nineteenth century to discuss the impact of the rise of industrial capitalism on both the family ethic and laws affecting the poor. Chapter Four examines how the rise of a market economy, which separated home and market production, fostered the decline of the colonial family ethic and paved the way for a new one more suited to the times. This chapter details the terms of the industrial family ethic, its justification of the new gender division of labor which assigned men to the market and women to the home, and its differential impact on white middle-class and white working-class women, and black female slaves. Chapter Five shows that the weaknesses of the colonial poor laws and their growing inability to serve the changing needs of the rapidly developing market economy paved the way for poor law "reform." The resulting redefinition and less tolerant view of poverty, the attack on outdoor relief, the rise of institutions, the removal of children from the home, and the activities of private charity organizations are examined for their impact on women's work and family life.

Chapter Six brings us into the twentieth century and analyzes the emergence of the Mothers' Pension program and Protective Labor Laws. The failures of earlier poor law reform, that is, the rapid deterioration of instititional care for orphaned children, the mentally ill and criminals, the restriction of public aid, and the unwillingess of private charities to provide financial assistance weakened the nineteenth-century social welfare system and introduced the need for a more active state. The growth of a wage-labor force dependent on an unstable market for its economic security and the increased labor force participation by women, both of which undermined patriarchal structures in the market and at home, further necessitated state intervention. Protective Labor Laws, which regulated the labor force participation of young women, and the Mothers' Pension program, which enabled mothers to remain at home and care for their children, enforced the family ethic. These laws reflected new ways of mediating the conflicting demand for women's home and market work and also marked a shift in the source of patriarchal authority from the male head-of-household (private or familial patriarchy) to the state (public or social patriarchy). Chapter Seven describes the changes in the political economy that paved the way to the Depression of the thirties and that gave rise to the 1935 Social Security Act. This landmark legislation, usually considered an effort to correct market dislocations and to control political unrest, must also be understaood as a response to the strong sense that the family system was in crisis. The Social Security Act included the major cash assistance programs discussed in this book, the Social Security Retirement program, Unemployment Insurance, and the Aid to Families With Dependent Children. The passage of the Act legitimized the Federal govemment's role in social welfare, gave birth to the modem welfare state, and institutionalized social patriarchy and the family ethic. Chapter Eight traces the various impacts of the family ethic in the Social Security retirement program from 1935 to 1980. Chapter Nine does the same for Unemployment Insurance, while Chapter Ten examines the development of the more controversial AFDC program. Chapter Eleven, takes us into the 1980s and the 1990s when, once again, economic dislocation has revived strident efforts to "reform" the welfare state.

The historical approach used in this book reflects my own fascination with history. History offers a view of events and their context not otherwise available, one that both informs and corrects our perceptions. In this case, we discover, for example, that neither women's impoverishment nor its causes are very new. The glance backwards also reveals a long history of social welfare "cutbacks." Like today, most of the assaults on the social welfare system, particularly those in the 1820s, 1870s, and 1950s accompanied major changes in the political economy and fell heavily on women who have always been highly represented, if not over-represented, among those receiving such benefits. Even "workfare" programs, which force women to work for wages outside the home as a condition of receiving public aid, have a long record. Only the means of channeling women into the low paid labor force have varied, shifting from strict eligibility rules that disqualified all but the most "deserving" poor women to closing programs down to the current reliance on voluntary and mandatory work requirements.

It is increasingly clear that the time has come to reconceptualize the dynamics of the U.S. social welfare system from the perspective of gender, race, and class. The analysis presented here represents a synthesis of several strands of scholarship. it draws on the published work of social welfare historians, feminist historians, women's studies scholars, and some primary sources to re-interpret social welfare history using a gender-lens. Reliance on secondary sources entails some problems, however. It limits the researcher to the materials, interests, biases, and research skills of previous scholars. in the case of social welfare history, this results in an urban if not a northeastern bias. Most social welfare histories reflect life as it developed in major Eastern seaboard cities. These areas contain more accessible records, but their predominance in the literature creates a distorted view; until the twentieth century the United States was a nation of mostly rural people. The condensation of long centuries into single chapters is another limitation of this book. Broad sweeping descriptions of major trends sacrifice detail and complexity and may result in omissions and some distortions.

The focus on women may also be seen as paying too little attention to the experiences of children. The differential treatment of women and children in no way minimizes the impoverishment of children, which is historically parallel to women's. Rather, it seeks to compensate for the long standing practice of studying about and planning for families or children without ever mentioning the female caretaker. This book's focus on women, I hope, will benefit children as well, since the two groups remain inextricably linked.

A strong effort was made to incorporate the experience of black women which is frequently missing from, or only briefly mentioned in, social welfare literature and historical accounts of women. Black women who first arrived in America in the early seventeenth century as indentured servants and slaves are the only women of color included in this book for several reasons. First, next to white women, black women were the second largest group affected by social welfare policies during the long period covered by the book. Second, however sparse information about the lives of poor black women and their experience with the social welfare system may be, it is more abundant than that of other women of color. Finally, it is likely that the response of the welfare state to black women paralleled its treatment of other women of color, despite the important cultural differences among them. Nonetheless, an examination of primary sources for information about the social welfare system's treatment of Native American, Hispanic, Asian-American, as well as black women is sorely needed.

The Family Ethic Today

The family ethic appears to be under assault once again. This time, it is the feminization of the labor force, reduced marriage opportunities for many women, no-fault divorce, single-parenthood, childless couples, alternative methods of conception, and the struggles for lesbian and gay rights which threaten the ideology of women's roles. Almost universally, the ever-increasing demand for married women and young mothers in the labor market has led to a widespread acceptance of women's work outside the home.

These challenges to the ideological *status quo* have engendered at least two mainstream policy responses: one attempts to restore while the other hopes to reformulate the family ethic; neither, however, threatens its central premise. Rather, each strategy perpetuates the terms of the family ethic to the extent that it accepts female economic dependence on men, the sex segregation of the labor market, and the gender division of society, or otherwise supports the conditions that underpin female subordination in both the public and private sphere. The "pro-family" platforms of the New Right, the Moral Majority, and the Reagan administration, the rise of religious fundamentalism, the moralistic response to AIDS, the media spotlight on research telling single women over thirty that marriage is out of their reach, and the amount of media attention given to professional women who have interupted their careers to return home are just a few of the better known attempts to focus women exclusively on marriage and family rather than work and other independent pursuits.

The liberal program, in contrast, seeks to reform the family ethic so that women will be better able to manage their work and family responsibilities. It accepts women's paid labor but encourages the idea of "supermom." It supports pay equity ("comparable worth"), corporate day care, and other workplace reforms such as flextime, paid maternity leave, child care leave, and laws preventing discrimination against pregnant women, all of which usefully take into account the pressures faced by working parents. Many of these proposed reforms help mothers and wives to stay at work without having to give up their role at home, and as such they still reflect the idea that domestic responsibilites are women's. Liberals may believe that women should be "supermoms" who can do and have "it all" but they make no similar requirement of working men. Indeed, recent research reports that most husbands of employed wives do not increase their share of housework very much, if at all. Some of the terms of the family ethic are undergoing change to match new social and economic trends, but its core—a gender division of labor that assigns only women to caretaking roles in the home—does not appear to be in serious jeopardy.

Reflecting changing conditions, the most current version of the family ethic holds women exclusively responsible for the home even when they work outside. This view of women's "place" is still functional to the wider social order, serving the interrelated goals of lowering production costs and supporting male domination of women both at work and at home. The age-old belief that assigns childrearing and homemaking responsibilities to women no longer keeps women out of the labor force, but it continues to justify their unequal treatment on the job, sustaining the market supply of low-cost labor and its patriarchal hierarchies. If, in the past, female poverty and dependency on men derived from the exclusion of all but poor women from the labor force, today female poverty and economic dependency persist *despite* women's entry into the labor force. The family ethic which previously justified the exclusion of white middle-class women from the labor market is now invoked to support the sex-segregation of the labor market and other arrangements that reduce the value and status of women's waged labor. Women still receive less pay than men for comparable work and continue to be relegated to low-status, women's jobs. The resulting economic insecurity helps to keep women tied to marriage, the family, and financially, if not emotionally, dependent on men. The process is circular for the idea that women belong in the home in turn rationalizes the conditions producing the low economic status that keeps them there.

The critique of the family ethic is not meant to devalue the experience of sharing one's life with a partner or that of bearing, raising, and loving children. Rather it suggests that institutionally enforced rules of family organization do not necessarily enhance family life and they frequently disadvantage women. To the extent that the family ethic endorses laws and customs that treat women and children as male property, idealizes marriage and motherhood while devaluing women at home and on the job, and permits societal institutions to view non-nuclear families as deviant and unworthy, the family ethic supports conditions that promote female oppression, discriminate against many families, and are destructive to healthy family life, a productive family system, and a humane family policy.

Social policy based on the traditional family ethic has served women poorly, failing to reflect their needs and those of their families. Instead, we need social welfare policies that reject the belief in the primacy of women's responsibility for the home and family while encoding a positive family ethic that recognizes equal rights and responsibilities within the family, and assures that the needs of all family members are satisfactorily met. Such a family policy would accept and respond to the needs of *all* families—single-parent, gay and lesbian, interracial families and communal families as well as the two-parent nuclear families. Policies reflecting this version of the family ethic would also enhance the autonomy and independence of women by strengthening women's position in the labor market and allocating greater resources to the caretaking role whoever carries it out. Unless the prevailing family ethic which devalues and degrades women is purged from all social policy, the historical record detailed in this book

as well as experiences in other nations suggests that even the best intended reforms reproduce the primacy of women's responsibility for
family and the home.

The paradoxical character of the welfare state makes it one arena
for such struggle. Although social welfare benefits support the interests
of capital and patriarchy—helping to lower the cost of reproducing and
maintaining the labor force and the non-working members of society
and to reinforce patriarchal norms—they also can strengthen the political and economic power of women, persons of color, workers, and the
poor. Indeed, welfare state benefits represent what the British refer to
as a social wage, that is, a source of income that enables people to survive while avoiding unsafe and insecure jobs as well as unsafe and insecure marriages. Thus, trade union, civil rights, women's, and poor
people's movements have struggled for years to secure welfare state
protections against the abuses of living and working in a capitalist
society and for a fairer share of the economic pie. More recently, as the
idea that biology is destiny loses its appeal, as large numbers of working women protest inequities on the job, as the already meager social
wage continues to shrink, as women begin to understand their poverty and continued economic dependency on either men or the state, the
struggle has increasingly focused on the ways in which the welfare state
mediates the conflicting demands for women's home and market work
and thus *regulates the lives of women.*

Notes to the Introduction

1. U.S. Bureau of the Census, Current Population Reports, Series P60-1988, Income, Poverty and Valuation of Non-Cash Benefits: 1993, U.S. Government Printing Office, Washington, D.C. 1995, p.22, T D-6.

2. Elizabeth Fox-Genovese, "Placing Women's History in History," *New Left Review,* No. 133 (May-June 1982), p. 19.

3. For a discussion of this dynamic in another country, see for example, Jennifer G. Schirmer, *The Limits of Reform: Women, Capital and Welfare* (Cambridge: Schenkman Publishing Company, Inc., 1982) which examines the impact of the Danish national program for social equality on the lives of women.

1

A Feminist Perspective on the Welfare State

Gender, like race and class, structures the organization of social life. Its study, only recently taken into account by students of the welfare state, is critical for it changes our perception of reality. Using a gender-lens uncovers previously ignored information, introduces new understandings of social interactions, and exposes how the construction of knowledge itself supports the *status quo*.[1] The two major political theories of modern times—liberalism and Marxism are gender-blind and uninformed by an understanding of patriarchy, and have consequently failed to explain women's experience. However, growing out of (and perhaps in spite of) these theories is a range of new and exciting feminist analyses which address women's oppression and begin to explore the relationship between women and the welfare state.

The first part of this chapter reviews the traditional political theories and the responses to them by liberal, radical, and socialist feminists. It gives special attention to the socialist-feminist perspective which informs this book. The second part the chapter moves from the theory of the welfare state to the ideology of women's roles, positing an important and largely unrecognized relationship between the two. It is argued that the ideology of women's roles, referred to here as the "family ethic," became encoded within the rules and regulations of the welfare state where it, along with the work ethic, has shaped public policy and regulated the lives of thousands of women who, from colonial times to the present, have turned to social welfare programs for support.

Traditional Political Theories: Liberalism and Marxism

Liberalism and Marxism are critical to our understanding of the political economy. Like other political theories, they analyze and explain regularly observed societal patterns. One such pattern, the role and function of the government or "the state," is especially relevant to social welfare policy which operates within and presumes the existence of the state. The following brief review of these two theories seeks to place the emerging feminist views of the welfare state into an historical and theoretical context. By no means does it capture the full complexity of each school of thought, do justice to the many important internal debates within each, or provide a major critique of them.

Liberalism

Classical liberalism[2] originated in seventeenth-century England, took root in the eighteenth century, and with the rise of industrial capitalism, became the dominant political theory of twentieth-century Western societies. Reflecting new views of human nature which placed selfishness, egoism, and individualistic self-interest at the center of the human psyche, liberalism held that the competitive pursuit of individual self-interest in a market free of government regulation would maximize personal and societal benefits. In *The Wealth of Nations* (1776),[3] Adam Smith described the market as an "invisible hand" impartially channelling naturally selfish motives of human beings into mutually consistent and complementary activities that would best promote the welfare of all. Smith's views were soon expanded into what became known as laissez-faire doctrine, the view that the market, rather than the state, should be the regulator of society.

The pressure to limit state power arose, in part, because the prevailing philosophy of more active government involvement, known as mercantilism, had begun to impede the development of the capitalist economy. Government subsidies, the granting of state charters and monopolies, the imposition of high tariffs, the seizing of overseas markets, and other interventionist practices which had usefully promoted trade and commerce now operated as a constraint. Earlier experiences with despotic monarchs and undemocratic parliaments also inspired opposition to state activism.

Laissez-faire doctrine restricted the responsibilities of the state without eliminating its regulatory role as protector of capital, property, and national security. The new doctrine defined legitimate state activity to include (a) securing the country against internal disorder and external threats; (b) protecting private property, enforcing contracts, and maintaining public institutions necessary for commerce but too costly for single firms to operate; (c) using naval and military power to control trade routes and develop an overseas empire; and (d) guaranteeing individuals freedom from undue interference and their right to be represented in government, to form associations, and to travel, speak, worship, and publish freely.

Liberalism also defined the state as the arbiter of societal conflict, a role that became necessary because the possibility of such conflict existed within the principles of liberalism itself. Indeed, one person's right to individual freedom might contradict another's, as might the maximization of individual self interest. To promote social cohesion, liberalism charged the state with setting and enforcing the general conditions governing social relations, establishing the means to reconcile various differences, and the methods for enforcing compliance. Classical liberalism, in effect, asked the state to do what the market could not do—to act as a neutral mediator, to reconcile competing interests on behalf of the common good.[4]

Liberty, was the political value that gave liberalism its name. But as it evolved, the complex and never singular political theory of liberalism also embraced the values of equality and justice, which were potentially competitive with the value of liberty. Departing radically from earlier political philosophies that accepted social hierarchies as natural and God-given, liberal theory opposed political institutions that treated individuals unequally by subordinating them to the will or judgment of another. Thus, it also charged the state with assuring formal or legal equality and with promoting justice, ie., the social distribution of economic benefits and obligations. Since nineteenth-century liberalism tolerated government regulation but discouraged direct state involvement in the political economy, the distribution of economic resources was left to the market. When it failed, these social welfare activities were picked up first by local and then state governments and private charitable agencies.

As liberalism evolved, the unregulated "liberty" of the twentieth century produced unequal access to economic resources and interfered with the individual's ability to maximize self-interest and to secure the liberty, equality, and justice that liberalism promised. As liberalism began to call for a broader state role in managing this and other problems, the nineteenth-century view of the "night watchman" or non-interventionist state became known as conservatism. Twentieth-century or contemporary liberalism, in turn, gradually accepted more government involvement on behalf of business, but also the working class and the poor. It began to justify limited state intervention to mitigate the worst effects of the market economy on business and industry and to provide a minimum standard of living for the poor. While the idea of state regulation, rather than direct intervention, remained a central feature of contemporary liberal thought, the shift toward a more active state became the ideological basis for the acceptance of state-provided social welfare benefits as a way to promote economic justice. According to liberal theory, the essence of the welfare state is government-protected minimum standards of income, nutrition, health, housing, and education assured to every individual as a political right, not as charity.[5] Viewing the rise of the welfare state in terms of collective responsibility, Richard Hofstadter, a liberal historian, stated that

> It has been the function of the liberal tradition in American politics...at first to broaden the numbers of those who could benefit from the great American bonanza and then to humanize its workings and help heal its casualties. Without [the] sustained tradition of opposition and protest and reform, the American system would have been, and in times and places it was, nothing but a jungle, and would probably have failed to develop into the remarkable system for production and distribution that it is.[6]

Marxist Political Theory

Marxists dispute liberalism's definition of the origins, functions, and political neutrality of the state. Marxist political theory views the state as pro-capital, not a neutral mediator of conflicts whose only interest is to allow all individuals their private pursuits. The state, according to Marxism, is the institution through which those with power rule; it helps to create the conditions necessary for the profitable accumulation of capital and for the legitimization of a social structure based on unequal social economic and political power relations. With the emergence of classes based on private ownership, the state was needed to maintain the power of the dominant class. Because the rule of the owning class was neither immutable nor self-maintaining, state power was necessary to protect it.[7] In addition to the use of force and repression, the modern state strengthens the dominance of the ruling group by creating the conditions necessary for profitable economic activity, citizen loyalty, and class harmony. James O' Connor, a Marxist economist, calls these economic and political activities of the state its accumulation and legitimization functions.[8] Although contemporary Marxists agree that the state serves capital, they debate whether it does so as a "handmaiden" taking instructions from the dominant class or as a "relatively autonomous" body that looks past the short-term interests of individual capitalists and their internal rivalries to act on behalf of the long-term interests of the capitalist class as a whole.[9]

In either case, and contrary to liberal theory, Marxists believe that the welfare state arose, not to cushion individuals against the worst excesses of the market economy, but to protect prevailing class and property relations. The state's accumulation and legitimization functions became necessary due to troublesome contradictions that Marxists define as built into the system of capitalist production. According to Marxist theory, the welfare state appeared when the imperatives of capitalist production contradicted the requirements of accumulation, stability, but also reproduction, creating problems that became too expensive, economically and politically, for individual capitalists to absorb.

The problems giving rise to the welfare state centered on what Marxists call, "the reproduction and maintenance of the labor force:" the need found in all societies to develop and maintain a healthy and productive labor supply that is properly socialized and readily available for work and to provide for the care of those who cannot support themselves. The incessant drive to accumulate capital necessary for the survival of capitalism, they say, intensified the processes of production in ways that often generated social unrest and interfered with the reproduction and maintenance of the labor force, including both the working class' ability to labor, procreate, properly socialize family members, and otherwise maintain itself and its non-working members.

According to British Marxist, Ian Gough,[10] the defining feature of the welfare state is "the use of state power to modify the reproduction of labor power (the capacity to perform labor) and to maintain the non-working population in capitalist societies."[11] The expansion of the welfare state, he says, shifted the costs of socializing and maintaining workers from private capital to the public sphere. These publicly-supported services are made available (a) through tax-supported programs of cash and in-kind assistance that enable families to purchase the food, housing, education, training, health care, and other services needed to bear and raise children and to prepare all family members for another day of productive labor; and (b) through publicly subsidized services that enforce patterns of thinking and behavior appropriate to the needs of a capitalist economy. These same welfare state programs maintain the non-working population by absorbing the costs of home or institutional care of those unable to support themselves due to old age, poor health, childcare responsibilities, or market dislocations. At times, the provision of these social welfare benefits operates as a concession in the face of mounting social unrest.

Building on Gough, James Dickinson,[12] a Marxist sociologist, argues that the welfare state became necessary to capital because the changing requirements of production gradually undermined the ability of the working class to carry out its reproductive and maintenance tasks. He argues that although capital accumulation depends on the supply and regeneration of labor in households, capitalism has not always generated the levels of wages and employment needed for the successful formation and maintenance of families. Instead, changes in the system of production designed to increase profits and labor productivity and to lower production costs frequently produced negative consequences that undercut the health, economic security, and general fitness of workers and their families. Low wages, illness, and unemployment, for example, not only deplete the ability of workers to labor, but historically have diminished the working class' ability to carry out its reproductive role in the home.[13] Influenced by the feminist thinking described below, which argues for attention to the family as well as the market, Dickinson's analysis suggests that the welfare state lowered the reproductive costs to capital by mediating tensions between family and the economy on behalf of capitalist reproduction.

Drawing on the British experience, Dickinson's description of the welfare state's evolution suggests a periodization that can be applied to the United States. In the pre-industrial United States, when both production and reproduction occurred within the home, the state, operating through colonial governments (there was no welfare state *per se*), helped to assure the formation of families, an adequate supply of labor, and the productivity of all community members. In the early nineteenth century, once industrialization separated household and market production, changing demands on the family and the development of an industrial labor force led the state to become more involved in enforcing ideas of proper family functioning and in disciplining the labor force. A century later, the negative consequences of capitalist development on labor productivity, and on the health, safety, and economic security of the working-class family combined with workers' demands for protection against abusive working conditions, to produce social legislation. Statutory protections such as Workers' Compensation, Protective Labor Laws, and Mothers' Pensions began to limit the over-exploitation of labor and to strengthen the reproductive capacity of the household. The modern welfare state emerged in the United States in 1935.The signing of the Social Security Act that year signaled acceptance of the idea that the state had to transfer at least some economic resources from households in surplus to those in deficit if the market's failure to provide enough income and jobs was not to become too disruptive to the smooth functioning of the political economy.

In contrast to liberal political theory which suggests that the welfare state represents collective responsibility and the public interest, Marxists argue that the welfare state arose to protect capital from the negative effects of the "class struggle." The class struggle is inherent to the capitalist system because, in the Marxist view, the structure of capitalism produces two opposing classes: a ruling class whose members own and control the means of production and a working class whose members, lacking such ownership, sell their labor power to capital in order to survive. Because profit depends on the owners' ability to exploit the workers, the interests of these two classes are in fundamental conflict. Members of the working class have collectively fought low wages, unemployment, occupational illness, and other negative consequences of capitalist production. Their unions, strikes, political candidates, and street protests represent a potential challenge to prevailing property relations that capital wants to preserve. The welfare state developed, in part, because capital, at various times and under various conditions, seeking to maintain internal harmony and the political loyalty of the working class, concedes to such pressure with economic and social reforms. According to Paul Sweezy, a Marxist economist,

> economic legislation has. . . had the aim of blunting class antagonisms so that accumulation, the normal aim of capitalist behavior, could go forward smoothly and uninterrupted. . . For the sake of preserving domestic peace and tranquility, blunting the edge of class antagonisms, and ultimately avoiding the dangers of violent revolution, the capitalist class is always prepared to make concessions through the medium of the state.[14]

State-sponsored programs, developed in response to the demands of disadvantaged groups for a greater share of the economic pie, also promote the political and economic stability necessary for the smooth functioning of production. At any moment in time, however, the likelihood of state action and the nature of the reform that results is not predetermined. Rather, it reflects the outcome of a contest between the demands of capital and those of labor as mediated by the state as well as the relative power of labor and capital at the particular historical moment.[15]

For this reason some contemporary Marxists now define the welfare state as an arena for class struggle and argue that social welfare provisions, while pro-capital, are not without benefit to the working class.[16] Welfare state programs are seen as having paradoxical outcomes that simultaneously enhance and negate human potential. On the one hand, the welfare state intervenes in daily life to reproduce the conditions necessary for the perpetuation of capitalist social, economic, and political relations. On the other hand, programs that benefit the "powers that be" also meet "common human needs." If social welfare benefits absorb the cost to industry of reproducing the labor force and maintaining the non-working poor, they also help individuals and families to survive. Secondly, to the extent that welfare state programs emerged from struggles waged by workers, people of color, women, and the poor, they not only produced a redistribution of income, however slight, but also empowered members of the labor, civil rights, women's liberation, and community organizations whose actions often create "pressures from below" that can force social change.[17] Third, the resulting package of benefits, which the British call a "social wage," operates as economic leverage, increasing the bargaining power of workers relative to capital. The social wage enables workers to take the economic risks involved in fighting for improved wages and working conditions and to consider resisting pressure to take any availiable job to survive. Thus, it is in their interest to fight for more generous social welfare benefits and to demand that capital, not labor, absorb the cost.

The Feminist Response To Liberal and Marxist Political Theory

The gender-neutrality of liberal and Marxist political theory has elicited responses from liberal, radical, and socialist feminists. Each feminist school has applied a gender-lens to their respective theoretical heritages and contributed to a new understanding of women's oppression and the welfare state.

Liberal Feminism

Liberal feminism[18] accepts liberal political theory but argues that its practice excludes women. The denial of equal rights to women and their differential treatment on the basis of sex without regard to individual wishes, interests, abilities, or merits interferes with women's free pursuit of self-interest, constrains their economic opportunities and deprives them of the benefits of full political participation. Arguing that this societal treatment of women violates liberalism's guarantee of liberty, equality, and justice for all, liberal feminists maintain that every individual must receive equal consideration regardless of sex, except when sex is relevant to the ability to perform a specific task or to take advantage of a certain opportunity. Extending the idea of the state as a guarantor of rights to include women's rights and family life, liberal feminists call on the state to take positive steps to compensate women in the market and at home.

Liberal feminists see blocked opportunities, the denial of rights, and sex discrimination as the keys to women's oppression. They historically have fought for formal equality under law including the right to vote, to enter the market, to receive an education, to own property in marriage, and to control their own bodies. Since the mid-nineteenth century, liberal feminists have also called for the elimination of protective labor laws that barred women from better paying jobs, the end to special exemptions from jury duty, and greater access for women in business, politics, and education. Their agenda has included laws that prohibit discrimination against women in relation to wages, hiring, promotions, credit, and social welfare programs, among other things. The capstone of these campaigns for gender-blind laws is the not yet ratified Equal Rights Amendment (ERA) to the Constitution which states that "Equality of rights under the law shall not be denied or abridged by the United States or any State on account of sex."

Reflecting a belief that the attainment of liberty, equality, and justice depends on the presence of certain material pre-conditions, traditional liberalism concluded that poverty may prevent individuals from exercising their rights. In this spirit, liberal feminists have stressed that the historic "feminization of poverty" has left women economically dependent, socially unfree, and unequal to men in most arenas. Their political goals include improvements in public programs serving women and expansion of the welfare state. Trusting to "reasoned" arguments and legislative change, liberal feminism relies heavily on the state to incorporate women into mainstream contemporary society.

Viewed as a neutral arbiter of conflicting interests, the state is assumed to be the proper and the only legitimate authority for enforcing justice.

Liberal feminists accept considerable state intervention in family life. In addition to economic and political rights for women, they have fought for day care centers, reproductive freedom, maternity leaves, and more equitable divorce laws, and against pregnancy discrimination, rape, incest, wife battering, and other features of family life that negatively affect women. Moving still further away from traditional liberal concepts, some liberal feminists argue that the achievement of equality of opportunity for women requires an end to unfair social expectations and to exclusive childrearing by women.

The impact of the liberal feminist agenda on family life has led Zillah Eisenstein to suggest that it harbors a radical potential.[19] Arguing that liberal feminism contains an implied and often undefined analysis of women's oppression as flowing from their status as a distinct sex-class, Eisenstein suggests that the logical conclusion of liberal feminism is that liberty, equality, and justice for women requires an end to patriarchal arrangements in the market and the home. Their demand for laws that guarantee women the same opportunities as men promotes equal opportunity but also the conditions for women's economic independence which contains the potential for destabilizing patriarchal power relations. Their call for state protection against domestic violence, marital rape, and other issues of family life extends the realm of public concern to matters traditionally regarded as private and beyond the realm of state intervention.[20] While the demands of liberal feminism do not directly challenge the state, Eisenstein also concludes that their thrust may be incompatible with aspects of liberal theory and the operation of the state. Liberal feminists' heavy reliance on legislative redress reflects the definition of the state as a neutral protector of all citizens' rights. But their strong dependence on government action contradicts the liberal tenet that state interventions undercut individual freedom and their demands risk exposing the state as biased against women.

Radical Feminism

Radical feminism emerged in the late 1960s as a break with both liberal feminism and traditional Marxism. Its understanding of women's oppression as rooted in patriarchal power relations of male domination and female subordination has forced a new conceptualization of the state. In contrast to liberal feminism which sees the denial of rights and blocked opportunities as the source of women's oppression, radical feminism points to the domination of women by men. Locating the imbalance of power between women and men in the biological differences between the sexes, most radical feminists ground male domination or patriarchy in the social relations of reproduction, i.e. the work women do bearing and raising the next generation. Male control of institutional arrangements, but also of women's bodies, enables men to define women's roles and traits, to exploit women's labor and sexuality, and to diminish women's control over their choices about childrearing, mothering, laboring, and loving. Viewed as "other," women have been excluded and devalued.

In this analysis, gender, more than race or class, structures every aspect of human nature and social life. It becomes the most important determinant of a woman's life experience. The gender-based division of society is patriarchy's overarching tool. The distinction between the sexes, according to radical feminism, pre- and post- dates capitalism, making it the deepest and most decisive social division. The resulting assignment of public and private life to men and women respectively appears in different forms in different societies, but everywhere it legitimizes excluding women from the public arena of the market and politics, privatizing family life, and ultimately devaluing all that is associated with women.[21] The gender division of labor also creates a social relationship of dependency between biological females and males capable of reproducing offspring together and thus enforces marriage, heterosexuality, and the nuclear family system.

The radical feminist analysis of women's oppression focuses primarily on the private sphere and the gender domination of women's reproductive capacity, sexuality, mothering, family life, interpersonal relations, and culture. Here, the private and the personal is defined as political. In its illumination of the power of patriarchal arrangements and its development of a woman-centered perspective, radical feminism has focused special attention on male violence against women (rape, incest, wife abuse, pornography), homophobia, and sexual politics at home and on the job. It supports the creation of an alternative women's culture and in some cases espouses female separatism. Radical feminism's biological explanation of the gender division of labor, its tendency to universalize the female experience, to posit the moral superiority of women, and to focus nearly all its attention on the private and personal spheres of life has resulted in criticism of its analysis as veering toward biological determinism, ignoring differences of race, class, and ethnicity among women, and divorcing its understanding of patriarchy from other features of the political economy. But implied in the radical feminist analysis, if not yet fully developed, is an account of the state as a patriarchal substitute for male control of women in the family. Whether it is a welfare mother referring to "the state" as "The Man" or Mary Daly claiming that "patriarchy appears to be everywhere,"[22] the idea that patriarchy is the cause of women's subordinate status has become part of feminist consciousness.

Socialist Feminism

The socialist-feminist response to the theories of liberalism and Marxism integrates the radical feminist analysis of patriarchal power relations and the Marxist analysis of capitalist class and property relations. The resulting understanding of female oppression helps to pave the way for a feminist analysis of the welfare state. The emerging synthesis locates the oppression of women in the ways that the power relations of capitalism (class domination) and patriarchy (male domination) together structure ideology, the social relations of gender and class, and the overall organization of society. The dynamics of racism have also recently begun to be factored into this complex equation.

Socialist feminists share the Marxist critique of liberal political theory as obscuring the class relations of the state. However, they find the Marxist analysis limited by its failure to include the experience and perspective of women. The lack of attention to women in Marxist theory is problematic, both descriptively and analytically, according to socialist feminists. Descriptively, it ignores that from colonial times to the present many women received social welfare benefits. Moreover, most of the reproductive tasks assumed by the welfare state correspond to those historically assigned to women in the home. Analytically, the Marxist analysis pays too little attention to the private sphere of reproduction in the home and to the overall role of patriarchy, both of which structure the lives of women. Although Marx and his followers did consider the "woman question,"[23] they focused primarily on the dynamics of capitalist production and did not develop their rudimentary discussion of patriarchy, reproduction, and the labor of women into a full account of female oppression. To correct for this, socialist feminists expanded the Marxist analysis to include the impact of patriarchy, the gender division of labor, and the sphere of reproduction.

Patriarchy

The early Marxists understood patriarchy and what they called the "world-historic defeat of women," as a product of the emergence of private property, the state, and class relations at a particular point in capitalist development. Under a system of private property, women as a group became property, that is, "mere instruments of production" to men who owned women's ability to labor. The oppression of women and their status as the property of men derived from their exclusion from the process of production which left women economically dependent and thus vulnerable to exploitation. The emergence of private property, classes, and the state also gave rise to monogamy and the nuclear family to assure the inheritance of individually-owned wealth by male offspring. Only the elimination of class and the private ownership of property would eliminate women's "wage slavery" in the market and their "domestic slavery" in the home. Viewing capitalism as the source of male domination, Marxists did not consider patriarchy to have an autonomous influence on women's lives.[24]

In contrast, socialist feminism, influenced by radical feminism, gives patriarchy equal standing with capitalism as a source of female oppression. While radical feminists stress the direct, personally exercised, and legitimized dominance of individual men over women, socialist feminists expanded the concept of patriarchy to include the male dominance that is structured into social arrangements, that indirectly secures male interests, and that gives men control over women. This broadened terrain permits a discussion of both the individual and society, and focuses on both the private and the public sphere. As a result, the influence of patriarchy in the home, on the job, in societal institutions, and throughout the wider social order is explored. More historical than radical feminism, socialist feminism also examines how patriarchy changes over time.

Patriarchy is grounded in relations of power as well as in the biological differences between the sexes. It consists of a social system that establishes the shared interests and interdependence among men that enables, if not requires, them to dominate women. Characterized by male domination and female subordination, patriarchy permits men as a group to control women's sexuality as well as their productive and reproductive labor. Under patriarchy, some men have more power than others and while all men benefit from patriarchy, privileges vary sharply by class and race.

Socialist feminism defines patriarchy as an autonomous system of social relations but insists on its inseparability from capitalism. The societal divisions by gender, class, and race thus reflect a synthesis of patriarchy and capitalism and are not determined primarily by one or the other alone. So for example, socialist feminists suggest that capitalist production is shaped by the forces of male dominance and that male dominance is organized by capitalist class relations. By insisting on the inseparability of capitalism and patriarchy, socialist feminism articulates the need to struggle against both. The understanding of the differential impact of capitalism and patriarchy on women of color that is now emerging (see below) provides a way to incorporate the dynamics of racism into this analysis.

The Gender Division of Labor

Patriarchal dominance is established and maintained by a gender-segregated society which assigns certain spheres and tasks to women and others to men. The early Marxists acknowledged this but did not develop the concept of patriarchy or the gender division of labor very fully. They viewed pre-class gender divisions as a "natural" (ie. biologically based) product of the sex act which extended outward to organize the rest of society. With the development of classes and the transformation of the family into an economic unit, the class structure became dominant. That is, instead of the gender division of labor shaping societal patterns, capitalist class relations now determined the gender division of labor.[25] Making gender division secondary to capitalist class relations prevented the early Marxists from seeing the social order as structured both by capitalism and patriarchy, and recognizing gender divisions as an independent source of female oppression.[26]

Socialist feminism makes society's gender division co-equal with its class divisions and central to its analysis of the political economy. In this view, when the rise of capitalism moved economic production from the househod to the market, domestic and economic production were separated. Patriarchy then caused the resulting division of *production* to be structured by gender: the assignment of the private sphere of family and reproduction to women and the more power-laden public sphere of market and production to men. Furthermore, the work within each sphere was divided along gender lines as well.[27] The new gender divisions and the accompanying ideology which sanctioned a public\private split served capital's need for discrete "homemakers" and "breadwinners" (see Chapter Four). At the same time they sustained patriarchal authority, which the rise of capitalist social relations threatened to undermine.[28]

The Sphere of Reproduction

The identification of the gender division of society as central to female oppression led the socialist feminists to examine the labor of women in the home as well as in the market. Their analysis of women's oppression forced them to look at women's domestic labor and the sphere of reproduction—both largely ignored by the early Marxists and other economists. Although most economists recognized that all societies needed to reproduce the labor force, they did not think of the family as the place where daily and generational reproduction of labor took place. Instead they analyzed reproduction as a characteristic of production. In standard Marxist usage, reproduction refers to the reproduction of capital (the replacement of machinery and capital equipment), the reproduction of wage laborers as factors of production, and to the reproduction of capitalist social relations by cultural and ideological institutions such as the family, education, and religion which, among other things, socialize individuals to capitalist norms.[29]

If the early Marxists had pursued their insights about the reproduction of labor further, they might have developed an understanding of the importance of women's reproductive labor in the home and uncovered the relationship between women's domestic labor, the process of capitalist production, and the oppression of women.[30] Their singular interest in the system of production, however, led them to focus only on the reproduction of wage laborers on the job, that is, the means by which the relationship between wage laborers and the capitalist employers is sustained. They asked what amount of labor must workers as a group expend and what wages must they be paid to assure that they will recreate themselves and continue to participate regularly in the process of production.

With regard to women's domestic labor in the home, the early Marxists recognized the importance of "individual consumption" to the reproduction of labor, assumed it took place in the working-class family, and suggested that the breadwinner's wage included a payment for the domestic labor of his wife. Indifferent to reproduction in the home, they failed to understand the ways in which the daily maintenance of workers depended on women's domestic labor and the structure of the family system. Thus, their analysis did not include the relationship of women's domestic labor to capitalist production, nor did it define the reproductive sphere as a potential source of female oppression.[31] While contemporary Marxists such as Gough and Dickinson pay more attention to reproduction in the home, they still fail to account for women's experience because they continue to subsume reproduction to production and to ignore patriarchy altogether.

Socialist feminists expanded Marxism by analyzing the sphere of reproduction in its own right. Instead of examining the dynamics of reproduction as a *response* to the needs of production or *vice-versa*, socialist feminists give equal attention to both spheres. They do so on the grounds that the survival of human society depends on the reproduction of the species as well as the production of commodities, that humans require the satisfaction of material, social, and emotional needs, and that attention to home and family life better explain women's experiences.[32] Production occurs primarily within the market and is the means by which society organizes and distributes the goods and services necessary for survival and for leisure. Reproduction, occurring within the family, organizes and distributes the means of satisfying the needs of procreation, socialization, sexuality, daily maintenance, and emotional nurturance.[33]

The earliest socialist-feminist discussion of the reproductive sphere stayed close to the Marxist focus on production. It analyzed women's unpaid domestic labor as essential to capital's need to reduce the costs of reproducing and maintaining the labor force and held capitalist relations responsible for the oppressive economic dependence of women on men.[34] But as socialist feminists incorporated ideas about patriarchy into their analysis, they began to examine the contribution of women's domestic and market labor to both systems. They found that women's labor provided benefits to individual men and employers, but also to the more systemic arrangements of patriarchy and capitalism. They concluded that the dynamics of women's home and market labor enforced female subordination in both spheres.[35]

More specifically, they argued that the need for women's labor in the home reinforced their exploitation in the market while their exploitation in the market helped to maintain their subordination in the home.[36] In its need for low paid workers, capitalism has maintained women (and other groups) as a reserve pool of labor that can be drawn into and out of the labor force as needed. The ready availability of cheap female labor benefits capital by exerting a downward pressure on wages, while the possibility of displacement helps to keep currently employed workers in line. The requisites of patriarchy, particularly the idea that women's primary place is in the home, act to reinforce this dynamic. At the same time, when women enter the market, employers rationalize paying them less for work in the least stable and most uninteresting jobs on the grounds that they are secondary earners, working temporarily or just for "pin money."

From the start, women's employment outside the home has also challenged the underpinnings of patriarchy. The early development of a sex-segregated labor market, however, helped to restore male domination and female subordination in the world of work. The sex-segregated labor market operates to keep labor costs down and to uphold male domination. By crowding large numbers of female workers into a small number of "women's jobs," occupational segregation increases competition among women, reduces their wages, and raises their unemployment rates. Occupational segregation by sex also supports the male\female wage gap, maintains male-dominated job hierarchies, and prevents women from competing with men for higher paying jobs.

The economic vulnerability resulting from work in low paid, low status women's jobs, in turn, helps to enforce women's subordinated place in the home. It promotes the economic, if not psychological, dependence of women on men, necessitates entrance into marriage, and locks women into their subordinate domestic roles. When women work without pay, doing the household and childcare tasks that assure the daily and generational renewal of the labor force, their labor benefits both men and capital.

Poor Women, Immigrant Women and Women of Color

While the socialist-feminist analysis has advanced the understanding of women's oppression in several ways, it has been accurately criticized for inadequately addressing the experiences of women from different racial, ethnic, and class backgrounds. To generalize from the lives of middle-class, native-born, white women to other groups of women as if no differences existed, creates distortions similar to those that result when scholars generalize research on male subjects to women. In recent years, socialist-feminist researchers, both white and women of color, have begun to reformulate their concepts by combining them with theories of racial oppression. Evelyn Nakano Glenn and Bonnie Thornton Dill,[37] for example, argue that the distinctions between public and private spheres and between productive and reproductive labor, drawn by socialist feminists, do not adequately reflect the experience of women other than middle-class white women. They re-examine these ideas to make them more applicable to the experiences of women with other backgrounds. Both Glenn and Dill point out that the notion of separate spheres is less useful for understanding the experiences of women whose poverty caused them to work for wages outside the home. Drawn by capital's need for cheap labor, women and children from native-born, immigrant, and families of color without means were a substantial part of the wage labor force. For these working women, the lines between private and public were not so distinct.

Glenn and Dill maintain that the line between productive and reproductive labor all but disappeared for the female members of oppressed groups. Like other members of racially subordinated groups, white society valued them primarily for their ability to work. During slavery, the reproductive labor of black female slaves belonged to their masters, who owned them as well as their children. Since then, the wage labor of women of color has continued to take precedence over their domestic labor. Viewed as workers rather than homemakers, the maternal and reproductive roles have been diminished and ignored. While patriarchal society "protected" white middle-class women as wives and mothers, women of color received little recognition, respect, or support for these roles. The family system of women of color, moreover, was regularly assaulted by the dominant society which not only refused to recognize its needs but often tore it apart. The slave trade, followed by certain immigration policies sometimes prevented and/or disrupted family formation among black as well as Chinese and Mexican-American workers. Low wages, irregular employment, and intensive internal labor mobility futher hindered the development of families among oppressed groups. Frequently these families, experiencing extreme exploitation on the job and having to struggle for cohesion in family life, were important sources of resistance to the *status quo*.

Finally, this analysis raises the issue of racial divisions among women.[38] As slaves and as domestic servants, women of color historically performed reproductive labor for white women and their families. When women of color entered the wider labor market, their jobs became tightly stratified by race.[39] Their nearly exclusive employment in the most menial personal service and cleaning jobs left more satisfying work for white women. Moreover, during economic downturns when jobs were few, white women often displaced women of color. Such labor market patterns led Glenn to argue that in the exploitation of women, race becomes a "second axis of oppression"—one that frequently brings benefits to white women. She maintains, however, that despite the benefits of racial oppression to white women and those of patriarchal oppression to men of color, white men remain the dominant exploiting group.

Socialist Feminism and the Welfare State

Socialist feminists have begun to apply their analysis of women's oppression and of the political economy to the welfare state. Elizabeth Wilson,[40] Mary McIntosh,[41] Hillary Land,[42] Carol Brown,[43] Zillah R. Eisenstein,[44] and Allison M. Jaggar[45] from the United States, Jane Ursell,[46] from Canada and others with an interest in the role of the state have started to account for complexities of the welfare state that contemporary Marxists and other gender-neutral theorists neither saw nor addressed.

Building on the Marxist analysis of capitalism and the radical feminist analysis of patriarchy, socialist feminism maintains that the state is neither a neutral mediator of interest group conflict nor simply pro-capital. Rather, the state protects the interests of both capital and patriarchy by institutionalizing capitalist class and property relations and upholding patriarchal distinctions. According to Zillah Eisenstein,

> The formation of the state institutionalizes patriarchy; it reifies the division between public and private life as one of sexual differences...The domain of the state has always signified public life and this is distinguished in part from the private realm by differentiating men from women...The state formalizes the rule by men because the division of public and private life is at one and the same time a male-female distinction...The state's purpose is to enforce the separation of public and private life and with it the distinctness of male and female existence.[47]

The state protects capitalism and patriarchy by enforcing their respective requirements, but also by mediating any conflicts that arise from the state's simultaneous commitment to both. The state steps in to create order and cohesion especially when the heterogeneous and frequently divided dominant class cannot agree on how best to resolve these tensions.[48]

Including patriarchy complicates the otherwise useful analysis of the origins and development of the welfare state put forward by Gough, Dickinson, O'Connor, and other contemporary Marxists who suggest that the welfare state operates to mediate conflicts between the capitalist requirements of production and reproduction. They see the welfare state as assisting capitalist accumulation and the legitimacy of the prevailing social order by assuring the reproduction of the labor force, the maintenance of society's non-working members, and securing the social peace. If Marxism argues that the welfare state arose to mediate reproductive relations on behalf of the productive needs of capital, socialist feminism holds that the welfare state originated to meet the changing requirements of patriarchy *and* capitalism and to mediate their conflicts. Drawing on various parts of the socialist-feminist discourse, a new but far from singular and still incomplete perspective can be envisioned which suggests that the origins and functions of the welfare state represent not only the need to reproduce and maintain the labor force as observed by the Marxists, but also to uphold patriarchal relations and to regulate the lives of women. From this perspective, the welfare state operates to uphold patriarchy and to enforce female subordination in both the spheres of production and reproduction, to mediate the contradictory demands for women's home and market labor, and to support the nuclear family structure at the expense of all others.

Upholding Patriarchal Control in the Family and the Market

Socialist feminists maintain that state intervention in work and family life reflects the changing requirements of patriarchy as well as those of capitalism and the historical intervention of the state on behalf of "proper" family life. Both Brown and Ursel[49] argue that the advance of capitalism gradually shifted the center of patriarchal control from the private family headed by a man to the state. In pre-industrial society, where the household was both the productive and reproductive unit, patriarchal authority was private or familial, that is, grounded in the gender organization of the family. Public or social patriarchy, rooted in the state, was more facilitative than direct, providing only the structural supports for private patriarchy in the home. By law, custom, and economics, male heads of household controlled the labor of women and other family members as well as their access to most economic resources. Marriage, property, inheritance, and public aid laws were local and operated primarily to enforce such control by the patriarch who, in turn, was obliged to maintain the nuclear family and women's place in the home.

Public or social patriarchy became stronger as the rise of industrial capitalism began to weaken the economic and political underpinnings of male authority. The separation of production and reproduction, the growth of factories, the creation of a wage labor force (which employed women and children as well as men), and the emergence of new ideas about individual freedom, equality, and opportunity shifted the basis of patriarchal authority from the male head of household to the employer and the state. As market relations slowly lessened men's ability to control the labor of family members and increased their wives' and children's access to economic resources, familial patriarchy alone no longer sufficed to maintain male domination and the gender division of labor.

The decline of patriarchal authority modified the state's relationship to private family life. As familial patriarchy gave way to social or public patriarchy, the state assumed regulatory functions previously confined to the family including greater regulation of marriage, inheritance, child custody, and employment.[50] The growth of the social welfare system and its "reform" in the early nineteenth century also marked the shift from familial to social patriarchy, at least for the poor. The transition, signaled by an attack on public aid (outdoor relief) and the rise of institutional care (indoor relief) made public aid very harsh and punitive. The Marxist explanation of these "reforms" suggests that state-regulated deterrence became necessary to discipline the newly industrialized labor force. The feminist analysis adds that the social welfare changes also operated to enforce new ideas about proper family life. Punitive relief programs assured that women chose any quality of family life over public aid. Welfare recipients whose families did not comply with prevailing norms were considered undeserving and treated even more poorly by the system. Given women's responsibility for maintaining the home, poor, immigrant, and female-headed households suspected of being unable to properly socialize their children were frequently defined as unworthy of aid. If an institutional placement resulted, it could tear "undeserving" families apart, often for reasons of poverty alone.

In the early twentieth century, the entry of more women into the labor force challenged patriarchal patterns and was viewed as competitive with men. The new labor and social welfare legislation that emerged enforced the gender division of labor and otherwise re-asserted patriarchal structures in the family and the market (see Chapter Six). Protective labor laws, Mothers' Pension programs, and other new social legislation excluded women from the labor market and relegated them to the home where they worked to reproduce and maintain the labor force. These and other laws also supported a sex-segregated occupational structure and established male-dominated hierarchies at the workplace (which mirrored and reinforced those already in place in the home).

During the rest of the twentieth century, the expanding welfare state continued to support patriarchal dominance while mediating reproductive relations on behalf of the productive needs of capital (see Chapters Seven through Ten). The emergence of the modern welfare state, marked by the enactment of the 1935 Social Security Act, signaled the institutionalization of public or social patriarchy. Instead of simply assuming patriarchal control, the state began to systematically subsidize the familial unit of production through the provision of economic resources to the aged, the unemployed, and children without fathers. The major income maintenance programs of the Social Security Act also incorporated patriarchal family norms. They each presumed and reinforced marriage, the male breadwinner/female homemaker household type and women's economic dependence on men. Mary McIntosh,[51] points out that even the special programs for female heads of households indirectly buttressed the ideal family type by substituting the state for the male breadwinner. By helping this "deviant" family approximate the "normal" one, programs for female-headed families "solved" one of patriarchy's major problems, that of the so-called "broken home" or female-headed home. At the same time, the program's low benefits and stigma penalized husbandless women for their departure from prescribed wife and mother roles. This kept unmarried motherhood and the breakup of the two-parent family from appearing too attractive to others. Until very recently, when they began to falter in this regard, the programs of the Social Security Act implicitly supported family structures that conformed to the patriarchal model and penalized those that did not. The historical intervention by the state on behalf of "proper" family life suggests the family's importance to the survival of capitalism and patriarchy. Indeed, families absorb the cost and responsibility for bearing and socializing the next generation, for managing consumption and other household matters, for organizing sexual relations, for providing care to the aged, sick, and young who cannot work, and for producing income to meet all these needs. The 1980 attack on the welfare state (described in Chapter Eleven), can be understood partly as an effort to restore the ability of the welfare state to uphold traditional patriarchal arrangements in face of recent threats derived from major changes in both the family system and the political economy.

Regulating The Labor of Women

Socialist feminists agree with contemporary Marxists that the welfare state helps to assure the reproduction of the labor force and the maintenance of the non-working members of the population. But they stress that from the start, programs serving women have had a more complicated role. The activities necessary to secure the physical, economic, and social viability of the working class depend heavily on women's unpaid domestic labor as do prevailing patriarchal family patterns. But because this competes with capital's ongoing demand for women's low paid market labor, socialist feminism forces us to see that the welfare state must regulate the lives of women in a unique way.

The demands for women's domestic and market labor have contradicted each other since the separation of household and market production in the early nineteenth century. Women's domestic labor assures capital fit, able, and properly socialized workers on a daily and a generational basis as well as the care of those unable to work. This unpaid domestic labor absorbs the costs that industry or government would otherwise have to pay to reproduce and maintain a productive labor force. Women's domestic labor also reinforces patriarchal arrangements. It relieves individual men of household tasks, services their physical, sexual, and emotional needs, keeps women economically dependent, stops them from competing with men in the job market, and defines women's place in the home. By the end of the colonial period, however capital's need for cheap market labor had combined with the impoverishment of the working class to draw increasingly large numbers of women into the wage labor market. Paradoxically, their entry conflicted with the benefits received by capital from women's unpaid domestic labor. Combined with fewer marriages and more female-headed households, the growing labor force participation of women, which held the possibility of greater economic independence, also contained a challenge to male dominance and patriarchal family patterns.

Socialist feminism argues that, from colonial times to the present, social welfare programs serving women have had to deal with these contradictory pulls. Given the twin benefits of female labor, the welfare state, in most historical periods, has played a central role in mediating the resulting conflict, especially among poor and working-class women. As this book details, social welfare policies have always regulated the lives of women, channelling some into the home to devote full time to reproducing and maintaining the labor force and others into the labor market where they also create profits for capital. By distinguishing among women as "deserving" and "undeserving" of aid, the policies also reinforced divisions among women along lines of race, class, and marital status.

Arena of Struggle

Like some Marxists, some socialist feminists conclude that the paradoxes of the welfare state make it a productive arena for feminist as well as class struggle. On the one hand, welfare state policies assist capital and patriarchy by reproducing the labor force, regulating the competing demands for female labor, enforcing female subordination, maintaining women's place in the home, and sustaining the social peace. On the other hand, welfare state benefits threaten patriarchal arrangements. They redistribute needed resources, offer non-working women and single mothers a means of self-support, and provide the material conditions for the pursuit of equal opportunity. Welfare state benefits that help women to survive without male economic support subsidize, if not legitimize, the female-headed household and undermine the exclusivity of the male-breadwinner, female-homemaker family structure. As a social wage, welfare state benefits increase the bargaining power of women relative to men. Eisenstein[52] argues that the very existence of the welfare state, especially its deep involvement in family life, is potentially subversive to capitalism, liberalism, and patriarchy. Whether or not and how the welfare state carries out its abstract tasks or exposes its roots in patriarchal capitalism, however, is not predetermined. Rather it reflects the degree of prevailing struggle over who (capital or labor) "pays" for these benefits and the extent to which the welfare state policies can be made to change rather than reproduce the conditions necessary to perpetuate patriarchal capitalism. In the final analysis, the outcome of the struggle reflects the relative power of the contesting forces at any moment in time.

The Role of Ideology: The Family Ethic and the Regulation of Women

The welfare state functions identified by socialist feminists are carried out, in part, by the codification of the family ethic or the ideology of women's roles in its rules and regulations. Indeed, the family ethic is one way in which the welfare state regulates the lives of women. Ideology, or the relatively coherent system of beliefs and values about human nature and social life generated by a society for itself, is found in the realm of ideas, the actions of individuals, and in the practices of societal institutions, including the welfare state. The power of ideology lies in its ability to influence the thinking and behavior of individuals, the practices of institutions, and the organization of society. In the case of women, the family ethic articulates expected work and family behavior and defines women's place in the wider social order. Embodied in all societal institutions, this dominant norm is enforced by the laws and activities of the state.

The family ethic derives from patriarchal social thought that sees gender roles as biologically determined rather than socially assigned and from standard legal doctrine that defines women as the property of men. It is grounded in the idea that natural physical differences between the sexes determine their differential capacities. The idea of natural differences between the sexes causes individuals to see their femininity and masculinity solely as part of human nature[53] rather than as the product of socialization. The sense of "naturalness" legitimizes socially constructed gender distinctions and enables individuals to participate, without question, in gender-specific roles. The implication that biology is destiny also obscures the historical impact of differential socialization and unequal opportunities on the choices made by individuals of different sexes, races, and ages. By making these choices seem natural and rational, the family ethic helps to justify discrepancies between societal promises and realities, to rationalize prejudice, discrimination, and inequalities, and to promote the acquiescence of the oppressed in their oppression. Finally, the direct appeal to nature as the source of gender differences minimizes the cultural determination of women's sexuality, the significance of changes in women's position over time, and the importance of women's private domestic labor to both capitalist production and patriarchal arrangements.

Like most ideologies, the ideology of women's roles represents dominant interests and explains reality in ways that create social cohesion and maintain the *status quo*. The family ethic articulates and rationalizes the terms of the gender division of labor. Despite its long history, the lynchpin of the family ethic—the assignment of homemaking and childcare responsibilities to women—has remained reasonably stable.

A family ethic telling women about their proper place existed in colonial America. This pre-industrial code placed women in the home and subordinate to the male head of household. Women were expected to be economically productive, but to limit their productive labor to the physical boundaries of the home. Between 1790 and 1830, changes in the political economy that accompanied the rise of industrial capitalism caused a dramatic shift in women's roles. The emerging market economy removed production from the home and created gender-based separate spheres. As men took their place in the market, the work ethic followed them there; but the new "industrial family ethic" continued to define women's place as in the home.

The industrial family ethic resembled its colonial predecessor in many ways, except that it denied women a recognized productive role. Told not to engage in market labor at all, the family ethic defined women's place as exclusively in the home. Reflecting the needs of the new social order, their domestic work included creating a comfortable retreat for the market-weary breadwinner, socializing children to assume proper adult work and family roles, managing household consumption, offering emotional nurturance to family members, caring for the aged and the sick, taming male sexuality, and providing moral guardianship to the family and the wider community. At the same time, and reflecting patriarchal rules, women were viewed as the "weaker sex" in need of male support and protection. The subordination of women became grounded in their economic dependence on men and in the law. The latter continued to define women as male property and to grant men control of women's labor and access to resources.

The idea of the family ethic draws on what other scholars have labeled the "cult of domesticity" or the "cult of true womanhood."[54] But as developed here, the concept goes beyond earlier descriptions, to examine the codification of the ideology of women's roles in societal institutions and to analyze its regulatory powers. Indeed, the family ethic which "protects" the white middle-class family also operates as a mechanism of social regulation and control.

On the individual level, the family ethic keeps women in line. Fulfilling the terms of the family ethic theoretically entitles a woman to the "rights of womanhood" including claims to femininity, protection, economic support, and respectability. Non-compliance brings penalties for being out of role. Encoded in all societal institutions, the family ethic also reflects, enforces, and rationalizes the gender-based division of society into public and private spheres and helps to downgrade women in both. The ideology of women's roles helps to keep women at the bottom of the hierarchies of power in both the public and the private spheres.

Indeed, the idea that women belong at home has historically sanctioned the unequal treatment of women in the market. The resulting economic insecurity has channelled them back into the home. The need for women's domestic labor and the ideological presumption of a private sphere to which women rightfully belong has helped to rationalize their subordination in the public sphere. When industry's need for inexpensive labor drew women out of their "proper place," the idea that they belonged in the home justified channelling them into low-paid, low-status, gender-segregated sectors of the economy and into jobs whose functions paralleled those tasks traditionally performed by women at home. Women's inability to earn a livable wage made men, marriage, and family life into a necessary and a more rational source of financial support. Lacking a material basis for independence, women easily became economically, if not psychologically, dependent on men which, in turn, created the conditions for women's subordinate family role.

In brief, the family ethic, which locked women into a subordinate family role also rationalized women's exploitation on the job. By devaluing women's position in each sphere, the ideology of women's work and family roles satisfied capital's need for a supply of readily available, cheap, female labor. By creating the conditions for continued male control of women at home and on the job, the economic devaluation and marginalization of women also muted the challenge that increased employment by women posed to patriarchal norms.

Targeted to and largely reflecting the experience of white, middle-class women who marry and stay home, the family ethic denied poor and immigrant women and women of color the "rights of womanhood" and the opportunity to embrace the dominant definition of "good wife" and mother because they did not confine their labor to the home.[55] Forced by dire poverty to work for wages outside the home, they also faced severe exploitation on the job, having to accept the lowest wages, longest hours, and most dangerous working conditions. Instead of "protecting" their femininity and their families' social respectability, the notion of separate spheres placed poor and immigrant women and women of color in a double bind at home and reinforced their subordinate status in the market. Separate spheres, which recognized and sustained the household labor that white women performed for their families, offered no such support to non-white women.[56] Both Dill and Glenn point out that society's treatment of women of color clearly indicated that their value as laborers took precedence over their domestic and reproductive roles. On all fronts, the families of poor and immigrant women and women of color experienced a series of assaults not faced by middle-class white women.

Perhaps this is why some of the families of poor, employed, husbandless, immigrant women, and women of color tried so hard to comply with the terms of the family ethic. Indeed, working-class men struggled to keep their wives at home even when this involved major sacrifices in the organization and comfort of their family life. To stay out of the labor force, working-class women typically limited family consumption, sent their children to work, sacrificed the privacy of their homes to take in boarders, increased the production of household goods and/or took in paid piece-work which burdened their already long work day.[57]

The ideology of women's roles is deeply encoded in social welfare policy. It is well-known that social welfare laws categorize the poor as deserving and undeserving of aid based on their compliance with the work ethic. But, as this book suggests, the rules and regulations of social welfare programs also treat women differentially according to their perceived compliance with the family ethic. Indeed, conforming to the ideology of women's roles has been used to distinguish among women as deserving or undeserving of aid since colonial times. Assessing women in terms of the family ethic became one way the welfare state could mediate the conflicting demands for women's unpaid labor in the home and her low paid labor in the market, encourage reproduction by "proper" families, and otherwise meet the needs of patriarchal capitalism. Recognizing the role of the family ethic in social welfare policy permits us to uncover the long untold story of the relationship between women and the welfare state, to which we now turn.

Notes to Chapter 1

1. Virginia Held, "Feminism and Epistemology: Recent Work on the Connection Between Gender and Knowledge," *Philosophy and Public Affairs*, 14(3) (1985), pp. 296-307.

2. This discussion of liberal economic and political theory draws heavily from E. K. Hunt, *Property and Prophets: The Evolution of Economic Institutions and Ideologies* (New York: Harper & Row Publishers, 1981), pp. 36-50; and Alison M. Jaggar, *Feminist Politics and Human Nature* (Totowa, New Jersey: Rowman & Allanheld, 1983), pp. 27-50.

3. Adam Smith, *The Wealth of Nations* (New York: Modern Library, 1937), pp. 420-423.

4. For a clear contemporary presentation of this view, see Milton Friedman, *Capitalism and Freedom* (Chicago: University of Chicago Press, 1962), Ch. 2, "The Role of Government in a Free Society."

5. Harold L. Wilensky and Charles N. Lebeaux, *Industrial Society and Social Welfare* (New York: Russell Sage Foundation, 1965), p. xii.

6. Richard Hofstadter, *The Age of Reform* (New York: Vintage Books, 1955), p. 18.

7. Hal Draper, *Karl Marx's Theory of Revolution I: State and Bureaucracy* (New York: Monthly Review Press, 1977), pp. 237-262.

8. James O'Connor, *The Fiscal Crisis of the State* (New York: St. Martin's Press, 1973), pp. 5-10.

9. For this debate see Ralph Miliband, *The State in Capitalist Society* (New York: Basic Books, 1969); Ralph Miliband, *Marxism and Politics* (Oxford: Oxford University Press, 1977); Ralph Miliband, "Poulantzas and the Capitalist State," *New Left Review* 82 (1973), pp. 83-91; Nicol Poulantzas, "The Problem of the Capitalist State," *New Left Review* 58 (November/December 1969), pp. 67-78; Nicol Poulantzas, *Political Power and Social Classes* (London: Verso, 1978); Fred Block, "The Ruling Class Does Not Rule: Notes on the Marxist Theory of the State," *Socialist Revolution* 7(3) (May-June 1977), pp. 6-28; Paul M. Sweezy, *The Theory of Capitalist Development* (New York: Modern Reader Paperbacks, 1942); Paul A. Baran and Paul M. Sweezy, *Monopoly Capital* (New York: Modern Reader Paperbacks, 1966); Theda Skocpol, "Political Response to Capitalist Crisis: Neo-Marxist Theories of the State and the Case of the New Deal," *Politics and Society* 10 (2) (1980), pp. 155-201.

10. Ian Gough, *The Political Economy of the Welfare State* (London: MacMillan Press, 1980), p. 49.

11. *Ibid.*, pp. 44-45.

12. James Dickinson, "From Poor Law to Social Insurance: The Periodization of State Intervention in the Reproduction Process, " in James Dickinson and

Bob Russell (eds.), *Family, Economy, & State* (New York: St. Martins Press, 1986), pp. 113-149.

13. James Dickinson and Bob Russell, "Introduction: The Structure of Reproduction in Capitalist Society," in Dickinson and Russell (eds.) *op. cit.*, (1986), pp. 9-10.

14. Sweezy (1942) *op. cit.*, p. 249.

15. *Ibid.*, pp. 58-62.

16. Paul Corrigan, "The Welfare State as an Arena of Class Struggle," *Marxism Today* (March 1977), pp. 87-93; Gough, *op. cit;* Frances Fox Piven and Richard A. Cloward, *The New Class War* (New York: Pantheon Books, 1982).

17. Thomas Weisskopf, "The Current Economic Crisis in Historical Perspective," *Socialist Review* #57 (May-June 1981), pp. 9-54.

18. Jaggar (1983) *op. cit.*, pp. 34-35, 173-185.

19. Zillah Eisenstein, *The Radical Future of Liberal Feminism* (New York: Longman, 1981), pp. 4, 201-219.

20. Conversation with Joan Tronto, May 1987, Political Science Department, Hunter College, New York, NY.

21. Hester Eisenstein, *Contemporary Feminist Thought* (London: G. K. Hall, 1983), pp. 15-26.

22. Mary Daly, *Gyn/Ecology: The Metaethics of Radical Feminism* (Boston: Beacon Press, 1978), p. 326.

23. See *The Woman Question: Selections from the Writings of Karl Marx, Frederick Engels , V. I. Lenin and Joseph Stalin* (New York: International Publishers, 1951).

24. Natalie J. Sokoloff, *Between Money and Love: The Dialectic of Women's Home and Market Work* (New York: Praeger, 1981), pp. 115-119, 144-145.

25. *Ibid.*, p. 18.

26. *Ibid.*, p. 146.

27. *Ibid.*, p. 151; Jaggar (1983) *op. cit.*, p. 127.

28. Elizabeth Fox-Genovese, "Placing Women's History in History," *New Left Review* no. 133 (May-June 1982), pp. 22-23.

29. Louis Althusser, *Lenin and Philosophy* (New York: Monthly Review Press,1971), pp. 127-189; Jaggar, *op. cit.*, p. 156.

30. Sokoloff (1981) *op. cit.*, p. 12.

31. *Ibid.*, p. 120.

32. Jane Ursel, "The State and the Maintenance of Patriarchy: A Case Study of Family, Labour and Welfare Legislation in Canada," in James Dickinson and Bob Russell (eds.) (1986) *op. cit.*, pp. 150-192.

33. Jaggar (1983) *op. cit.*, p. 159; Sokoloff (1981) *op. cit.*, pp. 120-124; Ursel (1986) *op. cit.*, pp. 150-152.

34. For a review of the long theoretical debate among Marxists about the meaning of women's domestic labor see Sokoloff (1981) *op. cit.*, pp. 112-140 and references therein.

35. Jaggar (1983) *op. cit.*, pp. 139, 144-147; Sokoloff (1981) *op. cit.*, p. 145.

36. Sokoloff (1981) *op. cit.*, pp. 203-251.

37. This section draws heavily on: Bonnie Thornton Dill, *Our Mothers' Grief: Racial Ethnic Women and the Maintenance of Families*, Research Paper #4, May 1986, Center For Research on Women, Memphis State University, Memphis Tennessee 38152; Evelyn Nakano Glenn "Racial Ethnic Women's Labor: The Intersection of Race, Gender and Class Oppression," *Review of Radical Political Economics*, 17 (3) (Fall 1985), pp. 86-108.

38. Glenn, *op. cit.*, pp. 104-106.

39. Bette Wood and Michelene Malson, *In Crisis: Low Income Black Employed Women in the U.S. Workplace*, Working Paper No. 131, 1984, Wellesley College Center For Research On Women, Wellesley, MA 01281.

40. Elizabeth Wilson, *Women and the Welfare State* (London: Tavistock Publications, 1977).

41. Mary McIntosh, "The State and the Oppression of Women," in Annette Kuhn and Ann Marie Wolpe (eds.), *Feminism and Materialism: Women and Modes of Production* (London: Routledge and Kegan Paul, 1978), pp. 254-289.

42. Hillary Land, "Women: Supporters or Supported?" in Barker, D. L. and Allen, S. (eds.), *Sexual Divisions in Society* (London: Tavistock Publications, 1976); Hillary Land, "Who Cares For The Family," *Journal of Social Policy* 7 (3) (1978), pp. 357-384; Hillary Land, "The Family Wage," *Feminist Review*, 6 (1980), pp. 55-57; and Parket, R., "Implicit and Reluctant Family Policy—United Kingdom," in Kamerman, S. B. and Kahn, A. J. (eds.), *Family Policy: Government and Families in Fourteen Countries* (New York: Columbia University Press, 1978).

43. Carol Brown, "Mothers Fathers and Children: From Private to Public Patriarchy," in Lydia Sargent (ed.), *Women and Revolution: A Discussion of the Unhappy Marriage of Marxism and Feminism* (Boston: South End Press, 1981), pp. 239-267.

44. Zillah R. Eisenstein, *Feminism and Sexual Equality: Crisis in Liberal America* (New York: Monthly Review Press, 1984).

45. Jaggar (1983) *op. cit.*

46. Ursell (1986) *op. cit.*

47. Z. Eisenstein (1984) *op. cit.*, p. 92.

48. *Ibid.*, pp. 89-92.

49. Ursell (1986) *op. cit.*; pp. 154-155, 157; Brown (1981) *op. cit.*, pp. 239-267.

50. Ursell (1986) *op. cit.*, p. 158.

51. McIntosh (1978) *op. cit.*

52. Z. Eisenstein (1981) *op. cit.*, pp. 104-105.

53. Julie A. Matthaei, *An Economic History of Women In America* (New York, Shocken Books, 1982), pp. 3-7.

54. See for example: Nancy F. Cott, *The Bonds of Womanhood: "Woman's Sphere" in New England, 1780-1835* (New Haven: Yale University Press, 1977); Barbara Welter, "The Cult of True Womanhood: 1820-1860," in Michael Gordon (ed.), *The American Family in Socio-Historical Perspective* (New York: St. Martin's Press, 1978), pp. 313-333; Barbara Epstein, "Industrialization and Femininity: A Case Study of Nineteenth Century New England," in Rachel Kahn-Hut, Arlene Kaplan Daniels, Richard Colvard (eds.), *Women and Work: Problems and Perspectives* (New York: Oxford University Press, 1982), pp. 88-100; Barbara J. Harris, *Beyond Her Sphere: Women and the Professions in American History* (Westport, Ct: Greenwood Press, 1983), pp. 32-72; Laurel Thatcher Ulrich, *Good Wives: Image and Reality in the Lives of Women in Northern New England* (New York: Oxford University Press, 1982).

55. Dill (1986) *op. cit.*, pp. 48-49.

56. Glenn (1985) *op. cit.*, pp. 86-109.

57. Dill (1986) *op. cit.*, p. 15.

2

The Colonial Family Ethic

The Development of Families, the Ideology of Women's Roles, and the Labor of Women

Recruiting Women to North America

Only a few women accompanied the first exploring parties and trading companies that reached North America. Several dozen female names appeared on the passenger lists before 1616, but not until 1619 did the numbers begin to grow. The European nations and commercial trading companies expected to reap quick profits from the riches of America.[1] Presuming no need for permanent migration, they typically sent male traders, explorers, and fortune hunters to the New World. But once they discovered that commercial profits and economic development required stabilized communities rather than rapid exploitation,[2] the trading companies began to bring women to America to stimulate the formation of families. The need for women's reproductive and productive labor led to the recruitment of wives, indentured servants, and slaves to the colonies. Only a few settlers married Native American women who already lived on and worked what, for the European explorers, was a new land.

45

White Wives

The first free white women came to the New World with those male explorers who brought their families with them.[3] To induce bachelor farmers to marry and settle down and to keep unmarried fortune hunters from returning home, colonial leaders began to devise ways to increase the supply of free white women. The owner of the Virginia Trading Company of London, for example, proposed that brides be sent to the Virginia planters. "He wished that a fit hundred might be sent of women, maids young and uncorrupt, to make wives to the inhabitants and by that means to make the men there more settled and less moveable who by defect therefor (as is credibly reported) stay there but to get something and then to return to England." Such instability it was feared would "breed a dissolution and so an overthrow of the plantation."[4]

Trading companies devised a variety of incentives to induce men to marry and to attract white women to the New World. They paid the transportation costs for planters who took a recruited wife, provided additional land to men who married, and promised servants to new couples to help "preserve families and proper family men before single persons." In 1619, the Virginia House of Burgess allotted husbands an equal land share for their wives, declaring, "in a newe plantation it is not knowne whether man or woman be the most necessary." In all, the Virginia company sent 140 women to the colony between 1620 and 1622.[5]

Other colonies enticed women with the promise of property rather than a breadwinner. Pennsylvania offered seventy-five acres to women who came at their own expense and Salem, Massachusetts offered "maid lotts" to women without husbands.[6] This inducement had to be eliminated, however, when some independent female landowners chose not to marry. The Maryland legislature in 1634 introduced a bill threatening to repossess land from women who did not marry within seven years after receiving it.[7] The governor of Massachusetts refused land to Deborah Holmes, "being a maid"; he wanted to avoid "all presedents and evill of graunting lotts unto single maidens not disposed of." Holmes got a bushel of corn instead.[8] Georgia, settled a hundred years later, not only refused to grant women land, but denied them the right to inherit.[9]

The great need for women in the colonies also encouraged the "sale" of wives. A sea captain in the early seventeenth century brought 144 single women looking for husbands to Virginia and sold them as "wives" for 120 pounds of leaf tobacco—or about $80. While this captain advertised for women looking to marry, others simply kidnapped young women off the streets of London for sale as wives or indentured servants to men in the American colonies.[10]

White Indentured Servants

The indenture system accounted for one-third to one-half of all immigrants to North America until the American Revolution.[11] Owing to the scarcity of labor prior to slavery, female and male indentured servants from Europe became an important labor supply, especially in the middle-Atlantic and southern colonies. Forty percent of Virginia's population of about 1,100 were indentured servants in 1625.[12] By 1671, the colony's population of 40,000 persons included 2,000 black slaves and 6,000 white servants. In Maryland, too, nearly all the newly arrived unmarried women were indentured.

Many women voluntarily took advantage of colonial shortages of women and labor by agreeing to "indenture" themselves to a prosperous person for a fixed period of time (typically four to seven years) in exchange for transportation to America. Others, as noted above, arrived involuntarily, victims of organizations that kidnapped and sold servants in the colonies. The British government also "banished" displaced agricultural workers, felons, convicts, vagrants, prostitutes, and other "undesirables" into servitude in the colonies where they worked for the Crown.[13] In 1635, Charles I ordered the sheriff of London to send nine female convicts to Virginia to be sold as servants. In 1692, a judge ordered "fifty lewd women out of the house of corrections and thirty others who walked the streets at night" to be sent to America.[14] Britain used this colonial labor to develop its trade and commerce, to supply raw materials to the mother country, and to purchase finished products from it at a good price. Britain also used the colonies as a dumping ground for those who might cause social unrest.

Most indentured servants traveled to the New World on over-loaded vessels, crowded beyond capacity by shipmasters to assure that deaths en route did not lower their profits. One traveler reported that:

> During the voyage there is on board these ships terrible misery, stench, fume, horror, vomiting, many kinds of seasickness, fever, dysentery, headache, heat, constipation, boils, scurvy, cancer, mouth rot, and the like of which comes from old and sharply salted food and meat, also from the very bad and foul water, so that many die miserable...Add to this want of provisions, hunger, thirst, frost, heat, dampness, anxiety, want, afflictions and lamentations,

together with other trouble as e.g. the lice abound so frightfully, especially on sick people, that they can be scraped off the body. The misery reaches a climax when a gale rages for two or three nights so that everyone believes that the ship will go to the bottom with all human beings on board. In such a visitation the people cry and pray most piteously.[15]

Upon arrival in America, passengers paid their transportation before leaving the ship. Unlike free white women recruited to form families as well as to work the land, the colonies treated indentured servants as individual laborers. Buyers separated husbands from wives, and parents often had to sell their children into service never to see them again. "Soul Drivers" purchased other passengers, driving fifty or more servants through the countryside like cattle, offering them for sale to the highest bidder.[16]

Black Female Indentured Servants and Slaves

With the development of a large-scale plantation economy and the end of the Royal African Company's monopoly on the slave trade, slavery superseded white indentured servants as a profitable and sure source of labor.[17] However, the first black women to arrive in America were indentured servants. Twenty blacks, including three black women, traveled on a Dutch ship to Jamestown in 1619, a year before the *Mayflower* voyage. Prohibited by law to sell baptized blacks into slavery, the government bought their contracts and sold them as indentured servants to colonial administrators.[18] When their contracts expired, the early African arrivals became farmers, artisans, and landowners who voted, had servants, and even some slaves.[19] Former black servants contributed to the rise of a free black population in America. Representing 7.9 percent of all blacks in 1790, the free black population grew faster than the slave population until the 1820s and consisted as well of West Indian refugees and American slaves who gained their freedom by flight, purchase, or release from conscientious masters.

Most Africans, however, arrived in America as slaves. Philip Curtin, the first person to systematically analyze the available evidence, estimates that British North America imported about 5 percent of the nine to ten million Africans who reached the New World in the 350 years of transatlantic slave trade.[20] The majority of Africans went to Brazil and the Caribbean. Most slaves—the prisoners of tribal wars, those sold by chiefs to black slave merchants, and those kidnapped by white slavers—came from the West African coast between Senegal and Angola, a region extending 300 miles inland, whose rich culture was strongly influenced by that of the western Sudan, an important center in the development of human culture.[21] Those Africans who survived the voyage to America brought a multitude of languages, skills, crafts, and cultural heritages to the New World. The black population in the colonies (both free and slave) rose from twenty in 1619 to 16,700 in 1690 to 325,000 in 1760 when blacks accounted for 22 percent of the nation's population.[22] Like indentured servants, slaves were imported to the colonies to work. For black women this meant working the fields and reproducing the slave labor force. Instead of assisting the formation of families as colonial society did for free whites, the imposition of slavery tore black families apart.

The long journey to America was an extremely harsh one for black women and men. Unlike the trip by free whites and many indentured servants, the trip from Africa was involuntary, deliberately brutal, and, in effect, the initial stage of an indoctrination process meant to transform the free African into a docile and marketable slave. After examining Africans for health and physical prowess, slave traders, often Arab or black, marched their captives long distances to coastal warehouses where they were stored until a shipload was amassed.[23] Aboard ship the slaveowners chained their "cargo" in pairs and forced them to lie on their backs or on their sides in cramped spaces often only eighteen inches high. Lack of space, mobility, fresh air, and food killed 6 to 16 percent of the slaves en route.[24] Schools of sharks often followed slave ships across the Atlantic, feeding on the bodies of the dead and the sick thrown overboard to check the spread of infection, and those who tried to escape by jumping ship.

The first ships contained only a few African women, but over time their numbers grew to about one-third. Their experience aboard ship, like that of black men, foreshadowed the conditions of slavery in America. Both sexes were stripped and branded, although at times the women were freed from the chains used to confine black men. Some traders branded black women under the breast with smaller irons, so as not to jeopardize their future marketability and readily whipped women who cried out in pain or resisted the hot iron. The nakedness of the African females served as a constant reminder of their sexual vulnerability to any white male who might choose to physically abuse and torment them. According to one witness," The younger women fared best at first as they were allowed to come on deck as companions for our crew...Toward the end of the run, which lasted nearly six weeks, the mortality thinned out the main hold, and some scores of women were driven below as company for the males."[25] The crew often raped black women to torture them or to subdue the recalcitrant. Slavers also ridiculed captured women contemptuously, often brutalizing children just to watch the anguish of their mothers.

While some women were pregnant prior to their purchase, one observer explained that "…many a Negress was landed upon our shores already impregnated by someone of the demonic crew that brought her over."[26] Women who survived the early stages of their pregnancy received little food or exercise and gave birth in the scorching sun or freezing cold without any assistance during labor.[27] One traveler noted, "I saw pregnant women give birth to babies while chained to corpses which our drunken overseers had not removed."[28] The number of black women who died in childbirth or lost their babies will never be known, but a ship doctor reports high insanity rates, especially among the women:

> One day at Bonny I saw a middle-aged stout woman, who had been brought down from a fair the proceeding day, chained to the post of a black trader's door, in a state of furious insanity. On board the ship was a young negro woman chained to the deck, who had lost her senses soon after she was purchased and taken on board. In a former voyage we were obliged to confine a female negro about 23 years of age, on her becoming a lunatic. She was afterward sold during one of her lucid intervals.[29]

Many plantation owners continued to torture and terrorize slave women and men to force them to suppress their own needs, to accept their inferiority and dependence, to ally themselves with the will of the master, and to accede to their own enslavement.

The Colonial Economy

The work and family life of women in the colonies was shaped by the imperatives of the agricultural economy, the institution of slavery, and the ideology of women's roles. Nearly all of the initial white women and men who came to America settled in rural areas and engaged in farming and other agricultural pursuits. However, as increasing numbers of Dutch, English, German, and Scot-Irish immigrants established new settlements farther South, North, and West, colonial villages became diverse ranging from new outposts to century-old communities.

The shock of entry into a wilderness vitally conditioned life in this pre-industrial society. Some families lived in log cabins, lacked the equipment needed to weave, to make candles, or even to grind flour, and like Native Americans wore skin clothing and used grease and rags to provide light. By the end of the seventeenth century, improved production techniques permitted New England farmers to live in more substantial quarters and to grow some surplus for export. During the eighteenth century, men farmed and fished while women manufactured a variety of goods for both use and trade. A rural class structure composed of a landed gentry, small landowners, yeoman farmers, and landless peasants emerged.

Larger cities such as Philadelphia, New York, Boston, and Charleston also sprung up in the mid-eighteenth century around Eastern seaboard centers of commerce and manufacturing. Here, the merchant elite, the upper crust of "urban" society, exchanged the products of American farms and forests for English, European, and West Indian food and African slaves. Craftpersons, retailers, innkeepers, and small jobbers comprised the middle class, while the working class consisted of sailors, unskilled workers, and some artisans.[30]

The South was shaped by the plantation economy and the institution of slavery. Slavery became a key factor to both American industry and European commerce when colonial economic development, especially in the South, suffered from British economic restrictions, widespread labor shortages, and the refusal of the Native American population to be enslaved. Slavers imported more than two million Africans to the West Indies and America between 1680 and 1786, including many women.[31] The inhumane slave trade itself became extremely profitable with gains ranging from one-third to one-half or more on original investments.[32] That the English enslaved Native Americans · and Africans but never their white captives suggests that racism was deeply ingrained in America prior to slavery.[33] To the Puritans, blacks were barbarians, uncivilized, unchristian, and inferior persons not entitled to the same human rights as whites.[34]

Virginia, whose court records showed blacks in hereditary life service by 1640,[35] legalized slavery in the mid-1650s followed by Massachusetts, Maryland, New York, the Carolinas, Pennsylvania, Delaware, and Rhode Island. Most slaves worked on southern plantations. But slaves, distributed widely among small slaveholders, also began to supplement free white labor in northern cities.[36] Between 1710 and 1742, the number of slaves in Boston quadrupled, reaching 8.5 percent of the city's population, while the white population only doubled. Black slaves comprised more than 18 percent of New York's population in 1731 and over 21 percent in 1746.[37]

In both the North and the South, the pre-industrial household functioned as the center of economic production and social reproduction. Until the manufacturing economy of the early nineteenth century separated household and market activities, the colonial household was the basic unit of economic production as well as the place of procreation, socialization, maintenance, consumption, and recreation. It relied heavily on the labor of free white women, white indentured servants, and black female slaves. The nature and meaning of women's productive and reproductive labor in colonial society was governed by gender, race, class, marital status, and degrees of servitude; and by the colonial family ethic, that is, the prevailing ideology of women's roles.

The Colonial Family Ethic

The colonial settlers brought patriarchal ideas about the proper role of women with them to the New World. Although the intense interest in the ideals of male and female temperament, which accompanied the rise of industrialization did not yet exist, the European settlers did subscribe to an array of feminine stereotypes and role prescriptions including women as the "weaker vessel," the seductive Eve, the loose-tongued gossip—as well as notions of female meekness, wifely obedience, and the injunction to be a sturdy, orderly, and industrious helpmeet. Referred to here as the colonial family ethic, these ideas informed women (and men) about their proper work and family roles. Fulfilling the terms of the colonial family ethic established a woman's femininity, her womanhood, and her social respectability, and non-compliance brought penalties. Directed primarily toward white, married, middle-class homemakers, the colonial family ethic largely reflected their experience. As the dominant ideology encoded in the rules and regulations of most societal institutions, the colonial family ethic exerted considerable influence over the entire social order. Indeed, colonial society measured, valued, and rewarded indentured servants, free black women, and black female slaves according to their conformity to its terms.

The Family

Colonial society placed the patriarchal family at the center of the social order. Defined as "little cells of righteousness" that held a "watchfulle eye" over the conduct of every individual and enforced the laws of God,[38] families assumed the responsibility for teaching religion, morality, the work ethic, obedience to the laws, deference to authority, and general good conduct at home. Supported by prevailing norms and laws, the colonial family operated as the key unit for survival, socialization, and social stability.[39]

In this view, the father's unquestioned rule was the only assurance of a proper discharge of the family's obligations. A leading Puritan theologian of the time wrote, "in the good man or master of the familie resteth the private and proper government of the whole household, and he comes not unto it by election as it falleth out in other states, but by the ordinance of God settled even in the order of nature. The husband indeed naturally beares rule over the wife, parent over their children, master over their servants."[40] Colonial society expected free white women to marry, to bear and raise children, and to manage a household in which they were economically productive, but faithful, obedient, and subordinate to men. To be proper helpmeets, colonial women each had to acquire a husband and a family, and had to take up homemaking in her own home.

Marriage

Marriage became the lynchpin of the colonial family ethic. "True womanhood" required the presence of and dependence on a male breadwinner.[41] The association between women and wife was so close that in some English dialects the two words had the same meaning. In northern New England, for example, between 1650 and 1750, most women were called "Goodwife," usually shortened to "Goody," as in Goody Prince, Goody Quilter, or Goody Lee.[42] Reflecting the economics of survival as well as patriarchal rules, colonial laws encouraged white women and men to marry, divorced persons to remarry, and required bachelors, spinsters, and other unmarried persons to live within an established household. A 1669 Plymouth statute read:

> Whereas great inconvenience hath arisen by single persons in this colony being for themselves and not betaking themselves to live in well-governed families. It is enacted by the Court that henceforth no single person be suffered to live of himself [sic] or in any family but such as the Selectman of the Town shall approve of; and if any person or persons shall refuse or neglect to attend such order as shall be given them by the Selectman, that person or persons shall be summoned to the Court to be proceeded with as the matter shall require.[43]

Town courts fined single persons and couples who lived apart, and taxed bachelors and self-supporting single women for evading their civic responsibilities.[44] Unmarried women, in addition, faced social disapproval as dependent girls and incomplete women. Without a husband, a colonial woman was not a "real" woman. Single women with means and widows were respected somewhat more, but newspapers and town gossips often characterized single females as unattractive, disagreeable "old virgins" unable to catch a man.[45]

Subordination

Colonial society expected married women to be subordinate to their husbands who by law and custom controlled women's labor and access to economic resources. According to one historian,

> Control rested with the male head to whom all others were subordinate. His sanctions were powerful; they rested upon traditions that went back beyond the memory of man [sic]; on the instinctive sense of order as hierarchy, whether in the cosmic chain of being or in human society; on the processes of law that reduced the female to perpetual dependence and calibrated a detailed scale of female subordination and servitude; and above all on the restrictions of the economy which made the establishment of independent households a difficult enterprise.[46]

Justified by the Old Testament's patriarchal model and prevailing cultural assumptions of female weakness and inferiority, religious leaders held that submission to God and submission to one's husband were part of the same doctrine. Economics and civil law further enforced female subordination. The exclusion of women from economic activity independent of their husbands or fathers left them financially dependent and poorly positioned for self-support. Colonial law acknowledged women's economic importance in deeds and wills that typically granted some resources to wives, but this recognition did not extend to the basic rights of land ownership, political participation, or social equality.[47]

English Common Law, the basis of much American law, caused married women to suffer "civil death" by holding that in "marriage, the husband and wife are one person in law; that is, the very being or legal existence of the woman is suspended during the marriage, or at least is incorporated and consolidated into that of the husband; under whose wing, protection, and cover she performs everything."[48] A married woman's inheritance, property, income, and even her clothing belonged to her husband, who could sell her possessions without her consent. She could not buy or sell, make contracts, sue in court, or be sued without her husband's permission. Married women could not even claim their children in cases of legal separation.[49]

The obedience and submission of women to men was also evidenced in laws that required female chastity and sexual fidelity. According to religious doctrine, God told Eve, "Thy desire shall be to thy husband and he shall rule over thee."[50] Colonial society openly acknowledged female sexuality, including the sexual needs of married women whose "intemperate longings" a husband was duty-bound to gratify. Failure to do so, be it due to impotence or willful denial, could be grounds for separation.[51] The community, however, did not condone extra-marital sex. Harsh laws severely penalized adultery, pre-marital sex, and out-of-wedlock births.

Within the law, however, a double standard prevailed. Adulterous relations by or with a married woman received the most severe penalties and could result in a death sentence. Sex between a married man and a single woman or between two single persons received a harsh but lighter response. Public opinion also tolerated greater violation of sexual norms by men than women. Popular magazines advised women to conceal their husband's infidelities while engaging in none of their own. A 1771 issue of the *Ladies Journal* stated:

> A licentious commerce between the sexes. . .may be carried on by the men without contaminating the mind so as to render them unworthy of the marriage bed, and incapable of discharging the virtuous and honorable duties of husband, father and friend...[But] the contamination of the female mind is the necessary and inseparable consequence of an illicit intercourse with men...[W]omen are universally virtuous or utterly undone.[52]

According to Dr. Samuel Johnson, the double standard protected propertied men from passing their wealth along to a child fathered by someone else. He explained that "Confusion of progeny constitutes the essence of the crime; therefore a woman who breaks her marriage vows is much more criminal than a man who does it."[53]

Economic Productivity

Private homemaking became the centerpiece of colonial womanhood. The colonial family ethic defined free white women as industrious helpmeets, placed a great value on the average woman's productive labor in the home, and called upon them to make an. economic contribution to the family and the community. The expectation of such productivity from women meshed with the household economy's needs but also with Puritanism's strong negative sanction against idleness.

Household work followed a clearly defined but flexible gender division of labor.[54] Men worked largely outdoors and in the fields while women worked closer to home. Colonial homemaking included the supervision of the home, the manufacture of household goods, the planting and preparation of food, and the spinning and weaving of cloth. Women also assisted with the harvest, helped in the family store, and produced crafts. In cash poor and frontier families, men struggled to produce for the market, to build up capital goods, and to save cash income for future investment. Wives contributed by reducing family expenditures and providing for most of the family's basic subsistence needs. They fed, clothed, and cared for their large families, made household furnishings, and often defended their frontier homes against attack.[55] Many colonial women also functioned as "deputy husbands," shouldering male duties from the most menial to the management of the family's external business affairs. Women could assume almost any task as long as it furthered the good of their family, was acceptable to their husband, and remained close to the confines of the home. But in all cases, women's productive labor was defined as secondary to that of male providers.[56] Any income that resulted from women's work was seen as saving money by reducing the demand on their husband's overall capital.[57]

Reproductive Tasks

As caretakers of the family and the community, colonial wives attended to the ill, aged, young, and disabled family members as well as to the widowed, orphaned, and destitute. Childbearing, a central part of women's homemaking role, conferred status upon women in a world where high infant mortality rates and a heavy dependence on child labor dictated large families. While bearing many children helped to perpetuate the family and to strengthen the community, infertility signaled female failure. Given the limits of prevailing medical knowledge, however, childbearing was dangerous work. One out of every five women in seventeenth-century Plymouth, Massachusetts died from causes associated with childbirth.[58]

While pregnancy and childbirth occupied many of a woman's adult years, seventeenth- and eighteenth-century America did not idealize motherhood.[59] Expected to show affection and sentiment, colonial society discouraged undue indulgence as a troublesome invitation to disorder and disobedience. Puritan ministers warned against "a

Mother's excessive fondness" and the tendency of mothers to spoil their children. The conditions of colonial life reinforced these views. High infant mortality rates and large families left mothers with little time to dote on their children or to become too emotionally involved with them.[60]

Except for childbearing, breastfeeding, and the preliminary education of the very young, social conventions assigned few childrearing tasks exclusively to mothers. In wealthy families children were suckled and raised by wet nurses, servants, and black slaves. In all classes, considerable responsibility for parental governance also rested with fathers[61] who disciplined children and supervised their education, religious instruction, and vocational training.[62] This pattern meshed with the authority attributed to the patriarch and with the Puritan devaluation of women as less rational and requiring the guidance of men. The structure of the home economy also permitted these parenting arrangements. Men worked in sufficient proximity to their children to become involved in their development. Colonial women who lacked time for extensive involvement could care for infants while cooking, weaving, and keeping an eye on farm animals.[63] With both economic and domestic activities taking place in the home, there was no obvious line between women's productive and reproductive labor. Productive tasks associated with economic matters were intermingled with reproductive tasks associated with childrearing, consumption, and home maintenance.

Class Differences

Both geography and the class position of a free white woman's husband determined the character of her work.[64] Less marked than in Europe, class distinctions in the colonies were based on differentials in wealth and landholdings. Indeed, in the middle class and upper class, a second image of woman as a decorous object and charming companion began to emerge. Unlike the later Victorian lady of "leisure," however, the image of the colonial gentlewoman meshed with society's demand that women be industrious. What differentiated her from lower classes of colonial women was the greater availability of resources, greater household help, and greater attention paid to grace and style.[65]

Instead of producing food and clothes themselves, the homemaking duties of wealthy colonial wives involved purchasing goods and services in the market, managing the many details of a large household, and supervising the work of servants and slaves. Feminine graces and the charms of female social companionship also added to their utility.[66] Taught to be charming, fashionable, and accomplished in drawing, painting, and French, upper-class housewives also played a social, entertaining, and decorative role.[67]

In sum, colonial society expected white women to marry, to make an economic contribution to the family and the community, to bear and raise children, to remain morally pure, and to manage a household under male authority and control. Those who followed the rules—acquired a family and pursued homemaking according to the needs of the household economy and the norms of patriarchy—won social approval as a "true woman." Because profits and economic growth required the formation and protection of white families, colonial leaders encouraged their organization and development.[68] Although white women were not granted equal rights and full social participation, colonial society acknowledged and supported the contribution their productive and reproductive labor made to the growth and stability of the family, the community, and the wider social order.

White Servants, Black Slaves, and Colonial Womanhood

The structure of colonial society denied the stamp of respectable womanhood to unfree women, both white indentured servants who were owned temporarily and black female slaves who were locked into involuntary and lifelong bondage. The same profitable development of colonial society which necessitated granting the "rights of womanhood" to free white women, led owners to refuse them to servants and slaves, along with their legal and economic rights.

Colonial norms which encouraged white women to develop their own families defined female servants and slaves first and foremost as individual units of labor. Indeed, the productive labor that female servants and slaves performed for their master's household took precedence over the productive and reproductive activities conducted on behalf of their own families. Prevented by law from marrying, their own mothering and homemaking roles were subsumed to their laboring tasks and accorded little recognition or support in white society. Colonial society left servants and slaves vulnerable to sexual exploitation and rationalized this by viewing them as sexually available and morally impure.

Female Indentured Servants

The female servant's productive and reproductive labor was almost completely controlled by the master for the term of the indenture. Masters prevented servants from marrying, leaving, or even buying anything without permission.[69] Although practices varied by region, typically indentured servants were poorly compensated and deprived of good food and privacy. Servants who tried to escape, and many did try, faced severe punishment, including fines, whipping, and branding for a second offense, as well as extended service. They received similar penalties for theft and laziness. Unlike slaves, however, the white indentured servant received some protection under the law which specified the provision of certain amounts of food and clothing, banned corporal punishment,[70] and permitted servants to sue their owners, with the courts granting freedom or shortened service.[71] Most critically, the servitude of indentured servants was contracted and ended after a stipulated period of time.

The rules of indenture barred servants from doing anything that threatened to impair or interrupt their productive labor. A female servant who became pregnant, thus degrading her productivity, faced heavy fines and possible whipping for failure to pay. To compensate for her reduced service and to punish the sin, her term might be extended as much as two years, if the father of her child did not purchase her remaining years of labor. If impregnated by her master, as frequently happened, the town denied extra service to him, selling it to the town instead.[72]

Some women escaped servitude when prospective husbands purchased the remainder of their time,[73] but most completed their contracts. At the end of the indenture period, servants were entitled to freedom dues, typically a few barrels of Indian corn, some clothing, or a small parcel of land. Although written into the contract, such freedom dues were not always paid.[74] Given the shortage of women, former indentured servants tended to marry quickly. Some married "up"; others entered the working class as wives or as domestic servants; still others drifted off and joined the ranks of the colonial poor along with formerly indentured men.[75]

Black Female Slaves

White colonial society simply denied the "rights of womanhood" to black female slaves. The very notion of black womanhood under slavery contradicted the prevailing ideology of women's proper role. Enslaved black women never possessed the right to legal marriage, to family integrity, or to protection against economic or sexual abuse. In an economy dependent on subordinated labor, female slaves worked outside their own families and outside of a woman's homemaking role.

The productive and reproductive labor of black women, central to the slave labor system, was owned and regulated by white masters who used force or the threat of force to extract as much work as possible from them. Female slave labor contributed to the master's economic well-being in both the "big house" and in the field, while the capacity of black women to reproduce guaranteed the growth of the slave labor force.[76] On the large plantations, 70 to 90 percent of the slaves of both genders worked in the fields. Black women hoed, shoveled, plowed, planted, and harvested; they felled trees, split rails, drove and loaded carts, and otherwise assumed tasks defined by white society as "men's" work. According to one ex-slave, "it was usual for men and women to work side by side on our plantation; and in many kinds of work, the women were compelled to do as much as the men."[77] Indeed, planters considered the sexual division of labor to be economically inefficient and disregarded it when organizing the tasks of slaves.[78] With the rise of industry, some slave-owners began to "rent" female slaves to the builders of southern roads, canals, levees, and railroads and to owners of mines, iron works, factories, and lumbering companies.[79]

Less than 5 percent of all adult slaves worked in the elite corps of trained household servants, the advantages of which were exaggerated by whites, according to slave narratives. In the "big house," where labor was more likely to be gender-typed, black women worked as nurses, cooks, seamstresses, washerwomen, and dairy keepers, and provided the elbow grease for most domestic chores, although during harvests they were frequently sent into the fields. Housework was back-breaking, closely supervised, and as fast-paced as work in the fields. The black woman's proximity to the master in the "big house" created special problems for slave women. Masters sometimes kept them "on call," forced them to remain standing in the presence of whites, and made them sleep on the floor at the foot of their mistress' bed. Under these conditions, white owners could also rape and sexually assault their female house slaves more easily and with impunity.[80]

Minor infractions or failure to accomplish the expected amount of work might result in severe chastisement in both the field or the manor. Masters whipped black female slaves for burning the waffles or oversleeping. One female fugitive slave reported:

> One day I set the table and forgot to put on the carving-fork—the knife was there. I went to the table to put on a plate. My master said,—"Where's the fork?" I told him, "I forgot it." He says,—"You'd d--- black b-----, I'll forget you!"—at the same time hitting me on the head with the carving knife...I was frequently punished with raw hides,—was hit with tongs and pokers and anything. I used when I went out, to look up at the sky and say, "Blessed Lord, oh do take me out of this." It seemed to me I could not bear another lick. I can't forget it.[81]

According to another slave woman:

> When dey ready to beat you dey'd strip you stark mother naked and dey'd say, "Come here to me, God Damn you. Come to me clean! Walk up to dat tree and damn you, hug dat tree!" Den dey'd tie your hands round de tree, den tie you feets, den dey's lay de rawhide on and cut your buttocks open. Sometimes they's rub turpentine and salt in de raw places, and den beat you some more.[82]

The reproductive labor done by female slaves for their masters was indistinguishable from their productive labor. After the slave trade became illegal in 1808, the line blurred even more as plantation owners placed increased value on the fertility of their female slaves and "breeding" became more common. A southern white traveler observed:

> In the states of Maryland, Virginia, North Carolina, Kentucky, Tennessee, as much attention is paid to the breeding and growth of negroes as to that of horses and mules. Further south, we raise them both for use and for market. Planters command their girls and women (married or unmarried) to have children; and I have known a great many girls to be sold off because they did not have children. A breeding woman is worth from one-sixth to one-fourth more than one that does not breed.[83]

Owners often bribed or coerced female slaves to reproduce rapidly, although repeated pregnancies without proper care resulted in numerous miscarriages and sometimes death. Masters promised freedom to slave mothers who gave birth to ten or fifteen children. Slave women were given extra food, special clothes, small sums of money, or were physically coerced to reproduce regularly. Some masters mated black women with white men, as mulattoes often brought a higher price or were easier to sell.

The economic benefits of the female slave's productive and reproductive labor at times, contradicted each other. The extraction of maximum physical labor produced immediate profits, but long hours of back-breaking work could damage a woman's reproductive system and undermine the owner's long-term investment in black female slaves as childbearers.[84] To preserve their ability to breed, some slave-owners gave pregnant and post-partum women fewer or lighter tasks and limited their workloads or floggings. But others forced female slaves to work through most of their pregnancy and put them back to work shortly after their delivery. One ex-slave told of a master who beat nursing mothers whose full breasts slowed them down, "with raw hide so that the blood and milk flew mingled from their breasts."[85] Another tells of an overseer who stripped, tied, and beat a slave woman in an advanced state of pregnancy for three days in a row because she failed to complete her assigned task.[86]

In contrast to the support given to the formation and maintenance of white families, slave-owners and government officials ignored and, in some cases, destroyed the black family. A combination of economics, racism, and fear led slave-owners, particularly those with large plantations and many slaves, to callously separate black family members in sales and estate settlements, to deny recognition of slave marriages, to sexually exploit female slaves, and to degrade all slaves by preventing them from defending family members from abuse.[87] Not all slave-holders engaged in these severe practices or carried them out with the same brutality, but the practices were condoned by the law.

After working in the master's house, fields, and factories, slave women returned home to carry out the reproductive work needed by their family and community. But black women's own homemaking came second and took place under a wide range of cultural assaults.[88] To begin with, the black woman's double day left her chronically overworked. A former slave recalls,

> I never knowed what it was to rest. I just work all de time from mornin' till late at night. I had to do everythin' dey was to do on de outside. Work in de field, chop wood, hoe corn, till sometimes I feels like my back surely break...In de summer we had to work outdoors, in de winter in de house. I had to card and spin till ten o'clock. Never get much rest, had to get up at four de next mornin' and start again.[89]

Another slave described her work: "What did I do? I spun an' cooked, an' waited, an' plowed; dere weren't nothin' I didn't do."[90]

Black women's work in the slave quarters followed a traditional gender division of labor in which women cared for children and maintained the house. Where the constraints of slavery permitted, men functioned as providers and household heads.[91] Some[92] but not all[93] historians argue that black women were subject to chauvinism from black men. However, the subordination of both the slave homemaker and her husband to their owner renders the discussion of marital inequality difficult. Such subordination left both husband and wife powerless and introduced a strange equality to the slave marriage that was based on shared oppression. Often unable to carry out the role of family provider and protector and lacking the resources of patriarchal society, black men, even when they wanted to, were poorly positioned to turn gender distinctions into female subordination.[94]

Gender distinctions were, however, very significant when it came to white men's treatment of black women. In this relationship, black women were exploited not just because of their race but also because of their sex. Slavery denied black women the rights of motherhood and accorded them virtually no protection against sexual assault by white men. White male ownership of slave children made mothering by slave women a painful and complicated task and allowed a mother to protect her child only so far. In the words of a former slave: "Many a day my ole mama has stood by an' watched massa beat her chillun 'till dey bled an' she couldn' open her mouf."[95] Female slaves also risked losing their offspring to high infant mortality rates or sale in the slave market. Some mothers killed their babies to keep them from being sold down the river; others "descended into madness" or "donned a mask of stoicism" to conceal their inner pain.[96] Still others desperately tried to prevent the sale. Moses Grandy, born a slave, told how his mother resisted the sale of one of his brothers: "My mother, frantic with grief resisted...she was beaten and held down; she fainted, and when she came to herself, her boy was gone. She made much outcry, for which the master tied her up to a peach tree in the yard and flogged her."[97]

The threat of sexual assault from white masters and overseers constantly confronted the female slave. Virtually all the slave narratives contain accounts of the sexual victimization of slave women. One ex-slave reported,

> Ma mama said that a nigger 'oman couldn't help herself, fo' she had to do what de marster say. Ef he come to de field whar de women workin' an' tel gal to come on, she had to go, He would

take one down in de woods an' use her all de time he wanted to,
den send her on back to work. Times nigger 'omen had chillun
for de marster an his sons and some times it was fo' de ovah seer.[98]

Slave narratives refer to Henry Bibb's master who forced one slave
girl to be his son's concubine; M.F. Jamison's overseer who raped a
slave girl; and Solomon Northrup's owner who forced one slave,
"Patsy," to be his sexual partner.[99] Without the right of choice or refusal,
virtually any sexual contact between black female slaves and white men
with power over them became a form of rape. The child of a slave
recounted what happened when his mother tried to choose:

I don't like to talk 'bout dem times 'cause my mother did suffer
misery. You know dar was an overseer who use to tie mother up
in the barn wid a rope aroun' her arms up over her head, while
she stood on a block. Soon as dey got her tied, di block was moved
an' her feet dangled, you know, couldn't tech de flo'. Dis ole man,
now would start beaten' her nekked 'til the blood run down her
back to her heels. I asked mother 'what she done fer 'em to beat
and do her so? She said, 'Nothin 'other dan 'fuse to be wife to dis
man.'[100]

The sexual exploitation of black women by white men differentiated their oppression from that of male slaves. The sexual abuse of
black female slaves by white men became a weapon of domination
that worked to extinguish the slave woman's will.[101] According to Susan
Brownmiller, "Rape in slavery was more than a chance tool of violence.
It was an institutionalized crime, part and parcel of the white man's
subjugation of people for economic and psychological gain [in which]
the black woman's sexual integrity was deliberately crushed in order
that slavery might profitably endure."[102]

Despite these many assaults and contrary to popular stereotypes,
black slaves achieved considerable family stability. Recent research by
Gutman and others has uncovered evidence of strong and enduring
family ties among slaves.[103] A strict set of kinship norms prescribed
sexual mores, marriage ceremonies, and kinship patterns.[104] Most slave
families tried, within the limits of the system, to maintain the two-parent,
male-headed household quite prevalent in the Afro-American culture.
Unions between husbands and wives, and parents and children en-
dured for many years. Even when separated by owners over long distances and great time spans, slave family members, when possible,
reunited.

The relationship between the slave family and their masters was
a contradictory one. The slave family simultaneously supported and

threatened the institution of slavery. Stable slave families, it was hoped, would socialize children to their subordinate status[105] and enhance the productivity of the master's workforce. At the same time, strong family ties among slaves promoted allegiances other than to the slave-master. The wide protective kinship networks formed in the slave community created pride, cohesion, and also became a breeding ground for resistance.[106]

Black slaves—both women and men—resisted their subordination by preventing the full use of their labor, by organizing revolts, and by running away. Resistance began on the slave ships where slaves tried to escape by jumping overboard, drowning themselves, or organizing sometimes successful mutinies.[107] On the plantations, slave women and men deliberately withheld their labor by feigning illness, slowing down their work pace, destroying crops and equipment, and even injuring themselves, all the while assuming an obedient, compliant posture. One ex-slave reports, "I knew a woman who could not be conquered by her mistress, and so when her master threatened to sell her to New Orleans Negro traders, she took her right hand, laid it down on a meat block and cut off three fingers, and thus made the sale impossible."[108] Slaves also taught themselves to read and write in clandestine "midnight schools" often run by women.[109] But perhaps the most dramatic and least known act of resistance among slave women was their refusal to perform their most essential role, producing slave babies. Slave women fought forced mating and used contraceptives and abortive agents to resist the system.[110]

More direct forms of resistance included fighting with their masters or overseers, running away, and organizing slave revolts.[111] Though no one knows for sure, between 40,000 and 100,000 slaves escaped to the North and Canada via the Underground Railroad during the years preceding the Civil War. Harriet Tubman, the Railroad's most famous conductor, made nineteen journeys to the South after her own escape in 1850, bringing over 300 slaves out of Maryland alone.[112] Numerous revolts and rebellions and riots by free blacks during the 1700s and 1800s left the colonists in constant fear of slave insurrections.[113]

Because of their ties to children, slave women ran away less often than men. But from New York to New Orleans they became actively involved in slave uprisings where they fought alongside men, often with guns and knives, and at times committed suicide rather than face capture and execution. Women also committed arson, sabotage, and on occasion poisoned their owners.[114] In 1681, a Massachusetts town court tried a slave named Maria and two male companions for trying to burn down their master's home. One man was banished from the colony, the other hanged; but the town burned Maria at the stake because "she did not have the feare of God before her eyes," and her action seemed to be "instigated by the devil."[115] A small band of slaves who killed seven whites in Newton, Long Island in 1708 included one woman. In 1712, twenty-three armed male and female slaves prepared to set fire to a slave-holder's house in New York City; they killed nine whites and injured six others. A visibly pregnant black slave woman was among those arrested. Black female slaves were known to be involved in slave plots in Louisiana (1730, 1732), in Charleston, South Carolina (1730), in Charlestown, Massachusetts (1741) and many others up until the end of the Civil War.[116] Frequently caught, the men were banished or hanged but women such as Maria, having a "malicious and evil intent," often were burned at the stake—a hideous torture no doubt meant to deter women from participating in these revolts.[117]

Summary

Colonial leaders and traders brought women to the New World as wives, servants, and slaves because their productive and reproductive labor was needed for family formation and economic development. Upon arrival and thereafter, women's experience reflected the demands of the household economy, the strength of patriarchal norms, and their relationship to the institution of slavery. In addition to gender, the character and scope of women's productive and reproductive labor was shaped by their race, class, marital status, and degree of servitude. These characteristics determined not only the personal and economic safety and security of women, but also the value, respect, and support accorded to their reproductive and productive labor. The traits also governed white women's ability to fulfill the terms of the colonial family ethic and reap its rewards. For black women, denied even the opportunity to comply, the family ethic—the white family ethic—only deepened their oppression as women as well as blacks.

Poor women, whose numbers continued to grow despite the contribution of women's labor to the nation's economic growth, confronted the colonial family ethic in the rules and regulations of public relief to which they often turned for help. Embedded in the institutions of public welfare, the colonial family ethic became a means of determining which poor women were aided and how much help they received. By treating women who conformed to the terms of the family ethic more favorably than those who did not, could not, or chose not to do so, the colonial poor laws responded to women differentially. They also helped to support patriarchal family governance and the ideology of women's roles. Chapter Three, which explores the colonial poor laws, presents the first segment in the untold story of the relationship between women and the U.S. social welfare system.

Notes to Chapter 2

1. June Axinn and Herman Levin, *Social Welfare: A History of the American Response to Need* (New York: Harper and Row, 1975), p. 16.

2. Susan Estabrook Kennedy, *If All We Did Was To Weep At Home: A History of White Working Class Women in America* (Bloomington: Indiana University Press, 1979), pp. 3-4.

3. Barbara M. Wertheimer, *We Were There: The Story of Working Women in America* (New York: Pantheon Books, 1977), p. 7. The first white woman settler in America was the wife of a Spanish soldier who traveled with her husband to Florida and who later died in an Indian raid in 1541. White women, along with black male artisans and agriculturalists, participated in the Spanish and Portuguese colonizing expeditions that, in 1565, founded St. Agustine, the first permanent mainland settlement in the United States. Still others were among the 150 families who, in 1598, accompanied 400 Mexican soldiers into what became the southwestern United States. Seventeen women disappeared between 1587 and 1591. Kennedy (1979) *op. cit.*, p. 4. The second supply ship sent to Jamestown, Virginia in 1608 included at least two women: Lucy, the wife of Thomas Forest and her thirteen year old maid, Anne Buras.

4. Julia Cherry Spruill, *Women's Life and Work in the Southern Colony* (New York: W.W. Norton & Company, 1972), p. 8.

5. *Ibid.*, p. 9.

6. Alice Kessler-Harris, *Out To Work: A History of Wage-Earning Women in the United States* (Oxford: Oxford University Press, 1982), pp. 10-11.

7. Spruill (1972) *op. cit.*, p. 11.

8. Kessler-Harris (1982) *op. cit.*, p. 11, citing Robert B. Morris, *Studies in the History of American Law* (New York: Octagon Books, 1963 [1930]) pp. 131, 134.

9. Spruill (1972) *op. cit.*, p. 17.

10. Carol Hymowitz and Michael Weissman, *A History of Women In America* (New York: Bantam Books, 1980), p. 3; Axinn and Levin (1975) *op. cit.*, p. 17.

11. Wertheimer (1977) *op. cit.*, p. 11.

12. Lois Green Carr and Lorena S. Walsh, "The Planter's Wife: The Experience of White Women in Seventeenth Century Maryland," in Jean E. Friedman and William G. Shade (eds.), *Our American Sisters: Women in American Life and Thought* (Lexington, Mass.: D.C. Heath and Co., 1982), p. 55; Mary P. Ryan, *Womanhood in America: From Colonial Times to the Present* (New York: New Viewpoints, 1975), p. 24.

13. Marcus W. Jernegan, *Laboring and Dependent Classes in Colonial America, 1607-1783* (Chicago: The University of Chicago Press, 1931), pp. 46-48.

14. *Ibid.*, p. 48.

15. Rhea Dulles Foster, *Labor in America*, (New York: Thomas Y. Crowell Co., 1966, third edition), p. 6, cited by Wertheimer (1977) *op. cit.*, p. 11.

16. Jernegan (1931) *op. cit.*, p. 51.

17. August Meier and Elliot Rudwick, *From Plantation to Ghetto* (New York: Hill and Wang, 1976, third edition), pp. 42-43.

18. Paula Giddings, *Where and When I Enter:The Impact of Black Women on Race and Sex in America* (Toronto: Bantam Books, 1985), p. 34.

19. *Ibid.*

20. Julie Matthaei, *An Economic History of Women In America* (New York: Schocken Books, 1982), pp. 74-75; Wertheimer (1977) *op. cit.*, p. 27.

21. Meier and Rudwick (1976, third edition) *op. cit.*, pp. 3-26.

22. Axinn and Levin (1975) *op. cit.*, p. 17.

23. Cited by Meier and Rudwick (1976, third edition) *op. cit.*, p. 38.

24. *Ibid.*, p. 38.

25. Eleanor Flexner, *Century of Struggle: The Women's Rights Movement in the United States* (New York: Antheum, 1968), p. 19, citing George F. Dow, *Slave Ships and Slaving* (Salem, Mass., 1927), p. 242.

26. Bell Hooks, *Ain't I A Woman: Black Women and Feminism* (Boston: South End Press, 1981), p. 18.

27. *Ibid.*

28. Flexner (1968), p. 19, citing Dow, *op. cit.*, (1927), p. 242.

29. *Ibid.*, citing Dow (1927), p. 151.

30. Matthaei (1982) *op. cit.*, pp. 22-23.

31. Wertheimer (1977) *op. cit.*, pp. 29, 109.

32. Meier and Rudwick (1976, third edition) *op. cit.*, p. 40.

33. Gerda Lerner, *Black Women in White America: A Documentary History* (New York: Vintage Books, 1973), p. 5; June Schoen, *Herstory: Record of the American Woman's Past* (Palo Alto: Mayfield Publishing Company, 1981) p. 23; George Brown Tindall, *America: A Narrative History* (New York: W.W. Norton & Co., 1984), Vol. I, p. 100.

34. Lerner (1973) *op. cit.*, p. 5.

35. Tindall (1984) *op. cit.*, p. 98.

36. Meier and Rudwick (1976, third edition) *op. cit.*, pp. 27-28, 40.

37. Gary Nash, *The Urban Crucible: Social Change, Political Consciousness, and the Origins of the America Revolution* (Cambridge: Harvard University Press, 1979), p. 107.

38. Barbara A. Hanawalt, "Women Before The Law: Females as Felons and Prey in Fourteenth-Century England," in D. Kelly Weisberg (ed.), *Women and*

the Law: The Social Historical Perspective (Cambridge: Schenkman Publishing Co., 1982), Vol. I, p. 186.

39. Kessler-Harris (1982) *op. cit.*, p. 4.

40. Robert H. Bremner (ed.) *Children and Youth in America: A Documentary History, Vol. I: 1600-1865* (Cambridge: Harvard University Press, 1970), p. 27.

41. Matthaei (1982) *op. cit.*, p. 51.

42. Laurel Thatcher Ulrich, *Good Wives: Image and Reality in the Lives of Women in Northern New England, 1650-1750* (New York: Oxford University Press, 1982), p. 6, xiii.

43. William Brighan (ed.), *The Compact with the Charter and Laws of the Colony of New Plymouth* (Boston 1836), p. 156, excerpted in R. Bremner, Vol. I (1970) *op. cit.*, p. 49; Robert W. Kelso, *The History of Public Poor Relief in Massachusetts 1620-1920* (Montclair, N.J.; Patterson Smith, 1969), p. 31.

44. Ryan (1975) *op. cit.*, p. 38; Mary Sumner Benson, *Women in Eighteenth Century America* (New York: Columbia University Press, 1966), p. 233; Spruill (1938) *op. cit.*, p. 137.

45. Spruill (1938) *op. cit.*, p. 138.

46. Nancy Folbre, "Patriarchy in Colonial New England," *The Review of Political Economics,* 12(2) (Summer 1980), p. 6, citing Bailyn, B., *Education in the Forming of American Society* (Chapel Hill: University of North Carolina Press, 1969), p. 16.

47. Ryan (1975) *op. cit.*, pp. 26, 29-30.

48. Ulrich (1982) *op. cit.*, p. 7, citing Sir William Blackstone, *Commentaries on the Laws of England* (Oxford: Clarendon Press, 1765-1769), Vol. I, p. 442.

49. Carol Brown, "Mothers, Fathers, and Children: From Private to Public Patriarchy," in Lydia Sargent (ed.), *Women and Revolution: A Discussion of the Unhappy Marriage of Marxism and Feminism* (Boston: South End Press, 1981), pp. 250-251.

50. Matthaei (1982) *op. cit.*, p. 49, citing Cotton Mather, *Ornaments to The Daughters of Zion* (Boston: Kneeland and Green, 1741, third edition), p. 94.

51. Ryan (1975) *op. cit.*, p. 52.

52. Spruill (1938) *op. cit.*, pp. 172-173.

53. *Ibid.*, p. 173.

54. Historians of colonial America do not agree as to the status of women or the presence of a gender division of labor. Some such as Alice Clark, Elizabeth Dexter, and Alice M. Earle stress the presence of women in traditionally masculine jobs in this period and conclude that women did not suffer the confines of the division of labor in colonial America. Another group of historians, including Edith Abbott and Robert Smuts, finds a simple strict division of labor which assigned women to the home and men to the fields. Examples of women and men doing the same work are dismissed as exceptions. A third group, which includes Mary Ryan, ignores the issues of the presence of a gender

division of labor and points instead to an economic partnership between women and men characterized by an equality that was lost when nineteenth century development excluded women from work.

55. For more discussion of frontier women, see John Mark Faragher, *Women and Men on the Overland Trail* (New Haven: Yale University Press, 1979) and Joanna L. Stratton, *Pioneer Women: Voices From the Kansas Frontier* (New York: Simon and Schuster, 1981).

56. Ulrich (1982) *op. cit.*, pp. 13-34.

57. *Ibid.*, pp. 37-38.

58. Matthaei (1982) *op. cit.*, p. 38; Kessler-Harris (1982) *op. cit.*, p. 4.

59. The following discussion draws heavily from Ruth H. Bloch, "American Feminine Ideals in Transition: The Rise of the Moral Mother, 1785-1815," *Feminist Studies*, 4(2) (June 1978), pp. 101-127.

60. Ulrich (1982) *op. cit.*, p. 54.

61. *Ibid.*, pp. 157-158.

62. See also Ryan (1975) *op. cit.*, p. 60; Laural Thatcher Ulrich, "Virtuous Woman Found: New England Ministerial Literature, 1668-1735," in Nancy F. Cott and Elizabeth H. Pleck, *A Heritage of Her Own* (New York: Simon and Schuster 1979), p. 39.

63. Ulrich (1982) *op. cit.*, pp. 145-164.

64. The following discussion draws heavily from Matthaei (1982) *op. cit.*, pp. 15-49.

65. Ulrich (1982) *op. cit.*, pp. 68-86.

66. Bloch (1978) *op. cit.*, pp. 102-103.

67. Matthaei (1982) *op. cit.*, pp. 36-50; Spruill (1938) *op. cit.*, pp. 64-85.

68. Bonnie Thornton Dill, *Our Mother's Grief: Racial Ethnic Women and the Maintenance of Families,* Research Paper 4, May 1986, Center for Research on Women, Memphis State University, Memphis, Tenn. 38162, p. 6.

69. Jernegan (1931) *op. cit.*, p. 54.

70. Kessler-Harris (1982) *op. cit.*, p. 10.

71. Jernegan (1931) *op. cit.*, p. 54; Wertheimer (1977) *op. cit.*, p. 21.

72. Carr and Walsh (1982) *op. cit.*, p. 59; Kessler-Harris (1982) *op. cit.*, p. 9.

73. Carr and Walsh (1982) *op. cit.*, p. 60.

74. G.B. Brown (1984) *op. cit.*, pp. 13-15.

75. Wertheimer (1977) *op. cit.*, p. 21.

76. Angela Y. Davis, *Women, Race and Class* (New York: Vintage Books, 1983), p. 7.

77. Matthaei (1982) *op. cit.*, p. 87, citing Austin Steward, *Twenty-Two Years a Slave and Forty Years a Freeman* (New York: Negro Universities Press, 1968\1856), p. 14.

78. Jacqueline Jones, "'My Mother Was Much Of A Woman': Black Women, Work, and the Family Under Slavery," *Feminist Studies*, 8(2) (Summer 1982).

79. Wertheimer (1977) *op. cit.*, p. 118; Davis (1983) *op. cit.*, p. 10.

80. Jones (1982) *op. cit.*, pp. 243-245.

81. Hymowitz & Weissman (1980) *op. cit.*, p. 43, citing Norman Yetman (ed.), *Voices from Slavery* (New York: Holt, Rinehart and Winston, 1970), p. 121.

82. Benjamin Drew (ed.), *A Northside View of Slavery: The Refugee, or the Narratives of Fugitive Slaves in Canada, Related by Themselves* (Boston: John P. Jowett, 1896), pp. 31-32.

83. Hooks (1981) *op. cit.*, p. 39.

84. Jacqueline Jones, *Labor of Love, Labor of Sorrow: Black Women, Work and the Family from Slavery to the Present* (New York: Basic Books, 1985), p. 19.

85. Hymowitz & Weissman (1980) *op. cit.*, p. 45; Hooks (1981) *op. cit.*, p. 37; Wertheimer (1977) *op. cit.*, p. 111.

86. Hymowitz & Weissman (1980) *op. cit.*, p. 45; Hooks (1981) *op. cit.*, p. 37; Wertheimer (1977) *op. cit.*, p. 111.

87. Jones (1985) *op. cit.*, pp. 33-37.

88. Dill (1986) *op. cit.*, p. 2; Elizabeth Higginbotham, "Work and Survival For Black Women," Research Paper 1, September 1984, Center for Research on Women, Memphis State University, Memphis, Tenn., 38162, p. 4.

89. Hymowitz & Weissman (1980) *op. cit.*, p. 43.

90. Matthaei (1982) *op. cit.*, p. 94.

91. Jones (1982) *op. cit.*, pp. 235-36; Jones (1985) *op. cit.*, pp. 36-38.

92. Hooks (1981) *op. cit.*, p. 4; Rennie Simson, "The Afro-American Female: The Historical Context of the Construction of Sexual Identity," in Ann Snitow, Christine Stansell & Sharon Thompson (eds.), *Powers of Desire: The Politics of Sexuality* (New York: Monthly Review Press, 1983), pp. 229-235.

93. Davis (1983) *op. cit.*, pp. 7, 12, 18.

94. Dill (1986) *op. cit.*, p. 24.

95. Jones (1985) *op. cit.*, p. 36.

96. *Ibid.*

97. Cited by Wertheimer (1977) *op. cit.*, p. 109.

98. Dorothy Sterling, *We Are Your Sisters: Black Women in the Nineteenth Century* (New York: W. W. Norton & Company, 1984), p. 25.

99. Davis (1983) *op. cit.*, p. 25.

100. Sterling (1984) *op. cit.*, pp. 25-26.

101. Gerda Lerner, *The Majority Finds Its Past: Placing Women in History* (Oxford: Oxford University Press, 1981), pp. 71-72.

102. Susan Brownmiller, *Against Her Will: Men, Women and Rape* (New York: Simon and Schuster, 1975).

103. Dill (1986) *op. cit.,* p. 20; see also Herbert Gutman, *The Black Family in Slavery and Freedom: 1750-1925* (New York: Pantheon, 1976).

104. Herbert G. Gutman, "Marital and Sexual Norms Among Slave Women," in Nancy F. Cott & Elizabeth H. Pleck (eds.), *A Heritage of Her Own* (New York: Simon and Schuster, 1979), pp. 298-310.

105. Matthaei (1982) *op. cit.,* p. 81.

106. Jones (1985) *op. cit.,* p. 31.

107. Meier and Rudwick (1976, third edition) *op. cit.,* p. 36.

108. Sterling (1984) *op. cit.,* p. 57.

109. Davis (1983) *op. cit.,* p. 22.

110. Giddings (1984) *op. cit.,* pp. 45-46.

111. Matthaei (1982) *op. cit.,* p. 77-78; for a brief discussion of the debate over the extent and meaning of slave resistance, see Meier and Rudwick (1976, third edition), pp. 80-86.

112. Wertheimer (1977) *op. cit.,* p. 145.

113. David M. Schneider, *The History of Public Welfare In New York State, 1609-1866* (Montclair: Patterson Smith, 1969), p. 86.

114. Wertheimer (1977) *op. cit.,* p. 34.

115. Giddings (1984) *op. cit.,* p. 39, citing Lorenzo Johnston Greene, *The Negro in Colonial America* (New York: Atheneum, 1968, 1969, 1971, 1974), p. 154.

116. Herbert Aptheker, *Essays in The History of The American Negro* (New York: International Publishers, 1964), pp. 16-23.

117. Giddings (1984) *op. cit.,* pp. 40-41.

3

Women and the Poor
Laws in Colonial America

Poverty, including poverty among women, was not absent in the American colonies. Despite the availability of land and high wages relative to Europe, the new arrivals did not escape the social and economic problems that plagued them in the Old World.[1] Class stratification, though less intense than in Europe, was visible early on, especially in urban areas. In Boston, in 1687, the richest 15 percent of the population owned 52 percent of the taxable wealth. By 1771, the top 15 percent owned about two-thirds and the top 5 percent owned some 44 percent of the wealth. In Philadelphia the concentration of wealth was even more pronounced, while in less developed areas the gap closed somewhat.[2]

Initially the harsh conditions of immigration and settlement left most settlers destitute. While some traveled to the New World bearing resources provided by the English crown, many arrived ill, indentured, enslaved, or without any means of support. Natural catastrophes, warfare, and epidemics as well as normal life events such as old age and illness made many others poor. By the mid-seventeenth century, poverty had become a high risk for the unskilled and semi-skilled city dweller, the landless tenant farmer, and the husbandless woman.

Between 1630 and 1645, Plymouth Colony reported 57 permanent relief cases in a population ranging over this period from 500 to 700 persons. The petitions for aid in the Massachusetts Bay Colony rose from eighteen between 1630 and 1639 to about twice that number from 1640 to 1645.[3] Although still relatively low and of manageable proportions after 1650, Massachusetts town records show 164 relief cases during the 1670s, 130 in the 1680s, 63 in the 1690s and 157 from 1700 to 1709.[4] Between 1700 and 1735 New York's permanent poor rose from thirty-five to fifty-eight adults and countless children. The seemingly low numbers reflect the lack of accurate data and the smaller population, but also an undercount built into prevailing record keeping practices. In most towns the poor list typically included only the permanent poor. No record was kept of the larger group requiring temporary assistance during personal emergencies, economic downturns, and throughout the cold winter months. The records lack data on the number of dependents per case as well as on those eligible residents who did not apply for or receive relief.[5] Despite these low numbers, the cost of the expanding relief rolls placed a heavy burden on town treasuries. New York City's poor tax jumped from 250 pounds in 1697 to 438 pounds in 1714; between 1700 and 1715, Boston's relief costs rose from 500 to more than 2,000 pounds.[6]

Because the gender characteristics of the poor are only rarely discussed, it is not widely known that the povertization of women also dates back to colonial times. By the early eighteenth century, in some towns women comprised from one-third to one-half of a town's paupers.[7] Of the ninety-seven paupers listed in the incomplete records of the St. Paul's parish in Virginia between 1706 and 1749, one-third were women. Likewise, in the Blisland, Virginia parish, females made up over one-third of the sixty recorded dependents.[8] The records of a small Virginia parish show that in 1750, the town relieved forty-two men, thirty-five women, and twenty children.[9] The numbers were larger in the emerging cities. The Boston assessors reported in 1751 that over 1,000 of 1,200 widows, representing 30 percent of the city's adult female population ". . . are in low circumstances . . . and in need of relief."[10]

The poverty of white women derived largely from their marital status and lack of economic opportunities, in addition to the health and environmental factors noted earlier. Adult white women faced poverty if they did not wed, married a poor man, or lost their breadwinner. Without property, a craft, or some capital, and facing limited opportunities to earn a living, white women frequently turned to family members or to the town for support. Most black women were enslaved at this time, though among the free black population a small group of women and men secured some means.

Contrary to most historical accounts, colonial communities did not view all poor women as "deserving" of aid. Social welfare historians have routinely concluded that the poor law authorities aided all persons viewed as unable to work through no fault of their own (i.e. the young, the aged, the sick, disabled, and widows with young children) more willingly than the able-bodied who could labor. But this categorization failed to take into account that colonial officials also made distinctions among women based on their compliance with the family ethic.Women viewed as unable to work and those following the family ethic received more favorable treatment under the poor laws than those who appeared to choose idleness and those who could not or chose not to conform to prescribed wife and mother roles. In addition to carrying out their overt functions and enforcing the work ethic, the colonial laws—poor laws, family relations law, and the slave codes discussed below—also operated to uphold patriarchal family governance and proper family life.

The Colonial Poor Laws

The colonial poor laws governed the provision of relief. Influenced by English statutes, religious doctrine, and Old World traditions, the earliest colonial leaders accepted both the presence of poverty and the obligation of the family and the community to aid the poor. In contrast to later times (see Chapter Five), the need for relief did not necessarily suggest personal failure or create suspicion. If one's economic status represented the workings of God, economic need was a natural and inevitable part of the human condition and the well-ordered society. Puritan Calvinism considered economic rewards to be a sign of predestined grace, and class hierarchies provided an opportunity for the well-to-do to serve society and God by caring for those with less.

Still, poverty was a problem for the colonial social order. In the harsh and isolated wilderness, where survival and success depended on the strength and productivity of each individual and family unit, the presence of poverty threatened the structure of work, family life, and the general welfare. Limited resources and severe labor shortages, reinforced by Calvinist ideas about the virtues of hard work and the sins of idleness, left the colonies with little sympathy for the able-bodied poor. As early as 1629, The Massachusetts Bay Company instructed the governor that "Noe idle drone bee permitted to live amongst us, which if you take care now at the first to establish, will be an undoubted means, through God's Assistance, to prevent a world of disorders and many grievous sins and sinners." A 1692 Massachusetts poor law empowered selectmen "to set to work all such persons, married or unmarried, able of body, having no means to maintain them, that live idly and use or exercise no ordinary and daily lawful trade or business to get their living by."[11] Violators of the colonial work ethic could be sent to the house of correction or the workhouse.

Like productive community members, the smoothly functioning male-headed family was seen as critical to the survival of the commonwealth. Reflecting this, colonial poor laws supported the formation of white families, stable households, and disciplined home life. The law held male-headed households responsible for the productivity of family members, the socialization, and education of children, and the maintenance of those unable to care for themselves. As the linchpin of the commonwealth responsible for community well-being and governance, poorly functioning white households risked undermining patriarchal authority and the productive potential of family members. For this reason, if and when such a family failed to perform its reproductive tasks adequately, the authorities might intervene.[12] If necessary, they might remove individual members and place them under alternative family governance. Families that followed prescribed norms, in contrast, often were protected and aided as a unit.

Beginning in the mid-seventeenth century, as villages such as Boston, Philadelphia, New York, Newport, Rhode Island, and Charleston, South Carolina grew into towns, colonial poverty became more acute, widespread, and problematic. The presence of the poor and their need for relief, as well as incipient social unrest, increasingly concerned colonial leaders. Economically disenfranchised urban dwellers began to steal, drink, and engage in mob action and other forms of protest.[13] By the early eighteenth century, the landless worker, indentured servant, and tenant farmer fought against grain shortages, rising prices, and the monopoly of the land by large owners. Thereafter, white urban dwellers, both the poor and working class, took to the streets of Philadelphia, New York, and Boston to lodge their sometimes violent protest against inflation, price fixing, joblessness, imprisonment for debt, and other economic injustices.[14] Uprisings among free blacks and slaves (sometimes joined by Native Americans) also occurred with increased frequency in various northern and southern cities, beginning in the late seventeenth and early eighteenth centuries.[15]

The growth of poverty and its attendant problems led colonial towns to formalize their relief systems. English law, particularly the Elizabethan Statute of Artificiers (1562) and the Poor Law (1601) supplied the framework for colonial public aid legislation which first appeared in Plymouth Colony in 1642, Virginia in 1646, Connecticut in 1673, and Massachusetts in 1692.[16] As the poor laws developed, paid officials and mandatory tax collections replaced voluntary administration and revenue raising. The colonial laws of settlement, outdoor relief, congregate care, and child welfare, discussed below, emphasized local responsibility and family support. They provided differential treatment to the poor based on their status as neighbor (resident) or "stranger" (non-resident) and as deserving (helpless) or undeserving (able-bodied) of aid. Along with colonial family relations law and the slave codes, also discussed in this chapter, the colonial poor laws acted to maximize productivity and to regulate family functioning.

The Settlement Laws

The principle of local responsibility for the poor operated within distinct boundaries dictated by the community's social, economic, and political needs and concerns about the costs of maintaining the poor. Such responsibility, however, was not readily extended to outsiders or non-residents. Transients in search of work, seaborne paupers, refugees from frontier wars, immigrants from abroad, and other "strangers" might become a burden on the town. To prevent this, colonial leaders passed settlement laws which established a person's legal residence and per-mitted towns to restrict the entry of strangers deemed objectionable for political, religious, or economic reasons. Responsible for aiding only those persons who met statutory residence requirements, localities used settlement laws to deny legal inhabitancy to potential paupers and troublemakers and thus keep them from becoming a "charge" on the town.

The earliest settlement laws focused on the removal of un-desirable persons. Detailed rules of residence appeared later on. More common and stringent in the northern than in the southern colonies,[17] the early laws authorized town officials to scrutinize and report all visitors and immigrants in hopes of removing potential paupers before they gained settlement. Seaboard towns held shipmasters liable for im-poverished passengers and insisted that they be returned to their place of origin. All towns required newcomers without means or an occupa-tion to post bond against their becoming a town charge before receiv-ing legal settlement. To prevent inhabitancy, the law also prohibited property owners from selling land to strangers without prior approval of the authorities and prohibited residents from entertaining guests for any length of time without first obtaining official permission or secur-ing their status with a bond.

Persons with skills or resources were welcomed to apply for residence but others could be "warned-out" or told to leave by the selectman. If warned-out within a prescribed period of weeks or months, the newcomer lost the right to settle. Warned-out persons who did not leave voluntarily might be fined, transported ("passed on") at town or province expense to their last legal settlement, or forcibly removed.[18] Expelled persons who returned after removal risked a whipping: "if a man, not exceeding 39 lashes, and if a woman, not exceeding 25 lashes and so as often as he or she shall return after such transportation."[19] Perhaps most important, warned-out persons who did not leave town were ineligible for relief. Should they come to require help in the future, they had to furnish "security," or be bonded by a local sponsor.

To secure the mobility of those unable to find work in their legal settlement and to prevent settlement laws from unduly interfering with the development of a labor supply, some states later in the eighteenth century permitted poor residents to move to other cities within the state. To this end, towns granted certificates of legal settlement, which acknowledged their responsibility for the support of persons moving from one jurisdiction to another and authorized their return should they become destitute.[20]

The settlement laws, which encouraged the residency of able-bodied persons and barred newcomers without means, skills, or connections, were applied to both women and men. But given the limitations they faced earning an income and possessing property, women without resources or a male breadwinner found it especially difficult to satisfy the rules of settlement. Numerous accounts exist of officials sending widows traveling from town to town. The 1657 records of Warwick, Rhode Island report one Mary Percie, a widow with child, an inhabitant of Providence, as being there "destitute of any setled being." With no one willing to provide security for them, the town ordered the constable to return her to Providence "if she not go of her own accord within a fortnight."[21] The records of Dorchester, Massachusetts show "William Sumner was desired to speak with the widow Hims (who is lately come into this towne) to informe her that she must return to the place whence she came." Similarly, the Salem records of 1698/9 state, "If Belthiah Wilkenson doe com or be sent from Salem to this town, the Selectman of this town atend [the] law in sending her back again." If another town were willing to guarantee the return of a newcomer, she could remain temporarily. The Boston selectman sent a note to the Dorchester selectman in 1665 requesting that the widow Colins be permitted to pass the winter there and "engaging that her reception shall not disoblige Boston from the duty owed her as an inhabitant of that town."[22]

Towns which encouraged the entry of able-bodied persons and proper family units discouraged the settlement of husbandless women. Single women, divorced or abandoned wives, and especially unwed mothers had a more difficult time proving their self-sufficiency and convincing town officials of their moral character.[23] In addition to economic criteria, the authorities used a woman's compliance with the family ethic to determine her right to settle.

Johanna Harrad, a single mother, was called before the deputies of Providence "to see what securitye may be put to clear the Town of what Charges may arise from her. And if none will be put in sufficient Securitye. Then to send her back again to Boston."[24] Sarah Neale, pregnant, was warned-out of Providence in November, 1680 as a non-resident, having no consent to remain, and also because of her slandering the town. In 1692/3 the Providence town council examined the status of a stranger, Mary Clarke, with regard to her settlement status. Only after two townspeople gave a 100 pound bond did the town let this unmarried mother remain. Although the settlement laws typically defined an out-of-wedlock child's birthplace as their legal place of settlement, to avoid the cost of their maintenance some changed their laws so that the town or parish in which the woman was "begotten with child" would be charged.[25]

Abandoned women faced similar problems acquiring settlement. Mrs. Hayman, "great with child," bore the full brunt of these rules when she confessed to the Providence deputies that her husband had gone off to sea six months earlier, leaving her to wander from one Massachusetts town to another and then to Providence in search of a home. Upon learning this, the Rhode Island court ordered her removal to Boston. The letter to Massachusetts authorities explained that:

> ...we have ordered our Constable, in oder [sic] to her Removeall to the place of aboad to leave her with you, for shee appeares to be a person vagarent; And her condition is such that it Requires her to be under the care and Custody of authority; [If] we should had directed her to one of the Constables within [our] jurisdiction to be sent from Constable to Constable to [the] place of her abode its likely it would be Concluded that we had asumed Power in [your] Province and so [your] Constables disobeyed...[26]

As poverty and the migration of paupers intensified during the eighteenth century, settlement laws shifted from simple procedures of removal to more comprehensive rules for establishing a legal residence.[27] Eligibility for settlement generally included (a) legal residence for a specified amount of time without becoming in need (ranging from one to ten years); (b) the ability to earn a specified amount of income, to own or rent property of a specified value (the amount varied by state and time); and (c) to establish a record of paying taxes, or to provide security against future destitution. One might also obtain inhabitancy by (d) holding an elected position; (e) being an ordained minister; (f) being admitted to settlement by a town vote; or (g) being a servant or apprentice in a town for a specified number of years.[28]

Women's marital status also played a key role as seen in the provisions of the 1794 Massachusetts Law of Settlement which formalized earlier practices. Married women had the easiest time gaining legal residence as they automatically assumed the residence of their husband. "The effect of divergent settlement" for husband and wife, according to one observer, "would be the application of a centrifugal force to the solidarity of the family."[29] If the husband had no residence, his wife retained her own at the time of her marriage which was likely to be her place of birth or last legal residence. If an unsettled husband of a settled wife required public aid, he received it in the place of her settlement, with the state reimbursing the town in which they were located.

Upon divorce a woman's legal residence reverted to that of her settlement status prior to marriage, where she had to return if she needed public aid. Although the laws of domicile allowed widows to gain new residence after the death of her husband or by remarriage, towns frequently refused settlement on the grounds that their legal residence was that of their husband or their own place of birth.

Reflecting the patriarchal structure of colonial laws, children followed the settlement of their father until age twenty-one when they gained it for themselves. If their father had none, then children took their mother's legal residence. Some towns granted children settlement at the time of their birth, but allowed them to change with their mother if she remarried. The settlement status of out-of-wedlock children complicated matters. Children born out-of-wedlock had the same legal residence as their mother at the time of their conception, birth, or her last legal settlement, if she had any. As a result children of unwed mothers might not receive settlement in the town in which their mother resided. Neither legitimate nor illegitimate children could gain a settlement by birth in a town if neither parent had settlement there.

The procedures for removing disqualified relief applicants to their legal residence became increasingly costly and complicated, often involving litigation between towns seeking to avoid additional pauper expenses. Eventually the rising costs of litigation and the need for greater labor mobility rendered the settlement laws an inefficient and ineffective deterrent device and colonial towns gradually relaxed them. To some extent, in larger urban areas the deterrent function of the settlement laws reappeared in the policies associated with the workhouse and the asylum. Some type of residency requirements, however, remained active in many states until the Supreme Court declared them unconstitutional in 1965.

The Slave Codes

While settlement laws restricted and denied public aid to "undesirable" poor whites, the laws governing the colonial black population, known as "the slave codes," cost black women and men their freedom. The colonial black population consisted of both free blacks and slaves. As noted in the previous chapter, the initial population of free blacks was composed of indentured servants who completed their terms, slaves released as a reward for service rendered, runaway slaves, those who purchased their freedom, and refugees from the West Indies. For a short while, colonial leaders tolerated the growth of a free black population and in general treated Africans similarly to white indentured servants. Free blacks voted, intermarried with whites, held minor elective office, owned property, and a few amassed huge fortunes and became slave-holders.

As the colonial economy became more dependent on slave labor, an expanding free black population with civil rights became a threat to the institution of slavery.[30] By the 1750s, slave codes proliferated. They eroded the liberties enjoyed by free blacks, removed the few social and economic rights granted to slaves, and otherwise assured the subordination of both groups. The Virginia slave codes ended the practice of freeing slaves who converted to Christianity and restricted the grounds for manumission to meritorious service. Elsewhere the codes prevented blacks from owning slaves or joining the militia, and denied the vote and the right to hold office to those few free blacks with enough land to do so. Other codes denied slaves the right to marry under white law or to inherit property, and insisted, contrary to patriarchal white law, that the children of blacks follow the condition of their mother rather than their father.[31] Laws also discouraged social contact between whites and blacks, made it a crime to teach a slave to read or write, and obliged white southerners to help in the return of fugitive slaves. These highly restrictive laws locked the slave-labor force into place and undermined the formation of families among slaves.

When free and enslaved women and men throughout the North and the South rebelled against their lack of freedom, colonial leaders tightened these legal restrictions. As a result of slave plots and insurrections such as those in South Carolina in 1739 and 1740, blacks lost the right to assemble, to possess weapons, to beat drums or blow horns, to buy liquor, to leave the plantation without a written pass, to testify in courts, and to be tried by a jury of any kind. The Pennsylvania, New York, and New England slave codes were less severe due to Puritan beliefs and the lower demand for slave labor. However, New York also tightened its codes in 1712 upon the discovery of a slave plot and again after the 1741 slave insurrection.[32]

Outdoor Relief

The settlement laws reduced the number of poor white persons qualified to receive public aid, but towns still had to provide for their indigenous poor. The patterns of relief available to poor whites varied widely but initially were familial and neighborly. These characteristics reflected the small size of towns and the centrality of the family to the colonial social order but also the absence of other societal caretaking institutions. In small towns, the overseer of the poor personally knew those in need and could assess the ability of family members to provide care. The poor often regarded an application or reference for aid as an appeal to neighbors. At the same time, colonial officials distinguished between the deserving and undeserving poor based on their compliance with the prevailing work and family norms.

As the first line of defense against poverty, colonial poor laws held families legally liable for supporting their immediate relatives. The law required parents and grandparents to provide for indigent offspring and adult children to support their elderly parents. The local government assumed responsibility only when these family members could not. The most common method of aiding poor whites was "outdoor relief," the provision of aid (outside of the workhouse) to people in their own or in a neighbor's home. Outdoor relief went primarily to deserving paupers whom officials preferred to aid "in so private a manner that it is seldom known to any neighbors."[33] Deserving poor women included widows, the wives of sick, disabled or temporarily unproductive men, and other women seen as involuntarily lacking a male breadwinner. New York City, for example, in the early eighteenth century, provided outdoor relief to members of functioning households, such as couples with a temporarily ill partner, competent widows, and mothers with children in need of only temporary aid.[34]

The deserving poor also included aged, sick, and disabled women, and mothers of young children who could not work or take care of themselves. In need of physical care or supervision, town officials often boarded these white women with an established family at public expense. A 1687 Massachusetts town meeting voted that a certain widow should be sent "round the town" to live two weeks with each family "able to receive her."[35] The town record of Huntington, Long Island contains such items as "paid to ye widow Ester Titus for Sarah Chichester, 2 pounds, 6s., 8d; and to Nath Wickles for keeping Mary Gunnery, 4 pounds."[36] The Boston selectmen saw to it that during the winter months wood was delivered to the door of Widow Chambers who was old, infirm, and without children to care for her.[37]

The deserving female paupers who qualified for aid in their own or a neighbor's home received clothes, firewood, bread, medical care, or possibly a small weekly cash payment. The Newport Town Council, in 1747, supplied two cords of wood to each of four widows. In 1750, the vestry in Charleston, South Carolina provided the two children of Hanna Caesare with clothing and schooling; in 1754, they paid a midwife to care for the wives of two absent soldiers. Private charity supplemented public support for the urban poor. Gradually, religious institutions, mutual benefit societies, occupational groups, immigrant aid associations, and separate organizations of free blacks developed to supplement individual philanthropists in the care of the sick and needy. One of the first such societies, The Scots Charitable Society, founded in 1744 in New York, provided outdoor relief but also employed poor female Scots to spin cotton, linen, and wool.[38] The receipt of outdoor relief enabled poor white women to continue to fulfill the colonial family ethic's key requirement for women, that of productive and reproductive labor within the confines of the home. By continuing their work as "homemakers," deserving poor women could hold onto colonial society's mark of a "true woman." At home, colonial women bore and raised children to assume proper work and family roles, carried out the household tasks necessary for family maintenance, and otherwise performed their productive and reproductive tasks at minimal cost to the town while contributing to the colonial economy. If married, they remained economically dependent on and subordinate to the male head of the household. Unmarried women typically remained under the authority of another male. By rewarding poor women perceived to be in compliance with the family ethic in this way, outdoor relief also helped to uphold both the ideology of women's roles and the patriarchal family unit.

In some larger towns, and with the passage of time, the line between deserving and undeserving poor blurred. To assist in identifying if not stigmatizing the poor, some cities, such as New York City in the early eighteenth century, followed England's lead and directed each relief recipient to wear a badge or mark with the letter "P" on the shoulder of their right sleeve signifying pauper, along with the initials of the town. The New York Common Council decreed that "The Church Wardens of the City put A badge upon the Cloths of such poor as are Clothed by this City with this Mark N.Y. in blew or Red Cloath att their discretion."[39] Pennsylvania and Rhode Island likewise "labeled" those unable to support themselves.[40] In some colonies, paupers forfeited all civil and social rights; they could be jailed, sold at auction, or indentured at the discretion of local officials; and, like most of the landless, they had no right to vote.[41]

Indoor Relief

While most deserving female paupers could expect to receive aid in their own homes, undeserving poor women were forced to work in exchange for a place in the poorhouse. The Essex town records of 1640 charged Mary Boutwell "for her exorbitance not working but living idly."[42] In 1643, the town of Salem, Massachusetts "ordered that Margaret Page shall [be sent] to Boston jail as a lazy, idle loitering person where she may be set to work for her living."[43] In 1682, the Boston Town Council decided to erect a workhouse and provide employment, ie., indoor relief, for the undeserving town charges whose assistance it deplored.[44]

Like undeserving males, undeserving poor white women also were auctioned-off to the lowest town bidder, sent to work outside the home in a manufactory, or placed in the early poorhouse or workhouse in those larger towns where these forerunners of more widespread indoor relief first appeared. At a time when women were expected to confine their productive labor to the home, indoor relief effectively penalized undeserving female paupers for being out of role. Nor were women exempt from the harsh physical punishment meted out to the idle poor. In Massachusetts, Connecticut, and elsewhere an idle person could "be stripped naked from the middle upward, and be openly whipt on his or her body, not exceeding the number of fifteen stripes" and ordered to "depart the town or parish."[45]

Farming Out

Undeserving poor white women denied outdoor relief in their own or a neighbor's home, might instead have their services auctioned-off to the lowest town bidder. In this process of "farming-out," female paupers, like men, exchanged their labor for support in another's home—often that of a relatively poor stranger who did not necessarily treat them well. Some poor women actively resisted these arrangements refusing to be taken from their homes. Having lived decently if not "handsomely" before, they balked at giving up their lodgings, however cramped and cold, in favor the home of another town resident.[46]

By the mid-eighteenth century, auctioning-off, along with indenture and apprenticeship (initially a means of educating young persons), had become a punitive measure intended primarily to lower pauper costs and, in some cases, to assure a ready supply of cheap labor. According to one observer, once in the home of their owners, auctioned-off paupers were often treated "more like brutes than like human beings...Instead of applying the amount received from the poormaster for the comfort of the pauper," the owners "spend it to support their families, or which is too often the case, in purchasing ardent spirits under the maddening influence of which they treat these wretched pensioners, and not unfrequently their own wives and children, with violence and outrage."[47]

When the practice of auctioning-off individuals to a single bidder became cumbersome, larger towns replaced it with "contracting out" the poor *en masse*. This congregate method of housing public dependents pre-figured the use of the almshouse. For example, in 1714, New York City adopted the policy of sending indigent persons to a private dwelling house and paying the mistress or keeper for receiving and maintaining them. The first keeper in New York was a woman, "one Elizabeth Berger [who] the churchwardens were ordered to pay...Six pounds of New York Money for Supplying her with necessaries for the use of the poor and for her Care and trouble about them for one year."[48] In 1734, after a rapid increase in the number of poor, the Charles Town Vestry hired a house and provided "proper attendance [for] all such as are real Objects of Charity."[49] This practice resembled a privately owned and operated almshouse whose profits depended on the labor of the inmates.

Early Almshouses and Workhouses

Boarding women and men in private homes at public expense remained the primary method of aiding the poor in most places until the early nineteenth century. However, in larger towns where the indigent population grew more rapidly, officials began to find it efficient to provide centralized care for some of the poor in almshouses or workhouses. These early indoor relief programs cared for relatively few indigent persons until the mid-1840s. Much less repressive than nineteenth-century institutions, the first poorhouses, some of which maintained more women than men, functioned primarily as a means for providing substitute care for those who did not easily fit in with a neighbor. For women who could not support themselves and who were judged undeserving, indoor relief could be punitive, making it impossible for them to pursue the socially valued roles of mother and homemaker.[50]

The first almshouse built under church auspices in 1657 in Rensselaerswyck, New York, then under Dutch rule, continued to function after the colony came under British control. The Manhattan poor were usually put out to private families until 1736 when the city, after years of discussion, opened the first public poorhouse, a two story House of Correction, Workhouse, and Poorhouse. The new institution admitted disorderly persons, parents of bastard children, beggars, runaway servants, trespassers, rogues, vagabonds, and poor persons refusing to work.

Housing many women, its equipment included tools and materials typically used by women in the home: "four spinning wheels, one or two large wheels for making shoes, two pairs of woolen cards, some knitting Needles, twelve pounds of Flax, 500 pounds of old Junck, twelve points of wool, twelve pounds of Cotton, two or three Hatchells, and other such Tools, Utensils and Furniture as for the future shall be found needful and necessary from time to time." The town provided this equipment to set "such poor to work as are able to labor and to prevent their being a Charge and Burthen to the Publick by sloth and Idleness and for Carrying on Trades, Occupations and Manufactures." Within a few years, similar institutions were built in other parts of the province.[51]

The first person to enter Boston's new almshouse in 1665 was a widow, Mrs. Jane Woodcock. Twenty years later, after a fire, a combined almshouse, workhouse, and house of correction replaced this early almshouse. A separate workhouse, opened in 1739 to reduce Boston's poor population, sheltered thirty-eight women, ten men, and seven children in 1741.[52] Although three times as many paupers received support at home as in institutions, between 1764 and 1769, the workhouse admitted 236 women, 174 men, 25 couples and 72 unattached children. Of the 236 women, 35 were mothers with children, 24 were pregnant women (usually unwed), 26 were aged, 10 sick, 12 nonresident, 9 poor, and 5 widows with children.[53] That the workhouse included so many husbandless, primarily unmarried, expectant, or single mothers with children, and female strangers suggests that while less deliberatively punitive than in later times, the early work-house/almshouse housed the poorest of the poor and those perceived as undeserving of the more favored outdoor aid.

Married women often entered the poorhouse when their husbands failed to provide. In 1739, Boston town officials, ordered the family of an "idle and viscous" breadwinner to the workhouse where they could earn "something considerable towards their own support." They assigned women to do carding and spinning and provided an attendant for the children until they grew old enough to be placed out into good families.[54]

When migration of the indigent increased in 1732, Philadelphia constructed an almshouse which included an asylum for the poor, an infirmary for the sick, and apartments for the insane. In 1736, Charleston, South Carolina built a workhouse and hospital for the poor, into which the inmates of the almshouse and most of the poor lodged with private families were transferred in 1738.[55]

The Manufactory

In the early eighteenth century the manufacture of wool and cloth gradually moved from home production to a centralized work place known as the manufactory. The continued shortage of male labor, the rise in female pauperism, and the identification of textile production as "women's work" led some communities to tie the manufactory to the relief system, especially for young women. The emerging merchant class hoped that "hiring" poverty stricken women and children would improve profits, lower the local poor law taxes, and in so doing also reduce the landed gentry's strong opposition to the development of commercial manufacturing.

As early as 1720, Boston purchased twenty spinning wheels and opened a spinning school to train "such children (mostly girls) as should be sent from the almshouse."[56] Thirty years later, The United Society for Manufacturers and Importation of Boston conducted the first American experiment in female factory labor in hopes of employing its growing number of poor widows (and their dependent children), many of whom refused to enter the workhouse. In 1751, renamed the Society for Encouraging Industry and the Employment of the Poor, it opened a linen manufactory to hire "our own women and children who are now in great measure idle."[57] Unable to attract enough private capital, the linen manufactory, in 1753, received government funds largely because "The number of poor is greatly increased . . . and many persons, especially women, and children, are destitute of employment and in danger of becoming a public charge."[58]

Manufactories in New York and Philadelphia also employed poor women. The New York Society for the Promotion of Arts, Agriculture and Economy, formed in 1764 during economically hard times, offered special prizes to encourage domestic industries and farm production. It opened a trade school for pauper children and lent spinning wheels to women workers offering cash premiums to the ten who produced the most linen yarn. The Society was commended in 1766-67 for its linen manufactory which employed "above three hundred poor and indigent persons, [and relieved] numbers of distressed women now in the poorhouse."[59] The United Company of Philadelphia, using patriotic arguments to promote American manufacture, employed one hundred spinners and weavers. Later, it offered "spinning and other work" to four hundred women "who would otherwise have been destitute."[60]

Most "manufactory" workers were husbandless women and others viewed as undeserving of aid. This early version of "workfare" forced women to be out of compliance with the colonial family ethic which encouraged women to work, but only within the confines of the home. As a result, the wives, widows, and daughters of artisans, mariners and laborers showed "great reluctance of toil in the manufactory"[61] just as they resisted other efforts that tied relief to work outside the home. They preferred instead to spin at home, to take in boarders, and to engage in domestic service rather than accept work-relief as a means of support. Leaving home, even for daytime work, involved a new kind of labor discipline that separated work and family responsibilities in unfamiliar ways, that split the dual functions of laboring women into two separate spheres, and that challenged deeply held values.[62]

Poor Black Women

Few black women or men came under the jurisdiction of the colonial poor laws. Colonial law held slaves to be the property and responsibility of their masters, and free blacks relied largely on themselves or their own self-help systems for support. When they did enter the poor law system, mostly in the North, black men and women were treated as the most undeserving of the poor. In 1703, Massachusetts restricted the emancipation of mulattos and blacks to prevent them from becoming "chargeable." In 1726, Pennsylvania enacted a law for binding out able-bodied blacks who did not work.[63] Colonial officials in

New York allowed slave-holders, upon payment of fees, to use the poorhouse for the support or whipping of their unruly slaves.[64]

Most colonial towns arduously protected themselves against the cost of maintaining members of the black population. Although some masters provided their freed slaves with land or other resources, others could not afford this and\or simply freed aged, infirm, or unproductive slaves to avoid the cost of their care. Thus, towns required slave-owners to put up security for their manumitted slaves. New York Court Records for 1750 show that the town rejected as insufficient the security Susanna Bond offered against the possibility that four slaves she desired to free would later become public charges. The New York Assembly, in 1773, legislated a ten-pound fine for slave-owners who allowed their slaves to beg, thereby forcing the general public to help maintain them.[65] After the American Revolution, northern states that passed acts of gradual emancipation held masters responsible for the support of the black women and men they freed.

The Children of the Poor

Colonial law permitted the government to separate children from their parents for reasons of destitution, ungovernable conduct, and improper guardianship on the grounds that the state must intervene when the community welfare is threatened. Directed primarily at families that did not conform to the work or family ethic, these rules reflected a deep distrust of the ability of indigent parents to carry out the reproductive tasks assigned to all families. The poverty of these parents often led officials to conclude that they were "unfit parents" leading an "idle, dissolute and disorderly course of life" whose sloth and indulgence promoted economic dependency rather than industriousness, role compliance, and proper family government.[66] The prevailing view of children as naturally sinful, aggressive, and prone to vices, including idleness, only reinforced these views.

These attitudes caused colonial society to keep a close watch on community members, especially the poor. As towns grew in size, officials began to "inspect all families and persons" reporting the names of the able-bodied but non self-supporting to the poor law authorities who sent them to work or to jail.[67] Boston town officials walked through town for "the purpose of discovering disorders and conditions of living that might, if not changed, bring the inhabitants to dependency."[68] The Massachusetts legislature, in 1679, ordered each town to present the names of all disorderly persons, single persons living alone, stubborn children and servants, night walkers, tipplers, Sabbath breakers, non-church goers, and others who behaved improperly "…whether by omission of family government, nurture, and religious duties, [or] instruction of children and servant, or idle, profligate, uncivil or rude practice of any sort."[69]

Towns empowered poor law officials to indenture and apprentice orphans and children of indigent and presumed neglectful parents in order to place them in more responsible homes. As early as 1641, the officials of Plymouth Colony ordered "that those that have relief from the town and have children and do not employ them that then it shall be lawful for the township to take order that those children shall be put to work in fitting employment according to their strength and abilities or placed out by the town."[70] A 1646 Virginia law permitted justices of the peace to remove children from their homes and bind them out to tradesmen "to be brought up in some good and lawful calling…for the better educating of youth in honest and profitable trades and manufactures…to avoid sloth and idleness wherewith such young children are easily corrupted…[and]…for the relief of such parents whose poverty extends not to give them good breeding." The Boston Town Records in 1657 noted, "Itt is agreed upon the complaint against the son of goodwife Sammon living without a calling, that if she dispose nott of him in some way of employ before the next meeting, that then the townsmen will dispose of him to some service according to the law."[71] In 1726, Watertown, Massachusetts received complaints about a poor family whose children of both sexes were able to go to work, to school, and to church. "But through the willfulness Negligence and Indulgence of their parents they are brought up in idleness, ignorance, and without religion, and more are likely to prove a trouble and charge, than blessings in their Day and Generation if not timely prevented." The town ordered that the family place the children, "into such Religious families where both Body and Soul may be taken good care off." If they did not, "the Selectman will take Effectual care that Such Children be forthwith put into such Families where they may have good care taken of them."[72] In the 1740s, some 178 Boston children were bound out to other families, most often outside the town.[73]

In colonial communities governed by patriarchal family households, a poor woman without a male breadwinner was at high risk of being declared "unfit" and losing the right to care for her children. Lacking adequate resources, some women voluntarily indentured or apprenticed their children to other families in hopes they would receive care and acquire a useful trade. The grandfather and uncle of the children of the deceased Zachary Field petitioned the Providence Town Council in 1695 to bind the child out to some "good places where they may be well brought up and educated," in order that they "might not be in want and later might be able to earn their livelihood." With Mrs. Field's approval, this request was carried out.[74]

To avoid paying relief on their behalf, town leaders often simply separated children from fathers and mothers who they viewed as morally dangerous, undeserving of aid, and a threat to child and community welfare.[75] Town officials believed that the practice of child removal and indenture to other taxpaying families would "re-integrate" pauper children into society as useful working members rather than letting them learn from parents that life without work or proper family governance was the normal state.[76]

Virginia law instructed church wardens "to bind out illegitimate children of single white women," both free and servant, to avoid the town incurring charges for them.[77] St. Peter's Parish in Virginia ordered "that a thousand pounds of tobacco and cask be paid unto Mary Wilkinson for nursing a bastard child belonging to a servant woman of Capt. Joseph Forster this ensuing year."[78] Another child born to two unmarried indentured servants in 1662 was turned over to the parish until the father became freed and "...shall make satisfaction to the parish."[79] Under the black codes, to be discussed below, the illegitimate children of interracial couples could be bound out for more years than white children and in effect became virtually permanently enslaved.[80]

Family Relations Law

Colonial family relations law—laws of marriage, inheritance and paternity—were enacted, among other reasons, to enforce the structure of patriarchal control. They presumed the supremacy of the husband over his wife and children, who became his property under the law. These laws combined with those that denied women the right to own property and the opportunity to develop an independent economic status, left women at high risk for transferring their economic dependency from their fathers and husbands to the town. In part, then, to prevent women without male support from becoming town charges, the laws of marriage, inheritance, and paternity attempted to provide for the care for an absent male's dependent spouse.

Marriage

Given the strong emphasis on family governance, it is not surprising that colonial law encouraged white men and women to marry, unmarried persons to live in family units, and divorced persons to remarry quickly or risk a fine. Towns denied single persons the right to live alone without town approval. People without ties lacked someone to supply their needs and to hold them within the bounds of order, and otherwise posed problems for social stability. Never-married single women did not endear themselves to the colonial community, especially if they were poor. They threatened the institution of marriage, the moral code, and the public purse, as did the lack of family and resources among previously indentured female servants and freed slaves who did not marry upon the termination of their servitude.

Despite these strong incentives for family formation, marital discord was not uncommon in the colonies, if discussions lamenting the decadence of domestic virtues, public notices of absconding wives, and routine complaints of spouses in court are any clue. Colonial couples sued for divorce on the still familiar grounds of desertion, non-support, neglect, adultery, and cruelty. Marital dissolution, however, risked turning previously dependent wives and children into public charges. Although divorce was not easy, it was reasonably possible to secure. These divorce laws (considered liberal relative to England's) were thought to forestall desertion and separation and served to facilitate remarriage so that each party could be cared for in a new family unit rather than by the town.

Desertion was more common than divorce among the poor. To prevent it from imposing a financial burden on the town and to penalize men who departed from their prescribed breadwinner role, officials required that deserting husbands return to and support their wives, and post bond against future abandonment. For those women whose husbands did not return, laws were passed that permitted them to remarry if their spouses had not reappeared after three years. By freeing these deserted or widowed wives to remarry, colonial law removed them from the "path of temptation" and also prevented them from needing public support.[81]

Inheritance

Widowhood was a key source of female dependency in colonial America. Death, war, sickness, and harsh living conditions took the lives of many men, often leaving their wives in economic distress. The dependence of widows on the town was lessened by colonial norms which permitted wives to continue their deceased husband's work, by the sanction of rapid remarriage, and by inheritance laws which provided for a widow's upkeep at whatever level the estate allowed. Colonial inheritance laws granted widows at least one-third of the household goods. They also allowed her to use or receive income from a third of her husband's real estate until she died or remarried, at which time the property reverted to her male heirs. However, few estates were liquid or large enough to allow a widow the means to maintain her previous standard of living.

In line with prevailing patriarchal arrangements, the rules of inheritance reserved final control over family property to the son. A widow with minor children might retain practical control of the entire estate until her son came of age. But she had no final control of property including her house and yard and even the pots, beds, and cow which had once been her domain. Nor did widows have a legal say in the final disposition of family property which was settled by court order or by her husband's will. In some cases the courts had to order sons to support their widowed mothers. In the later seventeenth century in Suffolk County, Massachusetts, Sarah Burnell complained to the courts that her son "hath the Estate that was left by her [second] Husband in his hands & refuseth to relieve her or yield her any Succor or maintenance therefrom." The Court ordered that Sarah Burnell "bee forthwith put into possession of the Chamber she formerly had in her Son's house or other at the Judgment of Captain John Richards and Lieutenant Daniel Turill and bee paid five Shillings in money per weeke by her Son until the next Court of this County."[82]

The economic plight of a growing number of widows, especially the small size and lack of liquidity of most inheritances, eventually led them to demand a liberalization of inheritance laws. By the time of the American Revolution, widows had won the right to convert real property into capital for purposes of personal support or investment.[83] Less affluent widows made a living in one of the few occupations open to women at the time,[84] but many widows still had to ask the community for support.

Paternity Laws

Unmarried motherhood—a violation of the family ethic—was another major source of female dependency in the colonies. Several factors made births outside of marriage a rather frequent occurrence: in some areas there were more women than men (among both whites and blacks); marriage by indentured female servants was prohibited; sexual infidelity among (especially upper-class) men was tolerated; and there was almost no knowledge about effective birth control methods. To limit out-of-wedlock births and to prevent the dependency of father-less children and unwed mothers, colonial towns passed strict laws against bastardy, adultery, and fornication. Interracial coupling carried the most extreme penalties.

The main goal in white bastardy cases was to prevent fatherless children and unwed mothers from becoming town charges. To this end the courts sought to establish paternity and obliged fathers of all clas-ses to support their illegitimate children. A 1752 Providence, Rhode Is-land law required the father to furnish sufficient security to keep the town indemnified as well as to support the child as long as the child was chargeable. Subsequent laws also provided for the punishment of the mother and the putative father. However, in practice, women were viewed as more blameworthy than the absent father and were left to carry the full burden of community disapproval and actual child sup-port. Governed by expediency, the difficulties in locating alleged fathers, the greater ease in establishing maternity than paternity, and the ever-present sexual double standard, the colonial courts frequent-ly apprehended and imposed charges only on the unwed mother.

Even when courts pursued paternity, if a woman was unable to identify the father, she had to post bond for the child's support and she risked incarceration in addition to routine penalties. A Rhode Island court fined Mary Cory for having an out-of-wedlock child and ordered her to keep the town from having to maintain or bring up the child.[85] Should a father actually appear in court he usually received lighter sanc-tions than the unwed mother.[86] In one case, a Virginia court sentenced an unwed mother to thirty lashes on her bare back while ordering the father to make a public confession of his sin before his church's con-gregation. Likewise, a Maryland court imposed physical punishment on an unmarried mother, but ordered the father of her child, a married planter, to pay a fine and to post bond for the child's support and his good behavior.[87] Even when the courts fined both parties equally, women were often unable to pay and received a whipping instead. This double standard which enabled men from various classes to es-cape responsibility and punishment and left women to stand alone before colonial courts also appeared in the not unrelated statutes that penalized adultery and fornication.[88]

Unwed motherhood was especially common among indentured servants who were prevented by law from marrying until they com-pleted their servitude and who often became impregnated by their

master or a manservant.[89] In addition to the fines and punishments faced
by free unwed mothers, courts required indentured servants to compensate their master for his losses due to their pregnancy and confinement, usually in the form of money or extra service.[90] In 1706, a North
Carolina court sentenced Elizabeth Fitz Garret, convicted of having a
bastard child, to serve her master two additional years and her child to
serve the same master until age twenty-one.[91] Masters who impregnated
their female servants typically received only minimal penalties and were
able to maintain the servant's regular service.[92] Male servants who
fathered a child often had to pay for the female servant's reduced service or extend his own.[93]

Interracial coupling, rather widespread in colonial America, also
threatened to make blacks dependent on the town. The intermingling
of the races occurred across class lines but was especially great among
black slaves and white indentured servants who often worked in
proximity. White leaders gradually banned interracial coupling because
it was considered a threat to white supremacy and to the institution
of slavery. In this view, interracial coupling tarnished the purity of the
white race, made it possible for a black child to be free because one
parent was white, and risked enabling black slave children to inherit
property from white parents. Laws punishing interracial coupling
proliferated in the early eighteenth century for these reasons but also
to reduce the number of mulatto children born outside of marriage who
might need support from the town.[94]

Virginia imposed fines for fornication with a black person as early
as 1622, only three years after the arrival of the first blacks to the British
colonies. The colony's first judicial decision that referred specifically to
race involved sexual relations between a white man, Hugh Davis, and
an unnamed black woman. For lying with a black woman, Davis
received a sound whipping before a public assembly. In 1691, Virginia
restricted intermarriage and ordered the banishment of any white
woman marrying a black or mulatto, bonded, or free.[95]

Some colonies enacted laws to ensure the slave status of an interracial couple's offspring. These laws secondarily avoided the potential of such children becoming dependent on the town. Virginia denied
the possibility of freedom to the child of a black female slave and a
white man when, in 1662, the House of Burgess reversed English common law which held that children followed the status of their fathers,
and declared that children "got by an Englishman upon a Negro woman
shall be bond or free according to the status of their mother."[96] Some
historians suggest that giving the children of black female slaves and
white men the mother's status—a dramatic reversal of patriarchal pat-

terns—provided an incentive for masters to expand their slave-holdings by themselves impregnating or by breeding their female slaves.[97] The change also prevented such black children from inheriting the property of their white fathers.

The legal system also assured the bondage of children born to white women and black male slaves. In 1663, Maryland declared that any free white woman who married a slave became a slave as did her children. The statute stated "freeborn English women...forgetful of their free condition and to the disgrace of our nation, do intermarry with Negro slaves...shall serve the master of such slave during the life of her husband. And that all issue of such freeborn women so married shall be slaves as their fathers were." Pennsylvania took similar action in 1725.[98]

In 1705, Massachusetts imposed banishment on any black or mulatto man lying with a white woman, required whippings for a white man committing the same with a black or mulatto woman, and ordered that the black woman be sold out of the province.[99] The same legislature also banned interracial marriage.[100] In Pennsylvania, a white woman bearing the child of a black man risked twenty-one lashes on her bare back and the man was warned "never more to meddle with any white woman upon pain of his life."[101]

Eventually many colonies outlawed interracial marriage altogether. But these bans indirectly fostered out-of-wedlock births and exacerbated the problem of economic dependence on the town. To reduce the cost of maintaining dependent black children, colonial officials demanded child support, imposed severe cash fines, or indentured their parents.[102] The child—often bound out, apprenticed, or sold into servitude for periods far longer than those set for white children—virtually became a slave. Despite severe punishments, interracial coupling continued well into the eighteenth century in Maryland, Virginia, North Carolina, and in some northern colonies. On the eve of the Civil War, one-third of the free black population in the United States was of mixed racial ancestry.[103]

Summary

Colonial poor laws, family relations laws, and the slave codes influenced how the colonies coped with poverty and dependency. Each in their own way helped to assure the supply of labor, the formation of proper families, and white patriarchal governance. The laws codified the work and family ethics and treated women differently according to their perceived compliance with these dominant norms. The poor laws rewarded deserving female paupers by aiding them at home and in ways that permitted them to retain a homemaker status—colonial society's mark of a "true woman." But the rights of colonial womanhood were denied to "undeserving" poor women defined as failing to properly carry out their assigned productive and reproductive tasks. Settlement laws punished husbandless women, unwed mothers, and many men in need of public aid by refusing to help them and sending them back to their legal residence. Outdoor relief aided deserving female paupers and allowed them to combine productive and reproductive labor in the home. Undeserving female paupers, in contrast, had to separate these tasks as they were forced to exchange their labor for support in a neighboring household, the almshouse, the workhouse, or the manufactory. This assured the productivity of those who could work but limited their ability to engage in the reproductive tasks assigned to women in the home.

Other laws broke families apart. They farmed out adults and removed poor children from the care of their parents when defined as "unfit." By defining women as deserving or undeserving of aid based on their compliance with the family ethic and by aiding the former at home while preventing the latter from taking up homemaking, colonial poor laws protected the town coffers, as well as the work ethic and the reigning ideology of women's roles. The poor law system had virtually nothing to offer black women regardless of whether they were enslaved or free.

The laws of marriage, inheritance, and paternity that structured the formation of families and the patriarchal family unit, also reflected concerns about female dependency. Laws encouraging marriage kept community members within the patriarchal family structure and kept women dependent on men rather than the state. Divorce laws that permitted remarriage rather than promoting separation or abandonment also reduced the likelihood of female dependency on the town. Inheritance laws contained provisions for widowed women and children, while paternity laws sought to assure parental responsibility for support. Slave codes severely restricted the liberty and mobility of blacks to guarantee their subordination to whites and their availability as an enslaved labor force. Towns also worked hard to avoid becoming responsible for the care and maintenance of mulatto children and free black adults.

The advance of industrial capitalism after the American Revolution, combined with the abuses of the poor law system, gradually undermined both the colonial family ethic and the colonial system of relief. The emerging market economy changed the demands of the labor market, placed new requirements on the family system, and weakened the ability of the patriarchal family to regulate the community's work and family life. This paved the way for a redefinition of women's roles, the family, and state involvement in family life. Chapter Four describes the emergence of a new family ethic that accompanied these changes in the political economy. Chapter Five examines the poor law reforms which made the system of relief more suited to the requirements of the new social order.

Notes to Chapter 3

1. Walter I. Trattner, *From Poor Law to Welfare State: A History of Social Welfare in America* (New York: The Free Press, 1984, third edition), pp. 16-17.

2. George Brown Tindall, *America: A Narrative History* (New York: W.W. Norton, 1984), Volume I, p. 117.

3. Charles Lee, "Public Poor Relief and the Massachusetts Community, 1620-1715," *The New England Quarterly* 55(4) (December 1982), pp. 569-570.

4. *Ibid.*, p. 574.

5. Raymond Mohl, *Poverty in New York, 1783-1825* (New York: Oxford University Press, 1971), p. 42.

6. *Ibid.*, p. 42; Carl Bridenbaugh, *Cities in the Wilderness: The First Century of Urban Life in America 1625-1742* (New York: The Ronald Press Company, 1938), pp. 232-234.

7. Alice Kessler-Harris, *Out To Work: A History of Wage-Earning Women in the United States* (New York: Oxford University Press, 1982), pp. 16-19; Julie A. Matthaei, *An Economic History of Women In America* (New York: Schocken Books, 1982), pp. 51-53; David Rothman, *The Discovery of Asylum: Social Disorder in the New Republic* (Boston: Little Brown and Co., l971), pp. 33-34; Mary Ryan, *Womanhood in America From Colonial Times to the Present* (New York: New Viewpoints, 1975), pp. 100-101.

8. Rothman (l971) *op. cit.*, p. 34.

9. *Ibid.*, p. 319 (note 3).

10. Gary B. Nash, *The Urban Crucible: Social Change, Political Consciousness, and the Origins of the American Revolution* (Cambridge: Harvard University Press, 1979), p. 172.

11. June Axinn and Herman Levin, *Social Welfare: A History of the American Response to Need* (New York: Harper and Row, 1975), p. 24, citing The Acts and Resolves, Public and Private of the Province of Massachusetts Bay; Chapter 14, An Act of Supplement to the Acts Referring to the Poor, 1692-3, Ch. 28 & 7.

12. Lee (1982) *op. cit.*, p. 573.

13. Bridenbaugh (1938) *op. cit.*, pp. 55-78.

14. Carl Bridenbaugh, *Cities in Revolt: Urban Life in America 1743-1776* (New York: Alfred A. Knopf, 1955), pp. 114-118, 305-314; Bridenbaugh (1938) *op. cit.*, pp. 70-71, 382-384; Carter Godwin Woodson and Charles H.Welsey, *The Negro in Our History* (Washington, D.C.: The Associated Publishers, 1962), pp. 89-93.

15. August Meier and Elliott Rudwick, *From Plantation to Ghetto* (New York: Hill and Wang, 1976), p. 45; Carter G. Woodson, *Free Negro Heads of Families*

in the United States in 1830 (Washington, D.C.: The Association for the Study of Negro Life and History, Inc., 1925), p. xxii.

16. Trattner (1984) *op. cit.*, p. 18.

17. Elizabeth Wisner, *Social Welfare in the South From Colonial Times to World War I* (Baton Rouge: Louisiana State University Press, 1970), p. 32.

18. Originally the power to "warn-out" was seen as necessary because towns had no police forces to maintain control over potentially dangerous people. Trattner (1984) *op. cit.*, p. 20 (footnote 3).

19. Roy M. Brown, *Public Poor Relief in North Carolina* (Chapel Hill: The University of North Carolina Press, 1928), p. 19; Mohl (1971) *op. cit.*, p. 58; David M. Schneider, *The History of Public Welfare In New York State 1609-1866* (Chicago: The University of Chicago Press, 1938), p. 114.

20. Margaret Creech, *Three Centuries of Poor Law Administration: A Study of Legislation in Rhode Island* (Chicago: The University of Chicago Press, 1936), p. 52, Schneider (1938) *op. cit.*, p. 114.

21. Creech (1936) *op. cit.*, pp. 59-60.

22. Robert W. Kelso, *The History of Public Poor Relief In Massachusetts, 1620-1920* (Montclair: Patterson Smith, 1969), pp. 38-39.

23. Rothman (1971) *op. cit.*, p. 46.

24. Ryan (1975) *op. cit.*, p. 67.

25. Creech (1936) *op. cit.*, pp. 70-71.

26. *Ibid.*, pp. 73-74.

27. Nash (1979) *op. cit.*, pp. 185-186.

28. James Lieby, *Charity and Correction in New Jersey* (New Brunswick: Rutgers University Press, 1967), p. 9; Kelso (1969) *op. cit.*; Henry M. Shaw, M.D., *The Settlement Laws of Massachusetts* (Boston: George H. Ellis, 1900).

29. Kelso (1969) *op. cit.*, p. 74.

30. Meier and Rudwick (1976) *op. cit.*, pp. 4-5.

31. Woodson and Wesley (1962) *op. cit.*, pp. 87-89.

32. Meier and Rudwick (1976) *op. cit.*, pp. 45-47; Woodson (1925) *op. cit.*, p. 90.

33. Nash (1979) *op. cit.*, pp. 188-189.

34. Rothman (1971) *op. cit.*, p. 36.

35. Trattner (1984) *op. cit.*, p. 19.

36. Schneider (1938) *op. cit.*, p. 63.

37. Trattner (1984) *op. cit.*, p. 19.

38. Bridenbaugh (1955) *op. cit.*, p. 126; Mohl (1971) *op. cit.*, pp. 49-50.

39. Schneider (1938) *op. cit.*, p. 64.

40. Paul Tutt Stafford, *Government and the Needy: A Study of Public Assistance in New Jersey* (Princeton: Princeton University Press, 1941), p. 43; Axinn and Levin (1975) *op. cit.*, p. 14.

41. Stafford (1941) *op. cit.*, p. 47.

42. Bridenbaugh (1938) *op. cit.*, p. 82, citing Report of the Radical Commissioners of the City of Boston, Vol. 7, p. 158.

43. Edith Abbott, *Women in Industry* (New York: D. Appleton and Company, 1910), p. 32.

44. *Ibid.*; Harris (1982) *op. cit.*, pp. 16-19; Matthaei (1982) *op. cit.*, pp. 51-53; Rothman (1971) *op. cit.*, pp. 33-34; Ryan (1975) *op. cit.*, pp. 100-101.

45. Marcus W. Jernegan, *Laboring and Dependent Classes In Colonial America* 1607-1783 (Chicago: The University of Chicago Press, 1931), p. 201.

46. Nash (1979) *op. cit.*, pp. 188-189.

47. Schneider (1938) *op. cit.*, p. 223.

48. *Ibid.*, p. 72.

49. Bridenbaugh (1938) *op. cit.*, p. 396.

50. Rothman (1971) *op. cit.*, p. 40.

51. Schneider (1938) *op. cit.*, pp. 71-75.

52. Bridenbaugh (1938) *op. cit.*, pp. 81, 293.

53. Rothman (1971) *op. cit.*, pp. 39, 320 (footnote 14).

54. Kelso (1969) *op. cit.*, p. 115.

55. Bridenbaugh (1938) *op. cit.*, pp. 391-396.

56. Kelso (1969) *op. cit.*, p. 114.

57. Abbott (1910) *op. cit.*, pp. 21-22.

58. *Ibid.*, p. 22.

59. *Ibid.*, p. 38; Mohl (1971) *op. cit.*, p. 48.

60. Susan Estabook Kennedy, *If All We Did Was To Weep At Home: A History of White Working Class Women in America* (Bloomington: Indiana University Press, 1979), p. 21.

61. Nash (1979) *op. cit.*, pp. 194-196.

62. *Ibid.*, pp. 193, 335.

63. Ira Berlin, *Slaves Without Masters: The Free Negro in the Antebellum South* (New York: Oxford University Press, 1974), pp. 92-93; Meier and Rudwick (1976) *op. cit.*, pp. 53, 61; Woodson (1925) *op. cit.*, p. xxii.

64. Mohl (1971) *op. cit.*, p. 44.

65. Berlin (1974) *op. cit.*, p. 61; Schneider (1938) *op. cit.*, pp. 87, 206.

66. Jernegan (1931) *op. cit.*, p. 180.

67. *Ibid.*, p. 199.

68. Kelso (1969) *op. cit.*, p. 98.

69. Robert H. Bremner, *Children and Youth In America: A Documentary History, Volume I: 1600-1865* (Cambridge: Harvard University Press, 1970), p. 42, citing Edmund S. Morgan, *The Puritan Family* (New York, 1966), pp. 148-149.

70. Kelso (1969) *op. cit.*, p. 97.

71. *Ibid.*, p. 165.

72. Grace Abbott, *The Child and the State Vol. I* (Chicago: University of Chicago Press, 1938), p. 212, citing *Watertown Records Comprising The Third Book of Town Proceedings And the Second Book of Births, Marriages and Deaths to the End of 1737*, Vol. II, Historical Society, Watertown, Mass., 1900, pp. 340-341.

73. Nash (1979) *op. cit.*, p. 185.

74. Creech (1936) *op. cit.*, p. 80.

75. Axinn and Levin (1975) *op. cit.*, p. 12; Kelso (1969) *op. cit.*, p. 175; Bridenbaugh (1938) *op. cit.*, p. 388.

76. Nash (1979) *op. cit.*, p. 184.

77. Jernegan (1931) *op. cit.*, p. 180.

78. *Ibid.*, p. 187.

79. *Ibid.*, p. 180.

80. Woodson (1925) *op. cit.*, pp. vii-ix.

81. Barbara A. Hanawalt, "Women Before the Law: Female as Felons and Prey in Fourteenth Century England," in D. Kelly Weisberg, *Women and the Law: A Social Historical Perspective Vol. I* (Cambridge: Schenkman Publishing Company, Inc., 1975), pp. 187-189.

82. Nancy Cott, *Roots of Bitterness: Documents of the Social History of American Women* (New York: E. P. Dutton & Co., Inc.,1972), p. 64, citing Records of Suffolk County Court 1671-1680, Publications of the Colonial Society of Massachusetts, Vol. XXIX (Boston, 1938), pp. 1063-1064.

83. Joan Hoff Wilson, "The Illusion of Change: Women and the American Revolution," in Jean E. Friedman and William G. Shade (eds.), *Our American Sisters: Women in American Life and Thought* (Lexington: D.C. Heath and Company, 1982), p. 120.

84. *Ibid.*, p. 119.

85. Creech (1936) *op. cit.*, p. 70.

86. Julia Cherry Spruill, *Women's Life and Work in the Southern Colonies* (New York: W.W. Norton & Company, 1972), pp. 316-317.

87. *Ibid.*, pp. 320-321, citing *Archives of Maryland*, X, p. 516; XVI; p. 14.

88. *Ibid.*, p. 315; Carol Hymowitz and Michaele Weissman, *A History of Women in America* (New York: Bantam Books, 1980) pp. 111-112.

89. Lois Green Carr and Lorena S. Walsh, "The Planters Wife: The Experience of White Women in Seventeenth-Century Maryland," in Friedman and Shade (eds.) (1982) *op. cit.*, p. 59.

90. Bremner (1970) *op. cit.*, p. 51, citing W.W. Hening (ed.), Statutes at Large of Virginia, II (New York, 1823), pp. 115, 167, 168.

91. Brown (1928) *op. cit.*, p. 14.

92. Spruill (1972) *op. cit.*, p. 322.

93. *Ibid.*, p. 318; Bremner (1970) *op. cit.*, p. 51, citing Henning (1823) *op. cit.*

94. Woodson and Wesley (1962) *op. cit.*, pp. 110-116.

95. *Ibid.*, pp. 111-112; Peter M. Bergman, *The Chronological History of the Negro In America* (New York: Harper and Row, 1969), pp. 12, 21.

96. Woodson (1925) *op. cit.*, p. ix; Wm. T. Alexander, *History of the Colored Race in America* (Westport, Ct.: Negro Universities Press, A Division of Greenwood Press, Inc., 1970), p. 133 (Originally published in 1887 by Palmetto Publishing Company).

97. Woodson (1925) *op. cit.*, p. xv.

98. Alexander (1970) *op. cit.*, p. 137; Woodson and Wesley (1962) *op. cit.*, p. 111.

99. Bergman (1969) *op. cit.*, p. 21.

100. Woodson (1925) *op. cit.*, p. xi.

101. *Ibid.*, p. xii; Woodson and Wesley (1962) *op. cit.*, p. 113.

102. Woodson (1925) *op. cit.*, pp. vii, ix-x.

103. Berlin (1974) *op. cit.*, p. 178.

4

"A Woman's Place Is In The Home"

The Rise of the Industrial Family Ethic

The rise of industrial capitalism in the early nineteenth century and the concurrent separation of household and market production restructured both the labor market and the family system. The requirements of the new market economy gradually undermined the ability of the colonial family ethic to regulate the work and family life of white women. Indeed, the changing economy created a new gender division of labor, which assigned men to the market and women to the home. Women's new "place" in the home evolved as the changing economy moved economic production from the household to the market, a trend which developed first and considerably more rapidly in major urban areas. As women's domestic labor shifted away from production (the transformation of raw or unfinished material into finished goods) to reproduction and maintenance (the bearing of children, caring for family members, and managing household affairs), it significantly increased the time women spent on household and caretaking activities.[1] The symmetry of this exchange was imperfect, however, because both poverty and the needs of the new market economy required women's labor outside the home. Moreover, in rural areas, life remained virtually unchanged. Eventually, the changing role of white women and the conflicting demand for their reproductive and productive labor rendered the colonial family ethic obsolete. In the early nineteenth century, it was replaced by a new definition of women's roles—the industrial family ethic—more suited to the needs of the emerging economic order.

The Decline of the Colonial Family Ethic

The process of industrialization unsettled and transformed the organization of both work and family life. The growth of market production and its increased efficiency gradually weakened white women's role as an economically productive helpmeet. In 1790, for example, women produced all their own yarn and wove their own cloth. But the sharp fall in the price of manufactured brown shirting after 1815, from 42 cents to 7.5 cents a yard, made it less worthwhile for women to sit at the loom. The changing economy made cash income virtually indispensable to most families who increasingly purchased market goods, borrowed from banks, and needed more productive farm machinery. The need for cash led more and more men and some women to leave home-based agricultural work for paid market labor.[2]

The growth of the market economy also restructured women's role in the family, particularly in urban areas. The pull of men into the market, the increased consumption of manufactured rather than hand-made products, the reduced need for children's labor on the farm, and the growing importance of socialization to the success and productivity of the next generation all modified women's homemaking and caretaking activities. These changing conditions required someone to create a relaxing home for the market-weary breadwinner, to oversee the consumption of market-produced goods and services, and to spend more time rearing children. These expanded family-maintenance tasks were assigned exclusively to women, in part because declining household production freed them for other tasks. But the social assignment of family responsibilities to women also reflected prevailing ideas that a woman's nature made her suitable for the job.

Paradoxically, as the new economic order enlarged women's reproductive tasks in the home, it also increased the need for women's market labor. The conviction that an independent republic depended on land ownership, the resulting scarcity and high cost of male labor, concerns about the idleness of women displaced from the household economy, and the rising dependency of poor women on public aid all contributed to the demand for women workers outside the home. The emerging manufacturing class, desirous of cheap labor and seeking ways to counter the idea that the growth of manufacture threatened society's agrarian base, offered to employ women. In his famous *Report of Manufacturers* (1791), Alexander Hamilton suggested that one great advantage of the establishment of manufactures was "the employment of persons who would otherwise be idle." Manufacturing establishments enhance the productivity of the population and the land and make "women and children...more useful...than they otherwise would be," he added.[3] Poor women heard that failure to accept such work would leave them "doomed to idleness and its inseparable attendants, vice and guilt."[4]

The demand for women's market labor clashed with the terms of the colonial family ethic which favored economic productivity by women only if it occurred within the confines of the home. It also conflicted with the new industrial family ethic and the expansion of women's reproductive responsibilities in the home. However, since the early manufacturing system relied heavily on pre-factory, home-based production, married women could remain in compliance with the colonial and industrial family ethic by earning an income while working at home. Because merchants contracted for this labor through the male household head, these early manufacturing systems also protected prevailing patriarchal relations. The growing mechanization of manufacture disturbed this delicate balance by making centralized factory production more efficient and profitable than home production. The invention of the water-driven cotton mill in Pawtucket, Rhode Island in 1789 and the introduction of the power loom in New England in 1813 made it possible to consolidate the processes of power-driven spinning and weaving under one roof. By 1815, textile mills located mostly in New England numbered in the hundreds and eventually eliminated the profitability of home-based production.[5]

Because married women preferred to earn an income by working at home, the early factories had to rely heavily on young single women. Hoping to make factory work compatible with the colonial family ethic, the owners initially offered them "sheltered" living and working conditions. For example, mill-owners in Lowell, Massachusetts, the most-well known factory town in New England, created a system of strictly supervised boarding houses and jobs, and promised to protect a young woman's virtue, her availability for marriage, and the primacy of her place in the home.[6] Mill work actually conferred some status on "the Lowell girls" as they came to be called. Eventually, however, market pressures caused the factory owners to eliminate supervised lodgings, de-skill the labor process, reduce wages, lengthen the work day, increase the pace of work,[7] and essentially remove the respectability and appeal of factory work to the white, native-born, often middle-class farmer's daughter. Once factory conditions ceased to dignify womanhood, it became increasingly difficult to mediate the tension between the need for low-paid labor and the colonial family ethic's proscription of women's work outside the home. Both deteriorating work conditions and the availability of new jobs for women, such as teaching, sent many young women out of the New England mills.[8] Their places were filled by male and female farm laborers wiped out by poor soil, depressions, and the high cost of farm machinery, as well as by free blacks in need of work and, beginning in the 1840s, by newly arrived Irish immigrants, half of whom were women.[9] Owing to their poverty, the single and married mostly foreign-born women who replaced the "Lowell girls" became part of the permanent urban labor force whose survival depended on their labor and uncertain market conditions. Segregated by gender and ethnicity and paid less than the native-born workers, they could not return to the farm when factory work dropped off.

The efforts to protect native-born, white women who had to work against the stigma associated with departures from the colonial family ethic did not extend to black women. White society defined and treated black women as laborers rather than as homemakers and denied them the patriarchal "protections" accorded to white women. Black female slaves and free black women were "shoved into the brutal face of pre-capitalist and capitalist exploitation outside their homes."[10] In addition to working in the fields and in the "big house," a small number of owners rented both male and female slaves to outside employers, often to compensate for the rising price of slaves. The first southern cotton mill, opened in 1789, utilized rented slave labor from nearby plantations. Similarly, thirty-five bondswomen, aged fifteen to twenty, and six or seven young male slaves operated the Arcadia Manufacturing textile mill in Florida.[11] In the early nineteenth century, slave women built levees, laid railroad track,[12] and labored in mines, foundries, saltworks, sugar refineries, turpentine camps, and food and tobacco processing plants.[13] The practice of slave rental declined once it became less efficient than hiring free labor in the North. Racism and economic necessity forced free black women into the paid labor force. Attempting to abide by the family ethic, free black married women also took in wash and boarders so that they could be at home with their children.[14]

The restructuring of home and family life meant that the colonial family ethic was less applicable to the reality of women's lives. The decline of women's economically productive role in the home, for example, violated the colonial family ethic's mandate against idleness. Yet economically productive work, now available only through the marketplace, brought women out of the home, thus contradicting the family ethic's mandate that women not leave the domestic sphere. The simultaneous expansion of women's caretaking activities in the home only compounded these conflicts, especially since this new "work" was not defined as economically productive. These developments, which created new tensions between the demand for women's home and market labor, marked the decline of the colonial family ethic and the rise of a new one more suited to the changing times.

The Industrial Family Ethic

The industrial family ethic first appeared in the 1790s, became institutionalized in the 1830s, and was further refined after the Civil War. By making reproduction rather than production the centerpiece of women's life and defining women's paid labor outside the home as deviant, the new family ethic helped to explain and institutionalize women's new role, popularly referred to as her "place in the home." More suited to the conditions of industrial capitalism, the industrial family ethic provided the rationale needed to exclude women from economic productivity, to expand their reproductive and maintenance tasks, and to define the home as "women's sphere." Securing women's place in the home also re-established the family as a necessary "bulwark against social disorder" when everything else was adrift. Once again, the home became "the one institution that prevented society from flying apart."[15]

The industrial family ethic articulated the new arrangements of capitalism and patriarchy by linking the separation of household and market work to a sexual division of labor—a specific set of recognizable and not altogether unfamiliar gender roles in which male "providers" worked for wages in the market and female "homemakers" remained at home. Under these revised gender norms, women and men who previously shared, however unequally, responsibility for household production now legitimately occupied seemingly "separate spheres." Pious, inferior, subordinate, and confined to the home as before, the terms of women's role in the new industrial family ethic elevated marriage, motherhood, homemaking, and the overseeing of family life to new ideological heights. In addition to the loss of a recognized productive role, the industrial family ethic defined proper women as "moral mothers" and "asexual wives,"[16] and denied their previously acknowledged sexual needs.

Not all women were prepared to give up their role in household production, to accept their exclusion from the labor market, or to become singularly devoted to homemaking and childcare: they had to be convinced! The family ethic promised that domesticity would shield women from the evils of the outside world and bring them certain rewards of status. In the words of one women's magazine: "There is composure at home; there is something sedative in the duties which home involves. It affords security not only from the world, but from the delusions and errors of every kind."[17]

The terms of the industrial family ethic were conveyed to women by ministers, educators, and by the popular advice books and sentimental novels that began to flood the market after the invention of inexpensive printing machinery in the 1830s.[18] Reflecting the experience of white, middle-class women and targeted primarily at them, women from other classes and races had difficulty subscribing to the terms of the industrial family ethic. Nonetheless, it was eventually encoded in all societal institutions and, especially in urban areas, exercised considerable ideological power. Fulfilling the terms of the new family ethic, also known as the domestic code, "the cult of domesticity," and "the cult of true womanhood,"[19] established a woman's femininity, her womanhood, and her social respectability. Non-compliance brought penalties for stepping out of role.

Marriage

Marriage, the seat of private and personal service, remained essential to the proper exercise of domestic virtues under the industrial family ethic. Advice books encouraged women to "think of marriage...justly, to esteem it the most important act of a woman's life, and as involving the most important results." Trained as sisters and daughters to be disciplined, devoted, and self-sacrificing, young women were prepared to enter "that sphere for which woman was originally intended, and to which she is so exactly fitted to adorn and bless, as the wife." One mid-century author wrote that "woman is made for love, conjugal and maternal, and when the powerful sentiment which seeks this necessary completion of the end for which she was created...has been awakened...[h]usbands and children...become necessary to her moral organization."[20] On the marriage night, the single great event of a woman's life, she bestowed her greatest treasure upon her husband, and from that time on became completely dependent on him, an empty vessel, without a legal or emotional existence of her own.[21] Some observers regarded marriage as a cure for "difficult girls" counting on the "sedative quality" of a home to subdue even the most restless spirits.[22] On rare occasions the popular literature absolved a "woman of genius" from the necessity of marriage because her extraordinary nature exempted her from needing the security and status of wifehood.[23]

Subordination

The industrial family ethic also held women to be subordinate to men. According to one of the many prevailing family-life advice books:

> Every family is a little state, an empire within itself, bound together by the most endearing emotions, and governed by its patriarchal head, with whose prerogative no power on earth has a right to interfere. Every father is constituted the head of his household. God has made him the supreme earthly legislator over his children, accountable, of course to Himself, for the manner in which he executes his trust; but amenable to no other power, except in the most extreme cases of neglect, or abuse."[24]

The Ladies Repository suggested that man was "woman's superior by God's appointment, if not in intellectual dowry, at least by official decree." Therefore women should submit to men "for the sake of good order at least."[25] The *Ladies' Magazine* explained: "[Woman] was not formed for independence...But [she is] endowed with those peculiar properties which enable her firmly but steadfastly to adhere to her natural protector."[26] *The Young Lady's Book* proclaimed, "It is however, certain, that in whatever situation of life a woman is placed from her cradle to her grave, a spirit of obedience and submission, pliability of temper and humility of mind are required of her."[27]

The idea of female selflessness, which intensified in industrial America, underscored female subordination. Domestic tracts described woman as having "A pure true heart, a self-forgetful spirit...a wish and an effort to please," and a readiness to minister " to the wants of others." "It is seldom that [her] wishes cross the limits of the domestic circle which to her is earth itself."[28] Women were told to "lay aside all consideration of themselves" and to make their "joys...the results of the gratification of others."[29] Guidebooks advised a wife to adapt herself to the husband, to avoid conflict with him, and to assimilate all his views and opinions. "If he is abusive, never retort," advised one author. "Avoid a controversial spirit" and "do not expect too much."[30] Mothers knew "to bear the evils and sorrows which may be appointed us, with a patient mind."[31] Women learned that desires at odds with their family's happiness and well-being must be restrained.

Women also learned to repress their sexuality. In contrast to colonial norms which expected women's sexual appetite to be comparable to men's, if not greater, the nineteenth-century cult of purity denied that women had any sexual drives. The period's leading expert on sexuality wrote, "The majority of women (happily for them) are not very much troubled with sexual feelings of any kind. What men are habitually, women are only exceptionally."[32] Experts reminded women that "the best mothers, wives and managers of households know little or nothing of sexual indulgence" and that the only passions felt by proper women were love of home, children, and domestic duties. Women were warned to hold their own sexuality suspect:

> There is a species of love, if it deserves that name, which declines soon after marriage, and it is no matter if it does...There can be no objection to external love, where it is a mere accompaniment to that which is internal. What I object to is making too much of it; or giving it a place in our hearts which is disproportioned to its real value. Our affection should rather be based chiefly on sweetness of temper, intelligence and moral excellency.[33]

Exempt from sexual feelings and passions, society also charged women with disciplining unregenerate male sexual activity and with maintaining the purity needed to properly oversee the home and the community.[34] Those who failed were warned that they would be "left in silent sadness to bewail your credulity, imbecility, duplicity and premature prostitution."[35]

Women's legal status heavily reinforced their subordination to men. Not very different from the colonial era, the law disenfranchised women and denied them control of their property and even of their children. A wife still could not make a will, sign a contract, or bring suit in court without her husband's permission. Nor could she secure the custody of their children, if divorced.[36] In the view of a New York judge who, in 1837, advocated wives' rights, the laws of marriage gave the husband

> ...so much and such uncontrolled, indefinite, irresponsible and arbitrary power over [the wife's] person and subject[ed] her to such an abject state of surveillance to the will, commands, caprices, ill humours, angry passions, and mercenary, avaricious and selfish disposition, conduct and views of her husband that marriage for woman approximated slavery for the blacks.[37]

The Home

The industrial family ethic portrayed the home as a sanctuary, a tranquil retreat. It was to be a redemptive counterpart to the amoral, impersonal, commercial world outside where market-weary male workers could restore themselves for another hard day of work. Embodying all the worthy characteristics of a former era, this image helped to ease the transition from a pre-industrial to an industrial society. Within the home, mutual responsibility and family love would counter the cash nexus and the individualism of exchange—an antidote to the harsh reality of capitalist work relations. "Home," preached a New Hampshire pastor in 1827, is "where...man seeks a refuge from the vexations and embarrassments of business."[38] Popular magazines exclaimed, "Let us have a place of quiet...which the din of our public war never embroils." The homes of men should be "a realm into which the poor...fighters with their passions galled, and their minds scarred with wrongs—their hates, disappointments, grudges and hard-worn ambitions—may come in, to be quieted and civilized...It is this that gives repose to the anxieties of the statesman and soothes his troubled breast amid the bustles and turmoil of political strife." Another magazine told men that at home "your errors will meet ever with gentlest forgiveness...there your troubles will be smiled away."[39]

The sexual division of labor placed women at the center of the home. When asked, "What gives light and life to that home; what binds us by an indissoluble, sacred tie to that altar; what calls forth the full, warm gush of grateful affection; what imparts existence, name, worth to those domestic virtues?" America answered, "Woman!"[40] Indeed, in contrast to colonial times, the home now became women's exclusive domain. According to an 1845 poem,

> Where lieth women's sphere?—Not there
> Where strife and fierce contentions are,...
> Not in the wild and angry crowd,
> Mid threat'nings high and clamours loud;
> Nor in the halls of rude debate
> And legislation is *her* seat;...
>
> Where then *is* women's sphere? The sweet
> And quiet precincts of her home;
> Home!—where the blest affections meet,
> Where strife and hatred may not come!
> Home!—sweetest word in mother tongue
> Long since in verse undying sung! (emphasis in original)[41]

An 1854 literary magazine stated, "Man profits by connection with the world; but women never." A few years earlier the *Ladies Garland* declared that "the active scenes in which the attention of man is...engaged are unsuited to [woman's] gentler character" and that "her natural delicacy will shrink from the rude contact of such boisterous occupations."[42]

To create a "haven in a heartless land," the industrial family ethic extolled the virtues of domesticity and maintained that wives who did not learn to keep house jeopardized their marriages. As society is constituted, wrote Mrs. S. E. Farley, "True dignity and beauty of the female character seems to consist in right understanding and faithful and cheerful performance of social and family duties."[43] To another advisor, making beds was good exercise; repetitive tasks resulted in patience and perseverance; and proper home management was a complex art. "There is more to be learned about pouring out tea and coffee than most young ladies are willing to believe." Other experts suggested that the science of housekeeping affords exercise for the judgment and energy, ready recollection and patient self-possession, that are the characteristics of a superior mind."[44]

Domesticity included managing household consumption, the purchase of the growing number of manufactured goods and services, and numerous other tasks necessary to keep family members physically and emotionally fit. Women supervised children, cared for the aged, nursed the sick and disabled, and generally helped to maintain the non-working members of the family and the wider community. Wrote Dr. J.W. Corson in an article repeatedly published in leading mid-nineteenth century women's magazines, " I love to see her at the couch of sickness, sustaining the fainting head, offering to the parched lips its cordial, to the craving palate its simplest nourishment...and complying with every wish of the invalid."[45]

Motherhood

Motherhood, one of the Puritan woman's many tasks, became the central responsibility for women in the industrial era. Colonial magazines assigned little weight to mothering, either in relation to women's other duties or in contrast to the father. This began to change in the 1790s as the hours spent by men in the home fell while those of women rose and as new ideas about childhood emerged. Colonial parenting concentrated on the transfer of property and work skills from one generation to the next and arranging a fruitful marriage for one's children. In the industrial economy, parenting became more focused on socialization than imparting specific work skills. Indeed, the immediate value of children's labor decreased while their productivity and success increasingly depended on acquiring the character traits necessary for survival and success in the market economy.[46]

Reflecting this, nineteenth-century child-guidance literature suggested that "a youngster must be able to go out into the urban world, to capitalize on such opportunities as it may present, to carve out a life for himself [sic] which, in a rapidly changing society may require different tasks to be performed than were required of his parents. His is to be the active, manipulative approach to people and things."[47] Thus, boys learned to be self-seeking, self-motivated, competitive individuals with the drive and confidence to succeed in the market whereas girls were trained to be supportive wives and mothers.[48] Learning obedience to authority was critical, for when children go into the world "they will be called upon to exercise self-denial, patience and self-command under the most trying circumstances; if not fortified by home discipline how can they practice them when beset in their daily walks?"[49]

According to advice books, the proper development of children now depended on a prolonged period of love, warm understanding, and protection from the corrupting influences of adult life and the market environment. This was reinforced by Lockean ideas of the innocence and malleability of the child's character which replaced Calvinist notions of original sin and God's Will. The former defined children as persons with distinctive attributes such as impressionability, vulnerability, innocence—not simply as little adults. *The Mother's Book* (1831) claimed that, "the mind of a child is not like that of a grown person, too full and too busy to observe everything; it is a vessel empty and pure—always ready to receive, and always receiving."[50] On such grounds the well-being of children, no longer irrepressibly sinful, "naturally" required full-time, undivided adult attention. Innocent children had to be protected from society's corrupting influences, and to be reared as moral and trustworthy citizens.

With these changes, the authors of domestic education tracts shifted their emphasis from the father to the mother as the central parent. "To American mothers," stated the *Claims of the Country on American Females,* "is then committed, in a special manner, the solemn responsibility of watching over the hearts and minds of our youthful citizens who are soon to take their places in the public arena and to give form and individuality to our national character.[51] Drawing on biological differences between women and men, it was assumed that women were especially endowed with the characteristics—namely, innate warmth, gentleness, and morality—necessary to provide childcare.

The Ladies' Literary Cabinet asked in 1819, "Is there a feeling that activates the human heart so powerful as that of maternal affection? Who but a woman can feel the tender sensation so strong? The father, indeed may press his lovely infant to his manly heart, but does it thrill with those feelings which irresistibly overcome the mother?"[52]

The new family ethic also defined mothers and wives as the moral guardians of the family and the community. Advice books told mothers to imbue their children with the "little morals of life...rights of property and a faithful observance of the truth...It is in the daily and hourly family intercourse that these 'little morals' must be cared for."[53] The responsibilities of the mother as caretaker, socializer, and moral guardian extended from the home to the wider social order. The popular literature regularly asserted that in "every domestic circle woman is the center," responsible for "the good government of the family which leads to the...welfare of State." Moreover, the "strength of the country is found...in the quiet influence of the fireside."[54]

Female piety underpinned women's purity and their role as moral guardians. Nineteenth-century authors agreed that "there is no gem which so much adorns the female character, and which adds so brilliant a lustre to her charm, as unaffected and deep-toned piety." Some writers emphasized women's inherent inclination for holiness; others argued that women needed religion because of their role as "arbitress of taste and manners."[55] Reverend Spring declared in the *Ladies Garland* in 1837 that only "pious mothers" could raise children of a "moral and religious character" who would develop into virtuous citizens capable of governing the nation. Another religious leader told women, "Yours is to decide...whether we shall be a nation of refined and high-minded Christians, or whether...we shall become a fierce race of semi-barbarians before whom neither order, nor honor...can stand."[56]

The Industrial Family Ethic, White Working-Class Women, and Women of Color

The industrial family ethic described the ultimate nineteenth-century female, an imaginary woman whose traits increasingly defined the roles of white, middle-class women. But the wide discrepancy between ideology and reality meant that few women, even those in the middle class, could match its idealized terms. Nonetheless, the industrial family ethic became encoded in virtually all societal institutions and operated as a powerful social force influencing the norms of the white working class, the free black community, as well as those of the white middle and upper classes.

Nineteenth-century working-class families attempted to comply with the prevailing ideology of women's roles. Working-class men and their unions fought for the "family wage" that is, wages adequate for a man to support his dependents. The demand, met by only a few employers, represented male efforts to secure a decent standard of living for their families at a time when the wage paid to the average worker covered the subsistence of only one person and was being cut back. The ideal of "normal" manhood contained in the notion of a "family wage" was premised on the economic dependency of women on men and supported women's exclusion from the labor force. To promote the family wage, but also because working-class men worried that women's employment lowered male wage levels and took away male jobs, the working-class press regularly extolled the virtues of the home and women's place in it. As in the popular literature of the middle class, counsel, comfort, and consolation became the products of women's labor in the home.[57]

If compliance with the industrial family ethic was viewed as offering white middle-class women an opportunity to develop themselves as mothers and homemakers, such compliance intensified the domestic labor of working-class women and involved major sacrifices in the organization and comfort of their family life. Not being "allowed" to work outside the home, working-class women had to make up for the lost income by limiting family consumption and risking the health of their children by sending them to work. They also gave up the privacy of their home and increased their household tasks by taking in boarders, increasing the production of household goods, and taking in piece work.[58] Like those women who did enter the labor force, those at home also faced a double work day.

The black community also accepted the industrial family ethic and strived to meet its terms. Black men, both slave and free, defined their manhood in terms of male supremacy in the family. As early as 1773, male slaves petitioned for freedom on the grounds, among other things, that male slaves had no family authority. A convention of free black males in 1855 declared, "As a people we have been denied the ownership of our bodies, *our wives,* homes, children and the products of our own labor" (emphasis added). The vindication of their manhood and even the achievement of racial equality called for establishing conventional patriarchal relationships. "As evidence of the deep degradation of our race," a black physician and newspaper editor, Martin Delany, observed in 1855, "there are among us [women] whose husbands are industrious, able and willing to support them, who voluntarily leave home and become chamber maids, and stewardesses." Delany added, "Until colored men attain to a position above permitting their mothers, sisters, wives and daughters to do the drudgery of...other men's wives and daughters it is useless, it is nonsense...to talk about equality and elevation in society."[59] Black husbands also took pride in buying fashionable dresses, pretty hats, and delicate parasols for their women. A well-dressed wife legitimized their relationship and his role as a successful provider.[60]

Black men clearly incorporated the industrial family ethic in their struggle to assert their manhood, to reclaim the white man's proprietary "rights" over black women, to protect black women from exploitive wage-labor, and to otherwise to free blacks from white domination. After the Civil War, black families strived to keep women closer to home where they performed domestic chores, took care of children, raised vegetables, and tended to farm animals. When he withdrew his family members from the fields after the Civil War, a Tennessee freedman explained to his employer: "When I married my wife, I married her to wait on me and she has got all she can do right here for me and the children."[61] Boston cotton brokers attributed the disastrous cotton-crop losses in 1867-68 to the decision of "growing numbers of Negro women to devote their time to their homes and children." A South Carolina newspaper reported in 1871, that the withdrawal of black females from wage labor necessitated a "radical change in the management of [white] households as well as plantations" and proved to be a source of "absolute torment" for former masters and mistresses.[62] These patterns afforded families greater subsistence and offered black women some of the patriarchal "protections" historically available to white women.

The early black press echoed the patriarchal call. Black newspapers published numerous articles on the "women's sphere," some reprinted from white papers. One black paper, *Freedom's Journal,* editorialized, "Women are not formed for the great cares themselves, but to soften ours. Their tenderness is the proper reward for the dangers we undergo for their preservation. They are confined within the narrow limits of domestic assiduity, and when they stray beyond them, they move out of their proper sphere and consequently without grace."[63]

Free, middle-class, black women often felt that the best way to join white society was to comply with the family ethic. The militant black activist Maria Stewart advised black women to excel in "good housewifery," knowing that "prudence and economy are the road to wealth." To mothers she declared, "what a responsibility rests on you! It is you that must create in the minds of your little girls and boys a thirst for knowledge, the love of virtue, the abhorrence of vice, and the cultivation of the pure heart." To maximize their influence, "true black women" also had to be pious and pure. As among whites, black middle-class women fulfilled the terms of the family ethic with greater ease than poor black women, large numbers of whom continued to work as washerwomen, domestics, and seamstresses. Racism, however, complicated the ability of all black women to comply with the family ethic.

The idea of a domestic vocation spelled out by the industrial family ethic clearly suggested an unfounded commonality among women. Despite its widespread acceptance, the industrial family ethic failed to reflect the experience of many white working-class and immigrant women and women of color. The similarity even among white married women who shared an exclusion from the paid labor force quickly disappeared in the inequality of their husband's income. Women with means often substituted leisure for the rigors of domesticity prescribed by the family ethic. They became "ladies of leisure" who entrusted the care of their children and households to hired help. "It's not genteel for mothers to wash and dress their own children," they were told, "or make their clothing, or teach them."[64] The lady of leisure, typically an urban woman, also demonstrated her husband's or father's ability to support a homebound wife, to provide amply for his family, and to distinguish it from the urban masses. The delicate clothes worn by upper-class women prohibited strenuous exercise, made walking difficult, and testified to the wearer's exemption from or incapacity for any "vulgarly" productive employment.[65] To a British observer, the idleness of the American lady exceeded that of other countries. "There is in America," she wrote, "a large class of ladies who do absolutely nothing."[66] Instead, upper-class women were encouraged to develop the feminine charms and special accomplishments that turned them into decorous ornaments. One advice book explained that,

> Women's brows were not intended to be ploughed with wrinkles, nor their innocent gaiety damped by abstraction. They were perpetually to please and perpetually to enliven. If we were to plan the *edifice,* they were to furnish the *embellishments.* If we were to lay out and cultivate the garden, they were to beautifully *fringe* its borders with flowers. If we were to superintend the management of kingdoms, they were to be the fairest ornaments of those kingdoms, the embellishers of society and the sweeteners of life (emphasis in original).[67]

Women whose poverty, race, or lack of a male breadwinner forced them to work for wages outside the home could not conform to the family ethic. Although exact data do not exist, estimates suggest that the majority of the early factory workers were children and white women of limited means. Indeed, as early as 1816, women and children made up two-thirds of the nation's 100,000 cotton mill workers.[68] By 1840, when about 10 percent of all women over age ten worked for wages outside the home, women filled nearly half of all manufacturing jobs and 90 percent of those in shoe factories, textile mills, and millinery shops. Significant numbers of women also worked in factories producing shoes, furniture, gunpowder, buttons, gloves, shovels, and tobacco.[69] Increasingly they were foreign born. By 1860, for example, foreign-born workers comprised 62 percent of the Hamilton Company's workforce, up from 4 percent in 1836.[70] Immigrant men tried hard to achieve the economic security necessary to keep their wives out of the labor force,[71] but often could not. An 1855 study of a working-class area in New York City found from 25 to 33 percent of married immigrant women at work, although the numbers varied sharply by nationality.[72] Free black men also attempted to keep their wives at home whenever possible.[73]

Women without male breadwinners also worked outside the home. In the 1840s, an estimated 30,000 to 50,000 women—mostly unmarried, widowed, or deserted—worked for wages in New York City. Their low wages and periodic unemployment left them on the margin of existence. By 1870, 1.8 million working women or nearly 15 percent of the adult female population,[74] were excluded from respectability under the terms of the industrial family ethic.[75] Commentators began to complain about the "New Departure," that is, entrance of women into the rank of wealth-producers and wage-earners. "Calculated, by thwarting nature's evident design…to rob her of special gifts of grace, beauty, and tenderness," writers argued that the error of the day "lay in the thought that woman should be self-supporting" and she was implored "to stop and consider what homes would become…[if] woman was to take her place beside man in every field of coarse, rough toil." The Wisconsin Supreme Court ruled in 1875 that "The law of nature destines and qualifies the female sex for the bearing and nurture of the children of our race and for the custody of the homes of the world in love and honor."[76]

The industrial family ethic hardly reflected the experience of many black women who, owing to a lack of marriage and work opportunities, had even less ability to fulfill its terms. A demographic shortage of black men and their exclusion from all but the most menial jobs limited the marriage possibilities of black women relative to whites. Although the majority of black families contained husbands and fathers, many free black women, particularly urban women, headed their own households.[77] A study of Petersburg, Virginia's free black population found that in 1810, women outnumbered men three to two, and that black women married less than white women and headed more than half the town's free black households.[78] A later study of seven southern cities (1870-1880) reported that women outnumbered men by ten to eight. Despite a demographic surplus of black women, men headed the majority of black families. Gutman's study of the black family from 1855 to 1880 found more female-headed households in the South than in the North, but that a full 70 to 90 percent of black households in both regions were headed by men."[79]

Even when they married, poverty sent many free black women into the labor force, causing them to violate the family ethic. The Petersburg study mentioned above reported that, on average, black women participated in the labor force three times more than white women, and that the labor-force participation of married black women averaged almost six times that of their white counterparts.[80] Employed black women did not, however, receive what little protection employers offered to white women working outside the home. Virginia tobacco factories, for example, which employed white and black women in the 1850s, carefully placed white women in sex-segregated jobs suitable for "respectable ladies." Black women, by contrast, worked side-by-side with black men as they always had.[81]

After the Civil War, whites continued to deny black women the rights of womanhood under the terms of the industrial family ethic. The white stereotypes of black women typically held her to be a laborer, dominant in the family (indomitable grandmother or unnatural matriarch), and sexually loose—characteristics which put her in direct contradiction of the family ethic. The black homemaker drew derision, while employers contemptuously and hypocritically referred to freed women who refused to work in the fields as "playing the lady," as "most lazy," and as demanding that their husbands "support them in idleness."[82] White society also ridiculed the fancy dress of free black women associating it with indolent and "uppity" behavior that defied the traditional code of southern race relations. One southerner described a Charleston street scene "so unlike anything we could imagine: Negroes shoving white persons off the walk—Negro women drest in the most outre style, all with veils and parasols for which they have an especial fancy—riding horseback with Negro soldiers and in carriages."[83] Black activist Maria Stewart argued that white supremacy often stood in the way of black women's ability to be "true women" and she openly disputed the notion that any race or class possessed exclusive claim to that morality and worth.[84]

All Women Not Quieted by the Family Ethic

The power of the family ethic inhibited but did not totally forestall militant reactions. White, working-class women protested their wages and working conditions, and fought against their isolation and subordination; black women of both classes resisted the impact of racism on their lives. The first white women workers to strike on their own in America were the members of the United Tailoresses Society of New York who, in 1825, called their first meeting and demanded higher wages,[85] and, despite chastisement for "clamorous and unfeminine declarations of personal rights," struck for more than 5 weeks in 1831. In 1828, a protest by several hundred New Hampshire mill women against restrictive factory conditions was covered by the press from Maine to Georgia.[86] Sewing women also combined forces in New York, Boston, and Philadelphia throughout the 1830s.[87] One thousand women who bound shoes at home in Lynn, Massachusetts formed the Female Society of Lynn and Vicinity for the Protection and Promotion of Female Industry in 1833.[88] By 1845, female workers in Lowell had built The Lowell Female Reform Association, published their magazine, *The Voice of Industry*, and drew thousands of their sisters into the fight against pay cuts and for the ten-hour day.[89]

The protests and organization of women workers, which continued after the Civil War, provoked considerable public disapproval[90] and raised questions about women's proper role. Critics attacked the striking women for their lack of femininity, referred to them as "amazonian," and suggested a "gynocracy" would emerge if the militia were not called out.[91] The response signaled an emerging public concern with the tension between women's work and their "place in the home."

Societal disapproval also greeted the white middle-class women who became involved in various religious and social reform organizations and started a movement to secure women's rights. Some historians suggest that the isolation and frustration of middle-class women helps explain why so many more women than men participtated in the evangelical revivals that swept through New England and New York State in the early nineteenth century. The needs of the ministry and those of women, it is argued combined to make religion a women's domain. Women organized hundreds of church-related societies including charitable organizations, missionary groups, literary clubs, and maternal associations.[92]

Denied access to the vote, to formal education, and to most professional jobs, many white, middle-class women also stepped out of their "place in the home" to join moral reform associations and benevolent societies which attacked prostitution, the double standard, drinking, and other symbols of male domination.[93] Others focused on equity for women. The first petition for a Married Woman's Property Law reached the New York state legislature in 1836. Women held the first national Anti-Slavery Society convention of American women in 1837, after being denied the right to speak at abolition meetings organized by men. By 1848, the year of the first Women's Rights convention in Seneca, New York, middle-class women were actively involved in seeking property rights in the family and equal opportunity in the wider social order.[94] Their extension of women's terrain from the private to the previously exclusively male, public sphere challenged patriarchal norms. Like their working-class sisters, they were denounced as "unnatural," as "semi-woman and mental hermaphrodites" and were scorned for tampering with society and undermining civilization.[95]

Black women also fought poverty, white supremacy, slavery, poor wages, and dangerous working conditions. Black slaves who could not quit, organize, or strike, resisted their oppression by slowing down their work pace, laboring carelessly, and otherwise undermining the full use of their labor. Female field hands on a Louisiana sugar plantation in Union-occupied territory successfully conducted a slowdown and work stoppage for higher pay during the fall 1862 harvest.[96] Slave women educated themselves, engaged in sabotage, operated the underground railroad, refused to breed slave children for their masters, and risked being burned at the stake for their participation in slave revolts.[97] Some free black women attempted to organize as workers. Black washerwomen in Jackson, Mississippi, in the first known collective action by this group in America and the first labor organization of black workers in Mississippi, established a standard rate for their work in 1866.[98]

Free, middle-class black women formed organizations on behalf of "the race" throughout the nineteenth century. They organized missionary, temperance, and mutual-aid societies to pay sick and death benefits and to assist widows and fatherless children. The Female Benevolent Society of St. Thomas, the oldest among blacks, was formed in 1793, two years before its male counterpart. As a second generation of free black women emerged, their "African" societies became "colored," and "mutual relief" expanded into "mutual improvement."[99] During the nineteenth century and prior to similar efforts made on their behalf by whites, free, black women called for the abolition of slavery, started black grammar schools, and created formal organizations to fight for their rights and to deal with problems created by racism.[100] Katy Ferguson, an ex-slave, established a school in New York City for poor black and white children in 1793—some forty years before the well-known school for young black girls opened in Connecticut by the white teacher Prudence Crandall.[101]

Black women struggled with black men and white women to participate in abolition meetings. White, female anti-slavery groups typically ignored the condition of black women, although prior to the Civil War a few became integrated and black women assumed positions of leadership.[102] Black women in Salem, Massachusetts organized their first Female Anti-Slavery Society in 1832.[103] Although no black women (but one black man) were present at the reknowned Women's Rights Convention in 1848, they participated in similar women's rights meetings thereafter, until the turn of the century when the need of southern support for women's suffrage made them unwelcome.[104] Maria W. Stewart, became the first native-born, American woman to speak in public, anticipating the Grimke sisters by five years when, in 1832, she addressed a crowd in Boston's Franklin Hall.[105] Black men supported some activism by black women, but, in 1849, black women threatened to boycott the meetings of a black convention in Ohio unless granted a more substantial role in the proceedings. A Philadelphia convention admitted a black woman in 1855 only after a spirited debate in which she took part.[106]

The Industrial Family Ethic and the Political Economy

The industrial family ethic emerged at a time when the nation needed to adjust to the deep, disturbing, and often tumultuous changes that accompanied the development of capitalist production. The emerging economy required a new gender division of labor that assigned women to the private arena of home and community, and men to the more powerful public arena of work, politics, and society. It also became necessary for previously independent male farmers and craftsmen to accept the different rules, pace, and discipline of wage labor in an industrial workplace controlled by others. Finally, the basis of white men's patriarchal authority needed redefining as the dynamics of the market economy gradually undermined their sources of control. The industrial family ethic help to stabilize the social order by reformulating the gender division of labor and the ideology supporting women's subordination.

The industrial family ethic helped convince women as well as men to accept their place in the new social order. Its terms offered women a new status and the comforts of "patriarchal protection" while fostering women's oppression in ways that served the needs of capital and patriarchy. Unpaid caretaking and homemaking labor benefitted capital by cushioning the family from the effects of an increasingly ruthless and cut-throat market and assuring the reproduction of the labor force and the maintenance of the non-working members of society. The economy needed women to provide a tranquil retreat for market-weary men, socialize children to fulfill appropriate gender and class roles, and assure the consumption of market-produced goods and services. Largely unacknowledged and regularly devalued, this unpaid domestic work in fact greatly enhanced the productivity of labor, the growth of business profits, and the formation of personalities ready to accept their proper place in the hierarchy of capitalistic and patriarchal relations. But it required the exclusion of homemakers from the labor market,[107] which was justified by the idea that women *belonged* at home. This idea also rationalized giving working women largely low paid, low status jobs.

The devaluation of women at home and in the market went a long way towards restoring patriarchal power in both spheres. The unequal treatment of women in the market placed them at the bottom of male-dominated job hierarchies. The poverty that resulted from women's economic marginalization caused them to turn to marriage for support, reinforced their economic, if not psychological, dependence on men, and locked them into devalued and subordinated family roles. The pattern resulted in a self-perpetuating cycle in which the idea that "women's place is in the home" sanctioned their unequal treatment in the market which in turn reinforced the conditions that kept women at home.

The family ethic also harnessed the male work ethic, which encouraged the development and disciplining of a male labor force. "The only way to make husbands sober and industrious," observed the *New York Post* in 1829, "was to keep women dependent on them." By equating manliness with economic success the family ethic linked male identity as a provider to the dynamics of capital accumulation. The good breadwinner worked hard, supported his family, and competed effectively with other men in the race for wealth. Only if he failed did his wife go out to work. Combined with the pressures of economic survival and upward mobility, the economic responsibility placed on men reinforced industry's ability to exploit and control the male labor force.[108] This thinking simultaneously re-inforced patriarchal norms, helping to turn the lady of leisure into a male-status symbol. Writing in the late nineteenth century, Thorstein Veblen observed that the lady's sole function was "to put in evidence her economic unit's ability to pay." She was "evidence of conspicuously unproductive expenditure."[109] Wealthy men of the rising merchant class displayed their newly acquired wealth and status by keeping their wives idle; working-class men demanded the family wage so their wives would not have to work, and black men defended their manhood on similar grounds. This construction of the male work ethic obscured the growing ambiguity of the father's role in the family and the fact that the growing market role of men left them with less time, energy, and confidence to personally supervise their wives and children, to maintain control of their labor and access to key resources.

Finally, the family ethic rationalized the class stratification which became more pronounced in the nation's cities beginning in the late eighteenth century. The growing wealth of the industrial capitalists, regarded as vulgar, ambitious, and dangerously powerful by the agrarian gentry, contrasted sharply with the living standards of the urban laborers who worked for them. As if to deny this reality, the newly democratic social order rejected the idea of ascribed status and all classifications except "natural" ones which included gender, race, and achieved status such as "self-made" wealth. In this context, the idea of common domestic vocation for all women gained enormous appeal. The democratic possibility left those who failed to achieve this goal personally responsible for their departures.[110]

In the long run, however, the many female workers and female paupers in America became visible. Indeed, their growing numbers, along with other changes, eventually created a crisis for the colonial poor law system, paving the way for its "reform." The results, described in Chapter Five, were a set of punitive new ideas about the cause of poverty, an attack on outdoor relief, and the development of institutional care. In a period of intense social change, the emerging poor law system, which encoded and enforced the industrial family ethic, also helped to adjust workers to the rules of wage labor, to reinforce family discipline and to reconcile the competing demands for women's paid labor in the market and her unpaid labor in the home.

Notes to Chapter 4

1. Marilyn Power, "From Home Production to Wage Labor: Women As A Reserve Army of Labor, *Review of Radical Political Economics* XV (1) (Spring 1983), p. 75.

2. Alice Kessler-Harris, *Out to Work: A History of Wage-Earning Women in United States* (Oxford: Oxford University Press, 1982), pp. 25-27.

3. Edith Abbott, *Woman In Industry* (New York: D. Appleton & Company, 1910), p. 50.

4. Joan Huff Wilson, "The Illusion of Change: Women and the American Revolution," in Jean E. Friedman and William G. Shade (eds.), *Our American Sisters* (Lexington: D.C. Health and Company, 1982), p. 123.

5. Nancy F. Cott, *The Bonds of Womanhood: Women's Sphere in New England, 1780-1835* (New Haven: Yale University Press, 1977), pp. 25-26, 35-36; Abbott (1910) *op. cit.*, pp. 35-40.

6. For descriptions of the Lowell System, see Susan Estabrook Kennedy, *If All We Did Was To Weep At Home: A History of White Working Class Women in America* (Bloomington: Indiana University Press, 1979), pp. 25-26, 336-337; Ernest R. Groves, *The American Woman:The Feminine Side of a Masculine Civilization* (New York: Emerson Books, 1944), p. 126; Alice Kessler-Harris, (1982) *op. cit.*, pp. 36-38; Thomas Dublin, *Woman At Work: The Transformation of Work and Community in Lowell Massachusetts, 1826-1860* (New York: Columbia University Press, 1979), pp. 75-85.

7. Abbott (1910) *op. cit.*, pp. 125-130.

8. Gerda Lerner, "The Lady and the Mill Girl: Changes in the Status of Women in the Age of Jackson, 1800-1840," in Nancy F. Cott and Elizabeth H. Peck (eds.), *A Heritage of Her Own: Toward A New Social History of American Women* (New York: Simon and Schuster, 1979), pp. 188-189.

9. Kessler-Harris (1982) *op. cit.*, p. 47.

10. Elizabeth Higginbotham, *Work and Survival for Black Women*, Research Paper #1, Center for Research on Women, Memphis State University, Memphis, Tenn. 38152, September 1984, p. 4.

11. Robert Starobin, *Industrial Slavery in the Old South* (New York: Oxford University Press, 1970), excerpted in Rosalyn Baxandall, Linda Gordon, Susan Reverby (eds.), *America's Working Women: A Documentary History—1600 to the Present* (New York: Vintage Books, 1976), p. 34.

12. Barbara Mayer Wertheimer, *We Were There: The Story of Working Women in America* (New York: Pantheon Books, 1977), p. 111.

13. Starobin (1970) *op. cit.*, Baxandall et. al. (eds.), p. 34.

14. Paula Giddings, *When and Where I Enter: The Impact of Black Women on Race and Sex in America* (Toronto: Bantam Books, 1984), p. 48; Wertheimer (1977) *op. cit.*, p. 121.

15. Kessler-Harris (1982) *op. cit.*, p. 50.

16. A debate exists among historians as to the impact of the cult of domesticity on women. Some historians argue that the home became a trap for women, a prison that hindered female fulfillment while serving men's view of social utility and order. A second group suggests that women made use of the ideology of domesticity for their own purposes, to advance their educational opportunities, to gain influence and satisfaction, even to express hostility to men. A third group views women's sphere as a basis for a subculture among women that formed a source of strength and identity and afforded sisterly relations. They imply that the tenacity of the ideology owed as much to the motives of women as to the imposition of the wishes of men or the wider social order. For a fuller discussion of this debate, see Cott (1977) *op. cit.*, pp. 197-206.

17. Barbara Welter, "The Cult of True Womanhood: 1820-1860," in Michael Gordon (ed.), *The American Family in Social-Historic Perspective* (New York: St. Martins Press, 1978), p. 320.

18. Mary P. Ryan, *Womanhood in America: From Colonial Times to the Present* (New York: New Viewpoints, 1975), pp. 142-143.

19. Cott (1977) *op. cit.*, p. 1, credits the first use of the term "domesticity" in this sense by recent scholars to William R. Taylor, "Domesticity in England and America, 1770-1840," in a paper prepared for the Symposium on the Role of Education in Nineteenth Century America, Chatham, MA, 1964. Barbara Welter named the "Cult of True Womanhood," in an article of that title, in Gordon (ed.), (1978) *op. cit.*.

20. Barbara J. Berg, *The Remembered Gate: Origins of American Feminism: The Woman and the City 1800-1860* (Oxford: Oxford University Press, 1978), p. 88.

21. *Ibid.*, p. 89; Welter (1978) *op. cit.*, p. 315.

22. Welter (1978) *op. cit.*, p. 325.

23. *Ibid.*

24. Barbara Epstein, "Industrialization and Femininity: A Case Study of Nineteenth-Century New England," in Rachel Kahn-Hut, Arlene Kaplan Daniels, and Richard Colvard (eds.), *Women and Work: Problems and Perspectives* (New York: Oxford, 1982) p. 94, citing Herman Humphrey, *Domestic Education* (Amherst, 1840).

25. Welter (1978) *op. cit.*, p. 318.

26. Berg (1978) *op. cit.*, p. 72, citing *Ladies' Magazine* (1820), p. 59.

27. Welter (1978) *op. cit.*, p. 318, citing *The Young Ladies Book* (New York, 1830), p. 28.

28. Berg (1978) *op. cit.*, citing *Ladies' Magazine* (1830), p. 41; and James Fenimore Cooper, *The Crater or Vulcan's Peak* (New York: Stringer & Townsend, 1855), V. 2, p. 89.

29. Berg (1978) *op. cit.*, p. 85, citing J. A. Segur, *Influence, Rights and Appeal of Women* (Albany 1842), p. 97; Samuel Patterson "Female Piety," *Ladies Garland* (1837), p. 53.

30. Welter (1978) *op. cit.,* pp. 318-320.

31. *Ibid.*, citing "Rules for Conjugal and Domestic Happiness," *Mother's Assistant and Young Lady's Friend* (Boston, April 1843), p. 115; *Letters to Mothers* (Hartford, 1838), p. 199.

32. Berg (1978) *op. cit.*, p. 84, note 16.

33. Epstein (1982) *op. cit.*, p. 99, citing William Alcott, (1837), p. 85.

34. Nancy F. Cott, "Passionlessness: An Interpretation of Victorian Sexual Ideology, 1790-1850," in Nancy F. Cott and Elizabeth H. Pleck (eds.), *A Heritage of Her Own: Toward a New Social History of American Woman* (New York: Simon and Schuster, 1979), pp. 162-181; Cott (1977) *op. cit.*, pp. 126-159; Welter (1978) *op. cit.*, pp. 315-318.

35. Welter (1978) *op. cit.*, p. 375, citing Toman Branagan, *Excellency of the Female Character Vindicated* (New York, 1907), pp. 277-278.

36. Berg (1978) *op. cit.*, p. 103.

37. Cott (1977) *op. cit.*, pp. 77-78 (note 24).

38. *Ibid.*, p. 64, citing Charles Boroughs, *An Address on Female Education, Delivered in Portsmouth, New Hampshire, Oct. 26, 1827* (Portsmouth, 1827), pp. 18-19.

39. Berg (1978), p. 66, citing Horace Bushnell, *The American National Preacher* (1840), p. 107; William B. Taylor, Esq., "Home," *Ladies Garland* (1839), p. 243; Donald Grant Mitchell, *Reveries of a Bachelor: Or a Book of the Heart* (New York 1850), p. 59.

40. Berg (1978) *op. cit.*, p. 67.

41. *Ibid.*, p. 60, citing *Ladies Repository* (1845).

42. *Ibid.*, p. 70.

43. Welter (1978) *op. cit.*, p. 229.

44. *Ibid.*, p. 321, citing *Letter To Young Ladies* (Hartford, 1835), p. 27, and *The Young Ladies' Friend*, p. 230.

45. Berg (1978) *op. cit.*, p. 102.

46. William E. Bridger, "Family Patterns and Social Values in America, 1825-1875, *American Quarterly* XVII (1) Spring 1965, pp. 3-11; Carol Brown, "Mothers, Fathers and Children: From Private to Public Patriarchy," in Lydia Sargent (ed.), *Women and Revolution* (Boston: South End Press, 1981), p. 243.

47. Daniel Miller and Guy Swanson, *The Changing American Parent* (New York, 1958), p. 40.

48. Julie A. Matthaei, *An Economic History of Women In America* (New York: Schocken Books, 1982), pp. 108-109.

49. *Ibid.*, p. 109, citing Anonymous, *Women's Influence and Women's Mission* (Philadelphia: Willis P. Hayward, 1854).

50. Cott (1977) *op. cit.*, p. 91.

51. Matthaei (1982) *op. cit.*, p. 113, citing Margaret Coxe, *Claims of the Country on American Females* (Columbus, Ohio: Isaac N. Whiting, 1842), p. 6.

52. Ryan (1975) *op. cit.*, p. 126, citing Samuel Woodworth (ed.), *Ladies' Literary Cabinet*, Vol. VI, p. 5.

53. *Ibid.*; Matthaei (1982) *op. cit.*, p. 109.

54. Berg (1978) *op. cit.*, p. 68, citing, *Ladies' Literary Cabinet* (1822), p. 141; William Eliot, Jr., *Lectures of Young Women* (Boston, 1853), pp. 55-56; J.F. Stearns, *Female Influence and the True Christian Mode of its Exercise, A Discourse delivered in the First Presbyterian Church in Newburyport* (July 1837), p. 23.

55. Berg (1978) *op. cit.*, p. 79; Welter (1978) *op. cit.*, pp. 313-315.

56. Berg (1978) *op. cit.*, p. 68, citing *Ladies' Literary Cabinet* (1822), p. 141; William Eliot, Jr. (1853) *op. cit.*, pp. 55-56; Stearns (1837) *op. cit.*, p. 23.

57. Jeanne Boydston, "To Earn Her Daily Bread: Housework and Antebellum Working Class Subsistence," *Radical History Review*, 35 (1986), pp. 7-25; Hilary Land, "The Family Wage," *Feminist Review*, 6 (1980), pp. 55-77; Martha May, "The Historical Problem of the Family Wage: The Ford Motor Company and the Five Dollar Day," *Feminist Studies*, 2 (Summer 1982), pp. 399-460.

58. Matthaei (1982) *op. cit.*, pp. 120-123.

59. Giddings (1984) *op. cit.*, pp. 60-61.

60. Jacqueline Jones, *Labor of Love, Labor of Sorrow: Black Women, Work, and the Family From Slavery to the Present* (New York: Basic Books, 1985), p. 69.

61. Giddings (1984) *op. cit.*, pp. 57-64.

62. *Ibid.*

63. Dorothy Sterling, *We Are Your Sisters: Black Women in the Nineteenth Century* (New York: W.W. Norton & Co., 1984), p. 220.

64. Berg (1978) *op. cit.*, p. 98.

65. *Ibid.*, p. 62.

66. *Ibid.*, p. 98.

67. Epstein (1982) *op. cit.*, p. 88, citing Thomas Gisborne, *An Enquiry into the Duties of the Female Sex* (London, 1797).

68. Abbott (1910) *op. cit.*, pp. 89-90.

69. Kessler Harris (1982) *op. cit.*, p. 29, 47-48; Carl Degler, *At Odds: Women and the Family in America from the Revolution to the Present* (Oxford: Oxford University Press, 1980), pp. 367-368.

70. Kennedy (1979) *op. cit.*, p. 47.

71. *Ibid.*, p. 50.

72. Dublin (1979) *op. cit.*, pp. 147-149.

73. Giddings (1984) *op. cit.*, pp. 60-61.

74. Edward K. Spann, *The New Metropolis: New York City 1840-1857* (New York: Columbia University Press, 1981), p. 72.

75. Kessler-Harris (1982) *op. cit.*, pp. 53-54.

76. Sarah Eisenstein, *Give Us Bread But Give Us Roses* (London: Routledge & Kegan Paul, 1983), pp. 70-71.

77. Jones (1985) *op. cit.*, pp. 73-74.

78. Suzanne Lebsock, "Free Black Women and The Question of Matriarchy: Petersburgh Virginia, 1784-1820," *Feminist Studies* 8(2) (Summer 1982), pp. 271-292.

79. Herbert G. Gutman, "Persistent Myths About the Afro-American Family," in Michael Gordon, (ed.), *The American Family in Social-Historical Perspective*, (New York: St. Martin's Press, 1983, third edition), pp. 468-469.

80. Jones (1985) *op. cit.*, p. 74.

81. Delores Janiewski, *Subversive Sisterhood: Black Women and Unions in the Southern Tobacco Industry*, Working Paper #1, Center for Research on Women, Memphis State University, Memphis, Tenn. 38152, August 1984, p. 4.

82. Jones (1985) *op. cit.*, p. 59.

83. *Ibid.*, p. 69.

84. Giddings (1984) *op. cit.*, pp. 50-51.

85. Wertheimer (1977) *op. cit.*, p. 83.

86. Dublin (1979) *op. cit.*, pp. 86-107.

87. Wertheimer (1977) *op. cit.*, pp. 96-97.

88. *Ibid.*, pp. 87-88.

89. Kessler-Harris (1982) *op. cit.*, pp. 39-43; Dublin (1979) *op. cit.*, pp. 86-107; Degler (1980) *op. cit.*, pp. 370-371.

90. Degler (1980) *op. cit.*, pp. 370-371.

91. Kessler-Harris (1982) *op. cit.*, pp. 38-44; Kennedy (1979) *op. cit.*, p. 38.

92. Carroll Smith-Rosenberg, "Beauty, The Beast and The Militant Woman: A Case Study of Sex Roles and Social Stress in Jacksonian America," in Nancy F. Cott and Elizabeth H. Pleck (eds.), *A Heritage of Her Own: Towards a New Social History of American Women* (New York: Simon and Schuster, 1979), pp. 197-221.

93. *Ibid.*; Berg (1978) *op. cit.*, Chapters 7-11.

94. Nancy E. McGlen and Karen O'Connor, *Women's Rights: The Struggle for Equality in the Nineteenth and Twentieth Centuries* (New York: Praeger, 1983), pp. 16-17; Lerner (1979) in Cott and Pleck (eds.), (1979) *op. cit.*, p. 191.

95. William H. Chafe, *Woman and Equality: Changing Patterns in American Culture* (Oxford: Oxford University Press, 1978), pp. 24-25.

96. Jones (1985) *op. cit.*, p. 56.

97. Wertheimer (1977) *op. cit.*, p. 119.

98. Giddings (1984) *op. cit.*, p. 63; Jones (1985) *op. cit.*, pp. 56-57.

99. Sterling (1984) *op. cit.*, p. 110.

100. Eleanor Flexner, *Century of Struggle: The Woman's Rights Movement in the United States* (New York: Atheneum, 1968), p. 42; Angela Davis, *Women, Race and Class* (New York: Vintage Books, 1983), p. 102.

101. Davis (1983), *Ibid.*, p. 102.

102. *Ibid.*, p. 56.

103. Sterling (1984) *op. cit.*, p. 113.

104. *Ibid.*, p. xiii.

105. *Ibid.*, p. 154; Davis (1983) *op. cit.*, p. 58.

106. Giddings (1984) *op. cit.*, p. 59.

107. Boydston (1986) *op. cit.*, pp. 7-25; Natalie J. Sokoloff, *Between Money and Love: The Dialectics of Women's Home and Market Work* (New York: Praeger, 1981), p. 223.

108. Cott (1977) *op. cit.*, pp. 97-98; Kessler-Harris (1982) *op. cit.*, p. 51; Matthaei (1982) *op. cit.*, p. 105.

109. Lerner (1979), *op.cit.*, p. 191., citing Thorstein Veblen, *The Theory of the Leisure Class* (New York, 1962, first printing 1899), pp. 70-71, 231-232, and "The Economic Theory of Women's Dress," *Essays in Our Changing Order* (New York, 1934), pp. 65-67.

110. Cott (1977) *op. cit.*, pp. 97-98.

5

Women and Nineteenth Century Relief

The rise of industrial capitalism transformed poverty from a social into a political problem and threw the poor law system into crisis. Given the incompatibility between the colonial poor laws and the emerging economy, new means had to be found to assist families in distress while stemming rising relief costs, maintaining the labor supply, and enforcing the new family ethic. The key early nineteenth-century reforms—cutbacks in outdoor relief, the rise of institutional care, and the growth of private charities—accomplished these ends by mixing rehabilitation with deterrence and punishment. Both the coerciveness of the antebellum reforms and the hardship they imposed on the poor intensified as the nation entered still another period of rapid growth, change, and instability.

The Poor Law Crisis

The colonial poor law system fell into crisis in urban America early in the 1820s as the process of capitalist development began to move the United States from the fourth to the most industrialized country in the world.[1] Industrial output climbed from $149 million in 1810 to $1,886 billion in 1860.[2] Industry's increasing need to maximize profits and cheapen the price of labor, left few workers, regardless of gender, race, or ethnicity, with the share of the product that their labor produced. As the survival of workers became more dependent on wages than tilling the land, they faced low pay, irregular work, frequent unemployment, and a loss of control over their working conditions.[3] The debilitating new forms of economic insecurity which accompanied the shift from an agricultural to a wage-labor force also overwhelmed the capacity of the colonial poor laws to assist those in need. Unrelenting poverty increased the rolls, raised the cost of providing relief, and stretched the system beyond its capacity to respond.

At the same time, the process of economic transformation weakened important personal and community ties that had previously supported both the family and the poor.[4] The strict separation of private and public spheres, for example, limited the ability of families to provide economic support to relatives. With the decline of the household as the unit of production, particularly in urban areas and the rising cost of shelter, the number of large residences fell. With smaller dwellings, families and neighbors had more difficulty housing needy friends and relatives.[5]

Changing labor market conditions, particularly the increased labor mobility needed to match unemployed workers with available jobs, also undermined the family as a source of socio-economic support and as a foundation for the poor laws. Travel in search of jobs separated workers from their communities, reduced the availability of kin, and, in bad times, left families to fend for themselves. The overburdened relief system had increasing difficulty meeting the needs of family members—the women and children left behind *and* the male workers on the road. While isolated families strained the poor law coffers and its rules of relative liability, local settlement laws continued to bar strangers from public relief. Increased labor mobility, growing difficulty in defining a person's native community, and costly litigation between towns over questions of legal residence eventually rendered settlement laws obsolete.[6]

Rising Poor Law Costs

The high cost of relief was the most immediate cause of the poor law crisis. National relief statistics for this period do not exist, but the 1823 Yates survey of New York State poor laws found that 22,111 of the 1.3 million people living in the state received some type of public aid at a cost of over $250,000.[7] Between 1776 and 1825, social welfare was New York City's greatest single expenditure ranging from one-fourth to one-fifth of the total budget.[8] Municipal expenditures for outdoor relief alone averaged $85,650 a year between 1845 and 1857,[9] and annual increases far exceeded population growth. A series of regular depressions kept costs high through the end of the nineteenth century.[10]

The experience of most major cities paralleled that of New York. The 1821 Quincy Commission study of the Massachusetts poor laws reported that the town of Boston assisted 6,000 people a year.[11] During the 1857-1858 panic alone, Boston's public aid expenditures rose from $44,107 to $62,800.[12] Poor law outlays in cities in New Jersey,[13] Rhode Island,[14] and elsewhere paralleled those of New York and Boston. Although the high proportion of local budgets absorbed by relief expenditures reflected the small number of other functions performed by governments at this time, the absolute dollar amounts seriously burdened local treasuries.

Labor Discipline

Meanwhile, the crisis was heightened by the colonial poor laws' inability to regulate the labor force. Low wages and rising prices, long hours and less leisure, unemployment and job insecurity, but also a loss of dignity, independence, and control plagued the new industrial workforce. Many resisted these conditions by refusing to become wage-laborers or organizing to protect their interests in this changed work environment where economic control rested with owners of the industrial plant, rather than individuals. New means had to be found to harness the work ethic and assure the availability of a labor supply.[15]

Few labor unions had survived the economic downturns and employer attacks of the 1820s, but in the more prosperous 1830s, skilled workers once again began to organize. The historian Norman Ware observed that American workers did not oppose the introduction of machinery *per se*, but resisted "the method of its introduction for exploitative purposes, as they conceived it, in the hands of a group alien to the producer. For every protest against the machine industry, there can be found a hundred against the new power of capitalist production and its discipline."[16] In 1833, Baltimore mechanics declared, "It cannot but strike every reflecting and observing man [sic] that a spirit unfriendly to the standing and pursuits of the mechanic is fast gaining ground in this country…the result of which if not stopped in its onward course will be to bring them to a state of servitude less viable than that of the vassals of the feudal lords and princes—because they may hold the name but lose the rights of freemen." Philadelphia held its first general strike in 1835, and from 1834 to 1837 union membership increased nationwide from 26,000 to 300,000, representing about half of the urban workers in the country.[17]

Already confronted with labor agitation, the governing elite openly feared the political independence of recently enfranchised, white, male workers. Would the 1828 election of Andrew Jackson bring Europe's political turmoil to the United States? Charles Loring Brace, founder of the Children's Aid Society, warned that unattended young ruffians would mature into a "dangerous class" who might well threaten the value of property and the permanency of societal institutions. He predicted, "they will vote—they will have the same rights as we ourselves…They will perhaps be embittered at the wealth and luxuries they never share. Then let society beware when the outcast, vicious, reckless multitude of New York boys, swarming now in every foul alley and low street, come to know their power and *use it!*"[18]

Among the poor from the Northeast to the urbanizing West, both the jobless and the employed took to the streets to protest defaulting banks, soaring bread prices, unemployment, and the draft. The nearly "continuous disorder and turbulence among the urban poor presaged a potential social collapse to some observers."[19] In 1825, New York City's Mayor Hone worried that mass violence, class hatred, and the "poor and ignorant" were intent upon "pulling down the well-to-do and enlightened."[20] In 1849, a Baltimore church leader stated, "no man [sic] would be safe in our streets walking at night, nor…in his bed." In 1854, a Boston philanthropic society declared that "such scenes as have been once and again enacted in the streets of Paris would arise in America unless cities dealt with poverty."[21] Leaders often blamed rising poverty and unrest on the influx of immigrants who many Americans experienced as economic competitors, cultural and religious "foreigners," and as "carriers of anarchistic or socialistic doctrines."[22] To Mayor Hone, immigrants "bring disease among us; [or] may generate a plague by collecting in crowds within small tenements and foul hovels."[23] A Philadelphia committee studying the poor deplored the burden of maintaining "the host of worthless foreigners, disgorged upon our shores…[and felt they should not have to] incur so heavy an expense in the support of people, who never have, *nor never will* contribute one cent to the benefit of the community."[24]

At the same time, slave revolts, protests by free blacks, and the formation of anti-slavery organizations spread throughout the South. Gabriel's Revolt (1800) of Richmond, Virginia; the Denmark Vesey Conspiracy (1822) in Charleston, South Carolina; and Nat Turner's Insurrection (1831) in South Hampton County, Virginia[25] are only the most well-known of the many slave rebellions. Meanwhile in the North, legal restrictions and disenfranchisement sparked black conventions, mass meetings, and protests in many cities including Cincinnati (1827, 1836, and 1841), Providence (1831), Philadelphia (1834, 1838, and 1843), New York City (1834), and Pittsburgh (1839).

Plagued by widespread labor shortages, a disgruntled work force, racial tension, and political unrest, industrial capitalism needed new mechanisms to enforce its work norms. The colonial poor laws neither encouraged workers to enter the labor force nor enforced labor discipline strongly enough. Most pointedly, the old system no longer instilled the necessary degree of fear needed to make workers take any job regardless of its pay and working conditions. Other ways were needed to make sure that relief benefits did not compete with paid labor as means of support.

Family Discipline

Changing conditions also undermined the capacity of the colonial poor laws to enforce patriarchal family governance and to assure that families formed, maintained themselves, and properly renewed the supply of labor. Indeed, many working-class families earned little and lived in utterly miserable conditions. Moreover, by transferring control of women's and children's labor from the family patriarch to the factory owner, the changing market economy compromised the foundations of patriarchal power which had been grounded in male control over the household's economic resources and the labor of its members. As if to step in and replace the declining patriarchal authority in the home, state policy increasingly regulated work and family life.

Still largely a rural nation, U.S. cities began to grow between 1790 and 1840. Although Census Bureau definitions exaggerated the urban trend, more than one-third of the inhabitants of New England and the mid-Atlantic states[26] crowded into deteriorating seaboard slums and New England factory towns.[27] In 1856, the Holyoke, Massachusetts Board of Health reported that, "Many families were huddled in low, damp, and filthy cellars, and others in attics which were but little if any better, with scarcely a particle of what might be called air to sustain life. And it is only a wonder (to say nothing of health) that life can dwell in such apartments."[28]

Conditions were no better in New York City. The 1853 report of the New York Association for the Improvement of the Conditions of the Poor described fourteen families living in ten small apartments in a rear dwelling six feet by thirty, with three rooms on each of the first two floors, and four in the attic. The entrance "is through a narrow dirty alley and the yard and appendages of the filthiest kind." Another tenement house with five floors above the basement housed 120 families or more than 500 persons.[29] By 1860, New York City's "cellar" population included some 20,000 poor people living in wooden "shanty towns" on Manhattan's Upper West Side. A city inspector told an industrial commission in 1845 that their one-room shacks contained "the family, chairs, usually dirty and broken cooking utensils, stove, often a bed, dog or a cat, and sometimes more or less poultry. On the outside, by the door in many cases, are pigs, goats and additional poultry. There is no sink or drainage and the slops are thrown upon the ground."[30]

The poverty wages paid to men and the regular demand for women workers undermined the quality of life for working-class families, weakened the foundations of familial patriarchy, and literally made it almost impossible for working-class women to carry out the reproductive and maintenance tasks required by the family ethic. Exact data on the number of women wage earners prior to 1850 do not exist but estimates suggest that, by 1840, about 10 percent of all women over age ten worked outside the home. Most were young and single although many widows and poor wives also hired out. The 1850 *U.S. Census of Manufacturers* showed 225,992 women and 731,137 men in manufacturing industries alone.[31] Untold numbers of other women, not counted as gainfully employed by the Census Bureau, worked at home, selling household surplus or sewing garments and shoes in the putting-out system. The latter employment patterns, also highly exploitative, protected the patriarchal family by enabling working women to remain at home. Wherever they worked, however, women's low earnings barely supplemented a husband's income or supported a husbandless family. In 1836, the *National Laborer* estimated women's wages nationwide and in "every branch of business" at no more than 37.5 cents a day or $2.25 for a six-day week.[32] Urban newspapers reported women toiling at "starvation rates" and "in a constant fight with starvation and pauperism."[33]

The increase of female-headed households also took its toll on both patriarchal arrangements and the renewal of the labor force. Death, divorce, desertion, and a demographic imbalance between the sexes increased the number of husbandless women at this time. According to an 1830 report, 13 percent of white Massachusetts women did not marry before age fifty.[34] An 1820 survey of poor women in Philadelphia found that deserted wives comprised as many as one-fourth of the city's paupers.[35] In 1830, the secretary of Philadelphia's Female Hospitable Society reported that 406 of the 498 female paupers in Philadelphia were widows and that they made up three out of every four of its applicants. "The remainder are chiefly wives, deserted by their husbands, or whose husbands do nothing for the maintenance of their children, who are too young to do anything for themselves."[36] The majority of New York City relief baskets in the early nineteenth century were reserved for women with such notations as: "husband in prison"; "husband has broke his leg"; "husband bad fellow"; "her husband has abandoned her and she has broke her arm."[37]

Inadequate living and working conditions in urban America further weakened the underpinnings of patriarchal family governance. To the extent that these changes interfered with the family's ability to carry out the responsibilities assigned to it by the nineteenth-century family ethic, they bred a lack of confidence in the working-class household. Fueled by nativism and racism, the blame for the maladaptive family fell heavily on poor women. A poorly functioning family, it was believed, could be traced to a woman who was not strictly adhering to her prescribed roles of wife and mother. The employment of women outside the home which exacerbated this distrust also conflicted with the need for her domestic labor.

With the poor laws less equipped to support patriarchal families and less able to mediate the competing demand for women's home and market labor, close colonial ties between the family and the state gave way to the ideas of classical liberalism (see Chapter One) which favored more distance between civil society (individuals and their families) and the state, and which limited state interventions to those instances when private means failed. The family redefined from a societal governing body to a privatized self-supporting unit, was expected to be self-sufficient and not dependent on others or government aid.

Reflecting this, the early nineteenth-century poor law reforms mixed deterrence, punishment, and rehabilitation to regulate the contradictions that appeared between the systems of production and reproduction. Relief was made less attractive than work or family life by punitively reducing aid to the poor and denying help to those viewed as out of role. Other programs attempted to retrain and rehabilitate clients towards more effective participation in the labor market and the family system. The deterrent and rehabilitative reforms fell heavily on poor wives and husbandless women whose life circumstances defined them as deviant. Begun as a mixture of frugality, genuine reform, and as an adjustment to new conditions, by the end of the century, poor laws had largely deteriorated into repressive mechanisms of social control.

New Explanation of Poverty

The poor law reforms—the contraction of outdoor relief, the rise of institutional care, and the growth of private charities—conceived and implemented in the first half of the nineteenth century, represented a major shift in the provision and philosophy of public aid. A new explanation of poverty emerged at this time and helped to rationalize and justify the changes. Colonial society had viewed the indigent as unfortunate neighbors whose poverty was natural and endemic to the social structure, if not predetermined by God's will. It merited a familial and community response. The rise of the market economy brought forward a new individualistic and moralistic explanation which focused instead on the characteristics of the poor. Echoing the previously described strains in the poor law system, the new theory located the problem of pauperism in the lack of labor discipline (violations of the work ethic), the lack of family discipline (violations of the family ethic), and the provision of relief itself.

Lack of Industry and Moral Character

Reflecting the need for labor discipline, a key explanation for poverty focused on the individual's lack of industry, poor initiative, and weak moral character. Love of sloth, supposedly led depraved persons to prefer idleness and a parasitic life as recipients of alms. Little tolerance existed for the able-bodied poor, viewed as lacking initiative rather than an opportunity to work. During the deep economic downturn of 1819, for example, the New York Society for the Prevention of Pauperism, claimed that "no man [sic] who is temperate, frugal, and willing to work need suffer or become a pauper for want of employment." A social reformer added that the "sober and able-bodied, if industriously disposed, cannot long want employment. They cannot, but in their own folly and vices, long remain indigent."[38] Nineteenth-century reformers believed that removing the dread of want turned the provision of public aid into a disincentive to work and wrongly implied that assistance was a right.

Reformers linked weak moral character to lack of industry as a cause of poverty. "The chief evils of poverty," argued William Ellery Channing, a Unitarian leader, "are moral in their origin and character. One must never overlook 'the great inward sources' of their [the poor's] misery."[39] The 1818 report of The New York Society for the Prevention of Pauperism blamed poverty on ignorance, idleness, intemperance in drinking, want of economy, imprudent and hasty marriages, lotteries, pawnbrokers, houses of ill fame, the numerous charitable institutions in the city, and war.[40] The 1860 Annual Report of the New York Association For Improving the Conditions of the Poor (AICP) concluded that, "one of the primal and principal causes of poverty and crime is the want of early *mental and moral* culture.[41] Charity workers believed that patient and systematic efforts at moral uplift that "inculcated" the poor with ideas of "temperance, frugality, and industry" would raise them from the "idleness and sensuality" of their "low and groveling life" and guide them toward "higher hopes and nobler principles.[42]

Improper Families

Nineteenth-century thinkers also linked poverty to their perception of a family's ability to carry out it's reproductive and maintenance tasks. Workers, single women, and immigrant adults whose poverty prevented them from complying with the family ethic frequently were judged to be unfit parents. Charity workers held that children of the poor, "are not always cursed by poverty principally but by the ungoverned appetites, bad habits, and vices of their parents."[43] The American Sunday School Union, an early nineteenth-century moral reform society, declared that the evils by which "the peace of society is broken up" and "its heaviest burdens accumulated may be attributed to something wrong at home."[44] The presence of the children of working parents hustling in the streets became evidence that poverty and crime derived from improper family life rather than the unsavory living and working conditions of industrial capitalism.

The solution often was to tear families apart. The Boston Charity Aid Society sought to remove as many children as possible from such conditions by placing them in families where "the habits of industry and good order" would be encouraged.[45] The New York AICP believed that,

> To keep such families together either by occasional relief or employment, is to encourage their depravity...These nurseries of indolence, debauchery, and intemperance, are moral pests of society and should be broken up. The inmates, in the absence of a more suitable provision , should be sent to the Alms-House— the sick...to the Hospital—the children to be educated and apprenticed, and the able-bodied adults sent to work, under such discipline and regulation as would tend to correct their habits, and oblige them to earn their own subsistence.[46]

Dependency

Finally, poverty was attributed to the availability of outdoor relief itself. Classical liberal economics, which won dominance at this time, held the poor laws to be an artificial creation of the state. Taxation to support the indigent inappropriately interfered with the "natural right" to possess and accumulate property and wealth and, in addition, deterred private charitable giving. In this view, relief programs themselves caused pauperism. The Guardians of the Poor in Philadelphia deplored outdoor relief as "calculated...to destroy that noble pride of Independence" and "to create a dependence on the bounty of others."[47] The poor laws enforced bad habits, tempting recipients to give up their frugality and industry, to buy unnecessary articles, to lose thoughts of the future, and to become "degraded, dissolute, wasteful, profligate and idle."[48] In his 1834 *Manual of Political Economy* Thomas Cooper declared, "The more paupers you support, the more you will have to support."[49]

Although some observers recognized illness, injury, widowhood, unemployment, and other external factors as causes of poverty, they remained the exception to the general rule of "blaming the victim," a practice which intensified in the latter half of the century. By blaming poverty on the victim rather than on the dynamics of the market economy, the individualistic theory of poverty obscured its political and economic causes, weakened the commitment to caring for the poor, and rationalized harsh and restrictive poor law reform, particularly in urban areas.

The New Poor Laws

From the 1820s onward, the colonial poor laws became the target of widespread critical investigations in major Eastern cities. State commissions detailed the abuses of the colonial relief system and recommended reducing, if not abolishing, outdoor relief and transferring its functions to institutions and private charities. By restricting outdoor relief, rehabilitating the helpless poor in institutions, and placing the able-bodied, undeserving poor in the workhouse, these proposals promoted rehabilitative but also punitive measures to enforce work and family discipline. The differential treatment of families as deserving or undeserving of aid based on their compliance with the industrial family ethic also reflected growing concerns about deviant women, proper family functioning, patriarchal governance, and a deep distrust of the poor to properly carry out the family's reproductive and maintenance tasks. Women, held responsible for proper family functioning often bore the brunt of this response. The contraction of outdoor relief and the growth of private charities meant less cash aid even for the most deserving female pauper. Institutional care removed poor, frequently immigrant, women from their homes, often separated them from their own children, and otherwise punitively disrupted the lives of women perceived as out of role. As the following discussion shows, the reforms cost some of them the "rights of womanhood" as defined by the family ethic. The loss of relief and the unattractiveness of institutional care released poor women for work in the poorhouse or the bottom rungs of the labor market. Such policies denied women the right to care for their children at home at a time when the family ethic praised ladies of leisure and defined full-time homemaking and motherhood as the centerpiece of woman's proper role. By channeling the undeserving poor women in the labor market, nineteenth-century public aid also helped to reconcile the conflicting demand for women's home and market labor. But the treatment of work as a punishment for being out of role, supplied the labor market with low-cost female labor without challenging the idea that women belonged at home.

The Attack on Outdoor Relief

In the pre-industrial colonial era most poor persons received outdoor assistance in private homes. Towns aided the deserving poor in this way, but often auctioned off the undeserving to the lowest town bidder or housed them in one of the early poorhouses. By the nineteenth century this system had become ineffective, at times abusive. The simultaneous stiffening of attitudes towards the poor turned calls for reform into an attack on outdoor relief.[50]

The first direct assault on outdoor relief occurred before the Civil War when various Eastern states established commissions to investigate the operation of the poor laws. Josiah Quincy, Secretary of the Massachusetts Poor Law Commission, concluded in his 1821 report "that of all modes of providing for the poor, the most wasteful, the most expensive, and the most injurious to their morals and destructive to their industrious habits is that of supply in their own families."[51] In 1824, Secretary of New York State John V. N. Yates also recommended the prohibition of all begging and the abolition of outdoor relief for healthy males age eighteen to fifty.[52] Levi Woodbury's report on the New Hampshire poor laws likewise criticized outdoor relief. But the sharpest attack came from William Meredith of Pennsylvania who informed the legislature that the rapid and complete abolition of the system of public poor relief was the sole efficacious remedy for the evils attendant upon the poor. He recommended capping the relief expenditures at the 1825 level and denying aid to any able-bodied person without legal settlement.[53]

Most cities retrenched, but only a few totally closed down their outdoor relief programs. Philadelphia abolished outdoor relief from 1827 to 1839; Chicago did likewise from 1848 to 1858.[54] Baltimore and New York considered this route, but restricted their programs instead.[55] City expenditures for outdoor relief began to fall, often dropping below those for indoor relief. In 1838, New York City allocated $380,000 for indoor relief, twice the sum for outdoor aid. This funding ratio continued until the Civil War.[56] Although outdoor relief expenditures rose steadily in Boston in the late 1850s, indoor relief programs received more funds.[57] These cutbacks fell heavily on women, increasingly poor and foreign-born. As early as 1790, the town of Marblehead, Massachusetts reported 459 widows and 869 orphans on the relief rolls.[58] The 1823 Yates investigation of New York State poor laws found that women comprised 52.2 percent of the 22,041 recipients of indoor and outdoor public aid. One-third of the total recipient population, which also included many children, was foreign-born.[59] The Annual Report to the Governors of the Almshouse of New York City reported over 40,000 visits to provide mostly fuel and some cash to the outdoor poor each year between 1851 and 1854. In 1855 and 1860 the number rose to nearly 80,000. The recipients included three children for every two adults. At least one-half of the adults were listed as wives or widows.[60]

Problems of poverty and the negative response to the poor only intensified after the Civil War, a prosperous period of rapid economic growth, accumulation of individual wealth, and class polarization. Criticism of the poor laws grew stronger as Social Darwinism and the eugenics movement emerged to dominate social thinking. Social Darwinism applied the biological explanation of evolution presented in *The Origin of the Species* (1859) to social phenomena. It combined laissez-faire economics and Darwin's concept of the survival of the fittest to argue that the possession of wealth evidenced "fitness" and that its opposite, poverty, signaled inherent weakness. Eugenics maintained that acquired characteristics, such as destitution, could be biologically inherited. These new theories rationalized the accumulation of wealth, held the poor in contempt, and justified the rampant nativism and racism that developed following the Civil War. They also held that the poor must pay the price of failure exacted by nature from all the unfit.

Any interference on their behalf by the state or charity was pointless, even dangerous, because it protected the defective in the struggle for existence, permitting them to multiply and weaken the species. Popularized by Herbert Spencer and William Sumner and hailed by philanthropists as well as prominent university, church, and government leaders, Social Darwinism and eugenics, taken to their logical extreme, favored the elimination of outdoor relief and even the poor themselves. William Sumner described proponents of poor relief as failing to see "that if we do not like survival of the fittest, we have only one possible alternative, and this is survival of the unfittest." "The whole effort of nature," declared Spencer, "is to get rid of such, to clear the world of them to make room for better."[61]

This thinking combined with rising costs, political corruption in the public aid bureaucracy, the conflict between public and private agencies for control of the charities field, and an intensification of the belief that outdoor relief led to pauperism stimulated a second, more widespread and prolonged attack on outdoor relief after the Civil War. New York City suspended public outdoor relief completely from July 1874 to January 1875, resuming it only partially (e.g. coal to needy families and cash to the adult blind) thereafter until 1931. Sixty-thousand persons lost their benefits in the first year including large numbers of women.[62] In the winter of 1878, Brooklyn ceased providing public aid for several years. Soon Philadelphia followed suit as did Baltimore, San Francisco, New Orleans, Washington, D.C., Kansas City, Louisville, and other cities.[63] Still others restricted their programs. Spending on outdoor relief in Boston fell from $80,341.89 in 1877 to $64,502.42 in 1900; in Buffalo it dropped from $73,237.00 in 1875 to a low of $ 29,292.00 in 1880, and then rose to $64,586 in 1900.[64]

We do not know for sure what happened to women once outdoor relief was contracted or abandoned but cutbacks both before and after the Civil War must have sent women (and men) into the labor force or looking for a spouse for support. Some also turned to prostitution. Those who went to private charities discovered that the charities preferred to aid only those they thought could be re-socialized to accept proper family roles. The remainder became separated from their families as they entered the institutions or the workhouses that had proliferated during the period. Free blacks continued to be excluded from, or only minimally served, by public outdoor relief programs prior to the Civil War. After the War, the federally funded Freedman's Bureau aided southern blacks (and later whites). Established in 1865 to manage abandoned and confiscated property, to find jobs for freed blacks and to maintain those who became transient and homeless, the Bureau distributed food rations and medical supplies, established forty-six hospitals, set up orphan asylums and schools for black children as well as institutions of higher learning. But widespread opposition from whites interested in preserving the old ways restricted its work. The Bureau was forced to rescind its relief and job creation programs on the grounds they created idleness and pauperism. The promise of "forty acres and a mule" to free blacks proved illusory as the government returned confiscated lands to plantation owners. Many of the contracts for black labor turned out to be exploitative. The largest single category of grievances initiated by black women under the Freedmen's Bureau "complaint" procedures, for example, concerned non-payment of wages. These and many other problems led to the Bureau's demise in 1872.[65] Clarke Chambers, a social welfare historian, speculates that the federalization of welfare may have been delayed until the 1930s, partly because the first major program established by the Federal government had aided blacks.[66]

The Federal government's failure to institute a comprehensive land redistribution program after the Civil War, the refusal of southern whites to sell property or extend credit to former slaves, and the lack of jobs open to black women and men in the North and the South left the majority of freed blacks of both sexes vulnerable and dependent on former white masters. After the War, all the confederate states but one enacted black codes to regulate the lives of ex-slaves and to maintain control over the black labor force. The laws, such as those passed in South Carolina, permitted corporal punishment, restricted labor mobility ("vagrancy"), extended apprenticeship into enslavement, and otherwise degraded blacks into an inferior caste.[67]

Private Charity

Private charities began to proliferate in the early nineteenth century. Efforts to introduce order into the chaos of private philanthropy existed prior to the emergence of the well-known Charity Organization Society (COS) and the "scientific charity" movement in the 1870s. Both the Boston Society For The Prevention of Pauperism founded in 1835 by Joseph Tuckerman and The Association for Improving the Condition of the Poor founded by Robert M. Hartley in 1843 anticipated the COS movement by many years. Each organization divided its respective city into districts and sub-wards to coordinate numerous relief-giving societies, assigned male "visitors" to investigate applicants for aid, and sought to prevent indiscriminate almsgiving.[68]

The early private charities assisted many women, and promoted proper family life, with some established solely for that purpose. As early as 1797, The Ladies Society for the Relief of Poor Widows in New York City granted aid to 98 widows and 223 children. The numbers grew to 152 widows and 420 small children by 1800.[69] In 1814, the Female Assistance Society in New York City relieved more than 1,500 poor women while the Association for the Relief of Respectable, Aged, Indigent Females assisted 150 women over age 60. In November 1821, the pension list of the Society for the Relief of Poor Widows included some 254 widows and 667 children under age ten.[70] New York's largest charity, the Association for Improving the Condition of the Poor (AICP) reported in 1858 that it aided 27 percent more women than men.[71] The number of families aided by AICP, many female-headed, jumped from 5,292 to 24,091 during the depression of 1873-1874.[72]

The private charities made sharp distinctions between women they regarded as "deserving" and "undeserving" of aid which assured the moral stature and independence of the poor and preserved the patriarchal family as the fundamental unit of society. They favored married women or previously married women who lacked a male breadwinner through no fault of their own—widows, the wives of sick, disabled, and temporarily unemployed men, and\or others defined as deserving of help. In contrast, they frequently denied aid to, separated, or otherwise penalized unwed mothers, abandoned wives, and wives of permanently unemployed men. Like the poor law authorities, charity workers distrusted the family management abilities of women who lacked a male breadwinner, whose breadwinner failed to provide steady support, or who herself failed to remain within the prescribed wife and mother role. The New York Society for the Relief of Poor Widows with Small Children, formed in 1797, would not aid a woman without evidence of her husband's death or proof of at least a twelve-month absence from the home. It removed widows from their pension list for "intemperance, promiscuity, begging, dancing, selling liquor, and even living in a disreputable neighborhood." The Female Assistance Society (1813) annually aided between 500 and 1,500 dependent but "upright" women.[73]

The AICP, which typically served more women than men,[74] preferred to help the "deserving" poor by providing moral advice rather than financial aid. They hoped this would "keep the recipients from degradation and vice, preserve their self-respect, and by sustaining them in the respectable position that they had previously maintained, save them from sinking perhaps irretrievably, into the gulf of pauperism."[75] Detailed lists of those served, such as the following one from the agency's 1858 annual report, reveal what cases the agency regarded as deserving of help: (1) "indigent widows and deserted wives with young children—a very numerous class—who in struggling to support and properly train their families were often overtaken by want"; (2) "educated and even accomplished females reduced from comfortable, perhaps affluent circumstances to dependence or to earning a scanty subsistence by the needle"; (3) "females once in comfortable circumstances, who have been reduced to poverty by the death or misfortunes of their husbands and relatives or by other causes (e.g. wives of shipmasters or other sea-faring men, and such as have sick and bedridden husbands or children, widows of tradesmen or mechanics having children and, perhaps aged fathers and mothers depending on them for support). These are mostly American born, from the great middle-class, and generally deserving of commiseration and aid"; (4) "the sick and bereaved generally, who had been brought by their misfortunes and the times, to temporary want"; (5) "mechanics who usually provide their own support but by sudden loss of employment were compelled to apply for aid." Later in the century, the AICP openly refused to serve applicants with claims on other charities, those viewed as professional paupers or impostors, those fit only for the almshouse, and recent immigrants legally entitled to support from shippers.[76]

Even as the environmental causes of poverty began to be recognized in the late nineteenth century, private charity workers continued to focus on "defects" in family life. Mary Richmond, a prominent social worker, wrote that any household that violated the prescribed gender division of labor would quickly become a "breeding place of sin and social disorder."[77] The Charity Organization Society (COS), the leading private welfare agency known for applying "scientific" principles to the delivery of social services and refining the method of "friendly visiting," also perpetuated the individualistic interpretation of poverty supported by Social Darwinism and eugenics. It encouraged the maintenance of proper families by rewarding only the most deserving female pauper. Of all the applicants in 1886, the COS found only 6.4 percent worthy of continuous aid. Another 24.4 percent merited temporary relief, but 52.2 percent, needed work not charity. Sixteen percent deserved no assistance at all. That year it assisted only 30.8 percent of the applicants of whom only 6.5 percent received more than temporary aid.[78]

A similar pattern developed the following year. Of 3,119 applications received by the COS from January to May 1887, only 658 or about 20 percent were served. Of the remainder, "943 were ineligible for relief, 1,044 needed work and not charity, and 274 were completely unworthy of aid." In 1889, more than half of the 1,843 new COS clients were married couples and 26.8 percent were widows. This compares to 6.6 percent deserted wives and 3.2 percent single women. Deserted husbands, widowers, single men, and relatives of clients comprised the remaining 11.6 percent of the cases.[79]

The COS instructed its "friendly visitors" to strengthen "true" home life among the poor, to help the husband who "lost his sense of responsibility toward wife and children to regain it," to "dissuade restless wives from seeking outside employment," and to introduce messy housekeepers to "the pleasures of a clean, well-ordered home."[80] Women whose male breadwinners failed to provide steady support received especially harsh treatment from private charity. The COS refused to aid a drunkard or his family unless the wife left home, whereupon she was aided as a widow. Deserted wives, however, were not treated as widows because this would encourage desertion by other men. By penalizing their wives, charities might harness the male work ethic and convey to men that desertion and non-support does not pay. Non-supporting men should be forced to support their families, wrote Josephine Shaw Lowell, a COS leader in the late 1880s,

> but where he has escaped entirely, the mother and children should be left to be maintained by the constituted authorities and the family broken up and distributed to different institutions, unless they can support themselves. It ought to be understood in every community that where a man deserts his wife and children and neglects his most pressing duties to them and to the public, that they will be left to suffer the fate he has prepared for them.[81]

The COS showed little tolerance for women perceived as immoral. Lowell declared that , "the unrestrained liberty allowed to vagrant and degraded women" was "one of the most important and dangerous causes of the increase of crime, pauperism, and insanity." Regarding such women as "the visible links in the direful chain of hereditary, pauperism and disease," Lowell asked:

> What right have we today to allow men and women who are diseased and vicious to reproduce their kind and bring into the world beings whose existence must be one long misery to themselves and others. We do not hesitate to cut off, where it is possible, the evil of insanity by incarcerating for life the incurably insane: Why should we not also prevent the transmission of moral insanity as fatal as that of the mind?[82]

Reflecting this sentiment, Lowell recommended long-term commitment to reformatories for all women under age thirty arrested for misdemeanors or upon birth of a second illegitimate child. Once incarcerated they would be "re-educated through physical, moral, and intellectual training," and "taught to be women." That is, "They must be induced to love that which is good and pure, and wish to resemble it; they must learn all household duties; they must learn to enjoy work;...they must be *cured* both body and soul, before they can be safely trusted to face the world again."[83]

Few white-dominated private charities aided black women or men, despite the high rates of poverty among blacks. Prior to the Civil War, most slaveowners maintained their slaves, while free blacks often had to fend for themselves. Black leaders discouraged their followers from relying on white charity and urged them instead to establish their own beneficial associations. Middle-class free blacks in the North formed hundreds of societies to provide sick and death benefits to members. In Philadelphia alone 100 such organizations existed in 1830. Twenty-seven female mutual benefit societies in Philadelphia paid $3,616.58 in benefits and sixteen male societies paid $2,202.71 that year.[84] Fewer formed in the South where white fears of insurrection limited the assembling of blacks.[85]

Individual whites did assist the black community after the Civil War, but the white-dominated charitable societies did little to help blacks secure their social, political, or economic rights or otherwise address their needs. Private, white charities continued to ignore the needs of blacks due to their location in northern and midwestern cities with smaller black populations, but also due to racist inattention. Despite sympathy for problems of blacks found in the COS literature,[86] one study concluded that blacks benefited less than other segments of the population from COS's ongoing services and subsequent reform efforts.

The overwhelming burden of charitable work for blacks fell to other blacks. According to an 1898 report on black self-betterment efforts, few black charitable societies existed at this time. Instead, blacks cared for their own in their families, and communities, and through the churches, secret societies, beneficial and insurance associations formed by the developing middle class.

> They have few charitable societies but they give much money, work and time to charitable deeds among their fellows; they have few orphan asylums, but a large number of children are adopted by private families, often when the adopting family can ill afford it; there are not many old folks homes, but many old people find shelter and support among families to whom they are not related.[87]

Black women's organizations, like their white counterparts, formed day care centers to help poor working mothers, as well as nursery schools and kindergartens for young black children.[88]

Institutional Care

A major shift arising from the pre-Civil War poor law reforms was the increased importance of institutions. The commissions investigating the colonial poor laws in the 1820s regularly discussed replacing outdoor relief with congregate care. Josiah Quincy's 1821 report on the poor laws to the state of Massachusetts, recommended: "That the most economical mode [of relief] is that of almshouses having the character of workhouses or houses of industry, in which work is provided for every degree of ability in the pauper, and thus the able poor made to provide, partially at least, for their own support, and also to the support or, at least the comfort of the impotent poor."[89] He recommended denying public provision except on condition of admission into a public institution.[90]

The Secretary of New York State, John Yates, also proposed more indoor relief after his investigation of the state's poor laws. He recommended the establishment of "one or more houses of employment, under proper regulation...The paupers there to be maintained and employed at the expense of the respective counties, in some healthful labor, chiefly agricultural, their children to be educated, and at suitable ages, to be put out to some useful business or trade." Each house of employment was to be "connected to a workhouse or penitentiary for the reception and discipline of sturdy beggars and vagrants. The discipline to consist either of confinement upon a rigid diet, hard labor, employment at the stepping mill, or some treatment equally efficious in restraining their vicious appetite and pursuit."[91]

Following the Quincy and Yates reports, many towns revitalized their little-used almshouses and workhouses. Others built their first institution for indoor relief. While the large majority of poor people continued to receive outdoor relief at home, the provision of institutional care—viewed as more efficient, economic, and morally correct than public aid—mounted especially in the larger urban areas. Poor houses existed in all but four of New York State's fifty-five counties by 1835. These institutions occupied nearly 8,000 acres of land in 1840, up from 4,000 in 1830. Between 1830 and 1850, the number of poorhouse inmates rose from 4,500 to nearly 10,000. Similar patterns obtained in Pennsylvania, Maryland, Rhode Island, and other states in the mid-West. By the end of the Civil War, four out of every five persons in Massachusetts who received extended relief remained within an institution. By 1890, almshouses in the United States contained 73,045 inmates. In 1903, there were 81,764 inmates nationwide.[92]

According to the historian Michael Katz, of all the residential institutions that emerged at this time, the almshouse or the poorhouse probably cared for more people and touched the lives of the very poor most directly. The new almshouse designed to correct the abuses of the colonial poor law system, sought to serve the poor, to alleviate distress, and to discourage pauperism. Reformers who located the cause of social problems in the increasingly squalid, competitive, and otherwise unsavory urban industrial environment hoped to rehabilitate the poor by removing them "from an environment in which they live in idleness and dissipation," by separating them from families that could not keep them from succumbing to temptations, and by exposing them, in institutions, to new habits, discipline, and values.[93] With this in mind, the poorhouse would provide compassionate care to the helpless and the ill, offer work to laborers who became jobless through no fault of their own, and impose hard physical labor on the idle who wanted only the dole. Most important, these policies of deterrence would keep all but the most needy from seeking aid. The rules and regulations forced able-bodied women and men to adjust to the discipline of wage labor at any cost and, by breaking up "improper" families, channeled others, mostly women, into marriage and family life regardless of its safety or security.

The poorhouse sheltered large numbers of women throughout the nineteenth century. In 1821, more than 60 percent of the residents of the first almshouse in New York City, known as Bellevue, were female.[94] In each year between 1851 and 1865, women numbered nearly 50 percent of all the almshouse inmates statewide. The figure ranged from a low of 1,109 or 42.3 percent of the inmates in 1852 to a high of 3,147 or 54.5 percent in 1865. During these pre-Civil War years, large numbers of women also entered the city's workhouse whose female population grew from a low of 422 or 29.7 percent of the residents in 1854, to a high of 8,024 or 65 percent in 1865. After 1850, foreign-born women predominated among the female almshouse inmates. Native-born women accounted for over 49 percent of the New York State almshouse inmates in 1842. Ten years later nearly 60 percent were foreign born,[95] far exceeding their proportions in the general population.[96]

Katz's examination of the Erie County Poorhouse records from 1829 to 1866 provides rich detail about the demography of such an institution. While Katz emphasized the ways in which people used institutions for their own purposes, the utilization patterns he reports also reveal the impact of poverty, nativism, and the industrial family ethic on the lives and choices available to poor women. For them, the Erie County Poorhouse evolved from a refuge for entire families into a shelter and maternity hospital for young unwed, largely immigrant mothers. That is, it soon housed primarily the "undeserving" female pauper, likely to have been denied aid from other sources.

The female population of the Erie County almshouse rose from 30 percent in 1829 to over 40 percent in 1859, peaking at 47 percent during the Civil War. During this time, women comprised about 40 percent of the inmates less than fifteen years old, and more than 50 percent of both those aged fifteen to nineteen and those aged twenty to twenty-nine. Contrary to many impressions, older women did not predominate in the almshouse during most of the nineteenth century. Except for 1853-1854 and the Civil War years, most thirty to forty-nine year olds were men while women always made up a very small share (10 to 25 percent) of those over age fifty. The low number of elderly women probably reflects the greater willingness of children to take in aged mothers than fathers and the greater ease with which poor law officials aided women.[97] Past their reproductive years and less likely to be judged by the terms of the family ethic, older and previously-married women no doubt were viewed as more deserving of aid than young single mothers or older men.

Many more women than men entered the poorhouse with a relative, usually a child. Initially and until the 1840s, the large number of families and individuals that entered the Erie Country Poorhouse were native-born. Between 1840 and 1860, the foreign-born—largely Irish—population climbed from 60 percent to 80 percent of the inmates. With this shift, young unmarried women unable to obtain other sources of help replaced families as the predominant group in the almshouse.[98]

Many almshouse residents stayed for only a short time, most less than six weeks. But as a group, women tended to remain longer than men due to their childcare responsibilities and lack of job opportunities.[99] Likely to have been considered undeserving by private charities and outdoor-relief agencies, entry into the poorhouse became a source of shelter but also punishment for these mostly foreign-born young women.

In most almshouses, the officials put women and men to work using a traditional gender division of labor. In 1795, the New York City almshouse reported that "the Business of sewing, spinning and picking oakum is daily attended to by all who are able to work and are not employed in the Wash House[,] the Cookery[,] the Bakery[,] or the Nurseries." Of the 1,563 paupers in Bellevue in December 1821, a total of 145 men worked at twenty-one occupations. Some 232 women performed such tasks as knitting, sewing, spinning, cooking, nursing, sweeping, washing, and scrubbing.[100]

Almshouses continued to shelter large numbers of women after the Civil War, but the group as a whole was older. Although he does not label them as such, Katz's re-examination of Hoyt's late nineteenth-century survey of New York State poorhouse inmates reveals that most of the women—unmarried, first generation American, and old—fell among the undeserving poor. In the post-Civil War years, two-thirds of the poorhouse women of all ages were husbandless. Twenty-seven percent were single; over 37 percent widowed or divorced. Of the widows, 78 percent had no living child or only one. By this time many paupers were native-born, but the majority had immigrant parents. The data also point to the greater economic vulnerability of women. Many more women than men had received outdoor relief prior to their residence in the poorhouse and women tended to enter the poorhouse at a younger age than men.[101]

With reform in mind, the early nineteenth-century almshouse was designed to bear no resemblance to its colonial predecessor which, according to most critics, confirmed rather than corrected habits of idleness and dissolution. Rather, a new policy of re-education through confinement set out to rehabilitate inmates towards self-sufficiency and self-support. The new almshouses would inculcate the work ethic stressing order, discipline, and an exacting routine. Inmates would learn constancy and diligence, obedience and respect, and other behaviors needed by wage laborers in a setting that emphasized reformation, health, cleanliness, and the acquisition of industrious habits. Distrust of poor families also was apparent. Not only were large numbers of women found in the poorhouse, but there was widespread acceptance of the idea, articulated in the Quincy Report, that in institutions the lives of the poor would be "more comfortable and happy," and above all, "temptations rendered less generous than if suffered to remain…in their own families."[102]

But in practice many almshouses, particularly those in large urban areas, soon deteriorated into poorly financed, custodial warehouses that often indiscriminately herded the "insane," the ill and the well, young and old, male and female paupers into the same unheated, unclean, and overcrowded quarters in need of repair.[103] Some poorhouses remained clean and orderly places, but a mid-1850 investigation of an upstate New York almshouse found that, "The ill and the maimed, the filthy and the diseased are crowded in the same rooms and in many cases lie on the floor together wrapped in wretched blankets more like beasts than human beings."[104] Poorhouse superintendents often resorted to force and strict confinement to maintain order. The failure of most almshouses to produce a special environment in which to rehabilitate the poor reflected limited knowledge, a lack of financial resources, the negative effects of using the almshouse to frighten the poor into independence, and the overall punitive disregard for this population.[105]

The almshouse and workhouse were part of a broader nineteenth-century movement towards institutional care for the non-working members of the population, that also included orphanages, juvenile reformatories, houses of refuge, insane asylums, and penitentiaries. The movement towards specialized institutional care reflected various reforms designed to correct the abuses of the undifferentiated poorhouse by separating the young, the sick, the insane, and the criminal from each other and from the able-bodied pauper. Lacking the "character" to resist the evils and the temptation of the squalid and evil city, individuals in need of care would be removed from this unsavory environment to specialized asylums governed by rehabilitative regimens of order, industry, and proper family life. The reformers also hoped to lower local relief costs by transferring the worthy paupers from town relief rolls to state or county institutions. This would leave towns responsible only for the unworthy and able-bodied who would be forced to find jobs or face forced labor in the local workhouse.[106] Pressures to develop more indoor and less outdoor relief also reflected systemic needs for a low paid labor force dependent on wages rather than relief, and for greater control over the family life of "dangerous classes." Since only those in desperate need would seek institutional care, its presence would deter the working poor from leaving the labor market or family life for relief. By removing the poor who entered the asylums from the temptations of the taverns, the gambling halls and the houses of prostitution that filled many cities, institutional care not only protected the poor from the evils of city life but also protected society from the poor.

Women also predominated among those found in mental institutions up to the Civil War and afterwards. Although the gender difference was not extremely large,[107] women exceeded the number of men admitted to New York City's Lunatic Asylum and Insane Asylums in virtually every year between 1849 and 1860.[108] The aggregate statistics for the Uttica and Willard Asylums in upstate New York from 1843 and 1860 show the same pattern. Over 53 percent of the patients admitted by these institutions were female. These figures parallel the late nineteenth-century figures of 55 percent female and 45 percent male reported by the New York State Board of Charities for all institutions—state, county, local, and private.[109] Similar patterns obtained outside New York State.[110] The reports of the Eastern State Hospital in Virginia show that the female patient population rose steadily from 32 percent of the total in 1832, to 54 percent in 1870, after which it fell, reaching 45 percent in 1890.[111]

The mental hospital also became a place to house the "undeserving" female pauper. Although the reasons why so many women were classified insane remains unknown, the demographic record suggests that economic factors could have played a more important role in confinement than psychological considerations. Moreover, before the 1880s, women could be legally committed to mental asylums more easily than men.[112] Before long, poor and immigrant women became overrepresented among mental asylum inmates especially in public facilities, where conditions also rapidly deteriorated. Between 1842 and 1851, the Worcester Asylum reported a sixfold increase in the admission of state paupers compared to a two-fold increase in the total inmate population. Similar increases in the institutionalization of the indigent occurred in Rhode Island, Ohio, Kentucky, Tennessee, and other states.[113] Institutionalized immigrants far exceeded their numbers in the population. They constituted 77 percent of the 11,141 admissions to the Lunatic Asylum in New York City between 1847 and 1870, 53 percent of the resident population of the Boston Lunatic Asylum in 1846, and 68 percent of the residents of Longview Asylum in Cincinnati in 1875.[114]

The strong, anti-foreign sentiment that accompanied the influx of immigrants into mental hospitals helped to shape institutional rules. To maintain the quiet, routine, and order called for by the therapeutic model in use then, hospitals segregated the foreign-born in separate and usually inferior quarters. From the perspective of the superintendent, "Opposite in religion and all the notions of social life, it would not be well to class the two races [native and foreign born] in the same wards, where each must bear from the other what was considered troublesome and offensive while in health."[115] The harmonious relationship between the doctor and patient, it was maintained, also required such class and ethnic homogeneity. The growing number of poor and immigrant patients in public mental hospitals in the 1840s, however, sped the decline of the therapeutic institution. Combined with insufficient resources and minimal understanding of insanity, xenophobia helped to transform the "asylum" into a custodial warehouse with social control as a key objective.[116]

Few mental hospitals admitted mentally ill black women and men. Reflecting the times, those that did adopted strict policies of segregation. Before the Civil War, southern states generally ignored free blacks and assumed that slaveowners arranged for the care of "disturbed" slaves. Some state hospitals in the South, however, did receive applications from free blacks and slaveowners. The State Hospital for the Insane in South Carolina refused to admit "insane negroes" in 1828-1829 as no special provision had been made for them by the General Assembly.[117] So did the Virginia Western Lunatic Asylum. Hospitals in Georgia, Tennessee, Mississippi, and Louisiana provided no rooms for blacks, although public officials connected to these asylums favored admission of blacks, but in segregated quarters. In contrast, South Carolina accepted free black women and men and some slaves after 1848 as did the hospital in Williamsburg, Virginia. The latter opened its doors to free blacks and slaves, segregating only the females until public pressure caused the director to discontinue mixing the races.[118] After the Civil War, southern hospitals admitted blacks more readily, but to strictly segregated and inferior wards.[119]

Northern mental hospitals tended to follow southern admission and segregation policies. In 1836, the trustees of the Massachusetts General Hospital reported facing the "painful necessity" of rejecting black applicants, because of the "unwillingness of the ward patients to admit among them individuals of that description."[120] The Indiana and Ohio state hospitals refused admission to blacks while Cincinnati officials confined insane blacks in the county jail. Hospitals that did admit blacks housed them in separate and unequal wards. Prevailing opinion in 1855 held that,

> in regard to what is suitable provision for col'd insane agree, & that our views are that it *is the duty* of all State, County, & City Hospitals for Insane, situated in communities composed in any considerable part of blacks, whether slave or free, to receive col'd patients; that they sh'd be accommodated in special cottages or lodges situated near the main edifice for whites, but so entirely distinct from them that all desirable separation of the races may be maintained.[121]

The small number of black women and men in hospitals outside the South reflected smaller black populations elsewhere and prevailing discriminatory practices. An 1863 survey by the American Freedmen's Inquiry Commission reported that mental hospitals in Maine, Michigan, Illinois, Iowa, New Hampshire, Pennsylvania, and Vermont admitted less than ten black persons per hospital from the time each opened to

1863. At the time of the survey, blacks accounted for three out of 531 residents at the Utica Hospital, four out of 340 in New Jersey, twelve out of 8,411 in Northhampton State Lunatic Hospital in Massachusetts, and thirty out of 1,764 for the Boston Lunatic Hospital. The largest number of blacks were admitted to the New York City Lunatic Asylum which admitted ninety-eight blacks and 3,813 whites between 1853 and 1862. The pattern at the private hospitals did not differ.[122]

A dominant goal of psychiatric rehabilitation, like that of the almshouse, became internalization of the work and family ethics. With regard to the former, one official explained in 1844 that mental hospitals were:

> places of refuge for the unfortunate, where a spirit of industry is fostered and a healthful mental activity maintained by various forms of useful employment. If every employable insane person was provided with useful labor under intelligent and proper supervision, he added, the entire world would learn that rational & useful work is a means of averting insanity; a means of keeping a sane mind sane; a means of lessening insanity of the mind & etc.[123]

The mental asylum movement defined enforced labor as central to rehabilitation.[124] "Moral treatment," or the re-education of the patient within a proper atmosphere sought to counter, if only symbolically, the irrational, pre-industrial habits of the laboring poor.[125] Industriousness, frugality, self-discipline, and productive labor became defined as the outward measures of sanity.[126] Keeping inmates busy also helped to reimburse the state for the growing costs of confinement.

The mental hospital regimen also hoped to reverse maladaptive family functioning. According to the historian David Rothman, superintendents made it clear that the asylum would bear "no resemblance to the casual, indulgent and negligent household that failed to discipline its members or to inculcate a respect for order and authority."[127] Echoing the family ethic, the administrators instead conceptualized the asylum and its procedures in terms of a well-regulated home and family. The historians Walkowitz and Eisenstadt suggest that the private asylum "tried to create a peaceful environment to counteract the baleful effects of urban industrial society." It tried to "become a rural, middle-class home for patients, a bourgeois alternative to the disintegration associated with the immigrant, working-class family, and a familiar environment for the more well-to-do patients." Nurses were employed to create a homey environment, to nurture and discipline disordered minds, and to guide patients to their proper places in an ordered industrial society.[128]

Work in the mental asylum followed the prevailing sexual division of labor. Officials assigned men to agricultural pursuits, carpentry, painting, and general maintenance work. Women performed many of the domestic chores.[129] The Boston Lunatic Asylum, for example, assigned outdoor work to male patients and washing and ironing to women. At the private Hartford Retreat, men worked at farmwork or in the joiners' shop while women knit stockings, made shirts, and did domestic duties.[130] Walkowitz and Eisenstadt indicate the possibility of class differences in the use of work therapy among women. Granting the difficulty of assessing this, they suggest that given the prevailing ideology of women's roles, doctors probably prescribed work therapy to insane working-class women whose cure required that they learn how to work in a properly disciplined way. The "lady's" mental health problem was not a matter of work discipline, but overexcitement and overwork, which recommended rest cures and medical treatments varying from drugs to clitorectomies.[131]

What began as an improvement over the colonial poor laws quickly succumbed to considerations of economy and terror. Private charities served mostly the deserving female pauper, leaving mental institutions, to become the shelters for isolated persons existing on the margins of society, without friends or family to care for them. The poor, female, foreign-born, and chronically ill institutional population continued to rise, but few "got well" as had been hoped. By mid-century, the asylum, the almshouse, and virtually all other institutions had deteriorated into warehouses for sheltering the ill, disabled, criminal, and homeless. Overcrowding, rising operating costs, and the increased admission of poor, immigrant, working-class and chronically-ill patients undermined the therapeutic model of treatment. Rothman suggests that custodial warehousing and punishment of inmates also became an attractive means of social control.[132] That is, institutions became places to hold those segments of the population viewed as troublesome and dangerous to the wider social order.

Orphan Asylums and Placing-Out

Nineteenth-century child-welfare policy reflected numerous concerns about women's roles and proper family management. Indeed poor law officials continued the colonial practice of removing children of "unfit" mothers from their homes, indenturing them, or placing them in the almshouses. Eventually, deteriorating poorhouse conditions led to the development of alternative means of caring for children.

The colonial almshouse mixed young children with insane, criminal, and pauper adults and did not feed, clothe, or care for them very well. Over time, reformers concluded that the failure to adequately maintain the future labor force risked swelling the ranks of vagrants, petty thieves, and other troublesome members of society. The Ohio State Board of Charities, in 1857, warned, "Let those who appreciate the importance of early impressions, who acknowledge childhood as the seedtime of life...estimate...what it must be to have these impressions formed by association with...the loathsome moral corruption so common to our poorhouses. Let them calculate the harvest not only to the future individual life of the child, but to the State, which must be gathered sooner or later from such sowing."[133] Three years later, Ohio called for mandatory removal of all children from county almshouses. New York made it unlawful to commit children over three and under sixteen to the poorhouse in 1875.[134] Other states quickly followed suit.[135] Officials also hoped that the threat of separation from their children might deter adults from seeking public aid. "Refusal to admit children," it was suggested, "would act as a deterrent to parent(s) who might hesitate to enter a poorhouse if they know that their children could not accompany them."[136]

Once children were banned from the almshouse in the mid- to late nineteenth century, alternative methods of "child-saving" arose, particularly the establishment of separate institutions for children (e.g. orphan asylums, juvenile refuges) and the removal of children from corrupt city homes and streets to free "foster" families in the country (e.g. "placing-out"). The number of institutions for children grew from just four before 1800 to seventy-five on the eve of the Civil War. By 1890, there were about 600.[137] The number of children supported in New York State institutions increased by 139 percent, between 1875 and 1900 compared to a 55 percent rise in the state's overall population.[138] The overwhelming majority of children's asylums, sponsored by religious groups or private non-sectarian charities, received public subsidies. Placing-out agencies, such as the Children's Aid Society founded in 1853, shipped children to homes in the mid-west. The New York Children's Aid Society placed 814 children in 1860, 2,757 in 1870, and 3,764 in 1880. Between 1853 and 1890, the Society sent over 92,000 children to free foster homes "in the country" where children often exchanged hard labor for support.[139]

Both the child caring institutions and the placing-out agencies embodied the twin goals of child welfare and social control, as well as the demand for child labor that had played a more significant role in colonial child welfare efforts. Although they differed sharply as to the means, both groups deeply believed that neglected or poorly socialized children should be protected by removing them from their homes. The Orphan Society of Philadelphia, in 1831, hoped, to shelter children from both "the perils of want and the contamination of example." In 1851, the Boston Children's Friend Society sought to remove children of intemperate, depraved, and pauper parents "from those baleful influences which inevitably tend to make them pests to society and ultimately tenants of our prisons." After the Civil War, the central aim of the Boston Children's Aid Society was to remove as many children as possible from the conditions that produce...viciousness by placing them in families where "the habits of industry and good order" would be encouraged. Charles Loring Brace, the founder of the Children's Aid Society, hoped the immigration plan he devised would "connect the supply of juvenile labor in the city with the demand from the county and to place unfortunate, and destitute, vagrant and abandoned children at once in good families in the country."[140]

Most institutions appropriated all parental authority to themselves, either to minimize contact between children and their "indiscriminate" parents or to discourage parents from abandoning their children or using the orphanage as a temporary boarding home.[141] The orphan asylum in Philadelphia, for instance, required destitute parents placing their child in the orphanage to sign a pledge declaring, "I do hereby surrender to the Orphan Society of Philadelphia, the child A.B. to be provided for...I will not demand or receive any compensation...or in any way interfere with the views or directions of said society." The District of Columbia denied parents and friends the right to remove any institutionalized child before the age of twenty-one. Some states, such as New York, actually legislated parental loss of prerogatives for delinquent children placed in a house of refuge.[142]

Child caring institutions also restricted contact between inmates and their relatives. The New York Juvenile Asylum, in 1831, permitted parents to see their children solely at the discretion of a special trustee committee. The Baltimore Home of the Friendless allowed family visits only on the last Saturday of each month. The Boston Children's Friend Society billed itself as a "place where the most respectable poor may feel perfectly safe in placing their children, as all intercourse will be cut off between the family, as such, and the connection of any that are unwise." Even stricter rules prevailed in houses of refuge which frequently made it quite inconvenient for parents to visit on the rare days in which visiting was allowed.[143]

Once removed from the "improper" influences of their families and the streets, the asylum and the refuge hoped to train, rehabilitate, and reform their charges. Like other institutions of the time, they placed a premium on obedience, discipline, hard work, education, and precision in an effort to prepare the children for their later place in the community. Officials from a South Carolina institution for children maintained that strict training "disciplines them for...various walks of life," enabling them to become "practical men [sic] of business and good citizens in the middle class of society."[144] Institutions rewarded children who adapted to their norms with less work, more rapid release, and more desirable apprenticeships. They held the recalcitrant longer and in some cases bound them out to the captain of a ship for a life on the sea.[145]

Child caring institutions also exposed the young inmates to the discipline of ideal family life. Like the mental hospital, they modeled themselves on the well-ordered family still viewed as the chief, if not the last barrier between the proper citizen and the life of vice and crime, between the nation and rampant disorder. The Baltimore Home of the Friendless, for example, strictly enforced "the order and decorum of a well-regulated Christian family." The St. Louis Reform School based its program on

> assimilating the government...as nearly as possible to that of the *time honored* institution which guided the infancy of nearly all of the truly great good men and women—that model, and often humble institution—the *family*...'God's University'...the well-ordered Christian family.[146]

Reflecting their critique of the family life of the poor, the directors of the Boston Asylum and Farm School for destitute and vagrant children, declared that "it is almost astonishing how readily boys hitherto accustomed to have their own way, and to dispute supremacy with inefficient or indulgent parents are brought into habits of respect and order by a system of uniformly firm discipline."[147] To its directors, the Boston Farm School, was superior to "the mis-government or non-government of the weak and careless parent."[148] Rothman concludes that the quasi-military quality of the institution was a rebuke and an example to the lax family.[149]

The ravages of poverty combined with officialdom's profound distrust of the poor meant that children of poor, immigrant, and single mothers were overrepresented among those removed from their families. Some mothers (and fathers) who could not care for their children placed them in institutions voluntarily. Other children were removed from their homes due to legitimate discoveries of abuse and neglect. But large numbers of poor parents lost the right to raise their own children because they were seen as deviating from prescribed homemaker (and breadwinner) roles.

By 1850, 88 percent of the inmates of the New York House of Refuge were children of immigrants, mainly from Ireland. Likewise, two-thirds of the residents of the Philadelphia refuge and over half of those in Massachusetts and Cincinnati came from foreign-born and destitute parents.[150] The Philadelphia House of Refuge reported a preponderance of unskilled and semi-skilled workers among the delinquents' fathers, while almost half the fathers of inmates in the New Hampshire House of Reformation were not steadily employed.[151] Single mothers were at especially high risk of losing their children. Sixty percent of the 257 children at the New York House of Refuge, in 1847, for example, had lived only with their mothers. Between 1830 and 1855, only 27 percent had lived with both natural parents prior to admission.[152]

Negative views of family life among the poor intensified after the Civil War reflecting the popular philosophies of eugenics and Social Darwinism. The 1875 Hoyt Report[153] on the causes of pauperism in New York City suggested that most cases were due to factors "which are frequently if not universally hereditary in character...Families dependent on private charity" it concluded, "seem to exist only to rear children like themselves. To keep such families together is contrary to sound policy; the sooner they can be separated and broken up, the better it will be for the children and for society at large. Vigorous efforts must be instituted to break the line of pauper descent."[154] Another charity leader, in 1888, stated:

> True charity must seek not only to rescue the home from all base conditions, but often must *break-up the unworthy family,* and so far as possible, create for those taken from these base households an environment most like the true home, in order that the highest interests of society and the State may be served...The best legal codes declare that a child is to be taken from a base parent, and put where it can lead a useful and honest life; and we may go farther, and say that society is recreant to its duty when it allows a child to remain with a parent that persistently teaches it beggary and crime (emphasis added).[155]

The law increasingly sanctioned the practice of breaking up families to "help" them. In the 1890s, state legislatures increased the power of the courts to take custody of children, if it could be shown that their parents or guardians were exercising an anti-social influence on them. In 1894, Massachusetts empowered the Court to remove a child from its family if it was evident that the child by reasons of "neglect, crime, drunkenness or other vice of the parents is growing up without salutary control and education or in circumstances exposing such child to an idle and dissolute life."[156] However, the line between state intervention to protect abused and neglected children and state intervention simply to discipline families often became blurred.[157] At the peak of the asylum and placing-out movements, the mere prospect of future social disruptiveness was enough to justify transferring children from their own homes to an institution or a foster home in the country where a truer and finer "family life" might be experienced. City governments authorized child-saving agencies, such as the Society for the Prevention of Cruelty to Children (SPCC), to investigate cases of abuse and neglect. The agencies, in turn, actively scoured slum streets for children who, in their view, needed protection from a degenerate home life.

Official distrust of the poor, the negative impact of poverty on the single mother's ability to parent, and the burden of xenophobic, racist, and sexist assumptions fell heavily on women at a time when the diagnosis of family maladaption often derived from a perception of the mother as not adhering to prescribed female roles. Single and working mothers faced an especially high risk of involuntary child removal. Gordon's study of the records of the Massachusetts Society for the Prevention of Cruelty to Children (MSPCC) between 1880 and 1920 found an over-representation of single-mother households in child-neglect cases. During that period, 28 percent of all MSPCC cases involved single-mother households compared to a much higher 52 percent for the child-neglect cases. Single parenthood occurred in 50.5 percent of child-neglect cases, 25 percent of child-abuse cases, but only 19 percent of Boston families were headed by a woman. In cases of comparable severity, the agency removed children from 75 percent of single-mother homes and 54 percent of two-parent homes. Child removal against the wishes of single mothers occurred much more often than among two-parent families.[158]

Economic deprivation and employment clearly affected the single mother's ability to parent. But agency bias against single mothers also contributed to the large number accused of neglect. MSPCC workers diagnosed women as immoral 68.9 percent of the time compared to

31.1 percent for men, even though more men than women engaged in extramarital affairs. Agency workers also labeled single mothers immoral more often than other women even though the non-marital sexual relationship of single mothers frequently occurred in long-standing, common-law marriages not recognized by the agency.[159] According to Gordon, "The very definition of child neglect arose as part of an ideology about proper family life that automatically conceived of single mothers as inadequate."[160] Stansell, another historian of the same period, concluded, "Like, prostitutes mothers of street children became a kind of half-sex...outside the bounds of humanity by virtue of their inability or unwillingness to replicate the innate abilities of true womanhood."[161]

Reflecting such views, private charities offering "not alms but a friend" often encouraged widowed mothers having to work to surrender one or more of their children to an asylum. Many did. Indeed, asylums and child-placing agencies routinely accepted the children of poverty-stricken, intemperate or deserting parents who still were alive (e.g. half-orphans) along with children of deceased parents (e.g. full-orphans). Many institutions contained more half- than full-orphans. Most of the 1,894 children housed in Chicago's Protestant Orphan Asylum in 1875 had "one parent who for various reasons cannot care for children in a home of their own, yet can contribute to their support in the asylum by paying a small amount for board."[162] Disobedient or delinquent children not sent to orphanages went to juvenile reformatories without necessarily being convicted of a specific crime.[163]

Black children rarely appeared in the early child-welfare institutions of white society. Before the Civil War, slave-holders maintained or sold the orphaned children of black slaves while towns indentured the parentless children of free black women. The laws enacted by southern states after the War to regulate their ex-slave labor force often perpetuated the enslavement of black children. In 1865, Mississippi made all orphaned black children under age eighteen and those whose parents could not support them available for apprenticing. Former masters received preference. One law permitted the state to apprentice the children of deceased or impoverished freed slaves and free blacks to a competent and suitable person "*provided* that the former owner of said minor shall have the preference when in the opinion of the court, he or she shall be a suitable person for that purpose."[164] But the law denied black children the guarantees of food, clothing, and education written into indenture contracts for white children.[165]

After the Civil War, a small number of orphanages for black children appeared, mostly sponsored, if not managed, by whites. A few, supported at first by the limited resources of the black community, eventually received public funds.[166] Less singularly focused on proper family life, black leaders organized orphanages to "create a home for some of the many parentless and neglected boys and girls of our race" and to "take them off the streets and train not only their heads but hearts and hands as well, that they may become useful men and women." Like their white counterparts, blacks formed juvenile refuges as well to remove black children from the ignorance, vice, and shame of the late nineteenth-century city.[167]

Supposedly an improvement over the undifferentiated almshouse, orphan asylums and homes for juveniles housed large numbers of children under rigid and punitive conditions by the middle of the nineteenth century. Critics of institutional care also pointed to their extraordinarily high infant mortality rates, and low vitality and non-development among the children who survived. The rapid shift from "rehabilitation" to often abusive custodial care can be attributed to the prevailing theory of rehabilitation through incarceration and to the practice of incarcerating the children as well as the adults of "the dangerous classes."

Mounting criticism of the deteriorating asylums increased the popularity of the placing-out system, which used similar standards for judging parental competency. But this system, which shipped urban children to homes in the West and middle-West, also fell on hard times. Critics accused the placing-out agencies of not properly investigating their "foster" homes and of not following up on the children shipped to western farms. They also claimed that placing-out simply reproduced the colonial system of auctioning-off children: it created an informal indenture system in which farmers worked the children placed with them as seasonal labor and then drove them out or by maltreatment caused them to run away. Catholics regarded placing-out as a device for converting Catholic children by kidnapping them from the streets and placing them in mid-western Protestant homes. Western states complained that they became the depository for New York's vagrant, destitute, and delinquent children, most of whom ended up in reformatories, prisons, or as wards of the state.[168]

By the end of the century, after a long, sharp, and often bitter debate between the advocates of family versus institutional care, the thinking about the differential impact of home and institutions on children was reversed. The earlier preference for breaking up families as the most morally and economically efficient method of enforcing prevailing work and family norms and maintaining the future labor force lost some, if not all, of its favor. The criticisms of both asylums and the placing-out process paved the way for programs which encouraged the de-institutionalization of children and their placement in families. States began to regulate institutional care but also to support the placement of children in their own or a properly supervised foster home. Private agencies slowly replaced free placing-out with paid and supervised foster homes. In the early years of the twentieth century, states began to enact Mothers' Pension laws that provided financial support for poor children in their own homes. As the financial and political costs of socializing children and adults in institutions became too high, and as the rising labor force participation of women once again challenged patriarchal norms, the children of "worthy" parents were among the first to be de-institutionalized and sent back to be cared for by their mothers at home. This was made possible by renewed support for public assistance (outdoor relief) in the form of Mothers' Pensions. The campaign for Mothers' Pension was launched by middle-class women reformers who crusaded not only for mothers' aid but also for women's suffrage, labor laws to protect women at the workplace and maternal and child health programs. The shift toward Mothers' Pensions as a program just for worthy widows foreshadowed both the expanding role of government in social welfare programs. Products of their Victorian upbringing, the Progressive Era women reformers who led the successful campaigns were sympathetic to mothers and children but believed in the traditional male-headed family. Their disapproval of single mothers other an the "deserving widow, " helped to stigmatize both divorced, separated and unmarried women as immoral and unworthy or aid and the programs serving them.[169] As Chapter Six shows, even the deserving widows who qualified for a Mothers' Pension remained suspect and faced intrusive monitoring and supervision. By retaining the industrial family ethic, the developing public assistance system continued to deny poor women the "rights of womenhood."

Notes to Chapter 5

1. Dario Melossi and Massimo Pavarini, *The Prison and the Factory: Origins of the Penitentiary System* (Totowa, N.J.: Barnes and Noble Books, 1981), pp. 108-109; George Brown Tindall, *America: A Narrative History,* Volume I (New York: W.W. Norton & Company, 1981), pp. 449-450; John M. Blum, Bruce Catton, Edmond S. Morgan, Arthur M. Schlesinger, Jr., Kenneth M. Stampp, C. Vann Woodward, *The National Experience: A History of the United States* (New York: Harcourt, Brace & World, Inc., 1968, second edition), pp. 437-438.

2. Norman Ware, *The Industrial Worker,* 1840-1860 (Chicago: Quadrangle Books, 1964) p. 2; June Axinn and Herman Levin, *Social Welfare: A History of the American Response to Need* (New York: Harper & Row, 1975), p. 79.

3. Raymond A. Mohl, *Poverty in New York, 1783-1825* (New York: Oxford University Press, 1971), pp. 28-40.

4. Michael B. Katz, *Poverty and Policy in American History* (New York: Academic Press, 1983), pp. 10-13, 200.

5. *Ibid.,* p. 10.

6. *Ibid.,* pp. 10-13, 200.

7. Melossi and Pavarini (1981) *op. cit.,* p. 119; David Schneider, *The History of Public Welfare in New York State, 1609-1866* (Montclair, NJ: Patterson Smith, 1969), p. 218.

8. Mohl (1971) *op. cit.,* p. 91.

9. Blanche Coll, *Perspectives in Public Welfare: A History* (Washington D.C.: U.S. Government Printing Office, 1971), p. 48.

10. David M. Schneider and Albert Deutch, *The History of Public Welfare in New York State, 1867-1940* (Chicago: The University of Chicago Press, 1941), p. 36, 53.

11. Melossi and Pavarini (1981) *op. cit.,* p. 119.

12. Coll (1971) *op. cit.,* p. 30; Leah Hannah Feder, *Unemployment Relief in Periods of Depression* (New York: Russell Sage Foundation, 1936), p. 21.

13. Paul Tutt Stafford, *Government and the Needy, A Study of Public Assistance in New Jersey* (Princeton: Princeton University Press, 1941), p. 71.

14. Margaret Creech, *Three Centuries of Poor Law Administration: A Study of Legislation in Rhode Island* (Chicago: The University of Chicago Press, 1936), p. 193.

15. Joseph G. Rayback, *A History of American Labor* (New York: The Free Press, 1966), pp. 76-92.

16. Ware (1964) *op. cit.,* p. xi.

17. *Ibid.,* p. xv, citing *Baltimore Republican and Commercial Advertiser,* September 13, 1833; also p. 56.

18. Charles Loring Brace, *The Dangerous Classes* (Montclair, NJ: Patterson Smith, 1967), p. 322.

19. Paul Boyer, *Urban Masses and Moral Order in America, 1820-1920* (Cambridge: Harvard University Press, 1978), p. 69.

20. Barbara J. Berg, *The Remembered Gate: Origins of American Feminism— The Woman and the City, 1800-1860* (Oxford: Oxford University Press, 1978), p. 33, citing Alan Nevins (ed.) *The Diary of Philip Home* (New York: Arno Press, reprint, 1976), p. 142.

21. Boyer (1978) *op. cit.*, pp. 89, 327 (note 8).

22. New York Association For Improving the Conditions of the Poor, *Twenty-Eighth Annual Report* (New York, 1871), pp. 50-60; *Thirty-First Annual Report* (New York, 1874), pp. 52-60.

23. Robert H. Bremner, *From the Depths: The Discovery of Poverty in the United States* (New York: New York University Press, 1964), p. 8.

24. Gerald N. Grob, *Mental Institutions in America: Social Policy to 1875* (New York: The Free Press, 1973), p. 234.

25. August Meier and Elliott Rudwick, *From Plantation to Ghetto* (New York: Hill and Wang, 1976), p. 81.

26. Blum *et. al.*, (1968) *op. cit.*, p. 463.

27. Mohl (1971) *op. cit.*, pp. 28-30.

28. Thomas C. Cochran and William Miller, *The Age of Enterprise: A Social History of Industrial America* (New York: Harper & Row Publishers, 1961), p. 64.

29. *Ibid.*.

30. Alice Kessler-Harris, *Out to Work: A History of Wage Earning Women in the United States* (Oxford: Oxford University Press, 1981), p. 120.

31. Edith Abbott, *Women in Industry* (New York: D. Appleton and Company, 1910), p. 70, 81.

32. Kessler-Harris (1981) *op. cit.*, p. 59.

33. Lynn Y. Weiner, *From Working Girl to Working Mother: The Female Labor Force in the United States, 1820-1980* (Chapel Hill: The University of North Carolina, 1985), p. 37.

34. Carl N. Degler, *At Odds: Women and the Family in America from the Revolution to the Present* (Oxford: Oxford University Press, 1980), p. 152.

35. Benjamin J. Klebaner, "Poverty and Its Relief in American Thought, 1815-1861," in Frank R. Bruel and Steven J. Diner (eds.), *Compassion and Responsibility: Readings in the History of Social Welfare Policy in the United States* (Chicago: The University of Chicago Press, 1980), p. 116.

36. Julie A. Matthaei, *An Economic History of Women in America* (New York: Schocken Books, 1982), pp. 137-138.

37. Mohl (1971) *op. cit.*, p. 25.

38. Walter I Trattner, *From Poor Law to Welfare State: A History of Social Welfare in America* (New York: The Free Press, 1984, third edition), pp. 53-54.

39. Boyer (1978) *op. cit.*, p. 90.

40. Schneider (1969) *op. cit.*, p. 213.

41. New York Association For Improving the Condition of the Poor, *Seventeenth Annual Report* (New York, 1860), p. 31.

42. Boyer (1978) *op. cit.*, p. 90.

43. Brace (1880/1967) *op. cit.*, p. 165.

44. Boyer (1978) *op. cit.*, p. 39.

45. Richard A. Meckel, "Protecting the Innocents: Age Segregation and the Early Child Welfare Movement, *Social Service Review,* 59 (3) (September 1985), p. 464.

46. New York Association For Improving The Conditions of the Poor, *Eighth Annual Report* (New York, 1851), p. 19.

47. Coll (1971) *op. cit.*, p. 31.

48. Klebaner (1980) *op. cit.*, p. 390.

49. Thomas Cooper, *A Manual of Political Economy* (Washington, D.C., 1834), p. 95.

50. New York City Governors of the Almshouse, *Annual Reports,* 1849-1860.

51. Massachusetts General Court, Committee on Pauper Laws, *Report of Committee to Whom Was Referred the Consideration of the Pauper Laws of the Commonwealth, 1821,* excerpted in Sophonisba P. Breckinridge, *Public Welfare Administration in the United States, Selected Documents* (Chicago: University of Chicago Press, 1927), p. 37.

52. New York State Legislature, *Report and Other Papers on Subject of Laws for Relief and Settlement of Poor* in *Assembly Journal* (January 1824), pp. 386-399, excerpted in Breckinridge (1927) *op. cit.*, pp. 50-51.

53. Cited in Klebaner (1980) *op. cit.*, pp. 128-129.

54. Axinn and Levin (1975) *op. cit.*, p. 42.

55. Coll (1971) *op. cit.*, pp. 29-33.

56. David J. Rothman, *The Discovery of Asylum: Social Order and Disorder in the New Republic* (Boston: Little Brown and Company, 1971), pp. 180-186.

57. Coll (1971) *op. cit.*, p. 29-33.

58. Mary P. Ryan, *Womanhood in America From Colonial Times To The Present* (New York: New Viewpoints, 1975), pp. 100-101.

59. New York State Legislature, *Report and Other Papers on Subject of Laws For Relief and Settlement of Poor,* excerpted in Breckinridge, (1927) *op. cit.*, pp. 50-51.

60. New York City Governors of the Almshouse, *Annual Reports,* 1849-1860.

61. Richard Hofstadter, *Social Darwinism in American Thought* (Boston: The Beacon Press, 1965), p. 41, 57.

62. Barry J. Kaplan, "Reformers and Charity: The Abolition of Public Outdoor Relief in New York City, 1870-1898," *Social Service Review*, 52 (June 1978), p. 210, citing Department of Charities and Correction, *Sixteenth Annual Report* (1875), p. ii, ix, 201; *Eighteenth Annual Report* (1877), p. vii.

63. Coll (1971) op. cit, pp. 43-44, 58.

64. Amos G. Warner, *American Charities* (New York: Thomas Y. Crowell Company, 1908), pp. 226-243.

65. Elizabeth Wisner, *Social Welfare in the South: From Colonial Times to World War I* (Baton Rouge: Louisiana State University Press, 1970), pp. 67-85; Axinn and Levin (1975) *op. cit.*, p. 84; Jacqueline Jones, *Labor of Love, Labor of Sorrow: Black Women, Work and the Family From Slavery to the Present*, (New York: Basic Books, 1985), pp. 53-54.

66. Personal communication, Clarke A. Chambers, Professor of History and Social Work, University of Minnesota, August 1986.

67. W.E.B. Du Bois, "The Black Proletariat in South Carolina," in Edwin C. Rozwenc (ed.), *Reconstruction in the South* (Boston: D.C. Health and Company, 1952), p. 65.

68. Bremner (1964) *op. cit.*, pp. 33-35; Brian Gratton, "The Invention of Social Work: Welfare Reform in the Antebellum City," *Urban and Social Change Review*, 18 (1) (Winter 1985), p. 4.

69. Schneider (1969) *op. cit.*, p. 188.

70. Mohl (1971) *op. cit.*, p. 28.

71. New York City Association for Improving the Conditions of the Poor, *Fifteenth Annual Report* (New York, 1858), p. 38.

72. Schneider and Deutch (1941) *op. cit.*, p. 36.

73. Mohl (1971) *op. cit.*, p. 149.

74. New York City Association For Improving The Conditions of the Poor, *Fifteenth Annual Report* (New York, 1858), p. 38.

75. New York City Association For Improving The Conditions of the Poor, *Ninth Annual Report* (New York, 1852), pp. 20-22; *Fifteenth Annual Report* (New York, 1858), p. 36.

76. New York City Association For Improving The Conditions of the Poor, *First Annual Report* (New York, 1845), pp. 20-21.

77. Cited in Boyer (1978) *op. cit.*, p. 160.

78. Kaplan (1978), p. 209, citing Edward Devine, "Public Outdoor Relief," *Charities Review* (May-June, 1898), p. 809.

79. New York City Charity Organization Society, *Eighth Annual Report*, (New York, 1889), Appendix D.

80. Cited in Boyer (1978) *op. cit.*, p. 160.

81. Josephine Shaw Lowell, *Public Relief and Private Charity* (New York, 1884), pp. 89-111, excerpted in David J. Rothman and Shelia M. Rothman, *On Their Own: The Poor in Modern America* (Reading, Mass.: Addison-Wesley, 1972), p. 9.

82. Josephine Shaw Lowell, "One Means of Preventing Pauperism," *Proceedings, Sixth Annual Conference of Charities*, Boston, June 1879, pp. 189-200.

83. *Ibid.*

84. Dorothy Sterling, *We Are Your Sisters: Black Women in the Nineteenth Century* (New York: W.W. Norton & Company, 1984), p. 75.

85. Meier and Rudwick (1976) *op. cit.*, pp. 106-107.

86. Alvin B. Kogut, "The Negro and The Charity Organization Society in the Progressive Era," *Social Service Review*, 44 (1) (March 1970), pp. 11-21; Axinn and Levin (1975) *op. cit.*, pp. 82, 86-87; Trattner (1984) *op. cit.*, p. 85; Stephen Diner, "Chicago Social Workers and Blacks in the Progressive Era," *Social Service Review*, 44 (December 1970), pp. 393-410.

87. W.E.B. Du Bois (ed.), *Some Efforts Of American Negroes For Their Own Social Betterment: Report of an Investigation Under the Direction of Atlanta University*, together with the proceedings of the Third Conference for The Study of the Negro Problems, held at Atlanta University, May 25-26, 1898, in *Atlanta University Publications* (Numbers 1-6: 1896-1901) (New York: Octagon Books, 1968), p. 28.

88. Gerda Lerner, *The Majority Finds Its Past: Placing Women in History* (Oxford: Oxford University Press, 1979), p. 84; *Black Women in White America: A Documentary History* (New York: Vintage Books, 1973), pp. 450-458.

89. Massachusetts General Court, Committee on Pauper Laws, *Report of Committee to Whom Was Referred the Consideration of the Pauper Laws of the Commonwealth, 1821*, excerpted in Breckinridge (1927) *op. cit.*, p. 37.

90. Gratton (1985) *op. cit.*, p. 3.

91. New York State Legislature, *Report and Other Papers on Subject of Laws for Relief and Settlement of Poor* (in Assembly Journal [January 1824], pp. 386-399, excerpted in Breckinridge (1927), *op. cit*, pp. 50-51.

92. Warner (1908) *op. cit.*, p. 196.

93. Rothman (1971) *op. cit.*, p. 169.

94. Ryan (1975) *op. cit.*, pp. 100-101.

95. State of New York, *Report of the Secretary of State Relative to Statistics of the Poor* (Albany 1855), p. 58.

96. *Annual Report to the Governors of the Almshouse* (New York, 1851), p. 9, (New York, 1870), p. 247.

97. Katz (1983) *op. cit.*, p. 76.

98. *Ibid.*, p. 246, T. A. 6.

99. *Ibid.*, pp. 72-86; 245, T. A. 5; 249, T.A. 9.

100. Mohl (1971) *op. cit.,* p. 95.

101. Katz (1983) *op. cit.,* pp. 267, T. A. 30; 113-119.

102. David Rothman (1971) *op. cit.,* p. 188, citing Massachusetts General Court, Committee on Pauper Laws, *Report of 1821,* p. 23 (aka the *Quincy Report*).

103. Schneider (1969) *op. cit.,* p. 244.

104. Rothman (1971) *op. cit.,* p. 187.

105. *Ibid.,* p. 195.

106. Rothman (1971) *op. cit.,* p. 187.

107. Katz (1983) *op. cit.,* p. 114.

108. New York State, Governors of the Almshouse, *Annual Report* (1880), p. 94. In 1871 the male patients housed at the Lunatic Asylum on Blackwell's Island, New York, were transferred to the new mental asylum on Ward's Island. The female inmates remained at the original site.

109. Ellen Dwyer, "The Weaker Vessel: Legal Versus Social Reality in Mental Commitments In Nineteenth-Century New York," in D. Kelly Weisberg (ed.), *Women and the Law: The Social Historical Perspective,* Volume One (Cambridge: Schenkman Publishing Company, Inc., 1982), p. 88.

110. Henry M. Hurd, *The Institutional Care of the Insane in the United States and Canada,* Volume III (Baltimore: The Johns Hopkins Press, 1916), pp. 710-713.

111. *Ibid.,* p. 713.

112. Personal communication with Clarke A. Chambers, Professor of History and Social Work, University of Minnesota, January 1987.

113. Rothman (1971) *op. cit.,* p. 284.

114. Grob (1973) *op. cit.,* pp. 231, 238.

115. *Ibid.,* p. 241.

116. *Ibid.,* p. 234.

117. Hurd (1916) *op. cit.,* p. 603.

118. Grob (1973) *op. cit.,* pp. 250-251.

119. *Ibid.,* pp. 252-254.

120. *Ibid.,* p. 244.

121. Quoted in *Ibid.,* p. 247.

122. *Ibid.,* pp. 245-246.

123. *Ibid.,* p. 178.

124. *Ibid.*

125. Grob (1973) *op. cit.,* pp. 168-169.

126. Daniel J. Walkowitz and Peter R. Eisenstadt, "The Psychology of Work: Work and Mental Health in Historical Perspective," *Radical History Review,* 34 (1986), pp. 8, 10.

127. Rothman (1971) *op. cit.,* p. 152.

128. Walkowitz and Eisenstadt (1986) *op. cit.,* p. 10.

129. Grob (1973) *op. cit.,* p. 178.

130. Walkowitz and Eisenstadt (1986) *op. cit.,* p. 11.

131. *Ibid.,* pp. 11-12.

132. See Grob (1973) *op. cit.;* David J. Rothman (1971) *op. cit.,* pp. 188; 192-205; Andrew T. Scull, *Decarceration: Community Treatment and the Deviant—A Radical View* (Englewood Cliffs, N.J.: Prenctice-Hall, Inc., 1977), pp. 20-29.

133. Ohio Board of State Charities, "Seventh Annual Report" [1867] pp. 249-250, in Robert Bremner (ed.), *Children and Youth in America,* Vol. II (Cambridge: Harvard University Press, 1971).

134. Mrs. C.R. Lowell, "One Means of Preventing Pauperism," *Proceedings, Sixth Annual Conference of Charities,* Chicago, June 1879, p. 194.

135. Meckel (1985) *op. cit.,* p. 469.

136. Schneider and Deutch (1941) *op. cit.,* p. 62, citing New York State Board of Charities, *Seventeenth Annual Report* (1883), pp. 44-45.

137. Trattner (1984) *op. cit.,* p. 113; Warner (1908) *op. cit.,* p. 280.

138. John Lewis Gillin, *Poverty and Dependency* (New York: The Century Co., 1921), p. 343.

139. Meckel (1985) *op. cit.,* p. 463; Warner (1908) *op. cit.,* p. 187.

140. *Ibid.,* p. 464, quoting Boston Children's Aid Society, *Thirteenth Annual Report* (Boston, 1877), pp. 3-4, and p. 463, citing Charles Loring Brace.

141. Schneider and Deutch, (1941) *op. cit.,* pp. 66-67; Warner (1908) *op. cit.,* pp. 274-277.

142. Rothman (1971) *op. cit.,* pp. 222-223.

143. *Ibid.,* p. 224.

144. *Ibid.,* p. 214, citing Orphan House of Charleston, South Carolina, *Proceedings of the Sixty-Sixth Anniversary* (Charleston, South Carolina, 1855), p. 50.

145. Rothman (1971) *op. cit.,* p. 230.

146. *Ibid.,* p. 220.

147. *Ibid.,* p. 214, citing Boston Asylum and Farm School, *Report for 1845* (Boston, 1845) pp. 6, 15; *Report for 1849* (Boston 1849), p. 12; *Report for 1842* (Boston, 1842), p. 7.

148. Rothman (1971) *op. cit.,* p. 214.

149. *Ibid.,* p. 236.

150. *Ibid.,* p. 262.

151. *Ibid.,* pp. 261-262.

152. *Ibid.*

153. See Michael Katz for a critique of this report and a re-examination of the data. Katz suggests that prevailing and largely negative predispositions toward the poor and methodological biases distorted the original study and its findings. Katz's re-examination of the data suggest a less victim-blaming, more accurate picture of poverty, its victims and causes.

154. Schneider and Deutch (1941) *op. cit.,* p. 27.

155. Rev. William Frederic Slocum, Jr., "Drunkard's Families," *The Council: A Monthly Essay on Organized Charity,* Vol. I, No. 5 (October 1888), pp. 2-3.

156. Meckel (1985) *op. cit.,* p. 471.

157. For the debate as to whether state intervention increased or decreased over time see among others Jacques Donzelot, *The Policing of Families* (New York: Pantheon, 1979); Kenneth Keniston and the Carnegie Council on Children, *All Our Children: The American Family Under Pressure* (New York: Harcourt Brace Jovanovich, 1978); Christopher Lasch, *Culture of Narcissism* (New York: Warner Books, 1977) and *Haven in a Heartless Land* (New York: Basic Books, 1979); Ann Vandepol, "Dependent Children: Child Custody and Mothers' Pensions," *Social Problems,* 29(3) (February 1982), pp. 221-235; Eli Zaretsky, *Capitalism, The Family and Personal Life* (New York: Harper and Row Publishers, 1973).

158. Linda Gordon, "Single Mothers and Child Neglect, 1880-1920," *American Quarterly* 37(2) (Summer 1985), p. 178.

159. *Ibid.,* pp. 178-179.

160. *Ibid.,* p. 174.

161. Christine Stansell, "Women, Children, and the Uses of the Streets: Class and Gender Conflict in New York City, 1850-1860," *Feminist Studies* 8 (Summer 1982), pp. 321-322.

162. Ann Vandepol (1985) *op. cit.,* p. 224, citing Robert H.Bremner (ed.) *Children and Youth in America,* Vol. 2, (Cambridge: Harvard University Press, 1972), p. 272; Grace Abbott, *The Child and the State* (Chicago: University of Chicago Press, 1938), p. 230.

163. Rothman (1971) *op. cit.,* p. 207.

164. John Hope Franklin, "Public Welfare In The South During The Reconstruction Era, 1865-88," *Social Service Review,* 44 (December 1970), p. 386.

165. Axinn and Levin (1975) *op. cit.,* p. 83.

166. Andrew Billingsley and Jeann M .Giovannoni, *Children of the Storm: Black Children and American Child Welfare* (New York: Harcourt Brace, 1972), pp. 51-55.

167. W.E.B. Du Bois (ed.), "Some Efforts of American Negeroes For Their Own Social Betterment," *op. cit.* (1896\1968), pp. 28-36.

168. Merckel (1985) *op. cit.,* p. 463; Schneider and Deutch (1941) *op. cit.,* pp. 72-74, 163-169.

169. Linda Gordon, *Pitied But Not Entitled: Single Mothers and the History of Welfare 1890-1935*. (New York: Free Press, 1994).

6

Poor Women and Progressivism

Protective Labor Law and Mothers' Pensions

At the turn of the century, as industrial capitalism once again transformed American society, heightened inequality generated widespread concern and unrest. The rise of giant corporations, the ruthless and unregulated pursuit of profits by "robber barons," and the growing concentration of wealth and power in the hands of a few contrasted sharply with increasingly hazardous working conditions and deepening poverty among the many. Despite an overall increase in the standard of living, low wages, irregular work, and unsafe jobs threw many women and men deep into poverty where, without needed resources, they experienced considerable difficulty in forming families, raising children, staying healthy, and simply surviving.

Between 1896 and World War I, social, economic, and political tensions intensified. The labor movement regained lost ground, the women's rights movement fought for the vote, and pressure to reform the urban-industrial environment spread to segments of the middle class.[1] Progressivism, the name given the social reform movement that emerged at this time, sought to modify the imperfections of capitalism without overthrowing it. Led largely by corporate leaders and middle-class reformers, Progressivism called for greater state involvement in the political economy in spheres where voluntary solutions seemed to have failed. Its program included state regulation of the market to prevent cut-throat business competition from undercutting industrial profits and state action to assure the maintenance and reproduction of the working class. The growing scarcity of labor, higher skill requirements, and capital's interest in economic stability heightened conflicts between the profitable accumulation of capital and the preservation of human resources. Reckless exploitation of labor became increasingly unprofitable, at least for the largest firms.[2] Progressives saw that, left to itself, the system of production—mechanization, the excessively long work day, and a record number of industrial accidents and deaths—reduced the efficiency of capital and the productivity of labor. Factory conditions weakened the health and stamina of employees, shortened their productive lives, jeopardized the reproductive capacity of the average woman, and otherwise threatened to "exhaust" the labor force faster than it could regenerate itself. Poor conditions also left workers less satisfied, less willing and able to work, and more interested in unionization. Overcrowded and unsanitary tenements in urban neighborhoods also made "productive" living very difficult. After private efforts to establish corporate benefit plans and harmonious labor-management relations met with only minimal success, big business turned to the state to absorb the costs of assuring the health, productivity, and longevity of the labor force.

The state also began to regulate the lives of working women, mediating the growing tension between the endless use of cheap female (and child) labor to keep profits up and the ever-present need for women's reproductive labor at home to maintain the working class as a whole. Low pay, long hours, and poor working conditions not only diminished women's physical capacity at work but risked interfering with reproduction. Working women also challenged patriarchal arrangements by seeming to threaten male jobs, the sex-segregation of the labor market, and the control of women's labor by individual men.[3]

The Progressive Era, often described in romantic terms, witnessed numerous efforts at social reform, including legislative campaigns for compulsory health insurance, workers' compensation, a shorter work week, minimum wages, public health programs, better housing, mothers' pensions, and an end to child labor. Even more universal and redistributive social insurance programs for the aged and unemployed, already developed in many European countries but not yet accepted in the United States, were explored.

With the emergence of Progressivism came the understanding that failing to allocate adequate economic resources to families interfered with patriarchal family life, the reproduction and maintenance of the working class, and the social peace. Perhaps more than individual suffering, dislocations in the spheres of production and reproduction gradually elicited state intervention. The profitable accumulation of capital and the maintenance of patriarchal arrangements increasingly depended on state policy to stabilize the market, protect workers against the worst abuses of individual employers, improve labor's capacity and willingness to work, secure the loyalty of the working class, and regulate women's home and work lives. The development of an increasingly complex, unstable, and interdependent economy intensified conflict between the needs of production and reproduction and fears of class polarization, the radicalization of labor, and general social unrest gradually rendered the laissez-faire doctrine of minimal state action less effective to the dominant class.

The broader understanding of poverty that emerged at this time justified state action on behalf of the poor. Most observers still explained poverty as the result of an individual's lack of industry, moral unfitness, or flawed genes. But by the end of the nineteenth century, changing conditions paved the way for a more social view. The irregular employment during the Depression of 1893, chronically low wages, poor housing, lack of health care, as well as advances in medicine, data gathered by scientific charity workers, a more skeptical attitude towards the rich, and the stark contrast between poverty and plenty all contributed to a new definition of poverty as a result of "social evils," circumstances outside and beyond the control of the individual.[4] In her 1910 study of wage-earning women, for example, Annie MacLean wrote,

> Under present industrial organization some groups bear an undue burden of the hardships of life, and in as much as this is largely the result of accident of birth or of training, it would seem that a truly democratic people would feel impelled to eliminate, wherever possible, the element of unfairness from the struggle, and remove the handicaps for which society is responsible.[5]

The Progressives, Working Women, and The Home

Fears about the reproduction and maintainenance of the working class as well as weakening patriarchal prerogatives in face of women's growing labor force participation underpinned Progressive Era interest

in the adverse effects of women's employment. Post-Civil War industrial expansion opened interesting new jobs for many middle-class
women as nurses, teachers, and clerical workers and increased the
demand for women in the domestic, service, and factory jobs they
already occupied.[6] Most of the beneficiaries were white, however, as
few of the new jobs were opened to black women. Despite their high
proportions in the urban labor force, less than 3 percent of all black
women workers held better paying manufacturing jobs, compared to
21 percent of foreign-born and 38 percent of native-born white working women.[7] Most urban black women simply continued to work as
cooks, domestics, seamstresses, laundresses, and unskilled laborers,
often in highly degrading circumstances.[8] The majority of black
women still lived in rural areas and worked with their families as
sharecroppers. Some middle-class black wives withdrew their labor
from the fields in favor of homemaking (and faced ridicule and
resistance from whites for their efforts to comply with the family
ethic),[9] while a few others worked as midwives and teachers, but the
black community could not support these services very well in 1900.[10]

The new and growing presence of white women in the labor force
stimulated Progressive Era concerns about women's employment.
Between 1880 and 1914, their wages and working conditions became
the topic of numerous government investigations, foundation reports,
and journalistic exposes, most of which painted a bleak picture of
economic exploitation or lost morality.[11]

Two legislative campaigns in the early years of the century—
for Protective Labor Laws and Mothers' Pensions-captured the
issues. Protective Labor Laws sought to regulate women's working
conditions while Mothers' Pensions were designed to enable single
women to raise their children properly by staying at home. The
Protective Labor law campaign which focused on the negative
impact of unregulated working conditions on women's reproductive capacity also revealed concerns that women's entry into the
labor market would disrupt the sex-segregation of jobs.
Reformers worried as well that the labor force might seduce
young, white, native-born, middle-class "girls" away from marriage and family life, leading the "respectable" single working
girl into a life of sin. The Mothers' Pension movement, which
highlighted the importance of maternal supervision to child
development, focused on previously married women without
means, most of whom were either widows or divorced mothers.
Mounting dissatisfaction with the children's institutions and
the foster-care system described in Chapter Five provided
additional support for the new program. But beneath these
issues lay deeper worries about competition by women for men's

jobs and about the "quality" of future workers. Despite the wide scope of both legislative efforts, they primarily favored women who approximated the terms of the family ethic. The Protective Labor Law reformers sought to protect "respectable" single working girls, while Mothers' Pension reformers hoped to assist "deserving" poor widows. In the end, reform helped to mediate the demands for women's home and market labor, marginalized women workers, and enforced the ideology of women's roles. The laws, in effect, protected women from the worst abuses of industrial development while benefiting capital and vesting more patriarchal power in the state.

Protecting the "Working Girl"

Concerns about the employment of single women surfaced shortly after the Civil War when commentators began to complain about the "New Departure," a term for the rising labor-force participation of young white women. By the turn of the century, 41 percent of all single women worked outside the home.[12] The simultaneous revolution in morals and manners among educated, middle-class women made working women even more threatening to the *status quo* and the durability of the family ethic.

Progressive reformers strongly believed that working and living away from home jeopardized the virtue of young single women. Without the anchor of domesticity, young working women risked succumbing to sin. An 1889 government survey of over 17,000 women employed in twenty-two cities exhorted women to avoid jobs that mixed the sexes because such jobs created "laxity," and threatened the virtue of even the best intentioned "young ladies." The document also discouraged racially mixed jobs. "The moral tendencies of the Philadelphia working women are of a distinctly high order," the Report observed, but in Richmond, "in the tobacco factories, where the races are mixed, immorality is much more noticeable than elsewhere."[13] After thirty-six public meetings and 258 witnesses, an 1895 New York State Assembly committee investigating the "condition of female labor" concluded that "from this terrible and unprecedented condition of affairs arises untold misery, immorality, and crime."[14] The U.S. Senate's nineteen-volume study of employed women and children, published in 1910, asked: "Is the trend of modern industry dangerous to the character of women?"[15] Rising employment among working-class women also generated widespread panic about white slavery and prostitution.[16]

Reformers also argued that employment distracted white women from marriage and motherhood: instead of looking for a husband and acquiring homemaking skills, young girls devoted their best energies to earning a living, learning useless tasks, developing a taste for extravagance, and nurturing dissatisfaction with mundane domestic life. The Birmington *Labor Advocate* declared that "the girl who works downtown every day cannot become much of a housekeeper." The writer added that only "Housekeeping makes housekeepers."[17] To another observer, working women risked becoming "mentally and morally unfit for [their] economic office in the family."[18] Work might also coarsen the feminine sensibilities necessary for marriage. Experts told white working women to avoid employments which might make them "bold, fierce, muscular, brawny in body or mind," and advised them instead to enter "women's jobs" which protected their morality and femininity.[19]

Others suggested that work by young daughters threatened the authority structure of the family, especially within immigrant homes. One observer noted,

> The girl accepts the standards of the new world rather than those of the home, not infrequently she becomes discontented with her home and ashamed of her parents. She chafes under the authority, becomes impatient with narrow conditions...seeks freedom from home responsibilities...and justifies herself by the claim, "I am earning my own and can do as I please."[20]

Parents feared their daughters' autonomy, even though many contributed money to their families and remained financially dependent on them. Finally, many authorities maintained that work interfered with women's ability to reproduce and parent. In *Muller v. Oregon* (1908), the landmark Supreme Court case that upheld the constitutionality of reducing the work day for women laundry workers to ten hours, Louis Brandeis and Josephine Goldmark argued that work endangered female reproductive and mothering capacities. Reflecting prevailing medical knowledge and the period's preoccupation with conserving human resources, they won their case by maintaining that

> women's physical structure and the performance of maternal functions place her at a disadvantage in the struggle for subsistence...This is especially true when the burdens of motherhood are upon her. Even when they are not, by abundant testimony of the medical fraternity continuance for a long time on her feet at work, repeating this from day to day, tends to injurious effects upon the body, and, as healthy mothers are essential to vigorous

offspring, the physical well-being of women become an object of public interest and care in order to preserve the strength and vigor of the race.[21]

Concerns about women living and working away from home rarely extended to the many young southern black women who had migrated alone to cities in the Northeast in search of new opportunities and a better life. A 1905 Census Bureau survey of 1,000 black female wage-earners in Manhattan found that nearly 42 percent were unmarried and less than twenty-four years old.[22] The large number of single, black women in northern cities produced an imbalanced sex ratio. In 1900, there were 116 black females to 100 males in Philadelphia and 124 to 100 in New York City. The majority of black families included two parents, but by 1905, fully one-quarter of all adult black women in New York City—many young and single—lived alone or in a lodging house.[23]

The contradiction between abusive working conditions and the family ethic's expectations for "respectable" white women led some middle-class reformers, many of them women, to find ways to protect the health, morals, and future family life of single, working women. Female benevolent societies such as The Working Women's Protective Union, the Working Girls' Society, and the Travelers Aid Society were established to shield young working women from the "evils" of city life. Settlement houses, which also appeared at this time, assisted women traveling from farm to town, provided supervised boarding homes to city dwellers, and established recreational clubs to keep young women away from dance halls, theaters, and saloons. While some settlement houses promoted unionization, legislative reform, and social action, most attempted to teach self-supporting women domestic values, distract them from the protests of their activist sisters, and reinforce general societal assumptions about women's proper role.[24]

Black reformers adopted similar strategies. Derived from "the historic self-help impulse that had characterized black communities since the era of slavery, the strategies were not just parallel or segregated versions of urban progressive reform."[25] The "Old Black Elite" (prosperous blacks, long-term northerners) and the wives of a new class of black businessmen and professionals assisted many young black working women in programs coordinated by the National Urban League (founded in 1911), the National League for the Protection of Colored Women, the National Association of Colored Women, and others. With chapters in numerous cities, these groups organized social clubs, employment services, recreation facilities, day nurseries, nutrition and hygiene courses, and homes for young working women and the elderly. Black service organizations also employed social workers and attempted to introduce domestic servants to northern standards of household maintenance.[26]

The White Rose Mission, for example, founded in 1897, protected domestics from exploitive city employment bureaus that preyed on newly arrived black female migrants from the South. It later became a settlement house, as did the Working Girls' Home Association, opened originally as a shelter for black women denied admission to Cleveland's YWCA.[27] The Phyllis Wheatly Home for black working women, one of the more well-known establishments, opened in Chicago in 1908 "to solve the problem of befriending the colored girls and women who come into this great city seeking work, often without relatives, friends or money."[28]

While some Progressive Era reformers focused on socializing young, working women toward marriage and motherhood, others lobbied for laws to improve women's low wages and hazardous working conditions. After the labor movement failed to secure a shorter work day for all workers, advocates of the ten-hour day made a strategic decision to seek redress on behalf of women workers alone. The above noted *Muller v. Oregon* decision handed down by the Supreme Court in 1908 legalized the ten-hour day and established the precedent for future protective labor laws. Armed with this court sanction, progressives lobbied states for higher wages, shorter hours, and safer working conditions for women as well as for upgraded domestic work. Between 1909 and 1917, forty-one states wrote new or improved hours laws for women, limited night work, restricted the number of pounds women could lift on the job, and required employers to provide seats to women workers and clerks in department stores.

In the end, the protections granted to women worked against them. Protective labor legislation based on motherhood, female frailty, and special privileges for the home became a justification for barring women from certain occupations (particularly the higher paid ones occupied by men) and segregating women into low paid "women's jobs." It contributed to the preservation of a sex-segregated labor market, the relative subordination of women to men, and the overall marginalization of women workers. To the extent that they created barriers, the laws channeled women back into the home and thus helped to mediate the conflict between production and reproduction.

Working-class women also organized on their own behalf, further challenging the family ethic's implied prohibition against social activism by women. They formed their own protective leagues, cooperatives, self-help groups, and trade unions, seeking support from one another as well as better pay on the job. Laundresses, cap makers, ladies' garment workers, shoe workers, and others united for action in the late 1880s, assisted at times by The Women's Trade Union League (WTUL), a federation of women's unions and middle-class sympathizers. The Knights of Labor, a national labor organization that opened its doors to women and blacks, claimed 500,000 members in 1886, 10 percent of whom were women. But when the American Federation of Labor (AFL) became the dominant labor organization in the late 1880s, the number of female unionists fell. A 1905 national survey of fifteen occupations found that 20 percent of the men but only 3 percent of the women belonged to unions. Only 1.5 percent of women in industrial jobs were union members in 1910, down from 3.3 percent in 1900.[29]

Women organizers faced ridicule from a public which equated trade unionism with communism and European revolutionaries and which regarded active women trade unionists as prostitutes and "unsexed female incendiaries."[30] Male opposition also helps explain the low numbers of unionized women. Samuel Gompers, the President of the newly formed AFL, and many of his followers, subscribed to the domestic code and opposed both work by wives and the organization of employed women. One labor paper argued, that "sisters and daughters" should not leave home, even for congenial workshops and factories, and vowed to check this "most unnatural invasion of our firesides."[31] Despite tight occupational segregation, white, working-class men feared the threat of underpaid female labor to their jobs as well as the challenge wage-earning women presented to patriarchal arrangements at home.

Despite a small and declining union membership, working women remained active. Chicago unions organized some 35,000 women in twenty-six trades in 1903.[32] Some 20,000 New York shirtwaist makers sustained a thirteen week walk-out in 1909. Another 40,000 Chicago garment workers struck Hart, Schaffner, and Marx in 1911. The following year, thousands of women textile workers, in what became known as the Bread and Roses strike, walked out of the mills in Lawrence, Massachusetts.[33]

Organization among black women was especially difficult because most worked individually as domestics in private homes rather than collectively in hotels and restaurants. Moreover, neither the AFL nor The Women's Trade Union League placed high priority on the unionization of the country's two million black women workers. Nonetheless, black domestics formed organizations such as the Association of Women Wage-Earners to promote self-reliance, assess wages and working conditions, teach domestic science, provide job placement services, and serve as agent between employers and employees. After World War I, some mainstream unions began to make efforts to unionize black female domestics.[34]

The Working Mother and Mothers' Pensions

In 1910, the majority[35] of all working women were single, but the employment of married women was on the rise. It jumped from 14 percent of all women workers in 1900 to more than 24 percent in 1910. That year, 11 percent of all married women worked for wages—double the number that had done so in 1900.[36] Nonetheless, as noted above, the Progressive Era controversy over female employment focused heavily on the young single "working girl." Lack of attention to married women reflected their smaller numbers but also their race, ethnic, and class characteristics: married women workers tended to be black, immigrant, and extremely poor.[37] Along with unwed mothers and older women, they could be easily dismissed as "heredity workers" and the "other girls."[38] It was the young, white, single woman that reformers viewed as temporarily caught in an unfortunate situation that required her to work.

One exception to this pattern of ignoring married women workers was the attention devoted to the small number of educated, middle-class married women who rejected prevailing sexual conventions, espoused sexual equality, and chose work as an alternative to domestic life.[39] Another exception was the poor but worthy widow forced to give up her children because she had to work to support them. Fifteen percent of all working women were widowed or divorced in 1910 due to shorter male life expectancy, very high occupational death rates, and the mounting divorce rate, which jumped from 53 per 100,000 in 1890 to 84 per 100,000 in 1906,[40] excluding separations and desertions, more common among the poor. Thirty-five percent of widowed and divorced women worked. The numbers were especially high in major urban areas. A 1914 study of 370 working women on Manhattan's West Side discovered that widows and deserted wives comprised 43 percent. Another survey of six working-class districts in Philadelphia reported 237 widows, 146 deserted wives, and 12 divorcees among 728 married women at work.[41] Husbandless women frequently entered the labor force because their families were poor. Working-class families had greater difficulty protecting themselves against the premature death or the loss of a male breadwinner because of the absence of savings, private pensions, and a social insurance program.

Public opinion about poor "widows" (many divorced women referred to themselves as widows at this time) focused more on their ability to care for their children than on their working conditions. By and large, the interest in the working mother reflected the Progressive Era's preoccupation with children as a national resource and the conservation of human resources rather than the needs of women themselves.[42] To Progressives, observed the historian Robert Wiebe, "the child was the carrier of tomorrow's hope...Protect him [sic], nurture him, and in his manhood he would create that bright new world of the progressive's vision."[43]

According to this view, a mother's employment negatively influenced her child's development. The United States Industrial Commission concluded in 1902 that married women weakened by hard work would give birth to sickly children, thus weakening the "physical and moral strength of the generation of working people."[44] The "prime function of women," concluded MacLean in her 1910 study of wage-earning women,

> was not to work for wages or to produce commodities, but "must ever be the perpetuation of the race. If these other activities render her physically or morally unfit for the discharge of this larger social duty, then woe to the generation that not only permits but encourages such wanton prostitution of function. The woman is worth more to society in dollars and cents as the mother of healthy children than as the swiftest labeler of cans.[45]

The 1914 Report of the New York State Commission on Relief For Widowed Mothers claimed that "No woman, save in exceptional circumstances can be both homemaker and the breadwinner of her family."[46] It concluded that,

> Many thousands of widowed mothers in the State of New York...are obliged to deprive [their] children of motherly attention and training in order to give themselves over to wage earning work...and...are unable to provide their children with a proper measure of the necessities of life...They cannot in such cases be successful mothers because they are too much distracted by wage-earning. They cannot be successful wage-earners because they are too much distracted by child life in their hearts and home. The children suffer in soul and body both. They get neither proper material care nor proper physical support.[47]

The Commission found that the work available to poor women "outside the home inevitably breaks down the physical, mental, and moral strength of the family and disrupts the home life through an inadequate standard of living and parental neglect, due to the enforced absence of the mother at the time the children most need her care."[48]

Although white commentators largely ignored their condition, black leaders made similar observations about destitute black mothers. A speaker at the second Atlanta University conference on "problems of negro city life," held in Georgia in 1900, attributed the high infant mortality among blacks "to the fact that negro mothers are, as a rule, obliged to work out [of the home], thus leaving their homes and children, which is not only the cause of infant mortality, but also of neglected child life." The conference recommended, among other things, "reform in the family life of the negro" and "greater care and attention…to the home and training of negro children.…It is desirable that parents' associations and mothers' meetings should be organized among them, and that day nurseries should be provided for negro children, in the enforced absence of their parents."[49]

The negative evaluation of maternal employment among both blacks and whites meant that working mothers were blamed for juvenile delinquency and other problems faced by children. The "lack of a mother's hand," it was argued, led children to roam the streets and fall into bad company. Judge Pinckney from the Chicago juvenile court favored home care over institutions because "Many of these unfortunate children who never had a decent chance…grow up into depraved manhood and womanhood and drift naturally into that great and ever increasing army of criminals who are a menace to society."[50]

Despite these perceptions, few day nurseries existed for the children of working mothers and most working mothers could not afford individual child care.[51] Strict eligibility rules excluded still others. One charity worker reported that nurseries did not admit "those cases where the mother works from a mere whim or the desire to have a little more in the way of a dress or furniture or even money saved, or for any reason wishes to shirk the care of her children. The mother's place is in the home except in cases of absolute necessity." Some centers required proof that the children had been born to married mothers.[52] Of the small number of subsidized day nurseries found mostly in large cities,[53] few were located in working-class or black neighborhoods. As late as 1933, less than forty day nurseries in the United States accepted black children whose access to public kindergartens was also blocked.[54]

To remedy the adverse effect of maternal employment, Progressives launched a campaign for Mothers' Pensions, a program of cash aid to indigent mothers without breadwinners to enable them to remain at home with their children—the future labor force. According to Grace Abbott, a social reformer at the time, the acceptance of Mothers' Pensions "constituted public recognition by the states that the contribution of the unskilled or semiskilled mothers in their own homes exceeded their earnings outside the home and that it was in the public interest to conserve their child-rearing functions."[55] However, as the program developed, it served only a small number of women in need. Most of those who qualified for aid turned out to be both widowed and white.

Concerns about working mothers and the quality of the future labor force actually appeared before the turn of the century, prior to the campaign for Mothers' Pensions. The 1890 National Conference of Charities and Correction heard speakers advocate "family aid so mothers could stay home with their children."[56] Ten years earlier, California had subsidized local relief programs to help mothers keep their children out of the labor market. In 1906, some California counties granted aid to children in their own homes and in 1911, the counties began to receive state reimbursement for this.[57] Only the successful opposition of the Charity Organization Society (COS) in 1897-1898 kept New York City from authorizing the Commissioner of Charities to place children in the custody of their mothers and provide them with an allowance equal to the amount otherwise allotted for institutional care.[58] In 1898, the New York City's Department of Public Charities arranged for COS to screen commitment petitions for those families deemed suitable to receive public aid at home instead of placing the child in an institution.[59] In 1908, Oklahoma provided "school scholarships" to the widowed mother of a school-age child in an amount equal to the earnings of the child when the child's wages were necessary for the support of the mother. In 1911, Michigan enacted a similar law requiring payment from school funds of a sum not to exceed $3 per week to indigent parents to enable their children to attend school.[60] New Jersey ruled in 1910 that the state could pay board to mothers for the care of their children.[61]

A key turning point in state responsibility for the care of dependent children occurred at the 1909 White House Conference on Children which officially sanctioned the idea that poverty alone should not disrupt the home. The often cited Conference Report concluded that

> Home life is the highest and finest product of civilization. It is the great molding force of mind and character. Children should not

be deprived of it except for urgent and compelling reasons. Children of parents of worthy character, suffering from temporary misfortune and children of reasonably efficient and deserving mothers who are without the support of a normal breadwinner, should as a rule be kept with their parents, such aid being given as may be necessary to maintain suitable homes for the rearing of children.[62]

This historic Conference which signaled a new relationship between women, the family, and the state focused almost exclusively on the white family. Only two black leaders, both southern males, were among the hundreds of invited participants. Both men, Dr. Booker T. Washington, President of Tuskeegee Institute, and Dr. Richard Carroll, manager of the South Carolina Industrial Home for Destitute and Dependent Colored Children, were known for their public acceptance of segregation. Conference participants not only ignored the large number of black women and men engaged in the provision of child welfare services (many of whom attended the Atlanta University conference on "Efforts for Social Betterment Among Negro Americans" held that same year), but their papers contained no mention of black children.[63]

The first Mothers' Pension law in the United States appeared in Missouri, two years after the White House Conference, but it was restricted to one county. Illinois enacted the first statewide program in June of that same year. The new legislation, which won ready support from all but the private charity organization societies, spread rapidly through the states after 1913. Twenty-seven of the forty-two state legislatures in session in 1913 considered Mothers' Pension legislation. Seventeen passed laws raising the total number of states to twenty, sixteen in the West or Midwest. Eight more states passed laws in 1915, and by the end of the decade there were thirty-nine, plus the territories of Alaska and Hawaii. By 1921, forty of the forty-eight states had adopted some form of Mothers' Pension law. The southern states with the largest concentration of blacks, however, were the last to join up. By 1933, neither Georgia, Alabama, nor South Carolina had legislated a pension program.[64] Comprehensive implementation of the laws lagged behind their quick passage since nearly all were permissive rather than mandatory. At no point prior to the 1935 Social Security Act did more than half the counties in the United States actually provide Mothers' Pensions.[65]

The success of the Mothers' Pension campaign reflected a convergence of several important social welfare trends including: (1) states' heightened interest in children as a human resource, (2) growing criticism of existing child-saving methods, (3) the emergence of the social work profession with new techniques for managing family life, and (4) the professionalization of public welfare.

The States' Interest in a Future Labor Force

President Roosevelt clearly expressed the states' interest in protecting the future labor force at the 1909 White House Conference on Children. Referring to the large number of children in institutions, he told Congress that

> The interests of the nation are involved in the welfare of this army of children no less than in our great material affairs. Each of these children represents a potential addition to the productive capacity and the enlightened citizenship of the Nation, or if allowed to suffer from neglect, a potential addition to the destructive forces of the community. The ranks of criminal and other enemies of society are recruited in an altogether undue proportion from children bereft of their natural homes.[66]

The New York State Commission on Pensions For Widows also underscored this as a governmental responsibility. "Normal family life," it declared in 1914, is the foundation of the State, and its conservation an inherent duty of government."[67] While one might debate the duty of the State of New York to aid the adult poor, it stated, "...that it is morally obligated to care for the dependent child cannot be doubted. This principle has always been recognized by our government; indeed, it is but the counterpart of its right to compel all children to be educated in its public schools."[68]

Likewise, in 1915, the Attorney General of Wisconsin concluded that its Mothers' Pension law was "passed in response to a rapidly crystallizing public sentiment that the state should not only take a human interest in the present welfare of [neglected] children, but that the interest which the state had in them as future citizens justifies it as a plain business proposition, in doing whatever may be necessary to promote their development into good and useful men and women saving them from a future of delinquency."[69]

Opposition to Institutional Care

Mothers' Pensions laws continued the nineteenth-century pattern in which the state interposed itself between parents and their offspring. However, instead of breaking up poor families by removing children from homes viewed as unfit, the twentieth-century strategy was to help families stay together on the grounds that no child should be removed from the home for reasons of poverty alone. The shift from institutional care and placing-out to Mothers' Pensions as a means to provide for the care, support, and socialization of poor children reflected the social welfare system's declining ability to accomplish these tasks. Increasingly, neither institutions nor private charity organizations could provide adequate care for destitute children. At the same time, the rise of new and more sophisticated social work methods for family management generated confidence in the practice of keeping children at home with their mothers.

Just as the appearance of institutional care was a response to the inability of colonial poor laws to meet the requirements of nineteenth-century capitalism, so Mothers' Pensions reflected the failure of institutional care and the placing-out system to assure the reproduction and maintenance of the labor force in the early twentieth century. As described in Chapter Five, the de-institutionalization of children began in the late nineteenth century in response to mounting criticism of child care institutions and the placing-out system. In 1910, one year before the enactment of the first Mothers' Pension program, the number of children housed in institutions peaked at more than 126,000, representing more than three per 1,000 of the child population. Another 17,000 lived in rudimentary foster-care arrangements. High infant mortality rates, outbreaks of contagious diseases, the exploitation of child labor, and the overall poor care provided to the children who survived discredited the original child-saving methods as a way to socialize children and conserve them as an important national resource.

Some blamed the large numbers of institutionalized children on the refusal of private charities to provide cash aid to single mothers.[70] According to the superintendent of one child-care institution,

> When the widow bereft of the support of her children, is left without funds, she cannot expect immediate relief from our present charitable system. Before her case is looked into and even becomes known, her children and herself are pretty nigh destitute and starving. Her first resort, therefore, is to place her children in a home, so that she may be able to go out and earn a meager livelihood. In most instances the charities do not give enough to keep the home intact; and then the amount is not fixed and regular. That is the reason most of these women place their children in institutions.[71]

In its 1914 report, The New York State Commission on Relief for Widowed Mothers concluded that government was the only solution because "private charity has not the funds, and cannot, in the future, raise the funds to give adequate relief in the home, nor to administer such funds in the efficient, wise and sympathetic manner which it has itself set up as the ideal." The Commission found "fundamental flaws" in private charity's philosophy, especially its continued belief that "financial aid was a minor, if not negligible, element in family rehabilitation," its attempts to force applicants for aid to secure it from relatives beyond those bound by law to support them, and its strong spirit of noblesse oblige.[72]

Others, like Judge Pinckney of the Chicago juvenile court, faulted both private charities and public relief for failing to keep families together. Judge Pinckney complained that because Cook County public relief provided only groceries and coal, he was continually forced to commit the children of poor but competent mothers to institutions. Likewise, private agencies often broke up families rather than provide emergency cash relief. Often, when it became obvious that a mother could not support her children even with aid, social agencies sent her to work and persuaded her to place one or two of her children.[73]

As a result, in 1900, children with at least one living parent comprised the majority of children in institutions and foster care.[74] These "half-orphans" were placed away from home because of poverty and the mother's need to work,[75] rather than the death of both parents. In 1912, Massachusetts concluded that such economic factors explained the institutionalization of 56.7 percent the children not living with their widowed mothers.[76] In 1913, nearly 1,000 New York State children ended up in orphanages due to the illness of widowed mothers; an additional 2,716 were committed because of family poverty.[77]

While most critics of institutional care decried its negative impact on "half-orphans," others focused on the consequences to the mother. They claimed that mothers who surrendered their children to institutions "open[ed] the door to graver dangers." Not only might the child do poorly, but in abandoning her child, the mother "has done an act of violence to her moral nature, from the consequences of which she cannot escape. If she be an unmarried mother, the surrendering of her child removes the one great influence towards a general restoration of her character thorough her maternal affection. Her love for children and fear of separation may prove her salvation."[78]

Rising costs and caseloads created additional pressures to de-emphasize institutional care especially since public subsidies to private child-caring institutions had soared. According to the 1904 census, forty-five states made public payments to private and ecclesiastical institutions which amounted to over $6 million or 27 percent of the total paid to all benevolent institutions. The rising receipt of public subsidies by private charities also alarmed many observers worried about maintaining a balance between public and private agencies.[79] Mothers' Pension advocates responded to these fiscal concerns by promising that keeping children at home would cost less than institutional care. In Illinois, they estimated that the monthly expense of maintaining a mother and six children at home fell below the $75 charged for the institutional care of the children alone.[80]

The Emergence of the Social Work Profession and Family Management Techniques

The emergence of the social work profession at this time, along with sophisticated family management techniques, also encouraged the move from institutions and placing-out to care for children at home. Both social casework and groupwork made it possible to organize the family and influence the training of the mother for the proper maintenance of children at home.

Settlement house workers, the forerunners of groupwork, often resided and lived in poor neighborhoods where they helped families improve their lives in practical ways and assimilate to American conditions. They taught white working-class, often immigrant, women how to cook, sew, and speak English. The settlements ran day nurseries and playgrounds, offered space for union meetings and medical dispensaries, and established cooperative boarding houses for working girls. Some, like those at Hull House in Chicago, eventually became heavily involved in lobbying for social reform. The Atlanta Neighborhood Union and other black settlement houses offered a similar range of social and educational services including orphanages, old age homes, summer camps, day nurseries, free kindergartens, street clean-up campaigns, recreational facilities, programs to train kindergarten teachers, educational reforms, and other programs to meet the needs of the black community.[81]

At the same time, Mary Richmond and other social workers began to conceptualize the process of casework with individuals which included study (investigation by a paid agent), diagnosis (case planning by a committee of volunteers), and treatment (rehabilitation by a friendly visitor). Called "social diagnosis," this was an "attempt to arrive at as exact a definition as possible of the social situation and personality of a given client." "The method and aims of social work," wrote Richmond in *Social Diagnosis* (1917), "were or should be the same in every type of service, whether the subject was a homeless paralytic, the neglected boy of drunken parents, or the widowed mothers of small children."[82]

The Professionalization of Public Welfare

The de-institutionalization of children was furthered by the professionalization of public welfare, especially the rise of the juvenile courts (which combined probation, separate hearings, and special judges in dealing with young offenders), the development of child-guidance programs (which provided expert diagnosis of the mental and physical condition of delinquents),[83] and the emergence of boards of public welfare (designed to professionalize the public sector through centralization, scientific research, and the use of trained personnel). Public welfare supporters hoped that these changes would enable public agencies to do preventive social work: to "effectively control the conditions of living and remove the causes of misery" and to replace custodial deterrence with efforts to create a "reasonably good environment in which to...live and...work and...play."[84] The 1914 Report of the New York Commission on Pensions for Widows concluded, "The formation of county boards of child welfare as recommended by this Commission should do much, not only to protect dependent children in their own homes, but also to bring together all the forces for good in every community, into an active harmonious group that would effectively drive out the evils resulting from the present system of incompetent poor relief and inadequate private charity in our villages, town and cities."[85]

Public welfare professionals favored the public provision of relief (such as Mothers' Pensions) on the grounds that the problem had become too large for private agencies and that the public sector now was as efficient and scientific, if not more so, than the charities.[86] The private charities vehemently disagreed. Opposed to Mothers' Pensions in part because they wished to retain control of their traditional turf, they favored a division of labor in which public agencies provided care for people in institutions and private agencies assumed responsibility for those aided at home. Defending themselves against the prevailing criticisms, private charities repeatedly claimed that Mothers' Pensions revived outdoor relief which they continued to oppose for all the same reasons as before.[87] The battle between the public and private sectors of the social welfare community was partially resolved as the staff of private charities and much of its philosophy was incorporated into and eventually came to dominate the Mothers' Pension program.

The Mothers' Pension Program, a response to the state's interest in conserving human resources and to changes in the social welfare system, represented a positive alternative to exploitative working conditions and child neglect. It also promised working mothers the respectability that the period accorded to women who remained at home. However, the Mothers' Pension assisted only a fraction of women in need. Favoring those who complied with the family ethic, the program primarily aided "deserving" female paupers deemed "suitable" to raise their children at home. The effective exclusion of so many poor women from the rolls prevented all but the most deserving from leaving the labor market. The program further enforced patriarchal norms insofar as it encouraged the economic dependence of women on men and defined child rearing as women's exclusive responsibility.

Enforcing Patriarchal Norms

At the 1909 White House Conference on Children, officials specified that the state planned to aid only the children of "worthy" parents. The Conference opposed breaking up homes "for reasons of poverty," but sanctioned family disruption for reasons of "inefficiency and immorality."[88] In a special message to Congress in February 1909, Theodore Roosevelt explained that the proposed Mothers' Pension program was for "parents of good character suffering from temporary misfortune and above all deserving mothers fairly well able to work but deprived of the support of the normal breadwinner" so that they could "maintain suitable homes for the rearing of their children."

The 1913 Massachusetts Commission on the Support of Dependent Minor Children of Widowed Mothers also indicated that its Mothers' Pension program would serve only "deserving" women who provided proper care to their children in "suitable" homes. The Commission stated that pensions were "not primarily for those with least adequate incomes under the present system of aid, but for the fit and worthy poor." It added, "no aid can be given, except under the poor-law and by private societies, to widows unfit to spend money for the improvements of their families."[89] After a "searching inquiry," the Illinois program accepted only those women who "can be trusted to make reasonably wise expenditures and to maintain fit homes for their children."[90]

In most states, "fit and deserving" mothers turned out to be widowed and white, that is, those most able to comply with the prevailing family ethic, leading many states to call the program "widows' pensions." In California, program recipients were dubbed "gilt-edged widows."[91] Only women with permanently absent husbands due to death, long-term imprisonment, and incurable insanity were routinely eligible in all states. Such eligibility rules distinguished among women according to their marital status and denied aid to other husbandless women viewed as departing from prescribed wife and mother roles.

These rules permitted a Mothers' Pension programs to avoid what they considered to be the twin headaches of non-supporting fathers and immoral mothers. A New York court, for example, upheld the denial of aid to a deserted mother on the grounds that the Act did not pension all classes of indigent mothers. The judge stated that the legislature "discontinued pensions to indigent mothers whose husbands had abandoned them because it concluded that to grant such pensions was not in accord with sound public policy."[92]

Over time, the states gradually relaxed their eligibility rules, but administrative decisions continued to favor women who conformed to the family ethic. By 1921, only six of the forty states with a Mothers' Pension program limited aid to widows. Seventeen states granted aid to children of deserted mothers and six assisted children of divorced mothers. Nonetheless, ten years later, widows still headed over 80 percent of the more than 60,000 families receiving aid nationwide. Five percent of the families were headed by abandoned wives and 1 percent by divorced women.[93] Unmarried mothers were the least likely to receive help. Just three states—Michigan, Nebraska, and Tennessee—officially aided unmarried women. Although the statutes of eight others were broad enough to include them, a 1931 survey found that only fifty-five families headed by unmarried mothers were receiving aid. Three years later a Michigan study of 2,000 Mothers' Pension families turned up only twenty-five unwed mothers.[94]

Mothers' Pensions served very few black women. Ninety-six percent of 46,597 families reporting race in 1931 were white. Of the 3 percent who were black, about half lived in just two states: Ohio and Pennsylvania. Many states aided virtually no blacks at all.[95] Of the 246 families receiving aid in North Carolina from 1924 to 1926, less than 2 percent were black, even though blacks represented about 29 percent of the state's population. Approximately the same percentage obtained between 1926 and 1928. Florida assisted only two black mothers in 1926. Although 21 percent of Houston's population was black, no blacks appeared in the Mothers' Pension caseload. Neither did Richmond aid black women.[96] Other minority groups fared no better. A 1922 Children's Bureau report found that eleven out of forty-five agencies gave smaller grants to Mexican, Italian, and Czechoslovakian families than to Anglo-Saxon families. One agency added 10 percent to the food

budget for "high type" or "deserving" families.[97] By excluding hundreds
of women viewed as "undeserving" of aid from the rolls in this way,
the Mothers' Pension Program, left them no choice but to find a breadwinner or to work for wages outside the home.

Despite the distinctions made between the "deserving" and "undeserving" poor, Mothers' Pension programs continued to distrust even
"deserving" families to properly carry out the family's maintenance and
reproductive functions. The Charity Organization Society (COS)
workers they hired offered economic assistance as part of a broader
plan of "social treatment" designed to reduce dependency by
rehabilitating families through "re-education of habit and emphasis on
right standards." Even "fit and deserving" widows who qualified for
help received regular visits from agency workers. The widowed mother,
it was argued, benefited from the supervision of a "friendly visitor" who
educated, guided, and carefully monitored her maternal job performance.

The New York City Board of Child Welfare required that each
pension recipient be visited quarterly by a Board representative but
defensively stressed that its advisory and counseling services were not
"meddlesome" or "policing." However, the investigator's review of pension appropriateness often turned out to be a loosely constructed judgement that reflected class and race biases. Reasons for rejection included
use of tobacco, lack of church attendance, dishonesty, drunkenness,
housing a male lodger, extramarital relations, poor discipline, criminal
behavior, child delinquency, and overt child neglect. Agencies even
forced families to move from neighborhoods with questionable reputa-
tions.[98]

A 1921 review of 212 Mothers' Pension records in Cook County,
Chicago found that over a two-year period virtually all the families had
received monthly visits from the probation officer. The field supervisor
who helped the mother improve her domestic skills (cleaning, cooking, sewing, and skillful buying) also made several visits. Such agency
visitors directed families to medical attention and improved housing,
and monitored the school attendance of children. They also withdrew
pensions from families who became ineligible. "Mother's failure," a
common disqualifier referred to such behaviors as untruthfulness, keeping roomers, and refusing to cooperate. Others who had been wrong-
fully accepted in the first place included "aliens,... three whose
marriage could not be proved,...two who could not prove the death
of their husbands,...two whose husbands were not totally incapacitated
for work,...a mother unfit morally, mentally or physically,...a woman

with an 'illegitimate child,'" as well as those who should have been judged financially capable.[99]

It was also hoped that the emphasis on "deserving" widows would help to mute public criticism of the new program. For the same reason, officials tried to distinguish Mothers' Pensions from outdoor relief. The New York State Commission on Relief of Widowed Mothers declared that "public aid to dependent, fatherless children is quite different in theory and effect from 'charity' or 'outdoor relief,'"[100] and placed the program under the jurisdiction of the county child-welfare board. The Massachusetts Commission concluded, "It seems not undesirable to create in the community a distinction between subsidy and relief. The family receiving the former may desire to live up to the special confidence reposed in it. Its income is regular and adequate. Supervision is less frequent than with other families."[101] The supervisor of the Pennsylvania Mothers' Assistance Fund hoped that the Mothers' Pension experiment would ultimately produce a "superior piece of public relief machinery...embodying all the principles of case diagnosis and treatment that have been worked out so carefully by private agencies in the past."[102] Many states located the administration of the former program in the juvenile courts and other special local boards rather than with public aid divisions to "utterly segregate Mothers' Pensions from public poor law outdoor relief."[103]

In theory, if not always in practice, the Mothers' Pension program discouraged maternal employment by "deserving" women. Most states required that children live with the mother and that she must not work outside the home. Ohio gave allowances to children "only when in the absence of such allowance, the mother would be required to work regularly...and when by means of such allowance, she will be able to remain at home with her children."[104] Since support of the indigent countered longstanding views that work was the best antidote to pauperism, some states permitted a limited amount of work, either homework or market work one day a week. Others left the amount of time a mother may be absent to the discretion of local officials.

By arguing that women belonged in the home and providing them a means for remaining there, Mothers' Pensions programs replaced male breadwinners and sanctioned the economic dependence of women on men or the state. The 1914 New York Commission on Pensions For Widows, for example, described the widows' pension as an "indemnity for the earning capacity of the husband, so that the mother may be enabled to bring up her children as they would have been brought up had their father lived and worked for them."[105] Josephine Shaw Lowell, founder of the New York COS, stated that "This sort of help [to poor deserving women] is not demoralizing nor pauperizing, if properly watched, because it only places the family in a natural position. Women and children ought to be supported, and there is no sense of degradation in receiving support."[106] The rules that defined eligibility in terms of a woman's relationship to a male bread-winner and the father of her child also implied dependency. The early state laws aided only children whose fathers could not support them due to physical or mental illness. Later grants became available to children of imprisoned fathers and divorced, deserted, or never married mothers.[107] The notion of female economic dependence, among other things, kept women at home but available for paid market labor on an as needed basis.

Paradoxically, while Mothers' Pensions maintained deserving poor women at home, the program's exclusionary policies and its low benefits channeled large numbers of women into the paid labor force, on a full- or part-time basis. Initially almost every state established a maximum pension which ranged from $9 to $15 a month for the first child and $4 to $10 dollars for each additional child. Some states limited the amount paid to any one family regardless of family size.[108] These monthly payments fell far below the $5 to $7 a week earned by working women and the amount an ordinary family needed to survive.[109] In 1931, the average monthly grant, higher in northern industrial states than in the South, varied from $4.33 in Arkansas to $69.31 in Massachusetts.[110]

The 1919 White House Conference on Children reported that "in many states allowances are still entirely inadequate to enable a mother to maintain her children suitably in her own home without resorting to...outside employment."[111] A 1923 study of 942 pensioned mothers in nine cities found 52 percent earning part of their family support.[112] A 1926 study of 783 families found 97 mothers working away from home 5 or more days a week, 229 at work part-time, and 138 working at home. Over one-third of the fourteen to sixteen year old children in these families had also gone to work, far exceeding their proportion in the general population.[113] A Michigan report on 4,000 families in the caseload concluded that low grants forced many mothers to lower standards and relinquish ideals for the care and training of their children.[114]

Following the family ethic, Mothers' Pension laws defined child rearing as the exclusive responsibility of women, a position that not only kept women at home, but enabled employers to rationalize the marginalization of those who entered the labor force. Except for Colorado, Florida, Minnesota, and Wisconsin, all the states permitted only the mother to receive a pension. Of the four exceptions, only Colorado supported any parent whose poverty prevented him or her from properly caring for a dependent child. Some other states allowed other female relatives to substitute for the child's biological mother.[115] But, in general, the laws regarded the care of children as women's work. When the Massachusetts Commission on the Support of Dependent Children of Widowed Mothers recommended that the state adopt "the principle of payment by way of subsidy for the rearing of children," it stated that, a "subsidy makes it feasible that children should stay with their worthy mothers in the most normal relationship still possible when the father has been removed by death."[116] When the Utah court declared the state's Mothers' Pension law constitutional in 1917, it observed that because the Act had

> ...for its object the better care and training, mental and physical, of children who are to become citizens of the state and...having in mind the public welfare by surrounding children of tender years with home associations, with the care and nurture of their natural protector, the mother, the Legislature by this act has determined that to be a policy of the state.

The Court continued,

> It will be conceded...that the proper rearing and bringing up of children, their education, their moral welfare, can all be subserved better by giving children the companionship, control, and management of their mothers than by any system devised by human ingenuity. The object of the act is to provide means where by mothers who are otherwise unable may be enabled to give such attention and care to their children of tender years as their health, education and comfort require.[117]

Although it denied aid to many women in need for moralistic reasons, the Mothers' Pension program helped an appreciable number of women avoid the worst jobs and in some cases abusive marriages. It enabled many women and children to survive. The flood of applications received each time a state introduced the new program exposed the inadequacy of the existing outdoor relief programs and the hardship produced by the economic system. In spite of strong efforts to distinguish the Mothers' Pension program from public aid, its development helped to pave the way for a renewed acceptance and the expansion of outdoor relief. This shift foreshadowed the inclusion of a program to aid dependent children in the historic Social Security Act of 1935.

Indeed, the Mothers' Pension program signaled a change in the nature of state intervention in family life. Instead of disrupting family life to assure the proper reproduction of the labor force and the maintenance of the non-working poor, the state stepped in to protect some husbandless women from the insecurities of the market. "The state and the mother entered a partnership," according to Winifred Bell, "in which both parties assumed certain responsibilities directed toward ensuring that a small group of needy children would remain in their own homes and be so supervised and educated as to become assets, not liabilities to a democratic society."[118] The state absorbed the costs of removing some mothers from the labor market and began to pay those associated with the maintenance and reproduction of the labor force at home. In this way, Mothers' Pension laws simultaneously praised the sanctity of the family and provided a rationale for continued state violation of that sanctity. They offered all children the opportunity to develop within a family environment while ensuring state control over their socialization.[119]

At the same time, Mothers' Pension laws continued the state's role in mediating the conflict between the demand for women's paid and unpaid labor. Maintaining women at home kept them in reserve until the demand for female labor expanded and provided income when the demand declined. When it did not maintain women at home as potential workers, the Program's low benefits and exclusionary eligibility rules channeled them into the low-paid female labor market. As discussed in the following chapters, the role of the state as overseer of family life and as regulator of women's paid and unpaid labor became institutionalized in 1935 with the passage of the Social Security Act by a Congress confronted with a collapsed economy and still another crisis in family stability.

Notes to Chapter 6

1. John H. Ehrenreich, *The Altruistic Imagination: A History of Social Work and Social Policy in the United States* (Ithaca: Cornell University Press, 1985), pp. 21-22.

2. For a discussion of the role of business in progressive era reform, see Gabriel Kolko, *The Triumph of Conservatism* (Chicago: Quadrangle Paperbacks 1963); James Weinstein, *The Corporate Ideal in the Liberal State, 1900-1918* (Boston: Beacon Press, 1968); Mimi Abramovitz, *Business and Social Reform: Workers' Compensation and Health Insurance in the Progressive Era*, unpublished dissertation, Columbia University School of Social Work, 1981.

3. Jane Ursel, "The State and the Maintenance of Patriarchy: A Case Study of Family Labor and Welfare Legislation," in James Dickinson and Bob Russell, (eds.) *Family, Economy, and State: The Social Reproduction Process Under Capitalism* (New York: St. Martin's Press, 1986) p. 134.

4. Robert H. Bremner, *From the Depths: The Discovery of Poverty in the United States* (New York: New York University Press, 1964), p. 131.

5. Annie Marion MacLean, *Wage-Earning Women* (New York: The Macmillan Company, 1910), pp. 160-161.

6. Susan Estabrook Kennedy, *If All We Did Was To Weep At Home: A History of White Working Class Women in America* (Bloomington: Indiana University Press, 1979), p. 94.

7. Jacqueline Jones, *Labor of Love, Labor of Sorrow: Black Women, Work, and the Family from Slavery to the Present* (New York: Basic Books, 1995) pp. 74, 80-94.

8. *Ibid.*, p. 55.

9. *Ibid.*, pp. 164-166.

10. *Ibid.*, pp. 45, 59, 71.

11. Alice Kessler-Harris, *Out To Work: A History of Wage Earning Women in the United States* (Oxford: Oxford University Press, 1982) p. 98; Kennedy (1979) *op. cit.*, pp. 93-94.

12. Weiner (1985) *op. cit.*, p. 6.

13. Kessler-Harris (1982) *op. cit.*, p. 101.

14. Weiner (1985) *op. cit.*, p. 38.

15. Kessler-Harris (1982) *op. cit.*, p. 101.

16. For a discussion of the response to prostitution during the Progressive period, see Ruth Rosen, *The Lost Sisterhood: Prostitution in America, 1919-1918* (Baltimore: The Johns Hopkins University Press, 1982).

17. Kessler-Harris (1982) *op. cit.*, p. 105, citing "Work is For Men," *Labor Advocate*, March 2, 1901, p. 1.

18. *Ibid.*, p. 105, citing Flora MacDonald Thompson, "Truth About Women in Industry," *North American Review*, 178 (May 1904).

19. Weiner (1985) *op. cit.*, p. 39.

20. Sarah Eisenstein, *Give Us Bread But Give Us Roses: Working Women's Consciousness in the United States, 1890 to the First World War* (London: Routledge & Kegan Paul, 1983), pp. 115-116.

21. 208 U.S. at 421 (1908) cited in Nancy E. McGlen and Karen O'Connor *Women's Rights: The Struggle for Equality in the 19th and 20th Centuries* (New York: Praeger, 1983), p. 158.

22. George Edmund Haynes, *The Negro at Work in New York City* (New York: Aras Press, 1968/1912), pp. 59-60.

23. Jones (1985) *op. cit.*, pp. 152-160. In contrast, midwestern cities received only a few hundred black southerners each year. Most of them young men without famiies; Frank F. Furstenberg, Jr., Theodore Hershberg, and John Modell, "The Origins of the Female-Headed Black Family: The Impact of the Urban Experience," *Journal of Interdisciplinary History*, VI (2) (1975), pp. 211-233.

24. Kessler-Harris (1982) *op. cit.*, pp.89-97; Weiner (1985) *op. cit.*, pp. 49-78.

25. Jones (1985) *op. cit.*, p. 190.

26. *Ibid.*, p. 190; Rosalyn Terborg-Penn, "Survival Strategies Among African-American Women Workers: A Continuing Process," in Ruth Milkman (ed.), *Women, Work and Protest: A Century of U.S. Women's Labor History* (Boston: Routledge & Kegan Paul, 1985), p. 142.

27. Gerda Lerner, *The Majority Finds Its Past: Placing Women In History* (Oxford: Oxford University Press, 1979), pp. 87-88.

28. Andrew Billingsley and Jeanne Giovannoni, *Children of the Storm: Black Children and American Child Welfare* (New York: Harcourt Brace Jovanovich, Inc., 1972), pp. 57-58.

29. Kessler-Harris (1982) *op. cit.*, p. 152.

30. Kennedy (1985) *op. cit.*, pp. 122-131; Weiner (1985) *op. cit.*, p.67; Kessler-Harris (1982) *op. cit.*, p. 86.

31. Kessler-Harris (1982) *op. cit.*, p. 84.

32. Kennedy (1985) *op. cit.*, pp. 122-131; Weiner (1985) *op. cit.*, p.67; Kessler-Harris (1982) *op. cit.*, p. 86.

33. Kennedy (1985) *op. cit.*, pp. 122-131.

34. Terborg-Penn (1985) *op. cit.*, p.144; Paula Giddings, *When and Where I Enter: The Impact of Black Women on Race and Sex in America* (Toronto: Bantam Books, 1984), pp. 144-145.

35. Weiner (1985) *op. cit.*, p. 6.

36. *Ibid.*, p. 6.

37. Weiner (1985) *op. cit.*, p. 84.

38. Weiner (1985) *op. cit.*, p. 47; Eisenstein (1983) *op. cit.*, p. 76.

39. Carroll Smith-Rosenberg, *Disorderly Conduct: Visions of Gender in Victorian America* (Oxford: Oxford University Press, 1985), p. 179.

40. Carol Brown, "Mothers, Fathers And Children: From Private to Public Patriarchy," in Lydia Sargent (ed.), *Women and Revolution: A Discussion of The Unhappy Marriage Of Marxism and Feminism* (Boston: South End Press, 1981), p. 249.

41. Leslie Woodcock Tentler, *Wage-Earning Women: Industrial Work and Family Life in the United States, 1900-1930* (Oxford: Oxford University Press, 1979), pp. 165-166.

42. Weiner (1985) *op. cit.*, pp., 8, 98-99.

43. Weiner (1985), *op. cit.*, p. 43, citing Robert H. Wiebe, *Search For Order, 1877-1920* (New York: Hill and Wang, 1967), p. 169.

44. Weiner (1985) *op. cit.*, p. 99, citing U.S. Industrial Commission, *Report,* Vol. 19 (1901).

45. MacLean (1910) *op. cit.*, p. 178.

46. New York State, Report of the Commission on Relief for Widowed Mothers, 1914, in Robert H. Bremner (ed.), *Children and Youth In America: A Documentary History, Vol. II: 1866-1932* (Cambridge: Harvard University Press, 1971), p. 379.

47. New York Relief Commission for Widowed Mothers, *Preliminary Report,* March 20, 1914, p. 1, quoted by Abraham Epstein, *Insecurity: A Challange to America* (New York: Harrison Smith and Robert Hass, 1933), p. 622.

48. New York State, Report of the Commission on Relief for Widowed Mothers, 1914, in Robert H. Bremner (ed.) (1971) *op. cit.*, p. 380.

49. "News and Notes," *The Charities Review,* 6(4) (May 1897), pp. 378-379.

50. Merritt W. Pinckney, "Public Pensions To Widows. Experiences and Observations Which Lead Me To Favor Such a Law," *Proceedings,* National Conference of Charities and Correction (1912), pp. 474-480, in R. Bremner (ed.) (1971), op. cit, p. 371.

51. Only 3 percent of the mothers interviewed in a 1914 survey reported use of day nurseries. Another study found them patronized by only 12 percent of the working mothers surveyed. Lacking any alternatives, working mothers, especially if heading a family alone, often left their children without adequate supervision during the day. A 1913 government study of Massachusetts found 968 employed widows responsible for 1257 children; of these children 59 attended day nurseries, 555 were in school, 188 were cared for by an adult relative, 121 were supervised by neighbors, 238 were in charge of older siblings, and 75 had no provision at all. In such situations not a few working mothers lost their children to institutions or foster homes as their very attempts to care for their children produced conditions of neglect. Weiner (1985) *op. cit.*, p. 129.

52. Weiner (1985) *op. cit.*, pp. 124-125.

53. The 1904 Census identified 166 day nurseries, 113 of them located in only four states. The Association of Day Nurseries, in 1910, recorded 450 centers nationwide.

54. White House Conference on Child Health and Protection, Report of the Committee on Socially Handicapped-Dependency and Neglect, *Dependent and Neglected Children* (New York: D. Appleton-Century Company, 1933), p. 303.

55. Grace Abbott, *The Child and the State,* Vol. II (Chicago: The University of Chicago Press, 1938), p. 229.

56. Walter I.Trattner, *From Poor Law To Welfare State* (New York: The Free Press, 1984), pp. 54-55.

57. Emma Octavia Lundberg, *Unto the Least of These: Social Services For Children* (New York: D. Appleton-Century Company, Inc., 1947), p. 134.

58. Roy Lubove, *The Struggle for Social Security, 1900-1935* (Cambridge: Harvard University Press, 1968), p. 101.

59. Trattner (1983) *op. cit.,* p. 55.

60. John Lewis Gillin, *Poverty and Dependency* (New York: Twentieth Century Fund, 1921), p. 372.

61. Epstein (1933) *op. cit.,* p. 625.

62. *Proceedings of the Conference on the Care of Dependent Children,* Washington, D.C., January 25-26, 1909, (Washington, D.C.: Government Printing Office, 1909), p. 9.

63. Billingsley and Giovannoni (1972) *op. cit.,* pp. 72-73.

64. Epstein (1933) *op. cit.,* p. 629.

65. Mark H. Leff, "Consensus for Reform: The Mother's Pension Movement in the Progressive Era," *Social Service Review,* 47 (September 1973), p. 260.

66. Special Message by the President of the United States, February 15, 1909, quoted in White House Conference on Child Health and Protection (1933) *op. cit.,* p. 55.

67. New York State, *Report of the Commission on Relief For Widowed Mothers,* 1914 (Albany, 1914), in Robert H. Bremner, (1971) *op. cit.,* p. 379.

68. *Report of the New York State Commission on Relief For Widowed Mothers,* Transmitted to the Legislature, March 27, 1914, p. 115, quoted by G. Abbott (1938) *op. cit.,* p. 252.

69. Letter Addressed to the Assistant District Attorney of Green Bay Wisconsin, November 30, 1915, quoted in G. Abbott (1938) *op. cit.,* p. 305.

70. Lubove (1968) *op. cit.,* p. 106.

71. The Commonwealth of Massachusetts, *Report of the Massachusetts Commission on the Support of Dependent Minor Children of Widowed Mothers,* January 1913, House Document No. 2075, pp. 153-160, quoted by Lundberg (1947) *op. cit.,* p. 128.

72. New York State, *Report of the Commission on Relief For Widowed Mothers,* 1914 (Albany, 1914), in R. Bremner (1971) *op. cit.,* pp. 381-383.

73. G. Abbott (1938) *op. cit.,* p. 265.

74. Linda Gordon, "Single Mothers and Child Neglect, 1880-1920," *American Quarterly,* 37 (2) (Summer 1985), p. 191.

75. Lundberg (1947) *op. cit.,* p. 127.

76. G. Abbott (1938) *op. cit.,* p. 249.

77. Weiner (1985) *op. cit.,* pp. 122-123.

78. State Charities Aid Association, Agency For Providing Situations in the Country for Destitute Mothers With Infants, *First Annual Report,* October 1894, p. 3.

79. Gillin (1921) *op. cit.,* pp. 196-213; Amos Warner, *American Charities* (New York: Thomas Y. Crowell, 1908), pp. 399-419.

80. Epstein (1933) *op. cit.,* p. 624.

81. Lerner (1979) *op. cit.,* pp. 83-93.

82. Kathleen Woodruffe, *From Charity to Social Work* (London: Routledge and Kegan Paul, 1964, 2nd ed.), pp. 105, 107, 108.

83. Lubove (1968) *op. cit.,* p. 97.

84. *Ibid.,* p. 96, citing L. A. Halbert, "Boards of Public Welfare and Good City Government," National Conference of Charities and Corrections, *Proceedings* (1913), pp. 213, 216.

85. *Report of the New York State Commission on Relief For Widowed Mothers,* Transmitted to the Legislature, March 27, 1914, p. 115, in G. Abbott (1938) *op. cit.,* p. 254.

86. Leff (1973) *op. cit.,* pp. 245-246.

87. For a review of these arguments, see Leff (1973) *op. cit.,* pp. 397-417; National Conference on Charities and Corrections, *Proceedings,* 1912.

88. *Ibid.,* pp. 56, 60.

89. G. Abbott (1938) *op. cit.,* p. 250.

90. Edith Abbott and Sophonisba P. Breckinridge, *The Administration of the Aid-to Mothers Law in Illinois* (Washington D.C.: Government Printing Office, 1921), p. 28.

91. Winifred Bell, *Aid to Dependent Children* (New York: Columbia University Press, 1965), p. 9.

92. G. Abbott (1938) *op. cit.,* p. 280-281.

93. Bell (1965) *op. cit.,* pp. 8-9; Emma O. Lundberg, "Aid To Mothers With Dependent Children, *The Annals of the American Academy of Political and Social Science,* XCVII (November 1921), p.97-105, in R. Bremner (1971) *op. cit.,* p. 389-390.

94. Bell (1965) *op. cit.*, pp. 8-9; United States Children's Bureau, *Mother's Aid, 1931*, Publication No. 220, Washington, D.C. (1933) pp. 6-24, in R. Bremner (1971) *op. cit.*, pp. 395.

95. Bell (1965) *op. cit.*, pp. 9-10; United States Children's Bureau (1933), in R. Bremner (1971) *op. cit.*, p. 396.

96. Bell (1965) *op. cit.*, p. 15; White House Conference on Child Health and Protection, (1933) *op. cit.*, pp. 302-303.

97. Irene Graham, "Family Support and Dependency Among Chicago Negroes," *Social Service Review*, III (4) (December, 1929), pp. 541-562; Haynes (1968) *op. cit.*, p. 80.

98. Leff (1973) *op. cit.*, p. 259; Bell (1965) *op. cit.*, pp. 12-13.

99. E. Abbott and Breckinridge (1921) *op. cit.*, pp. 30, 40-41, 73.

100. New York State, *Report of the Commission on Relief for Widowed Mothers* (1914), in R. Bremner (1971) *op. cit.*, p. 380.

101. Massachusetts Commission on the Support of Dependent Minor Children of Widowed Mothers, *Report* (Boston 1913), p. 12-13, in R. Bremner (1971) *op. cit.*, p. 389.

102. Lubove (1973) *op. cit.*, pp.107-108.

103. Quoted in Leff (1973) *op. cit.*, p. 259.

104. Ohio Commission to Codify and Revise the Laws of Ohio Relative to Children, *Report*, in R. Bremner (1971) *op. cit.*, p. 387.

105. G. Abbott (1938) *op. cit.*, p. 252.

106. Josephine Shaw Lowell, "Children" in William Rhinelander Steward, *The Philanthropic Work of Josephine Shaw Lowell* (New York, 1911), pp. 268-276 cited in R. Bremner (1971) *op. cit.*, p. 351.

107. G. Abbott (1938) *op. cit.*, pp. 234-235.

108. Leff (1973) *op. cit.*, pp. 248; Gillin (1921) *op. cit.*, p. 378.

109. White House Conference in Child Health and Protection, 1930, *Addresses and Abstracts of Committee Reports,* (New York: The Twentieth Century Co., 1931), p. 336.

110. Bell (1965) *op. cit.*, p. 15.

111. White House Conference on Child Health and Protection, (1933) *op. cit.*, p. 66.

112. Bell (1965) *op. cit.*, p. 16.

113. White House Conference on Child Health and Protection, (1933) *op. cit.*, pp. 194-195.

114. Bell (1965) *op. cit.*, p. 17.

115. Gillin (1921) *op. cit.*, p. 375.

116. *Report of Massachusetts Commission on the Support of Dependent Children of Widowed Mothers*, January 1913, p. 31 quoted in Epstein (1933) *op. cit.*, p. 624.

117. *Denver & Rio Grand Railroad Co. v. Grant County 51 Utah 294* (1917), quoted in Abbott (1938) *op. cit.*, pp. 277-278.

118. Bell (1965) *op. cit.*, p. 5.

119. Richard A. Meckel, "Protecting the Innocents: Age Segregation and the Early Child Welfare Movement," *Social Service Review* 59(3) (September 1985), pp. 456-457.

7

The Great Depression and the Social Security Act

The Emergence of the Modern Welfare State

The landmark Social Security Act became the centerpiece of the modern welfare state. Its original programs—social insurance (Old Age Assistance, Aid to the Blind, Aid to Dependent Children, Old Age Insurance, Unemployment Compensation, and Public Assistance)—offered cash assistance to retired and unemployed workers and to selected groups among the poor. It also provided for maternal and child health care. Enacted in 1935, when capital accumulation, patriarchal authority, and reproduction of the labor force, as well as the overall social peace, were threatened by the collapse of the economy, the rise of working-class militancy, and the destabilization of the family system, the Social Security Act institutionalized the role of the state in maintaining families, the labor force, and the general welfare of society.

By assuming responsibility for providing a minimum level of income below which no one was expected to live, the state began to address problems in the political economy that had been simmering since

215

the end of World War I. The provision of an income floor for some groups in the population implicitly acknowledged that the economic impact of old age, job loss, and the absence of a breadwinner were beyond individual control and that the market economy could not provide enough jobs for all those available and able to work. The Social Security Act expanded and made permanent the state's role in mediating conflicts between production and reproduction and sustaining patriarchal norms.[1] On the individual level, the income support programs of the Act, operating as a substitute wage, increased the federal government's role in relieving personal distress. By systematically distributing income from the working to the non-working members of society, the programs helped to assure the reproduction of the labor force, the maintenance of the non-working population, and the control of social unrest. By taking on key reproductive responsibilities previously assigned to the family and making access to income maintenance benefits conditional upon compliance with the family ethic as well as the work ethic, the Social Security Act also helped to forestall the challenges to the patriarchal family unit presented by the inability of male workers to support their families, the entry of more women into the labor force, and other changes in ordinary family life. Although less visibly and widely discussed, the Social Security Act also marked the institutionalization of social or public patriarchy in the contemporary welfare state.[2]

A Crisis in the Sphere of Production: Rising Economic Insecurity and the Collapse of the Market

The Depression exposed the roots of economic insecurity in the twentieth-century economy. Its causes, however, lay deep in social, economic, and political dislocations that underpinned the economic boom of the preceding decade. During the twenties, the nation's productivity soared, national income rose from $60 billion to $87 billion between 1922 and 1929,[3] and the economic expansion following World War I created jobs and higher wages for skilled and regularly employed workers with minimal inflation. Few listened to the rumblings of trouble that could be heard beneath the rapid economic growth, booming profits, and the giddy rise of consumerism.

Indeed, the general prosperity, the spread of new low wage industries, and an absence of national unemployment statistics masked sagging industrial employment. As mechanization increasingly improved the efficiency of production and raised profits, capital began to replace labor with machines. Between 1920 and 1929, according to one report, unit labor requirements dropped by 30 percent in manufacturing, 20 percent in railroads, 21 percent in mining, and 14 percent in telephone communications.[4] At the same time, excessive investments in the manufacture of automobiles, in the emerging service industries, and in international finance created an excess capacity that eventually translated into production cutbacks and fewer jobs.[5] By 1923, manufacturing output was 72.2 percent of capacity, dropping in other sectors of the economy as well.[6] The U.S. Bureau of Labor Statistics found that

> Industrial wage-earners in those states for which data are available lose about 10 percent of their working time through unemployment, mainly from lack of work and exclusive of idleness due to sickness and labor disputes...It appears that partial unemployment, due to part-time operation of plants, shut-downs, time lost on account of waiting, and related causes, is responsible for a loss of about 10 percent more of the working time of industrial wage earners.[7]

Only 80 percent of the economy was in use by 1929, according to a noted Brookings Institution study.[8]

Americans clearly benefited unevenly from the prosperity of the roaring twenties. Skilled workers made significant gains but their share of mounting national income did not compare to the rise of income enjoyed by the wealthy.[9] A 1929 Brookings Institution study found that 12 million of the 27 million families (or 42 percent of the total) had incomes below $1,500 while 36,000 (or only 0.1 percent) had annual incomes over $75,000. In effect, a tiny number of families at the top of the income scale collectively received almost as much income as the large number of families at the bottom of the scale.[10]

In contrast to the boom at the top, many wage earners suffered the consequences of the period's underlying economic problems. Many simply could not earn enough income to support their families. Family budget studies conducted at the time[11] found that, despite a 13 percent increase in real wages, the majority of workers never attained the $1,500-1,700 annual income needed for a family of five to live at a level of "health and decency." Twenty-one percent of low-income families lived below the estimated poverty standard of $1,000 per year. [12] "With the exception of a few isolated and exceptionally skilled trades," one researcher concluded, "the wages of American workers are insufficient, without supplement from other sources, to provide for the subsistence of a family consisting of a husband, a wife, and three minor children, much less maintain them in that condition of 'health and reasonable comfort,' which every humane consideration demands."[13] The report of the 1928 National Conference of Social Work stated that the income of unskilled and semi-skilled workers was not adequate, leaving many families unable to attain even the essential minimum living standard established by social agencies for families dependent on public or charitable relief.[14] Even some in the middle class felt excluded. Rising expectations and a psychology of abundance left many feeling that their standard of living failed to keep pace with the nation's economic growth. After the 1929 crash, the cost of living dropped sharply. But average income fell even further since during the Depression the work day became shorter. The purchasing power of the average wage earner in 1932 fell to 49.5 percent of its 1929 level although salaried workers experienced a less severe drop.[15]

According to one estimate, prior to the crash, unemployment was above 10 percent each year from 1924 to 1929, peaking at 13 percent in 1928. Another estimate of minimum unemployment produced somewhat lower but still troubling figures.[16] Depressed farm prices forced millions of people to migrate from the nation's farms to its cities, including 1.2 million blacks who left the South from 1915 to 1928. Temporarily absorbed in the labor market during World War I, these rural migrants replaced foreign-born immigrants as the largest pool of unemployed workers after the war, exerting a downward pressure on wages. Despite its intensification, the issue of unemployment received no more than passing attention in the 1928 presidential campaign. Many still believed that unemployment existed only in bad times, that only the thriftless suffered, and that jobs were available to those who tried hard enough.[17] One New Jersey man wrote to President Hoover in 1930, asking,

> Could we not have employment and food to Eat. and this for our children. Why Should we...Have foodless days...and our children have Schoolless days and Shoeless days and the land full of plenty and Banks bursting with money. Why does EveryThing have Exceptional Value. Except the Human being—why are we reduced to poverty and starving and anxiety and Sorrow So quickly under your Administration as Chief Executor. Can not you find a quicker way of Executing us than to Starve us to death.[18]

The median income of black families, both rural and urban, northern and southern, fell far below that of whites. Not counting the poorest
families on relief, the 1935 income of the majority of black families, but
only a small proportion of white families, was less than an emergency
budget of $903 a year for a family of four. Few blacks earned the $1,261
maintenance level income.[19] Black unemployment exceeded white unemployment by 30 to 60 percent.[20] A declining number of jobs provoked
racial competition for those that remained, weakening the already
tenuous hold black women and men had on employment in agriculture, industry, and the service sector. According to the Urban League,
prior to the Depression black workers sought to advance to positions
commensurate with their abilities. Now they just hoped "to hold the
line against advancing armies of white workers intent on gaining and
content to accept occupations which were once thought too menial for
white hands."[21] Activist and educator Nannie Bouroughs observed that
many of the jobs held by black women had "gone to machines, gone
to white people, or gone out of style."[22] The loss of jobs by black married women created severe strain since their families depended heavily on this income.

A Crisis in the Sphere of Reproduction: The Changing Role of Women and American Families

The Depression created a crisis in the family as well as in the
economy. It intensified the hard times for those at the very bottom,
pushed many in the working class into poverty, and destabilized some
in the middle class. Unemployment, hunger, evictions, and depleted
savings disrupted family patterns. Some families took to the open road;
others fell apart under the economic strain; still others just scraped by.
Jobless breadwinners frequently traveled long distances looking for
work or, in despair, deserted their kin. Evicted families sent children
to live with relatives and friends, while older children left home so that
younger ones would have more to eat. Married women and sometimes
their children took jobs. Prostitution rose.[23] Working-class families lived
with the threats of repossession, overcrowding, abuse, child neglect,
alcoholism, marital problems, desertion, sickness, malnutrition, starva-

tion, suicide, and premature death.[24] Meridel Le Sueur, a writer and activist in the thirties, observed in a 1934 short story,

> The working class family is going fast, the lower middle class family is also going, though not so fast. It is like a landslide. It is like a great chasm opening beneath the feet and swallowing the bottom classes first. The worker who lives from hand to mouth goes first, and then his family goes. The family rots, decays and goes to pieces with the woman standing last, trying to hold it together, and then going too. The man loses his job, cannot find another, then leaves. The older children try to get money, fail, and leave or are taken to the community farms. The mother stays with the little children helped by charity, until they too are sucked under by the diminishing dole and the growing terror.[25]

Conditions in the thirties also strained the ties that bound black women and men together. A Pittsburgh mother of six young children applied for city relief in 1931 when her husband lost the steel mill job he had held for several years. Shortly after the company told him that "he needn't trouble looking for a job as long as there are so many white men out of work," he left and never returned. His wife commented bitterly, "I guess us colored folks don't get hungry...like white folks." In 1930, about 29 percent of all black households were female headed, even more in northern cities.[26] One woman wrote to the President in 1934. "Pleas help Poor me i am a Colored woman 34 years old have 4 Children 3 Girls and 1 Boy. I have work awfully hard Every Senice i 9 years old." Having turned to drink upon the death of her husband, she had more difficulty finding work. "I have tried and tried to Get a Job But they are Scarse and City Releaf takes Care of my Children at Present."[27]

The crisis in the family, like that of the economy, was rooted in trends which the Depression intensified, especially the deterioration of the mechanisms that previously contained women—particularly white, married women—in the home. During the first thirty years of the twentieth century, declining birth and marriage rates and the solidification of white women's position in the labor market created new tensions between the demand for women's home and market labor, diminished the capacity of the working-class family to carry out its reproductive functions, and undermined patriarchal authority. Once again, the requirements of production and reproduction conflicted, although in new ways.

The birth rate dropped rapidly between 1910 and 1930, continuing a long-term trend toward smaller families. The lowered value of

children as an economic asset and the greater economic and emotional investment required for their care helped shrink family size, but
during the thirties the birth rate fell below the replacement level for the
first time.[28] Marriage rates among young adults which had been rising
during the previous forty years also fell sharply. By 1938, according to
one estimate, economic troubles had caused 1.5 million people to
postpone marriage. Although the divorce rate declined from 1929 to
1931, largely due to the legal costs, desertion..."the poor person's"
divorce...soared.[29]

The structure of family life was also affected by the male-female
sex ratio—a socio-demographic factor that shaped the likelihood of
marriage. In the early twentieth century, higher overall male death rates
produced a declining number of men for women to marry. In 1910,
there were 106 men for every 100 women, but the ratio dropped to
102.5 men to 100 women in 1930.[30] In the black community, higher
male death rates combined with migration patterns and differential job
opportunities for black women and men to produce an even greater
shortage of available men, especially in the cities.

Rising female employment further fueled the sense of crisis in the
family. The proportion of all women at work rose (with a slight drop
in 1920) from 20.6 percent in 1900 to 25 percent in 1930, where it
remained until World War II.[31] Working women disturbed the *status
quo* not only because women "belonged in the home" but also because
their numbers included many married women, particularly white, married women, whose labor force participation until this time, although
rising, had remained low.

Between 1900 and 1930, married women took jobs at a rate five
times that of other women so that the number of employed married
women increased four-fold compared to a two-fold rise for all
employed women. By 1930, nearly 29 percent of all working women
were married, compared to 15 percent in 1900. The proportion of all
married women who worked doubled, jumping from 5.6 percent in
1900 to 11.7 percent in 1930, six times the increase for single women.[32]
Most of the new working wives were white, although the labor force
participation rates of black women remained much higher and continued to grow albeit more slowly than before.[33] In 1940, when 14 percent of white and 32 percent of black wives worked outside the home,
the employment gap between black and white married women, still
large, had begun to narrow.[34]

The entry of more married women into the labor force prior to the Depression—neither accidental nor simply a matter of changed individual preferences—reflected ongoing changes in the economy. Rising economic expectations among the middle class, deepening economic need among the working class and the poor, and the new jobs in sales, advertising, and communications created by the nation's significantly expanded role in world markets and international finance drew married women into the labor force. As business recruited single women into the new clerical and sales positions, the demand for workers to fill less well-paid and lower-status jobs reached into the home. The supply of married women available to meet this demand [35] continued to grow in the thirties. By 1940, 28 percent of all women, 15 percent of married women, and 28 percent of all mothers with children under age eighteen worked in the paid labor force. The labor force participation rate of widows and divorced women ranged from 29.9 percent to 34.4 percent, comprising just under 20 percent of all women workers.[36]

The pre-Depression demand for women workers excluded black women who were kept out of white women's jobs in the expanding white-collar industries. Owing to strict occupational segregation by race and gender, less than 1 percent of all black women compared to 22 percent of all white women worked in white-collar jobs between 1910 and 1930.[37] The percentage of black female factory workers actually fell from 7 percent of all employed black women in 1920 to 5.5 percent in 1930.[38] Although a small number of black women made some gains in manufacturing, mechanical industries, and the professions,[39] racist and sexist employment patterns persisted throughout the thirties. By 1940, one-third of all white but only 1.3 percent of all black working women held clerical jobs.[40] Black women's employment in factories rose slightly to 6 percent, but remained below the 1920 level of 7 percent of all black women workers.[41]

Rising female employment during the thirties was accompanied by more than an 8 percent drop in the labor force participation rate of men.[42] Although working women also faced considerable unemployment, several features of the Depression economy improved their job opportunities relative to men: increased male unemployment, the sex-segregated labor market, and New Deal economic recovery policies.

High joblessness among male breadwinners, along with the high probability of their future unemployment, sent many women, including middle-class, married women, to work, some for the first time. Ironically, they found work because the jobs reserved for women in the sex-segregated labor market were not as prone to the ravages of cyclical unemployment that plagued male-dominated occupations. Indeed, after 1933, the clerical, trade, and service occupations employing large numbers of white women declined less rapidly and recovered more quickly than those employing mostly men.[43] Women workers also benefited from a government-influenced expansion of jobs in the public sector. On the one hand, the flow of federal funds for relief programs created thousands of low level clerical and human service jobs which were defined as women's work. On the other hand, the technological rationalization of production that followed from the economic slow-down, but also from the National Recovery Administration (NRA) loans to business, created new lower paying, often deskilled jobs which business filled with women, mostly white women. Women filled these jobs in part because men avoided them, and in part because business preferred to hire lower cost female labor.[44]

In contrast, New Deal recovery programs increased black unemployment. The Agricultural Adjustment Administration (AAA) reduced farm production by 40 percent to increase farm prices, causing the demand for farm labor to fall. AAA policies allowing landowners to invest their government cash subsidies in farm machinery stimulated the mechanization of southern agriculture which, from 1930 to 1940, displaced thousands of poor tenant farmers. The percent of black women employed in agriculture fell from 27 percent to 16 percent during this decade, but new jobs in expanding sectors of the economy were not open to them.[45] Combined with incentives for replacing sharecroppers with day workers, this policy also helped to transform southern farming into a wage labor system.

The rising employment of women conflicted with their role as homemakers and caretakers and challenged patriarchal norms. Public opinion held women responsible for male unemployment and for the family's financial and emotional distress.[46] It disparaged employed married women and strongly encouraged them to stay home.[47] A 1936 *Fortune* poll asked: "Do you believe that married women should have a full time job outside the home?" Fifteen percent believed they should, 48 percent did not, and 37 percent gave it conditional approval. The three most frequently cited reasons for opposing married women's work were that it took jobs away from men, that women's place was in the home, and that children were healthier and happier if women did not work.[48] One study concluded that "truancy, incorrigibility, robbery, teenage tantrums, and difficulty in managing children" resulted from a "mother's absence from the home."[49] In a letter to President

Roosevelt, a Kansas woman called employed women "thieving parasites of the business world." A Chicago-based civic organization urged that married women workers be forced back into the home because they were holding jobs that "rightfully belonged to the God-intended providers of the household."[50] Another social observer concluded that the very existence of job opportunities encouraged women to feel independent, which contributed to marital unhappiness.[51] Even Frances Perkins, the future Secretary of Labor, denounced the rich "pin money worker" as a "menace to society, [and] a selfish shortsighted creature who ought to be ashamed of herself." She added that any woman capable of supporting herself without a job should devote herself to motherhood and the home.[52]

The debate about working women was accompanied by strenuous efforts to expel married women from the labor force. Organized labor recommended denying jobs to women supported by a male breadwinner. The executive council of the AFL resolved that married women whose husbands have permanent positions…should not be hired. Railroads already notorious for discriminating against married women now began to fire them. In October 1930, the Northern Pacific Railway company dismissed all married women workers. Texas started a means test for women in transportation jobs—letting go wives with husbands earning more than $50 a month. New England Telephone and Telegraph Co. discharged married women workers in January 1931. A 1930-1931 National Education Association study of 1,500 school systems found that 77 percent refused to hire wives as teachers and 63 percent dismissed single female teachers who married. A 1939 survey by the National Industrial Conference Board showed that 84 percent of insurance companies, 65 percent of banks, and 63 percent of public utilities restricted work by married women.[53]

The federal government also barred the employment of married women. From 1932 to 1937, section 213 of the Federal Economy Act prohibited more than one member of the same family from working in the civil service. Within a year of enactment, more than 1,600 workers lost their government jobs, three-fourths of whom were women.[54] Nearly every state introduced (although not all enacted) bills to prevent the employment of married women; some cities embarked on crusades to fire working wives. Although some defended women's right to work, most Americans agreed with these practices. In response to a 1936 Gallop poll asking whether wives should work if their husbands were also employed, 82 percent said "no."[55] Feminists responded by suggesting that the debate over women's work "must not become a smoke screen to hide the real unemployment problems of providing work by shortening hours and increasing consumers' purchasing power by sharing the earnings of industry."[56] As noted above, married women continued to enter the labor force in record numbers, sometimes lying about their marital status to secure a job.

Researchers actively documented and thus legitimized the sense of crisis in patriarchal arrangements and in the reproductive sphere. Eminent sociologists such as William Ogburn and Joseph Kirk Folsom, among others, began to study the family only to confirm its decline. Their analyses warned that industrialization and urbanization had rendered the family's traditional functions obsolete except for the affectional tasks necessary to assure the happiness of children and spouses.[57] Saving the family, they concluded, required enhancing the traditional wife and mother role. This turned into a mandate for women to stay at home. As more men lost their jobs and more women went to work outside the home, sociologists wrote regretfully about the male breadwinner who no longer could provide for his family and the husband who washed dishes and made beds while his wife worked.[58]

The impact of the Depression on familial patriarchy became the topic of numerous research studies in the thirties. The studies expressed deepening concern about the shift in marital authority during the early part of the twentieth century. Samuel A. Stouffer and Paul E. Lazarfeld concluded that women increased their authority within the family because they fared better than men with respect to employment during the early years of the Depression.[59] Mirra Komarovsky found that unemployed husbands lost status in thirteen out of the forty-eight families she studied in the 1930s because of their joblessness, the deterioration of their personalities, and their continual presence in the home. She observed that wives' subordination to the unemployed husband might continue through habit. However, if the family's patriarchal structure depended on the man's role as provider, the loss of that role could undercut the husband's prerogatives.[60] John French and Bertram Raven argued that four out of five sources of a husband's social power in the family had declined in varying degrees since the turn of the century. But as long as he held on to referent power (that is, power referred to the husband out of respect and affection), his position was secure.[61] Wandersee, in contrast, suggests that women seldom became the dominant partner in a marriage unless their husbands defaulted on their family responsibilities.[62]

The raging debate over the propriety of working wives assumed that work by married women was a new and unusual development.

Thus the debate ignored the long history of work by poor, black, and immigrant wives and single women and expressed few worries that black women workers would deprive black men of their jobs. According to the historian Alice Kessler-Harris, until issues involving male and female roles affected the white, middle-class family, they went largely unnoticed.[63] Male unemployment and work by wives became issues to the extent that they encroached upon the prerogatives of white, middle-class men at home and on the job. Few researchers investigated the impact of married women's employment on the black male ego or black family relations. Interestingly, however, the still current debate over the matriarchal structure of black families began in 1939 with the publication of E. Franklin Frazier's *The Negro in Family Life in the United States*. Frazier, a pre-eminent black sociologist, effectively countered prevailing racist explanations of the condition of the black family. But owing to his dependence on a deeply racist printed historical record and selective oral histories, Frazier contributed to the idea that blacks lacked a stable family life. In research whose findings and interpretations Gutman and other historians have recently refuted, Frazier attributed the instability to the post-slavery formation of a large number of black female-headed families.[64]

The sociologists' warnings that the white family system was in decline was accompanied by efforts to strengthen it. New social services for families in trouble began to emerge at this time. The first marital clinic opened in Los Angeles in 1930 and the number of child guidance clinics grew. The visiting housekeeper, and a variety of home economics, parent education, birth control, and maternal and infant hygiene programs also appeared. New professional associations sprang up such as The New York State Conference on Marriage and Family (1936) and The National Conference on Family Relations (1938). The National Council of Parent Education changed its name to the Association for the Advancement of Family Life.[65]

The Political Crisis:
Social and Political Unrest

The sagging economy, loss of jobs, and changes in family life generated widespread political disaffection in the thirties. An increasingly politicized working class began to demand that the government provide for its economic security. The aged, the employed, the jobless, and the black community all organized and clamored for jobs or government relief, which helped to put the problem of economic security onto the national agenda. As Piven and Cloward note,

> mass unemployment that persists for any length of time diminishes the capacity of other institutions to bind and constrain people. Occupational behaviors and outlooks underpin a way of life and determine familial, communal, and cultural patterns. When large numbers of people are suddenly barred from their traditional occupations, the entire structure of social control is weakened and may even collapse...[I]f the dislocation is widespread, the legitimacy of the social order itself may come into question. The result is usually civil disorder—crime, mass protest, riots—a disorder that may even threaten to overturn existing social and economic arrangements. It is then that relief programs are initiated or expanded.[66]

Roosevelt's defeat of Hoover in 1932, and the Democratic Congressional victories in 1934 finally produced a governmental response. To restore order, Piven and Cloward conclude, the state must create the means to re-assert its authority, re-institute social control, and do so in ways consistent with normally dominant patterns. To this end, and to forestall a turn to independent or Left politics by organized labor, which now reached into every corner of the U.S. industrial system, business and government leaders attempted to win the cooperation of labor's more conservative wing.[67] Between 1932 and 1935, the federal government reversed its earlier support of anti-union laws, protected organized labor against hostile judges and employers, and endorsed labor's right to unionize. Roosevelt, who entered the presidency without an articulated labor program, supported Section 7a of the National Industrial Recovery Act (1933) (which guaranteed workers the right "to organize unions of their own choosing") and the National Labor Relations Act or the Wagner Act (1935) (which gave labor the right to bargain collectively). These new laws permitted unions to recover the ground they had lost since the twenties, renewed labor militancy, and gave rise to the Congress of Industrial Organizations (CIO), which unionized 3.7 million industrial workers, including many women, between 1935 and 1937.[68] By 1939, after years of militant struggle, 9 million workers or 7 percent of the civilian labor force belonged to a union, including 800,000 women, a 300 percent increase in female members over ten years.[69] The unionization of women, however, did not end male domination in unions or traditional patterns of sex discrimination.[70]

The Birth of the Welfare State

The need for order also led the federal government to involve itself, for the first time, in the provision of relief, most typically by assisting the states. That is, it began to systematically subsidize the familial unit of reproduction. After defeating Hoover, who opposed a federal response to the Depression, the Roosevelt administration, between 1933 and 1935, enacted several emergency relief programs for the poor and unemployed. Known as the first New Deal, the measures included the Federal Emergency Relief Act (FERA) (which provided federal grants to states for relief); the Public Works Administration (PWA) (which developed construction jobs in industry); the Civil Works Administration (CWA) and its successor the Works Progress Administration (WPA) (which organized work relief for able-bodied workers repairing roads, improving school buildings, and constructing stadiums, pools, parks, and airports); and the Civilian Conservation Corps (CCC) (which created jobs in the national forests at subsistence wages for 250,000 youth). Meant to be temporary, some of these relief measures remained operative until the early forties when the mobilization for World War II finally ended the Depression. Only when the 1935 Social Security Act made the federal government responsible for public relief and for a new, more comprehensive program called social insurance did the United States begin to develop a non-emergency, permanent welfare state.

The idea of federally sponsored relief and social insurance programs first entered American politics in the late nineteenth century when regular economic depressions and the mechanization of production caused increased joblessness. The failure of private charities, trade unions, company benefit plans, and poor laws to adequately protect workers against the loss of income due to unemployment first sparked interest in the provision of federal aid. From the 1870s to the 1890s, agrarian labor radicals and middle-class reformers who believed that society owed citizens the right to work called upon the federal government to settle idle workers in "unoccupied" Western lands, fund state public works programs, employ the jobless on internal improvement projects, and guarantee employment and a minimum wage. During the Depression of 1893-1894, some in Congress unsuccessfully sought direct federal aid for the unemployed. The failure of the United States to enact a social insurance program at a time when most European nations began to do so contributed to Wilensky and Lebaux's well-known characterization of the U.S. welfare state as a "reluctant" one.[71]

Despite political unrest and the strain of the Depression on the limited resources of public and private agencies, local responsibility for aiding the poor remained firmly established until the 1930s. State governments subsidized institutional care, but federal aid to states or localities remained rare except for disaster relief.[72] President Pierce reinforced the principle of local responsibility for the poor in 1854 when he vetoed the bill authorizing federal land grants to the states to build insane asylums. According to Pierce, if Congress provided for the indigent insane it would have "the same power to provide for the indigent who are not insane, and thus to transfer to the Federal Government the charge of all the poor in all the States." Pierce could "not find any authority in the Constitution for making the Federal Government the great almoner of public charity throughout the United States." He concluded that if Congress assumed this role, "the fountains of charity will be dried up at home, and the several States, instead of bestowing their own means on the social wants of their own people, may themselves, through the strong temptation which appeals to States as to individuals, become humble supplicants for the bounty of the Federal Government, reversing their true relation to this Union."[73] The veto remained firmly in place until the New Deal.

In the early twentieth century, changing conditions elicited interest in a more active role for the state. Rapid industrial and urban growth, the concentration of economic and political power, the continued market crises, the glaring discrepancies between wealth and poverty, the spread of unionization, worker interest in socialism, and populist unrest among farmers seemed to challenge both the economic and political order. To ward off major social change, Progressive Era leaders and social reformers began, as noted in Chapter Six, to seek ways to rationalize and regulate the economy. Some business and government leaders worried that industrial accidents and the lack of medical care for workers would lower productivity.[74] Others maintained that, "capitalism had to provide the wage earner with job security."[75]

In search of alternatives, reformers conducted research and held conferences, while business leaders introduced voluntary benefit programs to better organize and to stabilize the labor market. They also conducted state-level campaigns for workers' compensation, comprehensive health insurance, old age assistance, and mothers' pensions prior to World War I. These legislative activities involved the variously affected industrial, professional, and reform groups. With the exception of Workers' Compensation and Mothers' Pensions, few cash assistance laws were passed. During World War I and the ensuing period of political conservatism, interest in social insurance died down. Instead ideas of scientific management developed by Frederic Winslow Taylor raged, promising, among other things, that social engineering would do away with unemployment.

Meanwhile, in a search for ways to modify the abuses of production without tampering with prevailing class relations, government officials, business leaders, and social reformers all turned to Europe where, by the turn of the century, numerous countries had established social insurance programs. Germany under the rule of Bismarck was the first country to apply the concept of social insurance on a large national scale, but contrary to popular wisdom, Bismarck did not "invent" the idea. Even before it was enacted in Germany, agitation for social insurance already existed in Italy (1868), France (1880), and Norway (1881). Lengthy political struggles between the groups affected by the proposals delayed legislation in these and other nations.[76] Germany acted first because it had the necessary incentive, ideology, and institutional machinery. According to John Graham Brooks, an early twentieth-century economist, Germany not only experienced greater industrial growth than other European countries, but the German conception of the state was less influenced by the laissez-faire doctrine of the classical English economists. Moreover, German workers were among the first to seriously threaten the government in the name of socialism.[77]

Social insurance legislation spread rapidly through Europe before the turn of the century, significantly influenced by the German system. Legislation was passed in Czechoslovakia (1886), Austria (1881), Hungary (1891), Norway (1894), Finland (1895), Great Britain (1897), and Italy, Denmark, and France (1898). By 1915, most European countries had some type of social insurance program.[78] It developed later in the United States than in Europe due to a variety of economic, political, and ideological differences between the continents. The lack of a strong labor or socialist movement in the United States and the absence of an intense demand for social insurances also lessened the political pressure. Organized labor, that is the leadership of the AFL, remained opposed to government insurance until the Depression, although various union locals supported the idea.

The federal government began to investigate European social insurance programs prior to 1900. In 1893, the U.S. Commissioner of Labor, Carrol D. Wright, published a favorable study of the German system by John G. Brooks, entitled *Compulsory Insurance in Germany*.[79] Five years later, in 1898, the Department of Labor published *Workingmen's Insurance* by William F. Willoughby,[80] the first comprehensive, but less sympathetic, study of several European social insurance programs. The 1910 Annual Report of the U. S. Commissioner of Labor included an exhaustive, two-volume survey, *European Insurance and Compensation Plans,* by Isaac Rubinow. Also in 1910, the Russell Sage Foundation published a survey of the European systems, *Workingmen's Insurance in Europe,* conducted by Lee K. Frankel and Miles Dawson.[81] These early studies reflected emerging government and foundation interest in new solutions to prevailing industrial problems. Interestingly, many of the researchers later assumed leadership in the U.S. social insurance movement, although their positions on the issues varied. Business organizations such as the National Association of Manufacturers and the National Civic Federation also became interested in the question of social insurance.[82] Along with government and foundation leaders, those in business regularly attended the International Congress on Social Insurance formed in 1899 by European nations interested in sharing their experiences with their newly inaugurated social insurance systems.[83]

Proposals for a federal social insurance program were slowed by the 1854 Pierce veto and prevailing legal opinion holding such federal action unconstitutional. Nonetheless, some reform groups, business associations, and Congressional committees proposed legislation. Congress received bills for a federal old age insurance program in 1906 and 1911. In 1915, the U.S. Commission on Industrial Relations, created to investigate social and labor unrest, recommended a "Federal system of sickness insurance for all workers engaged in interstate commerce."[84] One year later, in 1916, Meyer London, a socialist New York representative to Congress, introduced a resolution to create a committee to draft a bill for a national unemployment insurance plan.[85] No further interest appeared until 1928, when rising joblessness and relief costs led to Congressional hearings on unemployment insurance. In 1931, after investigating European programs, another Congressional committee gave a qualified endorsement to the principle of compulsory unemployment insurance, but no bills ever came to a vote.

In the midst of the Depression, President Roosevelt formed the Committee on Economic Security (CES) to study the problems of insecurity due to unemployment, old age, and death. The CES proceeded to write legislation that became the 1935 Social Security Act and a quantum leap in U.S. social welfare policy was taken. To the already existing regulatory functions of the federal government, it added state intervention in the economy on behalf of the aged, the unemployed, and poor fatherless children and created a program for maternal and child health care. Health insurance, originally part of the package, was removed to deflect strong opposition from business, the medical profession, and the insurance industry. In 1937, the Supreme Court upheld the constitutionality of the Act which made the federal government's responsibility for social welfare permanent.

The final legislation, the outcome of intense political struggle, incorporated the principles of the more conservative and less redistributional Wisconsin model of social insurance, developed by the economist John Commons and supported by the more influential members of CES and President Roosevelt. The proponents of the Wisconsin model argued that their plan paralleled private insurance and meshed better with the dominant capitalist values of initiative, competition, and thrift because it stressed equity and used a financing mechanism that levied an old age insurance tax on both employers and workers and an Unemployment Insurance tax on employers. A more liberal and redistributional Ohio plan was spearheaded by Abraham Epstein, leader of the American Association for Social Security, and Dr. Isaac Rubinow, a social insurance expert. They saw social insurance as a means to protect workers from loss of income due to old age and unemployment, to foster a redistribution of income, and to promote social justice. The Ohio plan emphasized adequacy over equity and financing through general income taxation rather than joint employer/employee contributions—both of which shifted the program's fiscal burden from the working class to all members of society. The broader financing recommended by the Ohio plan implied that workers, employers, and the government each held some responsibility for the problem and that each would benefit from the solution. It was potentially more redistributional and reflected a strong belief that workers should have access to the program's policy- making process. It maintained that only this model assured adequate financial support.[86]

The original version of the Old Age Insurance program anticipated that the self-supporting system would require the addition of federal revenues in the mid-sixties, at which time the reserve fund, having reached its planned maximum, would be stabilized. These government contributions would eventually equal the annual amount of interest which the system lost in early years due to payments to retired workers who had not been in the system long enough to make full contributions.[87] At the last minute, however, the administration removed all future government grants to the Old Age Insurance program. According to Paul H. Douglas, a social insurance specialist at the time, it seemed that the Roosevelt administration opposed, "any levies upon wealth and large incomes in order to carry a portion of the cost of guarding against social insecurities."[88] Their differences notwithstanding, neither of these mainstream social insurance plans asked capital to pay.

The Wisconsin plan also favored joint federal-state operation of social insurance programs rather than an exclusively national program. The federal-state plan, it was argued, was administratively more practical, would quiet states' rights opposition to the bill, and might assure a favorable response from the Supreme Court. The fear that the Court might limit federal social legislation was not unfounded. The Supreme Court had recently held two federal child labor laws unconstitutional, one based on the taxing powers of the federal government and the other on the right of the federal government to regulate interstate commerce. The Social Security Act touched on the same legal issues.

Those in favor of a national system maintained that it permitted uniform rules and benefits, centralized and standardized administrative records, and meshed better with needs of a mobile labor force. A national system would also be more redistributional. Paul H. Douglas observed that such a plan would permit the federal government "to assess a larger part of the necessary expense upon individuals in the upper income brackets and upon the excess profits of corporations." He added that this would be largely impossible in a federal-state plan because the states lack effective income taxes and raise most of their revenues from regressive sales and local property taxes.[89] In the end, only the Old Age Insurance program became a national plan.

The exclusion of a group of occupations from both the Old Age Insurance and the Unemployment Insurance programs generated little ideological, but some practical, debate. The major exempted occupations included agricultural laborers, private domestic servants, local, state, and federal government employees, and workers in non-profit religious, charitable, scientific, literary, and educational institutions. Proponents justified these exclusions by suggesting that the program was meant to serve only industrial workers engaged in interstate commerce and by pointing to the administrative difficulties involved in collecting taxes from workers in highly decentralized occupations. The exemptions also represented some pragmatic political choices. Legislators excluded farm workers, for example, in order to win the vote of the farming interests, who they feared could defeat the entire bill by joining with industrial employers who opposed the Social Security Act. This, according to Edwin Witte, executive Director of the CES (1934-1935), was a more critical factor in the decision than the administrative difficulties involved in including farm workers. The decision was made easier because at this time agricultural and domestic service jobs were customarily excluded from all types of laws regulating employment conditions. Representatives from church pension funds fought hard to exempt their employees from the Old Age Insurance program to protect their own plans. Other non-profit organizations also argued that they could not afford the tax payments.[90]

The exemptions, especially of domestics, government workers, employees of non-profit organizations, and even farm labor, fell heavily on white women, black women, black men, and other persons of color. As late as 1940, the overwhelming majority of the 2.3 million domestics working in private homes (who represented 4.4 percent of the labor force) were female and black.[91] Large numbers of women also worked for non-profit organizations not covered by the law. Of the 1.8 million teachers, nurses, college faculty, physicians, clergy, social and welfare workers, and others employed by non-profit groups in 1945, 1.1 million or 61 percent were women.[92] Women still predominate among those employed by non-profit institutions today.[93]

In 1940, another 4.2 percent of the labor force or 2.2 million persons worked as farm laborers, many only seasonally employed. Ninety-one percent of farm workers were male and 70 percent were white. But in the South, where 95 percent of the non-white farm workers lived, more women and blacks filled these ranks. In 1940, 53 percent of southern tenant farmers were black, and 14 percent were female.[94] Today 3.9 percent of employed men and 1.1 percent of women work on farms with women accounting for nearly 18 percent of all farm workers.[95]

In the end, the social insurance model proved to be an effective way of integrating the reproduction of the working class with the ups and downs of capitalism without disturbing basic property relations. As a compulsory measure, it forced workers to save for future uncertainties that they might otherwise have ignored. The financing mechanism of the Act also reduced the redistribution of resources from the haves to the have-nots. To the extent that general revenues did not finance the insurance programs (they did finance the means-tested public assistance program), the costs of reproducing the labor force and main-taining the non-working members of the population were absorbed by the working class itself. Not only did the Old Age Insurance payroll tax transfer funds from the currently employed to retired workers, but most economists agree that employers ultimately shift their social insurance tax payments to workers in the form of lower wage increases and to consumers (who also are workers) in the form of higher prices. These financing methods effectively reduced previously higher taxes imposed on the wealthy by the poor laws and early state public assistance programs for the care of the poor.[96]

In sum, the 1935 Social Security Act, a response to the collapse of the economy, the destablization of the family, and the politicization of the working class, promoted economic recovery and security. As the following chapters detail, it also enforced traditional work and family roles. Recognizing that the market economy failed to provide adequate-ly for the economic support of older workers and in response to a variety of social, economic, and political pressures, the federal govern-ment, through the Social Security Act, assisted families in the reproduc-tion of the labor force and the maintenance of non-working members of the population. In so doing, the state institutionalized the pattern of intervening in family life when the conditions of production (this time rising economic insecurity and the market's inability to distribute in-come in ways that accounted for variation in family subsistence needs) threatened to undermine the sphere of reproduction.

In addition to mediating conflicts between the requirements of the spheres of production and reproduction, the programs of the So-cial Security Act mediated the competing demands for women's home and market labor, and enforced the structures of patriarchy which the increased employment by married women, the changes in the structure of family life, and the overall economics of the Depression seemed to undermine. The following chapters on Old Age Insurance, Unemploy-ment Compensation, and Aid to Dependent Children examine the in-corporation of the family ethic into these three programs. Despite many modifications, the ideology of women's roles encoded in the Social Security Act of 1935 remains conceptually unchanged today. For fifty years the gender bias structured into the programs has enforced the economic dependence of women on men, regulated women's labor force participation, assured women's role in maintaining and reproduc-ing the labor force, and, in general upheld patriarchal social arrange-ments.

Notes to Chapter 7

1. James Dickinson, "From Poor Law to Social Insurance: The Periodization of State Intervention in the Reproduction Process," in James Dickinson and Bob Russell (eds.), *Family, Economy, and State: The Social Reproduction Process Under Capitalism* (New York: St. Martin's Press, 1986), pp. 124-138.

2. Jane Ursel, "The State and the Maintenance of Patriarchy: A Case Study of Family, Labour and Welfare Legislation in Canada," in *Ibid.*, pp. 150-191.

3. Irving Bernstein, *The Lean Years: A History of the American Worker, 1920-1933* (Boston: Houghton Mifflin Company, 1960), p. 54.

4. *Ibid.*, p. 54.

5. Paul Sweezy, *Monopoly Capital* (New York: Monthly Review Press, 1969), p. 237.

6. Abraham Epstein, *Insecurity: A Challenge to America* (New York: Harrison Smith and Robert Haas, 1933), p. 47, citing C.W. Cobb and P.H. Douglas, *American Economic Review Supplement* 12 (1) (March 1928).

7. *Ibid.*, p. 192, citing United States Bureau of Labor Statistics, *Industrial Unemployment*, Bulletin No. 310, August 1922, p. 2.

8. Bernstein (1960) *op. cit.*, p. 59.

9. *Ibid.*

10. Wandersee (1981) *op. cit.*, p. 11.

11. For a list of these budget studies, see Epstein (1933) *op. cit.*, pp. 97-99; Winifred D. Wandersee, *Women's Work and Family Values 1920-1940* (Cambridge: Harvard University Press, 1981), pp. 6-26.

12. Wandersee (1981) *op. cit.*, pp. 6-26.

13. Epstein (1933) *op. cit.*, p. 96, citing Basil M. Manly, *Are Wages Too High?* People's Legislative Service, 1922, Washington, D.C.

14. *Ibid.*, p. 12.

15. *Ibid.*, pp. 29, 32.

16. *Ibid.*, p. 59.

17. *Ibid*, p. 62.

18. Robert S. McElvaine, *Down and Out in the Great Depression: Letters from the "Forgotten Man"* (Chapel Hill: University of North Carolina Press, 1983), pp. 42-43.

19. Richard Sterner, *The Negro's Share* (New York: Harper and Brothers Publishers, 1943), p. 87.

20. *Ibid.*, p. 362; Raymond Wolters, *Negroes and the Great Depression* (Westport: Greenwood Publishing Corporation, 1970), p. 292.

21. Wolters (1970) *op. cit.*, p. 92.

22. Jacqueline Jones, *Labor of Love, Labor of Sorrow: Black Women, Work and the Family from Slavery to the Present* (New York: Basic Books, 1985), p. 197.

23. Bernstein (1960) *op. cit.*, pp. 327-333.

24. *Ibid.*

25. Meridel Le Sueur, "Women Are Hungry," in *Ripening: Selected Work, 1927-1980*, in Elaine Hedges (ed.) (Old Westbury, New York: The Feminist Press, 1982), p. 144.

26. Jones (1985) *op. cit.*, p. 225.

27. McElvaine (1983) *op. cit.*, pp. 85-86.

28. Susan Ware, *Holding Their Own: American Women in the 1930s* (Boston: Twayne Publishers, 1982), p. 7; President's Research Committee on Social Trends, *Recent Social Trends In the United States*, Vol. I, (New York: McGraw-Hill Book Company, 1933), p. 40; Susan M. Hartman, *The Home Front and Beyond: American Woman in the 1940s* (Boston: Twayne Publishers, 1982), p. 17.

29. Ware (1982) *op. cit.*, pp. 6-7, 28; President's Research Committee on Social Trends, Vol. I (1933) *op. cit.*, p. 680.

30. President's Research Committee in Social Trends, Vol. I (1933) *op. cit.* p. 36.

31. *Ibid.*, p. 68.

32. Wandersee (1981) *op. cit.*, p. 68; President's Research Committee on Social Trends, Vol. I (1933) *op. cit.*, p. 715.

33. Lynn Y. Weiner, *From Working Girl To Working Mother: The Female Labor Force in the United States, 1820-1980* (Chapel Hill: The University of North Carolina Press, 1985), p. 89.

34. *Ibid.*, p. 89; Philip S. Foner and Ronald L. Lewis, *The Black Worker: A Documentary History from Colonial Times to the Present, Vol. VI: The Era of Post-War Prosperity and the Great Depression, 1920-1936* (Philadelphia: Temple University Press, 1981), p. 104.

35. Wandersee (1981) *op. cit.*, pp. 15-22; Julie A. Matthaie, *An Economic History of Women in America* (New York: Schocken Books, 1982), pp. 235-245, 252-253.

36. Wandersee (1981) *op. cit.*, p. 68.

37. Sterner (1943) *op. cit.*, p. 23.

38. Jones (1985) *op. cit.*, p. 208.

39. Sterner (1943) *op. cit.*, p. 23.

40. Jones (1985) *op. cit.*, p. 200.

41. *Ibid.*, p. 208.

42. William Henry Chafe, *The American Woman: Her Changing Social, Economic and Political Roles, 1920-1970* (London: Oxford University Press, 1972), pp. 55-56; Weiner (1985) *op. cit.*, pp. 5-9.

43. Samuel A. Stouffer and Paul F. Lazersfeld, *Research Memorandum on the Family in the Depression* (New York: Social Science Research Council, 1937), pp. 28-35.

44. Alice Kessler-Harris, *Out To Work: A History of Wage-Earning Women in the United States* (Oxford: Oxford University Press, 1982), pp. 250-272, 258-261; Ruth Milkman, "Women's Work and Economic Crisis: Some Lessons of the Great Depression," *The Review of Radical Political Economics*, 8 (1) (Spring 1976) pp. 73-98.

45. Wolters (1970) *op. cit.*, pp. 21-56; Jones (1985) *op. cit.*, pp. 200-202.

46. Wandersee (1981) *op. cit.*, p. 14.

47. The following discussion of attitudes towards women workers in the Depression draws on: Chafe (1972) *op. cit.*, pp. 107-109; Kessler-Harris (1982) op.,cit., p. 257; Jane Humphries, "Women: Scapegoats and Safety Valves in the Great Depression," *The Review of Radical Political Economics*, 8 (1) (Spring 1976), p. 107.

48. Ware (1982) *op. cit.*, pp. 27-28.

49. Kessler-Harris (1982) *op. cit.*, p. 255, citing Marion Elderton, "Unemployment Consequences on the Home," *Annals of the American Academy of Social and Political Science*, 154 (March 1931), p. 62.

50. Chafe (1972) *op. cit.*, p. 107.

51. Kessler-Harris (1982) *op. cit.*, p. 255, citing Paul Douglas, "Some Recent Social Changes and their Effect Upon Family Life," *Journal of Home Economics*, 25 (May 1933), pp. 368-369.

52. Chafe (1972) *op. cit.*, p. 107.

53. Stouffer and Lazersfeld (1937) *op. cit.*, pp. 55-56; Ware (1982) *op. cit.*, p. 28.

54. Stouffer and Lazersfeld (1937) *op. cit.*, pp. 55-56.

55. Ware (1982) *op. cit.*, p. 28.

56. Kessler-Harris (1982) *op. cit.*, p. 256, citing National Women's Trade Union League, News Release, December 21, 1931, in WTUL file box 4, Women's Bureau\National Archives.

57. William F. Ogburn, "The Family and Its Functions," in President's Research Committee on Social Trends, Vol. I (1933) *op. cit.*, pp. 661-708.

58. Bernstein (1960) *op. cit.*, pp. 327-333.

59. Stouffer and Lazarfeld (1937) *op. cit.*, p. 57.

60. Wandersee (1981) *op. cit.*, p. 108, citing Mirra Komarovsky, *The Unemployed Man and His Family: The Effect of Unemployment on the Status of the Man in Fifty-Nine Families* (New York: Dryden Press, 1940).

61. *Ibid.*, p. 109, citing John French and Berton Raven, "The Bases of Social Power," in Darian Cartwright and Alvin Zander, (eds.) *Group Dynamics* (New York: Harper & Row, 1968).

62. Stouffer and Lazerfeld (1937) *op. cit.*, p. 57.

63. Kessler-Harris (1982) *op. cit.*, p. 254.

64. Herbert G. Gutman, "Persistent Myths About the Afro-American Family," in Michael Gordon, (ed.), *The American Family in Social-Historical Perspective* (New York: St. Martin's Press, 1983), pp. 459-481.

65. Kessler-Harris (1982) *op. cit.*, pp. 252-253; Wandersee (1981) *op. cit.*, pp. 56-58.

66. Frances F. Piven and Richard Cloward, *Regulating The Poor: The Functions of Public Welfare* (New York: Pantheon Books, 1971), p. 7.

67. David Milton, *The Politics of U.S. Labor From the Great Depression to the New Deal* (New York: Monthly Review Press, 1982), p. 26; William E. Leuchtenburg, *Franklin D. Roosevelt and the New Deal, 1932-1940* (New York: Harper & Row, 1963), pp. 188-189.

68. John G. Rayback, *A History of American Labor* (New York: Free Press, 1966), p. 355.

69. Kessler-Harris (1982) *op. cit.*, p. 268; William Chafe (1972) *op. cit.*, p. 86.

70. Kessler-Harris (1982) *op. cit.*, pp. 266-269; Chafe (1972) *op. cit.*, pp. 64-85; Sharon Hartman Strom, "We're No Kitty Foyles: Organizing Office Workers For the Congress of Industrial Organizations," in Ruth Milkman (ed.) *Women, Work and Protest* (Boston: Routledge & Kegan Paul, 1985), pp. 212-213.

71. Harold L. Wilensky and Charles N. Lebeaux, *Industrial Society and Social Welfare* (New York: The Free Press, 1965), pp. v-lii.

72. "Federal Relief Legislation, 1803-1931," U.S. Senate, Hearings held before a Subcommittee of the Committee On Manufacturers, 72 Congress, 2nd. sess, February 2 and 3, 1931, reprinted in Edith Abbott, *Public Assistance*, Volume I, (Chicago: The University of Chicago Press, 1941), pp. 691-699.

73. June Axinn and Herman Levin, *Social Welfare: A History of the America Response to Need* (New York: Harper & Row, 1975), pp. 70-74.

74. Mimi Abramovitz, *Business and Social Reform: Workers' Compensation and Health Insurance During the Progressive Era,* unpublished Doctoral Dissertation, Columbia University School of Social Work, New York, 1981.

75. Roy Lubove, *The Struggle for Social Security 1900-1935* (Cambridge: Harvard University Press, 1968), p. 163.

76. Isaac Rubinow, *Social Insurance* (New York: Henry Holt, 1913), p. 20.

77. Charles R. Henderson, *Industrial Insurance in the United States* (Chicago: University of Chicago Press, 1909), pp. 4-5.

78. Rubinow (1913) *op. cit.*, p. 20.

79. John Graham Brooks, *Compulsory Insurance in Germany,* Fourth Special Report of the U.S. Commissioner of Labor (Washington, D.C.: 1893).

80. William F. Willoughby, *Workingman's Insurance* (New York: Crowell, 1898).

81. Lee K. Frankel and Miles M. Dawson, *Workingmen's Insurance in Europe* (New York: Charities Publications Committee, 1910).

82. For a discussion of the role of business in social welfare reform, see Abramovitz (1981) *op. cit.*

83. William F. Willoughby, "The Problem of Social Insurance: An Analysis," *American Labor Legislation Review*, 3 (June 1913), pp. 153-161.

84. Commission on Industrial Relations, *Final Report and Testimony* (Vol. I), Sen. Doc. No. 415, 64th Congress, 1st sess. 1916, p. 124.

85. U.S. Congress, House Committee on Labor, *Hearings on H.R. Res. 159,* 64th. Cong. 2nd sess., April 6 and 11, 1916.

86. Jerry R. Cates *Insuring Inequality: Administrative Leadership in Social Security, 1935-54* (Ann Arbor: University of Michigan Press, 1983), pp. 22-25; Arthur Altmeyer, *The Formative Years of the Social Security Act* (Madison: The University of Wisconsin Press, 1968), p. 11; Lubove (1968) *op. cit.*, pp. 33, 138-143.

87. Paul H. Douglas, *Social Security in the United States* (New York: Whittlesey House, 1939), pp. 56-68.

88. *Ibid.,* p. 68.

89. *Ibid.,* pp. 30-31.

90. Edwin E. Witte, *The Development of the Social Security Act* (Madison: The University of Wisconsin Press, 1963), pp. 152-156.

91. Paul H. Douglas, *Standards of Unemployment Insurance* (Chicago: The University of Chicago Press, 1933), pp. 424-428.

92. *Ibid.,* p. 62, T. 105.

93. *Ibid.,* pp. 55-56, T. II-3.

94. U.S. Congress, House of Representatives, *Issues in Social Security: A Report to the Committee on Ways and Means* (Washington, D.C.: Government Printing Office, 1946), p. 625, T. 101.

95. U.S. Bureau of Labor, Women's Bureau, *Time of Change: 1983 Handbook on Women Workers* (Washington D.C.: Government Printing Office, 1983), pp. 55-56, T. II-3.

96. Dickinson (1986) *op. cit.,* pp. 136-137.

8

Old Age Insurance

Growing old in America has never been easy. The graying of America began in the early twentieth century. With more senior citizens living longer but working less, prolonged retirement suddenly became a new stage in life, requiring additional supports, just when the reverence for age ebbed and the social roles of older people began to shrink. With financial self-sufficiency increasingly difficult for all but the most affluent, the next generation was confronted with the worries and burdens of caring for their parents. The problem only intensified when the Depression pushed more elderly out of the labor force and left many young families jobless and homeless. Given the economic collapse, widespread social unrest, and a working class less able to sustain ordinary family life, political pressures for government pensions for the aged mounted. The state eventually stepped in, and the resulting new programs for the aged had enormous implications for women both as workers and caretakers in the home.

The 1935 Social Security Act included two types of economic assistance for adults age sixty-five or older: Old Age Insurance (OAI), a social insurance program for retired workers regardless of need, and Old Age Assistance (OAA), a public assistance program for the elderly poor. These programs, which helped to maintain the senior segment of the non-working population, indirectly enabled members of the younger generation to devote more resources to their immediate families, the current and future labor force. Few thought of "Social Security"—the popular name for the Old Age Insurance—as a family program because the 1935 Act covered retired workers but not their dependents or survivors. But the architects of the Act, the Committee

241

on Economic Security (CES), clearly had families in mind. The 1935 CES Report to the President stated,

> Old age pensions are in a real sense measures in behalf of children. They shift the retroactive burdens to shoulders which can bear them with less human cost, and young parents thus released can put at the disposal of the new member of society those family resources he [sic] must be permitted to enjoy if he is to become a strong person, unburdensome to the State.[1]

The 1939 Amendments to the Social Security Act extended coverage to include a retired or deceased workers' dependents, converting the program into a major family policy. Ellen Woodward, one of the women leaders in Roosevelt's New Deal, later observed that the Social Security Act grew "out of the fight in which so many women have been engaged in for the past thirty years—the fight to protect and promote the well-being of the individual and his [sic] family."[2]

The new family policy affected women in many ways. A product of its times, the Old Age Insurance title of the Social Security Act incorporated the family ethic, regulated women's domestic and market labor, and encouraged the economic dependence of women on men. In general, it helped to enforce patriarchal arrangements whose stability had been undercut by the economics of the Depression, the entry of more women into the labor force and, in the long-run, by the economic plight of working-class families who could not earn or save enough for old age.

Maintaining the Aged Population

The social and economic marginalization of the aged which had begun prior to the Depression forced increased attention to their problems in the late twenties and early thirties. Demographic changes, increased financial insecurity, and the economic stress of caring for parents placed on the next generation all created political pressures for reforms on behalf of the aged.

Demographic Pressures

Demographics changes turned caring for the aged from a familial to a social problem. In each decade between 1880 and 1930, the growth rate of the population aged sixty-five and older exceeded that of the population as a whole. In 1930 the aged were 5.4 percent of the total, having increased at twice the rate of the overall population between 1920 and 1930.[3] The greatest growth was among foreign-born whites, followed by native-born whites and blacks.[4] Combined with a declining birth rate, increased longevity, and immigration patterns, forecasters accurately predicted that the population sixty-five and older would continue its fast growth well into the twentieth century.[5] Meanwhile, the number of years workers could expect to spend in retirement doubled from one and one-half years to three, while their economic resources declined or disappeared. The proportion of those who were gainfully employed dropped to 33.2 percent by 1930.[6] That year only 54 percent of males over sixty-five and 8 percent of the females were in the labor force.[7]

Economic Pressures

While both the aged population and the number of retired workers expanded, economic changes—especially the shift from dependence on the land to wage labor—conspired to undermine their means of support.[8] By the late twenties, the vicissitudes of the market economy had begun to eject the older worker. Economic fluctuations, the mechanization and routinization of production, and the greater premium placed on speed and dexterity rather than experience and judgement caused employers to favor younger workers as more productive. During the Depression, even more employers refused to hire or retain women and men over forty-five. Unemployed, older workers had more difficulty than younger workers becoming re-employed and their unemployment lasted for a longer time.[9]

Those earning low wages and acquiring little savings or property had difficulty protecting themselves against the loss of income in old age. In New York (1929) and in Connecticut (1932), for example, nearly 50 percent of the aged population did not earn even $25 a month, less than the $300 per year poverty line. Thirty-three percent of Connecticut's aged population had no income at all.[10]

Most of the aged lacked the economic cushion offered by a savings account, an insurance policy, or a pension. The number of saving accounts grew in this period, but the size of the average account fell 29 percent between 1913 and 1928. After 1929, business and bank failures all but eliminated the small accumulations of many families. At the end of the nineteenth century, workers began to purchase life insurance from fraternal societies, industrial insurance companies, or group plans, and from 1919 to 1929, the relatively new insurance industry sold $100 billion of insurance (1929 dollars) with 123 million policies in force.[11] But the low face value of the policies barely covered the costs of a funeral. Many policies never matured due to lapsed payments, surrenders, or expirations.[12] The 440 private pension plans in effect in 1929 offered some financial support to those who met their terms. However, the plans covered less than 15 percent of all wage earners, many of whom never vested due to requirements of twenty to thirty years of uninterrupted service. Not more than 140,000 retired workers, mostly in large industries, qualified for pensions in 1932. By 1933, the average per-capita payment had declined to $58 a month, and less than half of the plans guaranteed any payment at all. Pensions frequently rested on shaky financial grounds and many folded during the Depression. About 10 percent of those operating in 1929 were discontinued, closed to new employees, or suspended by 1932.[13]

Children and relatives provided the chief support to the elderly. A 1925 Massachusetts investigation estimated that children supported 74 percent of the dependent aged, while relatives provided for another 14 percent. In 1929, the New York State Commission on Old Age Security found that among the state's non-self-supporting population, 49.4 percent were over sixty-five and 55.6 percent of those over seventy depended on relatives or friends. A 1934 study by the District of Columbia reported that relatives supported 30 percent of the aged white population and 50 percent of the aged black population.[14] Married couples and people living with others fared somewhat better than single individuals,[15] but the economic dependency of the aged intensified family insecurity, reduced its purchasing power, and otherwise limited its reproductive capacities. The CES concluded that the Depression made family support of the aged increasingly difficult and in many cases impossible.[16]

The government provided only minimally for the aged poor prior to the Depression. The poorhouse remained a refuge for many of the indigent aged until well into the twentieth century. The 1923 U.S. Census of Institutions reported nearly 42,000 or 54 percent of the nation's almshouse inmates were sixty-five and older, representing 1 percent of the total aged population. Between 1929 and 1933, in some urban areas, the aged poorhouse population increased nearly 75 percent. The numbers found in other institutions for the ill and infirm also grew.[17] Other aged persons without means lived in the forerunner of today's nursing home, private homes for the care of the aged poor run by religious, fraternal, and ethnic groups, or trade unions.[18]

Only a few states legislated Old Age Assistance (OAA) programs prior to the thirties. In 1928, after six years of agitation, just six states and one territory aided the elderly poor. Not more than 1,000 persons received old age grants in these six states combined. Since permissive state legislation did not require counties to implement a program, in many places they remained inoperative or defective.[19] By 1934, programs existed in twenty-eight states and two territories, but monthly grants were low, ranging from 69 cents in North Dakota to $26.08 in Massachusetts. The average pension nationwide was $14.68.

OAA rules, in addition, disqualified many of the needy aged, including applicants with children or relatives "able" to support them, with small amounts of property and income, without U.S. citizenship, and without a specified length of residence in the state (up to fifteen years in some cases). States also refused to aid the "undeserving aged"— those who had deserted their husbands or wives, failed to support their families, had been convicted of a crime, had been a tramp or a beggar, or had not worked to their capacity as well as inmates of jails, prisons, infirmaries, and insane asylums.[20] In 1932, only 100,000 persons received OAA, a little over half of them living in New York state, many fewer in the South where large numbers of blacks lived. Two years later, as the Depression deepened, 236,205 persons over sixty-five in the United States or 9.6 percent of those eligible that year received an old age benefit, far below the number in need and below the number assisted in Europe, Canada, and Australia.[21]

An outpouring of letters to the White House poignantly told of the ineffectiveness of prevailing public and private relief programs. One middle-aged woman from Ohio wrote to Eleanor Roosevelt, "...Whether my mother ever gets anything or not, I hope all the other old people that is entitled to it gets it soon, because there is nothing sadder than old people who have struggled hard all their lives to give the family a start in life, then to be forgotten when they them self need it most."[22] A Georgia woman asked the President for help because, "Mr. President my father and mother's home will be taken away from them the first of January if I can't get up $50.00. My father is 83 years of age and my mother is 64 years of age, and I am all the dependents they have. I am a poor girl my salary is $3.00 a week and I have to feed myself out of that. I just can't raise it—I have no way on my salary and I can't borrow any on it...can you help me some—please oh please Mr. President don' t say no..." A young man from Michigan asked for a small pension for his father "so we would not starve. My father is seventy-six [too] old to work at the Antriim Co. furnace. I cant go away

and leave him alone to look for work and to stay here in such poverty I am so disturbed trying to know what to do."[23]

The elderly themselves also wrote to Washington for help. In a
letter to Eleanor Roosevelt asking for her support of more generous
state pensions for the aged, a seventy-two year old North Dakota
women said, "Its hard to be old and not have anything." Another elderly woman from Georgia wrote asking how "to put in for a pension." "I
am a Widow Lady no one to depend on I am losing my home I will
have no where to stay and not able at the present time to do any work
on account of my health. I tried to get my home in the Home loan but
they failed to get it in because I didn't have anyone to go my security."[24]

Political Pressures

The weaknesses of the economy paved the way for the development of a government-provided social wage to retired workers. The
failure of the economy to provide for the expanding aged population,
the consequent financial pressures on family life, combined with political agitation, slowly produced a governmental response. With unemployed workers over forty-five demanding jobs, retired workers
calling for pensions, and working-class children demanding help with
the support of their parents, social insurance was placed on the legislative agenda. State intervention became necessary to maintain the
elderly portion of the non-working population. By absorbing some of
these costs, the resulting policies enhanced the capacity of younger
families to maintain themselves and reproduce the labor force.

The CES hoped that old age pensions would support retired
workers, relieve younger working-class families, and secure the loyalty of both at a time of massive social unrest. The CES suggested that
the less tangible effects resulting from the gradual extension of social
insurance to many workers "would have considerable influence." It
predicted that the confidence and sense of security of a mature group
of citizens could not but affect the attitudes of younger groups."[25] The
availability of retirement income was expected to accelerate the displacement of superannuated workers from the labor market, increase
overall purchasing power and consumption, and let younger workers
know that the government would reward their own years of hard work
with a pension.

The problem of poverty in old age had been under investigation
prior to the Depression. In the early twenties, New York, Massachusetts,
and other states formed commissions to study the issue, as did major

business organizations such as the National Civic Federation and reform groups including the American Association for Old Age Security (later the American Association for Social Security) led by Abraham Epstein, and the American Association for Labor Legislation (AALL) headed by John Andrews. The earliest old age pension bills recommended a federal system. The first such bill, limited to military personnel (to avoid being declared unconstitutional), was submitted in 1906. Subsequent federal proposals attracted public attention, but little Congressional action. Pressure group campaigns later in the decade focused on state legislatures, rather than Congress. Alaska established one of the first pension plans in 1915. After the 1929 stock market crash, more states passed mandatory Old Age Assistance laws. By 1934, over half of the states had some type of program on the books.

The strong grassroots campaign for old age pensions launched by the Fraternal Order of Eagles (FOE) in the early twenties was largely responsible for the few state pension laws enacted during this period. Subsequently the FOE joined other groups calling for a national old age insurance program. More radical plans, however, also made a stir. The "Share Our Wealth" plan put forward by Senator Huey Long (D-LA) proposed to "soak the rich" (through heavy taxes on income, property, and inheritance) in order to establish a federally guaranteed annual income of $5,000. A poll taken by the Democratic National Committee in 1936 indicated that Long might capture 10 percent of the nation's Democratic vote, potentially endangering Roosevelt's reelection that year.[26]

Better known and less radical were the Townsendites, named for the movement's leader, Dr. Francis E. Townsend.[27] Begun in 1934 in California, the Townsend movement claimed to have mobilized the nation's elderly into a system of up to 7,000 local clubs with more than two million "members." They demanded a universal flat rate pension of $200 a month for all citizens sixty or older contingent upon withdrawal from the labor market and spending the entire check within one month. The plan would be financed by a federal sales tax, although subsequent versions of the plan added other sources of revenue. Despite the efforts of more moderate social insurance advocates to discredit the Townsend Plan as "unrealistic" (which in many ways it was), the Townsend movement crystallized tremendous popular sentiment in favor of old age security. If it evoked ridicule among social welfare experts, the movement popularized the idea of government-sponsored pensions and weakened conservative opposition to the more moderate proposals contained in the Social Security Act. The mounting public demand for old age insurance, a Townsendite petition bearing twenty-five million signatures, and the election of Townsend supporters to Congress caused President Roosevelt to tell the CES, "We have to have it...The Congress can't stand the pressure of the Townsend Plan unless we have a real old age insurance system nor can I face the country without having devised at this time... a solid plan which will give some assurance to old people of systematic assistance upon retirement."[28] The Townsendite movement, which peaked between 1935 and 1941, remained a significant oppositional threat to the new social insurance system for many years.

Social welfare experts involved in constructing the Social Security Act debated its provisions and struggled for leadership of the movement. The more influential CES members and President Roosevelt supported the conservative Wisconsin model of old age insurance which stressed equity, incentives, a contributory payroll tax paid by both employers and workers, and otherwise emphasized values supportive of the economic *status quo* (see Chapter Seven). The more liberal Ohio plan emphasized adequacy, redistribution, and social justice, and financing through progressive general income taxation.[29] In the end, the more conservative Wisconsin model prevailed. According to one sponsor of the Social Security Act, "Only to a very minor degree does it modify the distribution of wealth and it does not alter at all the fundamentals of our capitalistic and individualistic economy. Nor does it relieve the individual of primary responsibility for his [sic] own support and that of his dependents."[30]

The 1935 Social Security Act: Old Age Insurance for Retired Workers

The original version of the Old Age Insurance program reflected the ideological debate between the Wisconsin and the Ohio models, described above, a political battle in Congress, and concerns about the potential constitutionality of the Act.[31] The only exclusively federal measure in the Social Security Act—the Old Age Insurance program—protected workers sixty-five and over against the loss of income due to retirement. Beginning in 1942, retired workers would receive monthly cash benefits based on their wages and prior employment record. To qualify, a worker had to be sixty-five or older in 1942, employed in a covered occupation at least some day in each year between 1936 and

1941 and before age sixty-five, and earning not less than $2,000 in total wages during this period.

Strict eligibility rules and limited coverage disqualified many people from the program so that less than 50 percent of all workers, mostly those employed by large firms in industrial occupations, became eligible for a retirement pension.[32] White women and persons of color of both genders predominated among the excluded workers.

As described in Chapter Seven, the excluded were agricultural workers, domestic workers in private homes, casual laborers, government workers, those employed by non-profit religious, charitable, scientific, literary, educational organizations, and institutions for the prevention of cruelty to children or animals as well as employers covered by the Railroad Retirement Act. Covered workers who moved between covered and uncovered work also lost their insurance.

The benefits tied to wages ranged from a monthly minimum of $10 to a maximum of $85 per worker with no increments for additional family members other than a lump sum death benefit for the survivors of a deceased worker. The majority of industrial workers earned less than $125 a month, or $1,500 a year, making the top monthly benefit for many less than $20.[33] Persons over sixty-five who did not retire lost their full-monthly benefit payment for every month of employment. The benefit formula, weighted toward lower paid workers and those contributing only a few years did favor poorer workers. Although higher paid workers always received larger pensions, the proportion of wages covered was greater for those at the bottom.

This advantage for women and other low-paid workers partially compensated for the disadvantages they faced in the labor market. But other features undercut the gain. Because benefits were linked to wages, the pensions of low-paid workers were small. The program's benefit ceiling exerted a downward pressure on the $10 minimum benefit which hurt the lowest-paid workers and limited benefits to the poorly paid and those with large families, despite their greater need. Tying benefits to wages and imposing a cap on payments enforced the work ethic by leaving the family of a retired or deceased worker less well-off after the worker retired or died than while the worker was employed.

The pension program was financed by a flat payroll tax, shared equally by employees and employers. The payroll tax applied only to earnings up to a maximum amount per year ($3,000 in 1937), but the initial tax of 1 percent rose regularly thereafter. Tax collections to begin in 1937 would accumulate in a reserve fund until 1942 when the pension payments started. The single tax rate combined with the ceiling on taxable wages made the payroll tax regressive, taking proportionate-ly more dollars from the wages of lower paid than higher paid workers. The rapid accumulation of funds in the first years of the program even-tually became the basis for successful pressure from conservatives who wanted to replace the self-support financing model, in which past taxes paid for current retirees, with a pay-as you-go system, in which current taxes funded the benefits of current recipients.

The 1935 Old Age Insurance program provided little to women workers, despite their rising labor force participation. Women predominated among the occupations excluded from the Act. Of the 10.5 million women in the labor force in 1930, the largest number (29.6 percent) worked in domestic and personnel service. The rest were found in clerical jobs (18.5 percent), manufacturing (17.5 percent), professional service (14.2 percent), trade (9.0 percent), agriculture (8.5 percent), transportation and communication (2.6 percent), and public service (0.2 percent).[34] Domestic service, professional service, public service, and agricultural work accounted for over 50 percent of the female labor force, yet the Act excluded housework, private servants, teachers, nurses in hospitals, public welfare workers, and government secretaries, as well as workers in educational, religious, and charitable organizations, and agricultural laborers.

These occupational exclusions fell especially hard on black women (and men) who were overrepresented in domestic service and agricultural labor. In 1930, 40.7 percent of all black male workers were agricultural laborers, while 62.6 percent of all black women worked in private domestic or personal service. In 1937, the 2.2 million blacks who worked in jobs covered by the program represented only 6.9 per-cent of all covered workers. Eight percent of black males and 4.2 per-cent of black females worked in covered jobs. That year the system served only 377,000 black women.[35]

Women in covered occupations did not fare that well either. Policy makers and politicians considered white male wage levels and employment patterns as the norm, leaving many women workers unin-sured. Women became ineligible for a pension because they regularly had to move in and out of the labor force in response to marriage and family responsibilities. Their life circumstances also caused them to move from covered to uncovered occupations more frequently then men. Likewise, wage-based rules resulted in low benefits for women. Many earned less than $2,000 a year, qualifying them only for the $10 minimum monthly pension. Those earning up to $3,000 received $15.[36] Finally, the regressive tax structure meant that women, like other low-paid workers, paid a disproportionate share of their wages in Social Security taxes but received smaller payments from the program.

The 1935 Act provided no coverage to unpaid female homemakers, except for a small lump sum benefit paid to survivors of an insured worker. Non-working wives of retired or deceased workers received no benefits, although 75 percent of all adult women, 50 percent of single women, 65 percent of divorced and widowed women, and 88 percent of married women were not in the paid labor force at this time.[37]

An historic milestone in terms of the role of the state, the Old Age Insurance program did not satisfy everyone. From the start, the program's limitations elicited criticism from the Left and the Right, and almost immediately activated pressure for reform. The dissatisfaction of organized labor, whose members would both pay and benefit from the program, created a potential political problem early on. The AFL's belief in voluntarism and its long history of contending with government-supported anti-union drives left it with little interest in the program until the early 1940s when labor became an ardent supporter of the Social Security Act. The more militant Congress of Industrial Organizations (CIO), an early supporter of social insurance, however, favored its more progressive versions.

From the Right, Republicans opposed the basic social insurance concept and called for replacing the Old Age Insurance program with an expanded version of Old Age Assistance (OAA), the public assistance title of the Social Security Act directed to the aged poor. OAA was less popular with social insurance advocates who wanted social insurance rather than public assistance to be the centerpiece of the Act. The public assistance program was means tested, financed by general revenues, and administered jointly by the federal government and the states, while the more universal social insurance program was federally administered, financed by contributory payroll taxes, and available to workers "as a right," regardless of need. Republican preferences for OAA fueled the fears of social insurance advocates that the delayed (1942) implementation of the Old Age Insurance program would spur the growing popularity of OAA. OAA was operational in forty-two states by 1936, and its benefits already exceeded those that the insurance program would begin to pay in 1942, after five additional years of worker contributions. A Social Security Board official commented that if pressure to improve the OAA program continued, "it would seem ...to be practically impossible to put into effect the contributory [insurance] plan...If...in a five year period, the means test is lessened and the right of the individual is established for the non-contributory scheme, then the distinction between the two systems is eliminated."[38] The Board also feared that the liberalization of the state OAA programs "might have fanned the flames of the Townsend movement" which exerted significant influence in the 1936 presidential and 1938 Congressional elections. "The final result," stated another member of the Social Security Board several years later, "might very well have been to scrap the Old Age Insurance system before it ever went into operation."[39]

Throughout this period, the architects of the Social Security Act also worried about the growth of public support for more redistributional alternatives to the program, such as the Townsend plan. In December 1935, Edwin Witte, the executive director of the CES wrote,

> There is no doubt that this movement has made tremendous headway. The battle against the Townsend plan has been lost, I think, in pretty nearly every state west of Mississippi and the entire Middle Western area is likewise badly infected. At this time, the Republican Party organization is at least flirting with the Townsendites and I think it is mighty significant that not one of the major business organizations of the country has attacked the plan.[40]

In 1938, speculating about the next election, Witte wrote to Abraham Epstein, a major leader in the social insurance movement, that "the real issue is between the Social Security Act and the Townsend Plan."[41] These concerns were not unfounded. A 1939 Gallop poll indicated that 95 percent of the persons surveyed knew of the Townsend plan, 40 percent favored it, and 49 percent knew the exact amount of the proposed transfer. In contrast the poll uncovered a general lack of understanding of the Social Security program.[42] From the perspective of social insurance advocates, the concept of old age insurance was at a critical "juncture" requiring a "vigorous campaign" to avoid a "compromise between 'Townsendism' and 'national insurance.'" In 1939, four years after Congress passed the Act and two years after the Supreme Court upheld its constitutionality, the Old Age Insurance program underwent massive reform.

The 1939 Amendments: Family Policy and the Family Ethic

The 1939 amendments to the Social Security Act significantly reshaped the Old Age Insurance program. Freed from earlier worries about the constitutionality of the Act, faced with an unexpectedly large reserve fund, and seeking to make the program more attractive to workers, Congress revised it.[43] Among other changes, the 1939 Social Security Amendments expanded the Old Age Insurance program from one that provided a retirement annuity to individual workers to one that also protected family members. Arthur J. Altmeyer, member and chair of the Social Security Board (1935-1946), explained, "The essential purpose underlying the amendments to the old-age insurance program is clearly the desire to promote the security and stability of the American family." He added, "This system, formerly a plan to provide old-age annuities for individual wage earners, has become a broad system of family insurance, which protects not only the wage earner but his wife and children, and if they are dependent on him, his aged parents."[44]

The 1939 amendments liberalized the program. They made it easier for older workers to become insured, advanced the first pension payment from 1942 to 1940, increased benefit amounts by basing them on average rather than total wages, introduced pay-as-you-go financing, and provided supplementary grants to the members of a retired or deceased worker's family. The family policy that resulted from the latter change offered greater economic security to America's families. By moving from individual to family protection, the amendments also institutionalized state subsidization of families to carry out their reproductive and maintenance tasks, underpinned the state's role in mediating the conflict between women's home and market work, and reaffirmed the foundations of public patriarchy.

The 1939 amendments brought many more women into the Social Security system, but largely as the economic dependents of male workers. The Social Security Advisory Council had recommended that "the enhancement of the early old age benefits under the system, should be partly attained by paying...a married annuitant a supplementary allowance on behalf of the aged wife. The inadequacy of the benefits payable during the early years of the old age insurance program, it explained, "is more marked where the benefits must support not only the annuitant himself, but also his wife." The Council also recommended benefits for aged widows and widows caring for the children of deceased insured workers. The Council believed that supplementary benefits to wives and widows, at a time when all benefits were low, could meet "the greatest social need with a minimum increase of costs." Enhancing benefits by providing dependents a proportion of the wage earner's grant would also keep benefits tied to wage differentials set in the market.[45]

Reflecting this thinking, the amendments raised benefits to retirees by paying supplemental grants to their wives, widows, children, and, in some cases, parents. At the same time, these amendments further inscribed the ideology of women's roles—particularly the family ethic—into the Social Security Act. Intentionally or not, the 1939 provisions presumed and supported the male breadwinner/female homemaker family model, encouraged women to choose traditional family life over work or alternative family forms, affirmed women's economic dependence on men, and otherwise enforced patriarchal arrangements that perpetuated the subordination of women.

More specifically, the rules and regulations of the 1939 amendments treated women differentially according to their marital and work statuses, rewarding women whose lives conformed to the terms of the family ethic and punishing those who did not, could not, or chose not to do so. As a result they (1) penalized working women, (2) rewarded full-time homemakers, (3) punished husbandless women, and (4) neglected women once their reproductive and caretaking responsibilities declined. Through numerous subsequent amendments, and with some exceptions, the current provisions of the Old Age Insurance program continue to reflect and reinforce the family ethic in similar ways.

Work By Women Discouraged

The 1939 amendments continued to provide retirement benefits to women workers but did not encourage or reward female employment any more than in the 1935 Act. Women workers remained disadvantaged by rules that geared benefits to wages, reflected male work patterns, and ignored the impact of occupational segregation, sex discrimination, and family responsibilities on the labor force participation of women. Women still predominated in the occupations excluded from the Act. They continued to receive low benefits due to their low wages and fewer years on the job; and, as ever, they paid disproportionately high taxes relative to better-off workers and to the retirement benefits they eventually received.

The presumption of long and steady employment disadvantaged women. The benefit formula, for example, averaged earnings over the period a worker could reasonably be expected to have worked in covered employment. This favored workers with long work histories. Like the 1935 Act, it penalized women whose work lives were more likely to be interrupted by moves in and out of the labor force in response to homemaking and child care needs and who were more likely to move in and out of covered employment.

Because the benefit formula softened the impact of years of no or low-paid work, it was a plus for women given their low wage rates and frequent absence from the labor market. But the formula offered less protection to women than it seems. It increased benefit levels to poorly paid workers by dropping five years of no or lowest earnings when calculating their benefit base. But any years of zero or low earnings over five were counted and began to lower the benefit amount. Women easily accumulated more than five years of low or no earnings and their earnings record suffered accordingly.[46]

The "benefit gap" between women and men reflected their different earnings and family responsibilities. As late as 1976, 60 percent of working women but only 21 percent of working men received monthly benefits of less than $220. In sharp contrast, 21 percent of the women and 64 percent of the men had benefits of $280 or more that year.[47] In 1985, the $399 average monthly benefit paid to 10.5 million retired women workers fell far below the $521 received by 11.7 million retired men. Moreover, the retirement income of women is less likely to be supplemented by a private pension than that of men. In 1982, 73 percent of non-married, white women and 86 percent of non-married, black women received more than half of their income from Social Security benefits. A person who received only Social Security income is seven times more likely to be poor than an older person receiving wage and salary income.[48]

Many other countries do not count work force absence due to pregnancy and child care when calculating retirement benefits. If they do, they treat this time as covered employment and credit it to a woman's account with some ascribed earnings.[49] In 1983, the Senate-House Conference on the Amendments to the Social Security Act eliminated a proposal to provide two additional drop-out years for spouses who leave the work force to care for children under three and who have no earnings during that time.[50]

Although the labor force patterns of women of color resemble those of white men, they receive the lowest Social Security benefits. More than white women, women of color collect Social Security benefits based on their own wage records (rather than as dependent spouses), have high labor force participation rates (except for Hispanic women), long work records, and fewer moves in and out of the labor force. Nonetheless, in 1979, the average monthly benefit for all women of color was $230 compared to $260 for their white counterparts; for black women alone it was an even lower $192.[51] This differential reflects the low wages paid to women of color and the historic exclusion from the Social Security Act of the jobs they most often fill. The elimination in 1981 of the $122 minimum social security benefit hurt black and Hispanic women, especially those who worked as domestics or in other low-paid jobs.

Ironically, the effects of racism and poverty make women of color eligible for more if not higher Social Security benefits. Due to high male death rates and the greater reliance on the extended family in their communities, proportionately more elderly black than white women collect benefits as widowed mothers and for raising their grandchildren. Women of color also receive more Social Security disability benefits because their typically unsafe workplaces lead to higher rates of strokes, diabetes, heart disease, hypertension, and other debilitating conditions. Access to more benefits, however, frequently does not amount to much. Not only are the benefits low, but poverty and dehumanizing work that women of color must tolerate shortens the number of years they receive retirement income and other social security benefits, as well as their lives.

The regressive payroll tax with a single tax rate and a ceiling on taxable wages also penalizes women and other workers at the bottom of the earnings ladder. In 1937, with a $3,000 ceiling on taxable wages, 99.7 percent of working women and 95.8 percent of working men earned less than the maximum and therefore were taxed on their entire earnings. Workers taxed on their entire wages pay disproportionately more of their income in Social Security taxes than those taxed only on the portion of their earnings that falls below the ceiling. Over time, as the income ceiling rose, the proportion of men with incomes below it fell rather steadily until 1965 when only 51 percent of male workers earned less than the $4,800 maximum. After 1970, as the ceiling was raised, this percentage crept up so that in 1981, 87.5 percent of male workers earned less than the $29,700 ceiling. The female pattern, in contrast, remained dramatically stable. The proportion of women earning less than the annual Social Security tax ceiling, always higher than that for men, fell below 93 percent only twice during these years and moved back to 99 percent in 1981.[52]

The Social Security retirement program also incorporated the view that a working woman's income was secondary and unnecessary for family support. The resulting double standard penalized the dependents and survivors of working women, making it harder for them to collect benefits than dependents of employed men. For example, widows were insured on the grounds that wives were economically dependent on their husbands, that the extended family no longer cared for aged widows, and that younger widows needed to stay home with surviving children.[53] But the program denied comparable income protection to a working woman's husband age sixty-five or over and to young, male widowers with children. A 1946 Brookings Institution study of the Social Security program explained that, "The law is based on averages and normal conditions, and on the average or under normal conditions, a husband is not dependent on his wife for support." But the report adds even when he is, the program does not provide for his needs upon his wife's death.[54] Between 1939 and 1950, a working woman could not insure her husband nor, in most cases, could she insure her children.

During this period, the program acknowledged female support of the family only in the absence of male income. A child became economically dependent on the mother when "no parent other than such individual was contributing to the support of such child and such child was not living with its father or adopting father."[55] Until 1950, a woman's children received benefits on their mother's earnings only if the father was out of the home and contributed nothing to their support. As long as the family was together, or if the absent father contributed something, the program discounted the mother's wages and her economic role regardless of the amount of support she actually provided.

When the 1950 amendments granted benefits to the adult dependents and survivors of a deceased working women over sixty-five, they liberalized these discriminatory rules somewhat. But to qualify, a husband had to pass a "support test" that proved his financial dependence on his employed wife, a test not given to wives of employed men. The male widower, unlike the female widow, had to show that in the year before his wife retired or died his income was one-fourth or less of the couple's income. In contrast, a husband's earnings automatically qualified his wife to benefits as his dependent. Given women's low wages relative to men, many husbands failed the "support test." Unable to establish that they were supported by her, the dependents of a working woman received no Social Security benefits on her account even though she paid the same taxes as a working man.

In the mid-1970s, the Supreme Court outlawed this differential treatment of women relative to men on the grounds of sex discrimination. Long before this, however, the National Federation of Business and Professional Women had lobbied for legislation to remedy such inequities in the Social Security system. In response to the growing participation of women in the labor market and in electoral politics, and by way of thanking the many women who worked in his campaign and who elected him to office, President Kennedy established a National Commission on the Status of Women which included a special Task Force on Social Insurance and Taxes. The Task Force's 1963 report acknowledged pervasive discrimination against women in the Social Security program although little was done to end it.

The increased militancy of the women's liberation movement in the late 1960s and early 1970s kept women's issues on the Social Security agenda. At the 1973 hearings on the economic problems of women held by the Congressional Joint Economic Committee, Representative Martha Griffiths (D-MI) stated, "the real purpose of these hearings is to point out that Social Security has met the social concerns of the nation as defined by men. It has not met the social concerns of the nation as defined by women, or as defined by men and women. It has met them as defined by men."[56] In 1975, the Advisory Council on Social Security investigated long-term changes in women's socioeconomic status.[57] Under renewed pressure from the Women's Equity Action League (WEAL) and Women's Rights Project (WRP) of the American Civil Liberties Unions (ACLU), the Supreme Court invalidated the rules excluding male widowers with small children and those requiring a husband's proof of economic dependency on his wife. The Court held that such rules discriminated against working women because they offered women fewer benefits then those available to working men. In *Weinburger v. Wiesenfeld* (1975), the Court ruled in favor of a Stephen Wiesenfeld who claimed partial entitlement to benefits on the record of his deceased wife who had been employed as a teacher (in addition to survivors' benefits for his children).[58]

The recognition of sex discrimination in the Old Age Insurance program helped to equalize the value of women's and men's survivor benefits. But other measures of the program still differentiate among women based on their compliance with the family ethic and do not raise issues of fairness between women and men. Such provisions, which do not lend themselves to legal redress on the grounds of sex discrimination, will require other means of change. Women's dual entitlement to benefits as a worker or a dependent and the differential treatment of one- and two-earner couples, fall into this more troublesome category. By favoring homemakers and penalizing working wives, these regulations disadvantage one group of women relative to another. They also presume and enforce the patriarchal pattern of women's economic dependence on men.

With the concept of dual entitlement, the 1939 amendments recognized women's twin roles as worker and wife. Dual entitlement allows a woman to receive either a worker's benefit on her own employment record or a dependent spouse's benefit of 50 percent of her husband's award, whichever is higher. She cannot receive both. Widows receive 75 percent of their deceased husbands' grant. Until recently, most women became eligible as dependents. In 1952, only 36,000 women (or 2 percent of those over sixty-five receiving benefits) were eligible for both spousal benefits and retired workers pensions in their own right.[59] The dual entitlement rule which values women's homemaker services at half the income earned by their husbands[60] presumes and enforces their economic dependence. It also reproduces class differences as the wives of higher-paid men receive a larger grant than women married to lower-paid men.

Owing to women's work patterns and low wages, their benefit as wives frequently exceeded what they could claim on their own earnings record. That is, many working wives received a smaller pension as a paid worker than as a dependent spouse.[61] This left retired working women, who paid Social Security payroll taxes, no better off than wives who neither worked outside the home nor paid taxes to the system. In fact, retired working women, often less advantaged to begin with, were worse off. Not only did they receive the same amount of benefits as non-working wives, but they received no return on the social security taxes they paid when employed. In the mid-1950s, when disability benefits became part of the benefit structure, the homemaker advantage was reduced somewhat. But in general, the dual entitlement feature of the Social Security Act continues to devalue women's domestic labor and enforces their subordination to men.

The Social Security retirement program's differential treatment of one- and two-earner couples also presumes and preserves women's economic dependence. The program works best for the traditional married couple with a lifelong homemaker and a lifelong breadwinner; they typically receive a higher retirement benefit than a two-earner couple with the same combined earnings. The benefits of one-earner couples include the worker's earnings plus the 50 percent spouse benefit. In two-earner couples each spouse receives benefits based on his or her half of the couple's combined earnings. A one-earner couple whose breadwinner has an average wage of $750 a month, for example, receives a pension of $580 ($387 for the worker and $193 for the spouse). In contrast, a two-earner couple whose combined average monthly earnings total $750 receives a pension of only $532 ($225 for the spouse with an average monthly wage of $250; $307 for the spouse with an average monthly wage of $500). The surviving spouse in a one-earner couple also does better. This spouse is entitled to as much as two-thirds of the total benefits received by the couple, while the survivor of a two-earner couple may get as little as 50 percent.[62]

The inequities between working and non-working women under Social Security was the topic of many discussions during the mid-1970s, kept alive by continuing pressure from the women's movement. The 1977 Social Security amendments required a study of proposals to eliminate dependency as a factor in the determination of entitlement to a spouse's benefits and to bring about equal treatment for men and women. The resulting panels created by the Department of Health, Education, and Welfare (HEW) to assess policy options advanced by feminists, social security experts, and congressional leaders produced two reports: *Report of the HEW Task Force on Social Security* (1978) and *Social Security and the Changing Roles of Men and Women* (1979).[63] According to one observer, the 1979 Advisory Council on Social Security spent "more time reviewing the treatment of working and non-working women than on any other issue."[64] All this activity, however, resulted in little action.

With the election of Reagan and the rise of intense concerns about a potential fiscal crisis in the Social Security system, public attention to gender issues in Social Security died down. But it did not disappear, in part due to the efforts of The Older Women's League (OWL) and the Grey Panthers, both formed in the late 1970s to protect the interests of the elderly. The 1983 National Commission on Social Security Reform recommended a few incremental changes for disabled and divorced women. The 1983 amendments to the Social Security Act mandated the Department of Health and Human Services to develop legislative proposals for "earnings sharing," a plan which removes the idea of female economic dependence on men and creates an independent Social Security record for each spouse in his\her own right. With such a plan, married couple's total annual earnings is divided equally between the spouses for each year of marriage. Upon divorce or retirement, a spouse's earnings record would equal their share of the fifty-fifty split plus earnings received outside the marriage. Discussed in more detail in Chapter Eleven, the idea of earnings sharing promises to shape the future debate over women and Social Security. In the final analysis, these and other highly technical discussions need to be made understandable to the wider public, carefully assessed in terms of the family ethic, and broadened to include other innovative ideas.

Punishing Women Who Fail to Comply with the Family Ethic

Being a wife, mother, and homemaker is essential to any woman hoping to benefit fully from Social Security. Stepping outside of those roles by, for example, getting a divorce, working outside the home, or choosing an alternative family structure means real financial risk. The Social Security Act effectively punishes women who break out of its limited definition of a woman's proper role.

From the start the Social Security Act presumed and rewarded stable marriages. An elderly woman's marital status conditioned her entitlement to benefits. To receive dependent's benefits, she had to be a wife for at least five years, and living with the eligible worker at the time of application; or she had to be a widow for one year and living with her husband at the time of his death. Changes in a woman's marital status resulted in a loss of benefits. A divorced wife lost her spouse allowance and a remarried widow forfeited her survivor's benefits. These rules existed to protect the program against abuse by those who married solely to increase their benefits, but they also automatically favored married over unmarried women.

To finance the cost of the expanded benefits to married men, the Social Security Advisory Council penalized single persons. In 1939, when the Council recommended a reduction in the future benefits payable to single individuals, it explained that "to provide more adequate basic protection to the wage earners of the country and at the same time fit the pattern of benefits to the financial cloth," the old age benefit formula needed to be revised "in such a manner as to reduce the eventual benefits, but not the taxes payable, to individuals as single annuitants."[65] The Council viewed this plan to increase the benefits of married workers at the expense of single workers as "socially desirable" and not in violation of the principle of individual equity "since widowers, bachelors, and women workers will still receive benefits equal in value to their individual direct contributions invested at interest."[66] "To increase the annuity in all cases, regardless of marital status..." believed the Council, "would involve unwarranted costs."[67] Less attention was paid to the fact that such family protection distorted the equitable return on taxes to single persons, that the majority of working women at that time were single, and single women's low wages already translated into seriously inadequate benefits. Redistribution of benefits from single to married persons also presumed the former lacked dependents and therefore needed less protection. "It is true," the Council acknowledged, "that in some instances a single annuitant will need to support an aged dependent relative. To make such relatives eligible for allowances would create many administrative problems."[68] In the end, the program covered fewer dependents of single than married workers. Married workers received allowances for non-working spouses, children, and grandchildren, persons less likely to be among a single person's dependents. Moreover, except for their children, the dependents of single adults, such as siblings, aunts, uncles, and other non-nuclear family relatives, who frequently are cared for by single women, do not qualify for coverage as family members. Given all this, single workers received less value for their Social Security tax payment.

Although distinctions between married and single workers occur regardless of gender, they tend to hurt single women who, more than single men, become caretakers of relatives outside the nuclear family when they become old, sick, or disabled. In the late 1960s, the economists Pechmen, Aaron, and Taussig found that Social Security's differential replacement of income for married versus single persons was much larger than could be justified by the former's need for more income. Robert Ball, former Social Security Commissioner, concluded that of all social security beneficiaries, "the worst off are the non-married."[69] The program's bias against single persons failed to become a political issue, according to one policy analyst, because single persons were a small and politically inactive interest group.[70]

The original Social Security Act essentially ignored non-working divorced women and their children.[71] When retired wives, retired widows, and young widows with children became entitled to a dependent's allowance in 1939, the program excluded the 789,000 divorced women living in the United States at that time. Wives and widows had to be living with their husbands at the time he applied for benefits and lost them upon divorce. No provisions existed for divorced women until 1950 when "mother's insurance" was extended to divorced widows. To qualify, however, divorced widows had to be unmarried, caring for their children, and dependent on ex-husbands for at least one-half of their support (despite the fact that many states actually prohibited alimony).

Divorce *per se* was not recognized until 1965, when retired spouse and widow's benefits were extended to divorced women (and to divorced men in 1977). But eligibility was restricted to those women who passed stringent "marriage" and "support tests." To qualify, a woman had to be married to her former husband for at least twenty years (dropped to ten years in 1977), not remarried at the time of application, and until 1972 had to prove economic dependence on her husband when he qualified for benefits. Moreover, a divorced woman could not claim her benefits until her ex-husband retired. Testifying at 1973 Congressional hearings on the economic problems of women, Representative Martha Griffiths (D-MI) pointed out that the Social Security system denied pensions to a woman married to a man for forty-nine years, but permitted his wife of one day to claim survivors' benefits if he died.[72] Recent Social Security legislation has somewhat eased the problems faced by divorced women. Since 1984, a divorced woman over sixty who remarries can continue to receive benefits on her first husband's account. As of 1985, a divorced spouse is entitled to her retirement benefit at sixty-two even if her husband has not claimed his, but must wait two years after her divorce to collect them.

Finally, the benefits for divorced women remain inadequate. Even when a divorced (or separated) woman qualifies for benefits, the 50 percent spouse's allowance is insufficient to support a separate household. It was intended to supplement a worker's full benefit rather than to support a woman and her children alone. Meanwhile, a divorced woman's ex-husband continues to qualify for his full benefit which amounts to two-thirds of the 150 percent of the husband's earned benefits they received as a couple.

Paradoxically, even women who comply with the family ethic lose out once their reproductive and homemaking responsibilities decline. Benefits to married women under sixty-five effectively cease once both their husband and children have left home. The 1939 amendments limited dependents' benefits to women over sixty-five and to younger women caring for children. A woman qualified for benefits as the wife of a retired worker when she reached sixty-five and as his widow at sixty-five or younger if she was still caring for their children. A deceased worker's children under sixteen (eighteen if in school) also received an allowance. But younger wives of retired men, young childless widows, and young widows of deceased workers with older children received no benefits until they reached sixty-five.

The Social Security Advisory Council justified the exclusion of young wives and childless widows on the grounds of costs. But it also suggested that women with no reproductive tasks to perform were not a priority. In recommending this provision the Council stated,

> It is recognized that the wives of a considerable proportion of aged men are several years younger than the men themselves and that where this discrepancy in ages occurs, the payment of the wives' allowance will be delayed some time after possible retirement of the husband. After thorough consideration of all possible alterna-

tives, the Council is convinced that the minimum age requirement here proposed is necessary and justifiable...a large additional cost for this purpose [is] unwarranted so long as far more pressing needs exist.[73]

The Council justified the exclusion of young widows without children on similar grounds. "As contrasted with the payments to widows with dependent children," the Council argued, "benefits to *all* younger widows would not only greatly increase the cost of the total program but would, it is believed, divert funds from more pressing needs." "It is normal," the Council continued, "for a large majority of younger widows without dependent children to re-enter employment. To provide continuing benefits to such widows would not only create many anomalies and inequities, but serious administrative difficulties as well."[74]

Young widows with children, however, received insurance. When recommending widows' insurance, the Advisory Council stated,

Such payments are intended as supplements to the orphans' benefits with the purpose of enabling the widow to remain at home and care for the children...as soon as the last child attains the upper limit of age for eligibility for benefits, the payments to the widow shall cease...This is not intended to affect her eligibility to an old-age annuity on her attainment of age 65.[75]

The Council viewed benefits for the survivors of a young wage earner as "the counterpart of the protection of the wage earner and his aged wife or widow should he live to retirement after his children are grown."[76] But this protection ceased once her youngest child came of age.

These provisions created what is called today a "widow's gap," referring to the full-time homemaker's loss of benefits during the years between the time that a widow's youngest child turns sixteen (later raised to eighteen) and the time when she becomes eligible for old age benefits. Few other benefits are available to this group of "displaced homemakers," many of whom lack other resources and who may experience difficulty entering or re-entering the labor market. If they take their Social Security benefits early, at sixty-two rather than wait until sixty-five, their already low payments are permanently reduced by 28.5 percent. Some turn to general assistance, the only financial aid program available to single women without children. During the last ten years, as the problem has grown, some programs to train or retrain displaced homemakers for paid labor outside the home have emerged.

Recent changes in the Social Security Act have exacerbated the widow's gap. The 1981 Budget Act which terminated "widow's insurance" when the youngest child reaches sixteen instead of eighteen, lengthened the time before age sixty that a widow will be without Social Security protection. Likewise, phasing out students' benefits for the eighteen to twenty-two year old children of retired, disabled, or deceased workers increased the financial burdens of widows and grandmothers raising children. In 1979, 22 percent of benefits to students (age eighteen to twenty-two) went to families of color. Finally, Congress eliminated a proposal to shorten the widow's gap by providing widows aged fifty-five to fifty-nine a six month transition benefit equal to the benefit a widow would receive at age sixty immediately after a worker's death.[77]

It is important to note here that bringing young widows with children into the Old Age Insurance program in 1939 effectively removed families headed by widows from the rolls of the Aid to Dependent Children (ADC) program, one of the public assistance titles of the Social Security Act. The transfer of 43 percent of the 254,000 ADC families headed by a widow to the Old Age Insurance rolls left the less generous and more stigmatized public assistance program to cover women traditionally viewed as less deserving of aid. The Advisory Council stated that

> While the expansion of aid to dependent children under the Social Security Act has been gratifying, there is great need for further protection of dependent children. In many instances, the aid is insufficient to maintain normal family life or to permit the children to develop into healthy citizens. Many deserving cases are not able to obtain any aid. Above all, the relief method is not the most desirable way of meeting childhood dependency. Social insurance offers an improved method of dealing with the problem.[78]

Presumably the inferior program was adequate for the remaining 57 percent of the ADC caseload consisting of separated, divorced, deserted, and unmarried women and their children. (See Chapter Ten.)

In sum, as the market economy failed to provide adequately for the economic support of older workers and in response to a variety of social, economic, and political pressures, the federal government began to assist families in the reproduction of the labor force and the maintenance of the non-working members of the population. In 1939, the government broadened the Old Age Insurance program to include the wife, children, and in some cases the aged parent of a retired or deceased worker. This institutionalized state intervention in the family when economic insecurity threatened to undermine the workings in the sphere of reproduction.

At the same time, the provisions of the Social Security retirement program enforced the structures of patriarchal authority which the rise in the employment of married women and the economics of the Depression challenged. Through rules and regulations that incorporated the family ethic, the program presumed stable marriages, favored homemakers over working wives, one-earner over two-earner couples, and married over single persons. It ignored divorced women for many years and neglected women once their reproductive tasks declined. As a result, the provisions of the Old Age Insurance program encouraged married women to remain at home, discouraged paid labor by wives, penalized divorced and single women, and offered only small rewards to women who worked. The program conveyed the message that proper and deserving women belonged in the home. By helping them to stay there, the program, however unintentionally, enforced the economic dependence of women on men and regulated women's labor force participation according to the productive and reproductive needs of twentieth century patriarchal capitalism.

Notes to Chapter 8

1. The Committee on Economic Security, *1935 Report to the President,* in National Conference on Social Welfare, *The Report of the Committee on Economic Security of 1935 and Other Basic Documents Relating to the Social Security Act,* 50th Anniversary Edition, (Washington, D.C.: National Council of Social Welfare, 1985).

2. Speech by Ellen Sullivan Woodward, "Women's Stake in Social Security," September 1, 1940, quoted in Susan Ware, *Beyond Suffrage: Women in the New Deal* (Cambridge: Harvard University Press, 1981), p. 100.

3. President's Committee on Economic Security, *Social Security in America: The Factual Background of the Social Security Act as Summarized From Staff Reports to the Committee on Economic Security* (Washington, D.C.: Government Printing Office, 1937), pp. 139-142; Roy Lubove, *The Struggle for Social Security 1900-1935* (Cambridge: Harvard University Press, 1968), p. 114.

4. *Report of the President's Research Committee on Social Trends, Vol. I* (New York: McGraw-Hill Book Company, Inc. 1933), pp. 26-27.

5. President's Committee on Economic Security, Staff Reports, *Social Security in America* (1937) *op. cit.,* pp. 139-142.

6. Carolyn Weaver, *The Crisis in Social Security: Economic and Political Origins* (Durham, N.C.: Duke Press Policy Studies, 1982), p. 32.

7. U.S. Department of Commerce, Bureau of the Census, *Historical Statistics of the United States, Colonial Times to 1957* (Washington, D.C. Government Printing Office, 1970), p. 71.

8. President's Committee on Economic Security, Staff Reports, *Social Security in America* (1937) *op. cit.,* p. 143.

9. *Ibid.,* pp. 143-149; U.S. Bureau of the Census occupational data show that on the average while 7.78% of the general male population 16 years of age and over had passed their 65 birthday, only 5.15% of men 65 or older were still working. The figures varied by occupation with more professional and technical than manual workers employed over age 65. For example, in 1930, 8.41% of working farmers, 8.85% of lawyers, judges and justices, 6.5% of retail dealers, 5.91% of bankers, brokers and money lenders were 65 or over compared to 2.34% of miners, 1.32% of cotton mill operators, 2.61% of machinists, 2.21% of store clerks and 0.75% of locomotive firemen. See Abraham Epstein, *Insecurity: A Challenge to America* (New York: Harrison Smith and Robert Haas, 1933), pp. 491-492.

10. President's Committee on Economic Security, Staff Reports, *Social Security in America* (1937) *op. cit.,* p. 149.

11. Weaver (1982) *op. cit.,* pp. 45-46.

12. Epstein (1933) *op. cit.,* pp. 119, 125-129.

13. President's Committee on Economic Security, Staff Reports, *Social Security in America* (1937) *op. cit.*, pp. 167-178; Lubove (1968) *op. cit.*, pp. 127-132; Epstein (1933) *op. cit.*, pp. 141-148.

14. President's Committee on Economic Security, Staff Reports, *Social Security in America* (1937) *op. cit.*, pp. 149-153.

15. *Ibid.*

16. The Committee on Economic Security, Staff Reports, *1935 Report to the President,* in National Conference on Social Welfare (1985) *op. cit.*, p.44.

17. President's Committee on Economic Security, Staff Reports, *Social Security in America* (1937) *op. cit.*, p. 154.

18. Weaver (1982) *op. cit.*, p. 30.

19. President's Committee on Economic Security, Staff Reports, *Social Security in America* (1937) *op. cit.*, pp. 160-161.

20. *Ibid.*, pp. 162-163.

21. *Ibid.*, pp. 155-167.

22. Robert S. McElvaine (ed.), *Down and Out in the Depression* (Chapel Hill: University of North Carolina Press, 1983), p. 100.

23. *Ibid.*, p. 100.

24. *Ibid.*, pp. 104-105.

25. *Ibid.*, pp. 198-199.

26. Jerry R. Cates, *Insuring Inequality: Administrative Leadership in Social Security 1935-1954* (Ann Arbor: University of Michigan Press, 1983), p. 22.

27. Cates (1983) *op. cit.*, p. 22; Abraham Holtzman, *The Townsend Movement* (New York: Octagon Books, 1975), pp. 48-49, 86-121; Lubove (1968) *op. cit.*, p. 10.

28. Holtzman (1975) *op. cit.*, p. 88.

29. Cates (1983) *op. cit.*, pp. 22-25; Arthur Altmeyer, *The Formative Years of the Social Security Act* (Madison: The University of Wisconsin Press, 1968), p. 11; Lubove (1968) *op. cit.*, pp. 33, 138-143.

30. Cates (1983) *op. cit.*, p. 24, citing Edwin E. Witte, "Social Security: A Wild Dream or a Practical Plan?" in *Social Security Perspectives: Essays by Edwin E. Witte* Robert J. Lampman (ed.) (Madison: University of Wisconsin Press, 1962), p. 11.

31. For a description of the development of the Social Security Act see, among others, Altmeyer (1968) *op. cit.*; Cates (1983) *op. cit.*; Martha Derthick, *Policymaking for Social Security* (Washington, D.C: The Brookings Institution, 1979); Epstein (1933) *op. cit.*; Lubove (1968) *op. cit.*; Edwin E. Witte, *The Development of the Social Security Act* (Madison: The University of Wisconsin Press, 1962).

32. Eveline M. Burns, *The American Social Security System* (Boston: Houghton Mifflin Co., 1949), pp. 66-73; U.S. Congress, House of Representatives, *Issues*

in Social Security: A Report to the Committee on Ways and Means, 79th. Congress, 1st Session, 1949, pp. 26-30.

33. Maxwell S. Stewart, *Social Security* (New York: W.W. Norton and Co., 1937), pp. 152-153.

34. Winifred D. Wandersee, *Women's Work and Family Values 1920-1940* (Cambridge: Harvard University Press, 1981), p. 85.

35. Richard Sterner, *The Negro's Share* (New York: Harper & Row, 1943), pp. 214-215.

36. President's Committee on Economic Security, Staff Reports, *Social Security in America* (1937) *op. cit.,* p. 224.

37. Sophonisba P. Breckinridge, *Women in the Twentieth Century* (New York: McGraw Hill Book Company, Inc., 1933), p. 11.

38. Cates (1983) *op. cit.,* p. 105, citing Jane Hoey to Mr. Bane, October 15, 1936, File Folder 011.4, Sept. 1936, "Records of the Executive Director of the Social Security Board" (1935-1940), Record Group 47, National Archives, Washington, D.C.

39. Cates (1983) *op. cit.,* pp. 105-106, citing Louis Resnick to Frank Bane, July 26, 1937, File Folder 011, Central Files of the Social Security Board (1935-47), Record Group 47, National Archives, Washington, D.C.; Altmeyer (1968) *op. cit.,* p. 60.

40. Quoted in Weaver (1982) *op. cit.,* p. 108.

41. *Ibid.*

42. *Ibid.,* p. 255, footnote 22.

43. J. Douglas Brown, *An American Philosophy of Social Security* (Princeton: Princeton University Press, 1972), p. 56; Cates (1983) *op. cit.,* pp. 104-135.

44. Arthur J. Altmeyer, "The New Social Security Program," *School Life,* XXV (January 1940), pp. 103-104.

45. Advisory Council on Social Security, *Final Report 1937-1938,* in National Conference on Social Welfare (1985) *op. cit.,* pp. 187-189.

46. U.S. Department of Health, Education and Welfare, *Report of The HEW Task Force on the Treatment of Women Under Social Security,* February 1978, p. 11 (mimeo).

47. U.S. Department Of Health, Education and Welfare, *Social Security and the Changing Roles of Men and Women* (Washington, D.C.: Government Printing Office, February 1979), pp. 22-23.

48. Older Women's League, *Report on the Status of Mid-Life and Older Women in America,* Mother's Day, 1986, p. 3; 1325 G. St. N.W. LLB Washington, D.C. 20005.

49. U.S. Department of Health, Education, and Welfare, *Report of the HEW Task Force on the Treatment of Women Under Social Security* (1978) *op. cit.,* pp. 129-130.

50. Women's Equity Action League, *WEAL Facts,* "Social Security Amendments of 1983: Impact of Financing on Women," Social Security Fact Sheet #3 (805 15th. St. NW, Suite 822, Washington, D.C. 20005), April 1983, p.2.

51. Women's Equity Action League, *WEAL Facts,* "Social Security and Minority Women," Fact Sheet #2 (805 15th. St. NW, Suite 822, Washington, D.C. 20005), June 1983, p.2.

52. "Women and Social Security," *Social Security Bulletin,* Annual Statistical Supplement, 1983, p. 81, T. 23.

53. Advisory Council on Social Security, *Final Report 1937-1938,* in National Council of Social Welfare (1985) *op. cit.,* p. 192.

54. Lewis Meriam, *Relief and Social Security* (Washington, D.C.: The Brookings Institution, 1946), p. 122.

55. Amendment to Title II of the Social Security Act, 1939, sec. 202(c)(4).

56. Congress of the United States, Joint Economic Committee, *Hearings on the Economic Problems of Women,* Part 2, July 24, 25, 26, 30, 1973; 93rd. Cong., 1st. Sess. (Washington, D.C.: Government Printing Office, 1973), p. 321.

57. W. Andrew Achenbaum, *Social Security: Visions and Revisions* (Cambridge: Cambridge University Press, 1986), p. 131.

58. In 1975, in *Weinberger v. Wisenfeld,* 420 U.S. 636, 644, the Supreme Court struck down the provision that provided survivors' benefits to widows (less than 65 years of age) with small children but not to widowers (less than 65 years of age) with small children. In 1977, in *Califano v. Goldfarb,* 430 U.S. 199, the Court overturned the economic dependency rule for husbands, since such proof was not required for wives.

59. Achenbaum (1986) *op. cit.,* p. 128.

60. Dorothy Miller, "The 'Feminization' of Poverty: Women and the Proposed Social Security Cuts," *Washington Bulletin* 27 (16) (August 24, 1981).

61. U.S. Department of Health, Education and Welfare, *Social Security and the Changing Roles of Men and Women* (1979) *op. cit.,* pp. 28-29.

62. Barbara Mikulski and Ellyn Brown, "Case Studies in the Treatment of Women Under Social Security Law: The Need for Reform," *Harvard Law Journal* (1983), pp. 38-39; U.S. Department of Health, Education and Welfare, *Social Security and the Changing Roles of Men and Women* (1978) *op. cit.,* p. 29.

63. "Task Force Report on Treatment of Women Under Social Security," *Social Security Bulletin* 41 (May 1978), pp. 37-39; U.S. Department of Health Education and Welfare, *Social Security and the Changing Roles of Men and Women* (1979) *op. cit.*

64. Achenbaum (1986) *op. cit.,* p. 131.

65. Advisory Council on Social Security, *Final Report 1937-1938,* in National Council of Social Welfare (1985) *op. cit.,* p. 195.

66. *Ibid.,* p. 190.

67. *Ibid.,* p. 189.

68. U.S. Advisory Council on Social Security, *Final Report, December 10, 1938,* Senate Doc. 4, 76th Congress, Session 2 (1939), p. 17.

69. Cited in Martha Derthick, *Policymaking for Social Security* (Washington, D.C.: The Brookings Institution, 1979), pp. 260-261.

70. *Ibid.,* p. 261.

71. See Jean Taft Douglas Bandler, *Family Issues in Social Security: An Analysis of Social Security,* unpublished Doctoral Dissertation, Columbia University School of Social Work, New York, 1975, pp. 130-131; U.S. Department of Health, Education and Welfare, *Report of The HEW Task Force on the Treatment of Women* (1978) *op. cit.,* pp. 19-20; Women's Equity Action League, *WEAL Facts,* Social Security Fact Sheet #4, April 1983, p. 1.

72. U.S. Congress, Joint Economic Committee (1973) *op. cit.,* p. 321.

73. Advisory Council on Social Security, *Final Report 1937-1938,* in National Council of Social Welfare (1985), *op. cit.,* p. 190.

74. *Ibid.,* p. 193.

75. *Ibid.,* p. 192.

76. *Ibid.,* p. 192.

77. Women's Equity Action League, *WEAL Facts,* "Social Security Amendments of 1983: Impact of Financing on Women," (April 1983) *op. cit.,* p. 2.

78. U.S. Advisory Council on Social Security, *Final Report, December 10, 1938* (1939) *op. cit.,* p. 17.

9

Unemployment Insurance

Unemployment peaked in 1932 when thirteen million persons or 25 percent of the labor force was out of work, not including those left out of the official count because they had already given up ever finding a job. Depending on the city, the black unemployment rate exceeded that of whites by 30 to 60 percent.[1]

With so many families' survival now tied to market wages, unemployment caused widespread personal and social distress. Always a serious threat for the working class, unemployment became a massive disaster during the Depression, wiping out jobs *and* any small economic cushion that families had managed to create. Pervasive joblessness destabilized the functioning of families, the efficiency of the market, the foundations of patriarchy, and the overall political equilibrium. As early as 1914, John Andrews, the well-known Progressive Era economist, concluded that, "The time is past when the problem of unemployment could be disposed of either by ignoring it, as was the practice until recent years in America, or by attributing it to mere laziness and inefficiency. We are beginning to recognize that unemployment is not so much due to individual causes...as social and inherent in our present method of industrial organization."[2] But only after the devastation and unrest of the 1930s did the federal government respond. In 1935, Unemployment Insurance was included in the Social Security Act to protect workers against the loss of income due to temporary or involuntary joblessness.

Maintaining the Working Class

Even before the Depression, the market's inability to provide jobs for all those available for work resulted in high unemployment rates. From 1900 to 1930, the number of men and women wage earners about doubled to thirty million. They represented 62.2 percent of the civilian labor force in 1930 compared to only 50.7 percent in 1900. But their employment was often precarious. According to one account, America passed through fifteen business crises from 1812 to 1920 and sixteen alternative periods of prosperity and depression between 1885 and 1930.[3] Unemployment soared in the thirties from 3 million persons after the 1929 stock market crash to over 13 million in 1933. Despite strenuous and innovative New Deal programs, it stayed above 15 percent of the labor force until the mobilization for World War II finally absorbed most of those without work.

Unemployment weighed heavily on working people and worsened their already low standard of living. The collapse of the economy wiped out over 7 million savings accounts and millions of insurance policies. The number of attempted evictions in New York City rose from 203,271 in 1931 to 308,516 in 1932; and from 27,670 to 35,000 in five of Ohio's industrial centers. Malnutrition among children soared. Children in New York City drank 20 percent less milk from September 1930 to September 1931 and in some northern Illinois communities milk consumption dropped 30 percent. Malnutrition among children was above average in forty-eight Pennsylvania counties and increased by more than 33 percent between 1930 and 1932 in New York City schools. Unattended illness was rampant despite maximum use of existing free health services, according to the New York State Commissioner of Health in 1933. A leader of Chicago's Jewish Charities testified at Senate hearings held in 1931-32 that, "The visiting nurses are discovering in almost every home that they have entered a problem of illness that is unmet."[4]

Ongoing unemployment humiliated workers, broke up families, left women to fend for themselves, and otherwise undermined patriarchal patterns and the reproductive capacity of many families. Testifying before a Congressional committee, a relief worker described the shame experienced by a jobless man who came looking for work. When he heard that the agency had none to give, he asked, "Have you anybody you can send around to my family to tell my wife you have no job to give me, because she doesn't believe that a man who walks the street from morning till night day after day cannot get a job in this town. She thinks I don't want to work." Another social worker told of a laborer whose wife took their baby and ran off with a truck driver leaving a note that he could support them better than her husband could. "I did not prosecute," the husband explained, "she is right, I cannot support them."[5] The applications to settle domestic disputes rose from 18,442 in 1929 to 22,625 in 1930 in three New York family courts. They were still higher in 1931. Not unrelated, the number of children placed in institutions around the country increased 48 percent from 1930 to 1932, according to the Executive Director of the Child Welfare League of America.[6]

From the perspective of business, such high unemployment was unprofitable because it undercut the skill and efficiency of workers. As early as 1911, The Report of the New York State Employer's Liability Commission stated,

> From being unable to get steady work, the unemployed often become unable to do steady work—unreliable, inefficient, 'good for nothing.' During long periods of unemployment good workmen [sic] degenerate into tramps. They become habituated to a life of idleness and uncertainty so that when at least employment is once more to be had, they are unfit for continuous labor. The mere unemployed have become unemployable.[7]

Business leaders also worried that idle plants eroded their investments in capital equipment, that employed workers restricted their output to prolong their jobs, and that unemployment reduced consumer purchasing power.[8] They also worried that joblessness would radicalize workers. The 1932 Report of the California Unemployment Commission stated that "Idleness destroys not only purchasing power, lowering the standards of living, but also destroys efficiency and finally breaks the spirit. The once industrious and resourceful worker becomes pauperized, loses faith in himself [sic] and society. Society must provide his bread."[9] John Commons, a well-known University of Wisconsin economist, had much earlier described unemployment as a "critical defect of capitalism, the leading source of conflict between capital and labor...and the stimulus to both trade unions and socialism."[10]

Few resources were available to the unemployed. Some jobless workers turned to labor unions, among the first organizations in the United States to try and provide out-of-work benefits to their unemployed members. But these programs offered only rudimentary aid to a small minority of women and men and could not begin to meet the need. By 1928, union plans provided benefits to less than 35,000 workers or 0.8 percent of their total membership. Three years later, the

Bureau of Labor Statistics found stable unemployment benefit plans in only three international and forty-five local unions. They covered only 45,000 members or 1.5 percent of all trade union members nationwide, largely in the printing trades. During the Depression, many unemployment benefit plans simply collapsed. In 1934, the year before the Social Security Act was passed, such plans protected less than 100,000 people.[11] Few in number, they did not cover the majority of unskilled workers, including most employed women and blacks.

A small number of employer-sponsored and joint union-management benefit plans also existed. In 1931, only fifteen out of some 300,000 firms in the United States operated some type of program for jobless workers. They covered about 70,000 workers in the mid-1930s, more than half in one large company. Company programs, sometimes called welfare capitalism, were modest in scope, offering low benefits and short-term protection, primarily to laid-off seasonal workers. Joint union-employer benefit plans, found mainly in the garment industry, protected another 65,000 women and men. Many employer-sponsored plans, like those run by unions, simply contracted or collapsed under the weight of the Depression.[12] Prior to this, in the 1910s and 1920s, the business establishment had tried, without success, to prevent unemployment through employment exchanges, emergency public works programs, and voluntary efforts by employers to regularize work.[13]

Some of the jobless turned to public and private relief agencies. Private agencies, historically opposed to the provision of financial aid, were not prepared for the task. Moreover, the number of people in need soon overwhelmed local resources. Expenditures for relief doubled between 1929 and 1930 according to a Russell Sage Foundation study of eighty-one cities. Much of the relief dispensed by private agencies was paid for by public funds and provided by family agency workers on loan to public agencies.[14] By the fall of 1931, in virtually every U.S. city, large numbers of public and private municipal relief agencies went bankrupt. Some state governments began to assist overwhelmed cities in the provision of home and work relief.[15] Despite considerable agitation for it throughout the twenties, no state provided unemployment insurance until 1932 when Wisconsin enacted the first law. Most states feared that an unemployment compensation law would put their employers at a competitive disadvantage with employers in states without one. In 1933, the Federal Emergency Relief Administration (FERA) estimated that over fifteen million persons, including nearly three million families and 500,000 individuals, were receiving relief. The average monthly benefit per family ranged from $15.15 to $19.08.[16]

Others lacking any form of relief sold apples, depended on hand-outs, or traveled the open road, living in shantytowns of cardboard and tin sheeting ("Hoovervilles") at the edge of big cities. Many families lived on bread, water, and what they could scavenge from garbage cans. As millions sank into hopelessness and poverty, groups of workers once again took to the streets to demand that the government provide relief.

Pressure from Below

Agitation by jobless workers for work and relief has accompanied nearly every depression since the beginning of industrialization. Throughout the nineteenth and twentieth centuries, workers in all large cities clamored for work, the right to earn a living, and a fair share of the profits. Pressure from these and other groups led, in the thirties, to what Piven and Cloward describe as the largest movement of the un-employed in the history of the United States.[17] Jobless workers formed citizen committees and self-help groups, held outdoor meetings, demonstrated at relief offices, city halls, and state capitals, and marched to Washington, D.C. In their desperation, they also harassed local relief agencies, bootlegged coal, and organized the looting of food. While some workers resisted turning to public aid as long as they could, others, deeply angered, came to believe that they had a right to an income that would allow them to survive. According to a study by the American Public Welfare Association, "Relief offices were approached by large committees, numbering ten, fifteen, twenty, and sometimes more persons, which demanded an immediate audience, without previous appointment and regardless of staff members' schedules." Frequently neighborhood crowds gathered outside the relief office to buttress these large committees while they presented their "demands."[18]

Jobless workers also engaged in more organized forms of protest. In 1930, 3,000 unemployed persons stormed Cleveland's City Hall, 12,000 jobless workers marched to Chicago's seat of municipal government, and 35,000 rallied in New York. Similar demonstrations occurred in virtually every major city in the United States. During the early 1930s, the National Council of the Unemployed, a federation of local groups, held mass demonstrations, resisted evictions, reversed local relief cut-backs, secured public works jobs, and fought for social insurance. Petition drives—at least three gathering more than a million signatures each—demanded government work or relief. In Cleveland, Philadelphia, Chicago, Los Angeles, and Detroit, discontented workers rioted to be heard.[19]

Black men and women participated in these protests and also organized their own. Risking arrest and imprisonment, they withheld money from rent-raising landlords, blocked evictions, and protected black fugitives from law enforcement officials.[21] The NAACP, founded in 1910, organized twenty-three new chapters in 1934 and claimed a membership of 85,000 in 404 branches nationwide.[22] That year, Arkansas farmers formed the Southern Tenant Farmers' Union, in response to the eviction of sharecroppers brought on by the policies of the Agriculture Adjustment Administration (AAA). Its membership in 1936, from one-third to one-half black, included many women.[23] A few years earlier, in 1933, thousands of unemployed workers in Birmingham, Alabama, the majority black, demonstrated for jobs and civil rights.[24]

The leadership of the AFL initially opposed government relief, calling for "jobs, not a dole." But as the Depression deepened, the more militant rank and file unionists and many state labor federations began to demand public works programs and direct government relief for the unemployed. By 1932, the AFL leadership reversed its earlier opposition to social insurance and endorsed the idea of Unemployment Insurance to be financed by employers under the supervision of the states.[25] From the start, the rapidly growing CIO and the militant unemployed councils had strongly supported the more redistributive social insurance proposals. Even more threatening to top business and government leaders was the prospect that the national electoral realignment which marked the 1932 defeat of Hoover by Roosevelt would embolden organized labor to form an independent political party.[26]

Social reformers and business associations also tried to address the problem of unemployment. During the 1920s, they searched for alternatives to voluntary programs including private benefit plans, employment exchanges, and incentives for employers to regularize the labor market. They also favored emergency public works programs. Others, influenced by the enactment of Unemployment Insurance laws in England and Europe, unsuccessfully introduced Unemployment Insurance bills into state legislatures.

The government initially responded to the militancy of jobless workers with force. Police armed with rifles and riot guns greeted the 1931 hunger march to Washington, D.C. In 1932, the Detroit police opened fire on thousands of marchers who refused to halt, killing four and wounding several others. Later that year, 20,000 World War I veterans, known as the Bonus Expeditionary Force, marched from

Portland, Oregon to Washington, D.C. to plead with Congress for earlier payment of a wartime service bonus not due to them until 1945. Instead of meeting with them or passing the bill, President Hoover ordered the army to clear the marchers' camp. Men, women, and children fled as their shacks burned behind them. Terrorism and violence defeated a 1935 strike by black and white cotton pickers organized by the Southern Tenant Farmers' Union.[20]

At the same time, these "pressures from below" produced small steps towards reform. In the late 1920s and early 1930s, six states established unemployment commissions. In 1931, after twelve years of agitation, the nation's first Unemployment Insurance program was enacted in Wisconsin, and in 1933, at least eighty-three Unemployment Insurance bills were introduced in twenty-three states. Some motion, but very little action, occurred at the federal level. Since federal involvement in social welfare still lacked legal sanction, it's not surprising that a 1928 Congressional committee rejected the concept of Federal Unemployment Insurance, in favor of voluntary unemployment reserve funds established by employers. A Congressional committee did endorse the principle of compulsory insurance in 1931, but recommended that the federal government limit its role to allowing employers to deduct contributions to their state unemployment insurance reserve fund from their federal income taxes.[27]

A national Unemployment Insurance program did not appear in the United States until Congress enacted the Social Security Act in 1935, six years after the stock market crashed and well after the jobless rate had reached record heights. In the interim, however, Congress did legislate major work relief programs in response to the unemployeds' deepening desperation and continued agitation. As noted in Chapter Seven, these consisted of the Federal Emergency Relief Act (FERA), the Public Works Administration (PWA), the Civilian Works Administration (CWA) and its successor, the Works Progress Administration (WPA), and the Civilian Conservation Corps (CCC). Although "temporary," some of these programs remained operative until the mobilization for World War II ended the Depression. They also paved the way for the 1935 Social Security Act which included the Unemployment Compensation Program, Old Age Insurance, and Aid to Families With Dependent Children.

Work Relief and Women

Despite rising female labor force participation during the 1930s, women did not escape unemployment. The Women's Bureau estimated that at least 2 million women were out of work in January 1931. About 10 percent of jobless women also headed a household; 20 to 50 percent were responsible for dependents. As a general rule, about 20 percent of normally employed women were out of work at any given moment in the 1930s. Many had no place to live. The YWCA reported that 140,000 women were homeless in March 1933. That same year, the Women's Bureau counted almost 10,000 women hoboes in 800 cities, an increase of 90 percent over the previous year.[28]

Women in domestic and service employment—mostly black women—were overrepresented among the unemployed.[29] Indeed, joblessness fell especially hard on black women workers, 60 percent of whom worked in these two occupations.[30] Whites fired their black household servants and began to "do their own work," and white domestics displaced black women in many of the remaining jobs.[31] In what became known as a "slave market," groups of black women aged seventeen to seventy waited on sidewalks in various northern cities for white women to drive up and offer them a day's work.[32]

About 30 percent of black women worked as agricultural laborers at this time, mostly in the South. They too became unemployed owing to farm failures, rising food prices, New Deal crop limitation programs, and the mechanization of agriculture. By 1940, only 16 percent of black women worked as farm laborers, down from 27 percent ten years earlier. The number of black women employed in better paying factory jobs also fell from 7 percent of all black female workers in 1920 to 5.5 percent in 1930; it rose slightly to 6 percent in 1940.[33]

Women's experience of unemployment was a dismal one. Describing a domestic employment bureau, the author Meridel Le Sueur observes,

> We have been sitting here now for four hours. We sit here every day waiting for a job. There are no jobs. Most of us have had no breakfast. Some have had scant rations for over a year. Hunger makes a human being lapse into a state of lethargy, especially city hunger...There are many woman for a single job...Most of the women who come here are middle-aged, some have families, some have raised their families and now are alone, some have men who are out of work...There are young girls too, fresh from the country...There is a great exodus of girls from the farms into the city now...The girls are trying to get work. The prettier ones

can get jobs in the stores when there are any, or waiting on table, but these jobs are only for the attractive and the adroit. The others, the real peasants have a more difficult time...[34]

Other unemployed women become virtually invisible. Once again, Le Sueur paints a vivid picture.

> It's one of the great mysteries of the city where women go when they are out of work and hungry. There are not many women in the bread line. There are no flop houses for women as there are for men, where a bed can be had for a quarter or less. You don't see woman lying on the floor at the mission in the free flop houses. They obviously don't sleep in the jungle or under newspapers in the park. There is no law I suppose against their being in these places but the fact is they rarely are...Yet there must be as many women out of jobs in cities and suffering extreme poverty as there are men. What happens to them?...I've lived in cities for many months broke, without help, too timid to get in the bread line. I've known many women to live like this until they simply faint on the street from privation, without saying a word to anyone. A women [without dependents] will shut herself up in a room until it is taken away from her, and eat a cracker a day and be as quiet as a mouse so there are no social statistics concerning her.[35]

The initial New Deal work relief programs did not adequately recognize female unemployment. They focused primarily on the male breadwinner as the mainstay of family life and incorporated the family ethic. Official government policy stated that "needy women shall be given equal consideration with needy men," but in practice, the implementation of programs for women lagged behind those for men, with little happening at all for as long as six months after the establishment of FERA in May 1933.[36] At its peak in 1934, the short-lived Civilian Works Administration (CWA), one of the first work relief agencies, placed four million workers in large-scale construction and public works projects. Only 300,000 women participated, as most CWA jobs were considered unsuitable for them. Likewise for WPA projects in which women were 12.1 percent of all workers in December 1935 while comprising 25 percent of the total labor force.[37] Only 12 percent of the workers assisted by the Federal Emergency Relief Administration (FERA), which funded state relief programs, were female.

At a November 1933 White House Conference on the Emergency Needs of Women called by some of the women officials in the Roosevelt administration with the help of Eleanor Roosevelt, Harry Hopkins, a social worker and head of the New Deal's relief programs, acknowledged the government's lack of attention to four million unemployed women. "Women have had less attention than any other employed group," Hopkins stated. He added, "The government now has the money and the determination to care for them. It has the power to give, but it has not done what it should and it feels pretty humble about it."[38] In 1935, Ellen Woodward, head of the Women and Professional Projects for the new WPA program wrote to Eleanor Roosevelt to ask,

> Won't you please ask the President to emphasize in his talk Sunday night that employable women on relief will receive their fair proportion of jobs in the new program. I think this is important, Mrs. Roosevelt, for when the Civil Works was initiated, many people, including otherwise intelligent state administrators, interpreted the statement "four million men will be put to work" to mean literally men and not men and women. It took weeks of effort and thousands of wires and letters to correct the erroneous impressions...Since the projects mentioned in the press have been mainly projects on which only men work, there is much uneasiness felt by women all over the country.[39]

That same year, Eleanor Roosevelt reminded Hopkins about the lack of male support for women's programs. "I forgot today to say that I hope in some way you will impress on state administrators that the women's programs are as important as the men's. They are so apt to forget us!"[40]

Unfortunately, stereotypic attitudes toward women workers persisted. The WPA, which coordinated federal work relief programs, often restricted female enrollment. Its programs were "intended to conserve the skills, work habits, and morale of the able-bodied unemployed through work suited as far as possible to their abilities and of value to their communities." But as Ellen Woodward had warned, they focused mainly on men.[41] The rule limiting WPA jobs to only one member of a family routinely excluded women since it typically eliminated wives. The agency gave preferential consideration to male workers with heavy family responsibilities and prohibited the employment of "women, housewives, or mothers of dependent children," needed at home to care for children and invalids.[42] The program also denied jobs to women with able-bodied but jobless husbands, defining the latter as the household head.[43]

To be certified, women had to qualify as the economic head of the household. But other eligibility criteria reflecting male work patterns defined women with a weak labor force attachment or without appropriate work experience as "not in the labor market," or "unavailable" for steady employment and thus ineligible for work relief.

WPA reports justified these restrictions by citing "a desire to put some brake upon women's eagerness to be the family breadwinner, wage recipient, and controller of the family pocketbook" and "a desire to protect the WPA program against possible public criticism for employing 'too many women.'"[44] Consequently, as noted above, only 12 percent of all WPA workers were women, mainly female household heads. The proportion of women holding WPA jobs rose in the early 1940s, but only after men had left the rolls for private employment.[45] Before this, the WPA reported that the proportion of women eligible and available but not assigned to WPA jobs "is frequently so high as to make WPA officials wonder how they can possibly provide jobs for them."[46]

The majority of women included in WPA projects worked in traditionally female jobs, such as research and clerical work, recreational activities, library, health, nutrition and canning projects, and community service centers. The largest WPA program for women was the sewing room in which surplus material was used to make clothes and other items for relief clients, hospitals, and public institutions. Fifty-six percent of all women on the WPA worked in these sewing rooms in 1936.[47] In 1937, the WPA established the Household Service Demonstration Project to provide training to women seeking domestic employment. The WPA also employed some 30,000 women on housekeeping aid projects, and another 8,000 on school lunch projects. One-third of all women on WPA projects did, however, hold higher level white-collar jobs as clerks, technical workers, professionals, and project supervisors.[48]

In 1935, although 25 percent of all black women workers were on relief and two-fifths of them were household heads,[49] WPA agencies did not readily place black women in work relief jobs. Black women comprised only 2.1 percent of all WPA workers in 1939, compared to 11 percent for white women.[50] Local agencies justified denying work relief to black and Hispanic women and men (whose incomes fell far below those at which the program certified white workers) on the grounds that they were accustomed to lower standards of living. Black and Hispanic WPA applicants also faced deliberate application delays and racial quotas and often complained to the Roosevelt administration.[51] One letter to Harry Hopkins from Chicago described segregated work sites and asked, "We would like to know do the government insist on Jim Crow on the W.P.A. projects? "[52]

WPA rules requiring workers to accept private employment at prevailing community wages before seeking work relief were applied differentially by race. Black workers, for example, who refused to accept any private market job regardless of its pay were denied aid, while whites had more leeway. If WPA employment of black women competed with private domestic service, WPA rules permitted channelling them into the regular labor force.[53] In the South and Southwest, WPA offices placed black and Hispanic women for only some part of the regularly scheduled project hours, "to arrange matters so as to permit them to earn less than the standard monthly wages which was thought to be so high as to discourage acceptance of other employment that might be available to them."[54] For women who had worked before, the WPA required that "a careful check should be made to determine what change has taken place in her economic situation which has caused her to be in the labor market as contrasted with her former circumstances."[55]

Local WPA administrators discriminated against blacks in still other ways. They often assigned skilled, white-collar, and professional black workers to unskilled manual WPA jobs despite WPA rules that explicitly prohibited such de-skilling. Local agencies rationalized these practices by claiming that they had "trouble" placing black female manual laborers and found it "difficult to use" the skills of black domestics on WPA projects. While black and white males might work together on the same outdoor projects, southern WPA agencies segregated women's projects. Most white women worked indoors[56] while black women were sent to work in the fields, regardless of their previous work experience. Evoking images of slavery, an illiterate southern black woman protested this discrimination. In a 1937 letter to the President of the United States, she wrote,

> I am ritin of these few line to let you know the way they are doin in Savannah here between the white woman an the colord woman take all of the colord woman out of the sewing room and sent them on the fahm an in the worst field in all...to dig up skelton an dead body now Mr. Presendent, I dont think it is rite for the people of Georgia to treat colord women worst as they would treat mans the colord woman if they want to work they must go to the fahm or say we haven nothen for Fall for we are not goin to put no Negro in no sewing room there place is on the fahms cold an rain the colord woman haft to go no shelter for they to go out of the rain and till the trucks come from town for them sometime we get good an wet in the rain before a truck can get from town to get us...these thing ant fare if they are have fahm why dont white

woman an the fahm too an have colord woman the sewing room too...[57]

A black woman from North Carolina wrote to WPA Director, Harry Hopkins,

> As you know we all do not like to work in tobacco for good reasons. We are settled women mostly & different troubles that prevent us from riding in open trucks, standing up 20 odd miles twice a day, stand & work all day long, we're not given no notice but to quit work here and work no where not regarding nothing...We also wish you to investigate why that so many teachers unemployed and eligible to teach have not been employed by the Adult Education here, that these teachers can have classes as they once had & help the illiterate colored people...Mr. Hopkins, colored women have been turned out of different jobs projects to make us take other jobs we mentioned and white women were hired & sent for & given places that colored women was made to leave or quit.[58]

Some of the early New Deal work relief programs virtually ignored jobless women altogether. The Civilian Conservation Corps (CCC) provided work for thousands of unemployed young men but did nothing for unemployed young women wandering from city to city. Some critics noticed this and began asking for what they later dubbed "she-she-she" camps.[59] Taking the lead, New York State's temporary Emergency Relief Administration opened a camp for women in 1933, named Camp Jane Adams. A Conference on Camps for Unemployed Women organized by Hilda Smith, a FERA specialist in Workers' Education, supported by Eleanor Roosevelt, and hosted by the White House, led to the establishment of twenty-eight schools and camps for needy unemployed women as an experimental project. By 1937, ninety camps served 5,000 women. Unlike the CCC camps which paid wages to young men, the women received neither pay nor vocational training. Education became the main focus of the "she-she-she" camps until Congress eliminated them in 1937, as part of a New Deal program cutback. Government support for the women's camps always fell far below the millions of dollars for wages, education, travel, and supervision allocated to the male CCC camps. Indeed, few Americans even knew that camps for women existed.[60]

The National Industrial Recovery Act (NIRA), the centerpiece of the early New Deal recovery plan, both helped and hurt women. The program promoted recovery by discouraging price competition and wage cutting. To this end, it organized industry into trade groups, exempted them from anti-trust laws, and negotiated standardized wage codes. The NRA wage codes set maximum and minimum wage rates for all workers, raised the minimum wage, shortened the work day, and increased the employment of women covered by the codes. At the bottom of prevailing wage scales, women made important gains under the NRA, but the codes applied only to industries in or affecting interstate or foreign commerce and excluded half of all employed women, particularly domestics, laundresses not employed in laundries, dressmakers and seamstresses not in factories, and workers in agriculture, public, and professional service.[61] Codes were not approved for telephone companies employing more than 235,000 women nor the insurance industry which employed 150,000 women. Clerical workers benefited only marginally and black women barely at all because the codes excluded most of the jobs opened to them.[62]

The NRA codes also institutionalized the male-female wage gap, ignoring the single-wage standard recommended by the National Consumers' League and other leading women's groups.[63] Based on the principle that "women shall receive the same pay as men when they do substantially the same work," rather than the rule of comparable worth, more than 25 percent of the first 464 codes included a female minimum wage 14 to 30 percent below that of men. By 1935, seventy-one codes set a lower wage for women than for men employed in the same kind of work.[64] The official NRA explanation cited "long established customs" which allowed women to be paid much less than men for the same job.[65] Black female industrial workers, concentrated in southern commercial laundries and tobacco plants, made the very lowest wages permitted by the codes, a third of which set lower hourly wages for workers in the South.[66] By respecting local wage rates in the southern and rural areas where the majority of black women and men still resided, the NRA codes also maintained wage differentials among the races. (The codes were declared unconstitutional in 1935 albeit for other reasons.)

Despite some federal efforts to do otherwise, most New Deal work programs succumbed to racism. The Roosevelt administration, seeking to maintain southern support while wooing the increasingly important black vote in northern states, did nothing to help blacks in particular. Roosevelt held that programs in aid of the poor would benefit blacks since they were overrepresented among the poor.[67] But lack of an affirmative policy allowed old patterns to prevail. Following local customs and public pressure, the CCC maintained segregated camps throughout the South and in some parts of the North. Blacks stayed in CCC camps longer than whites due to lack of jobs, moved up into administrative posts less often than whites, and faced enrollment quotas despite unemployment rates twice that of whites.[68] As discussed in Chapter Seven, the AAA's acreage reductions displaced many black women and men from the land creating more unemployment within the black community. Although blacks were overrepresented on the FERA rolls which included 17.8 percent of the black population (580, 000 families) and 9.5 percent of the white population (2,550,000 families). Relative to their numbers among the poor, however, FERA seriously underrepresented blacks.[69]

Despite lower relief benefits and the barriers they faced in obtaining aid, even minimal relief made a big difference to black families in the thirties. Reflecting this, a black Mississippian wrote to President Roosevelt, "to Let you no how they are treating we colored people on this releaf. I went up to our Vister and replied for some Thing to do Some Thing to eat and She told me that she has nothing for me at all and to they give all the worke to White people and give us nothing an Sir I wont you to no how we are treated here. So please help us if you can."[70]

The Unemployment Insurance Program

In many ways, the design of the Unemployment Insurance program was highly insensitive to the needs of women, especially women trying to balance work and family roles. Designed with the male worker in mind, it has remained conceptually unchanged since 1935 when the labor force was predominantly male and when the ideology of women's roles defined paid work by women, particularly wives, as unimportant and deviant. Even more than the Old Age Insurance program, the Unemployment Compensation program reflects male work patterns and penalizes working women viewed as out of role.

Development of Unemployment Insurance

Congress enacted the Unemployment Insurance program in 1935 to provide temporary income to the unemployed, to help stabilize the economy by maintaining the purchasing power of laid-off workers, and to encourage employers to regulate employment. Like Old Age Insurance, Unemployment Insurance was widely debated in the United

States prior to its passage, and two of the opposing sides were represented by the Wisconsin and the Ohio plans.

The Wisconsin plan considered unemployment the responsibility of employers and assumed it could be prevented or limited by devising economic incentives to encourage individual employers to "stabilize" employment, by keeping workers on the job. Its bill, the "American Plan," broke sharply from European precedents which allowed a strong government role. It favored exclusive employer financing, individualized employer reserve accounts in a state-administered but employer-controlled benefit fund, and rate variation or "experience rating" which allowed employers to receive a tax credit for minimizing their company's level of unemployment.[70] Once established, the funds would serve a select group of regularly employed, but temporarily jobless, workers for a limited period of time with payments based on past earnings.

The Ohio plan, on the other hand, viewed unemployment as a chronic feature of capitalist production, assumed it could not be prevented, and focused attention on aiding the victims to achieve social justice. It favored a state administered fund which pooled rather than separated employer taxes, and used them to pay benefits to a broad rather than a narrow group of eligible workers. Individual employers, they maintained, could not prevent unemployment and individual employer funds would produce a wide variation in benefits due to differential volumes of unemployment in various industries and firms. The statewide fund would be under public, not employer, control with joint contributions from both workers and employers; it would not permit experience rating. It would cover almost all jobless workers for a significant period, with benefit levels high enough to prevent them from seeking supplementary public aid. Taxing workers as well as employees gave both groups access to policy decisions.

The Progressive Labor Action and the Socialist Party drafted more radical plans calling for government as well as employer contributions and longer benefit periods. The Lundeen plan, advanced later by the Communist and Farmer-Labor Parties, received wide attention including support from the AFL, local unions, and a variety of other groups. It called for Unemployment Insurance benefits for all unemployed persons over age eighteen for the entire period of any involuntary joblessness. Benefits equal to the local wage rate, but not less than $10 a week plus $3 for each dependent, would be funded by general revenues raised from taxes on inheritance, gifts, and income over $5,000 a year. It included no payroll tax on employers or employees. Instead of the government, a commission elected by the organization's workers and farmers would administer the program. The support the Lundeen bill received at the House Committee on Labor hearings led the Committee to recommend its passage. The Roosevelt administration subsequently blocked the proposal which nonetheless obtained fifty votes in the House.[72]

The Unemployment Insurance program that emerged from the legislative debate reflected a none-too-happy merger of the principles, if not the exact provisions, of the Wisconsin and Ohio plans. In general, however, the views of the more conservative Wisconsin group prevailed. President Roosevelt's letter transmitting the Social Security Act to Congress echoed the Wisconsin plan's goals: "an unemployment compensation system should be constructed in such a way as to afford every practicable aid and incentive toward the larger purpose of employment stabilization."[73]

The Unemployment Insurance program of the Social Security Act encouraged but did not require states to pass laws to aid the unemployed. The federal government imposed a 3 percent tax on all employers of eight or more persons working in interstate commerce except for those in exempted industries. As in the Old Age Insurance program, the law exempted farm workers, domestic servants in private homes and in small firms, and employees of local, state, and federal governments, and of non-profit religious, educational, charitable, agencies and scientific and literary organization.

As an incentive to the states, the federal government forgave or "offset" 90 percent of the tax on employers in any state establishing an Unemployment Insurance program that met federal conditions. Washington collected the remaining 10 percent and redistributed it to the states for administrative costs. Employers in those states without a program paid the full amount directly to the federal treasury. Known as the tax-offset plan, it included less federal involvement than two other proposals rejected by Congress: the "federal plan," which provided for a compulsory national system of Unemployment Insurance and the federal-state "subsidy plan" which provided federal grants to the states to pay unemployment benefits if they created unemployed insurance funds raised by a tax on employers. By 1937, all forty-eight states had an Unemployment Insurance program.

Administered by individual states, the program lacked uniform benefits and any guarantee that the level and duration of benefits would meet minimum living standards. Within broad federal guidelines, states determined their own eligibility requirements, rules of coverage, benefit levels, waiting periods, and financing systems (e.g. pooled funds, individual plant reserves, or industry-wide funds). Benefits, started two years after a state began to assess employers and were restricted to temporarily employed workers with a strong labor force attachment. They varied widely but typically included a minimum and maximum amount and a specified number of compensable weeks. Employers initially favored financing the program using individual reserve accounts, but by the early 1940s, owing to major administrative difficulties, nearly every state had shifted to pooled funds.[74]

The Unemployment Insurance program also sanctioned "experience rating," an advantage to employers with low jobless rates. Designed as an incentive to prevent unemployment, the experience rating had the opposite effect. The method for calculating an employer's unemployment history that was eventually adopted—the volume of jobless benefits drawn by their previous employees—led them to seek ways to reduce the number of jobless workers credited to their accounts, rather than to minimize lay-offs.[75] In 1973, Margaret M. Dahn, Director of the Office of Research and Actuarial Services, U.S. Department of Labor, testified to Congress that experience rating generates employer resistance to benefit increases and "engenders a constant search to find ways to deny benefits to individual claimants." In legislative bargaining, employers agree to benefit increases "only if qualifying requirements are made tougher, individual benefit computations less generous, and disqualifications rougher."[76]

Consequently, despite its broad coverage of occupations only a small proportion of all jobless persons qualified for Unemployment Insurance benefits. Sixteen percent of jobless workers received benefits in 1939.[77] The number rose after World War II and remained above 50 percent between 1940 and the mid-1970s, peaking at 81 percent in 1975 during a deep recession. Despite record high unemployment rates in the early 1980s, the number of insured workers fell sharply.[78] In 1985, with 90 percent of the employed covered by Unemployment Insurance, only 37 percent of the unemployed received benefits. In 1986, the percentage dropped to the lowest level recorded in the program's history with fewer than one out of every three jobless workers collecting benefits in an average month. This was the third consecutive year that the level of coverage fell below 35 percent, reflecting program cutbacks and tighter eligibility rules (see Chapter Eleven). Prior to 1984, the percentage of jobless workers receiving unemployment benefits in an average month fell below 40 percent only once.[79] If discouraged workers (those who have been out of work so long that they have given up looking for a job and who are consequently not reported in Labor Department estimates of the number of unemployed) are added, the number of jobless workers without benefits falls further.[80] Other countries provide more extensive compensation. In August 1984, for example, Sweden, Germany, and Japan provided benefits to over 60 percent of their unemployed compared to 31 percent in the United States.[81]

Such limited coverage is troublesome because the Unemployment Insurance program offers some important protections. It helps employers to maintain the skill level, health, and welfare of the temporarily unemployed labor force. It offers workers a relatively non-stigmatized source of income and the time needed to find a new job commensurate with their skills and past wages. In effect, it operates as a social wage that enables workers to refuse jobs that pay too little, engage in collective protest against poor wages and working conditions, and otherwise resist exploitation without having to worry about the next dollar.

Regulating The Female Labor Force and Maintaining Patriarchal Arrangements

The 1935 Unemployment Insurance program has remained essentially the same since it was passed. From the start, the rules and regulations of the program often have worked against women, persons of color, and the poor. In the 1970s, researchers estimated that in normal years, poor households received no more than one-fifth of all Unemployment Insurance payments and that only 16 percent of all households receiving payments were poor.[82] In the 1980s, women comprised over 40 percent of the unemployed, but only one-third of all Unemployment Insurance beneficiaries. Women continue to be underrepresented on the Unemployment Insurance rolls although female joblessness has equaled or exceeded that of men each year from 1948 to 1985.[83]

Like the Old Age Insurance program, the Unemployment Insurance system did not account for the ways in which women's employment patterns differ from those of men and how women's home and family responsibilities shape their labor force participation on which eligibility for Unemployment benefits is based. The bias against women found in the Unemployment Insurance program partially reflects the social norms and labor market patterns of the 1930s. But it is also firmly grounded in the contradictory dynamics that require women's labor in the home to reproduce the labor force and to maintain the non-working population, and in the low paid labor market to keep profits high. Like the other titles of the Social Security Act, the provisions of Unemployment Insurance tend to exclude women workers, provide them with lower benefits, and make it difficult for women trying to balance work and family roles.

Women Excluded

By the mid-1980s, nearly 88 percent of all employed persons worked in jobs covered by the Unemployment Insurance program.[84] But the program was slow to include occupations employing large numbers of women. Like the Old Age Insurance program, the occupations exempted in 1935 included large numbers of black, Hispanic, and white women, and men of color. Ironically, after World War II, as men entered and women left the labor market, many states increased benefit amounts and expanded the list of exempted occupations to include those employing many women: household workers in clubs, colleges, fraternities and sororities, and employees in other non-profit organizations. The subsequent inclusion of federal civilian workers (1954) and ex-servicemen (1958) expanded female coverage only slightly.

In 1973, over 90 percent of uncovered workers fell into three occupational groups in which women, especially women of color, predominated: agriculture, domestic household service, and state and local government. Despite changes made in 1970 that brought more state employees into the program, over 8 million state and local government workers still remained exempt in 1975.[85] Domestic workers who became entitled to Social Security pensions in 1951 received virtually no Unemployment Insurance protection until 1978. Only three state Unemployment Insurance programs (Arkansas, Hawaii, and New York) and the District of Columbia covered household workers prior to that year. In 1978, federal law required coverage of certain farm workers, most state and local government employees, and a small number of private, household workers whose employers pay wages of $1,000 or more during a calendar quarter for such services. This new provision incorporated mainly large employers and added only 128,000 private household jobs to the program.[86]

Strong Labor Force Attachment

An Unemployment Insurance program that requires applicants to demonstrate a substantial and continuing attachment to the labor force heavily disadvantages working women. To qualify, applicants must pass a "work test" that shows a recent and strong employment record. The currently unemployed must have worked in a covered occupation for a specified amount of time (usually fourteen to twenty weeks in at least two quarters of the base period) or earn its equivalent in wages within a certain time. In 1935, the Committee on Economic Security (CES), which designed the Social Security Act, explained that such work requirements protect the regularly employed worker by screening out first-time or new entrants into the labor force, those returning from home or school after an absence, the long-term unemployed, and intermittent workers.[87] These groups fail to qualify because they lack a recent and firm attachment to the labor market, and because their current joblessness is not considered to be work-related. Such work tests clearly penalize women who move in an out of paid jobs more than men (to carry out home and family responsibilities) and constitute about two-thirds of adult entrants or re-entrants to the labor force.[88] Because the work test refers only to waged labor, women who enter or re-enter the labor force from work in the home do not qualify for benefits while job hunting. If women's domestic labor were viewed as work, when they enter the labor market from home they would receive benefits just as men do when they are between jobs.

Available for Work

Unemployment Insurance applicants must establish their availability for work as well as their attachment to the labor force. That is, they must be willing and able to take a suitable job. If not, their joblessness is not due to a lack of work opportunities and cannot be compensated. They must be physically and mentally capable of work, register with the State Employment Service, and accept a "suitable" job. "Unsuitable" jobs—not commensurate with workers' skills, experience, and previous pay, too far away from home, or with unreasonable working conditions—can be refused.

The availability rule adversely affects women, especially women trying to balance work and family responsibilities. Women who cannot work certain hours due to child care problems or those choosing to work part-time so as to maintain their families, historically have been declared unavailable for work and thus ineligible for benefits. In 1944, for example, a state employment office denied benefits to a mother who had to leave her job on the third shift owing to her inability to find child care for her young children during those hours. Although the woman was willing to accept work on any other shift, the court declared her unavailable for employment because she could not work on the night shift, her employer's peak production period.[89] The mother's willingness to work under conditions that would also allow her to provide proper child care was not recognized by the rules. In another case, the

Court disqualified a working mother needing child care, because she had voluntarily left work for personal, non-work related reasons.[90]

The availability requirement, typically interpreted to mean available for full-time work, also penalizes casual workers, seasonal workers, and workers choosing part-time employment. When the framers of the Social Security Act considered disqualifying voluntary part-time workers they clearly had women in mind. Paul H. Douglas, a leading social insurance expert, argued for the exclusion of part-time workers saying:

> There are some, particularly women, who wish to be employed for only a few hours per day or per week. Such persons as these are only casual or incidental members of the real labor supply and do not need or deserve the same protection as those who are fully dependent on industry for employment. It would be well, therefore...that those who are normally involved in industry for at least half of the standard working hours should come under unemployment insurance, *but this should not be the case for those who have more than one leg in the home* (emphasis added).[91]

Employers pay Unemployment Insurance taxes on part-time workers, some of whom work enough hours to pass the program's work test. But those who work less or who voluntarily seek part-time jobs cannot claim benefits because the program requires that applicants be "available" for full-time work. In any one year, nearly three-quarters of all employed women work full-time. But 66 percent of all part-time workers are women.[92]Indeed, in a society that assigns family responsibilities to women, many women "choose" part-time work at some point in their lives. Although such "voluntary" part-time work by women fell sharply during the post-War period, women *are* more likely than men to "choose" to work part-time. More men are employed part-time "involuntarily" for reasons such as lay-offs and\or the inability to find full-time work. In 1981, 22 percent of all working women worked voluntary part-time schedules compared to 6 percent who worked part-time involuntarily. The rates were somewhat higher for married women living with their husbands.[93] Today's rapid expansion of part-time employment risks confounding the distinction between voluntary and involuntary part-time work. By creating conditions in which many women can choose only part-time jobs, it is possible that many women will begin to think they have no other choice.

The rules denying benefits to workers for refusing suitable jobs also handicap women who try to combine work, marriage, and motherhood. Under the suitable work provisions noted above, a worker can refuse a midnight-to-eight job if it is impossible to get public transportation at those hours or because the night working conditions are dangerous. But a similar right of refusal is not permitted if a worker cannot make child care arrangements during those hours. Likewise, a worker can refuse a job because it is too far away from home, but not because it is too far away from her children's day care center.[94]

Most states' regulations limit Unemployment Insurance benefits to persons who are actively seeking a job and who can establish that their unemployment is for a "good cause," that is involuntary, work-related, and not due to personal circumstances. The program does not assist workers unless their unemployment is considered to be the fault of either the community or the employer. Most state Unemployment Insurance programs disqualify workers who (a) quit a job voluntarily without good cause; (b) are discharged for work-related misconduct; (c) refuse a suitable job; (d) are directly involved in a strike or (e) make fraudulent claims. These actions typically are penalized by delaying (up to twenty weeks in one state), reducing, or cancelling benefits.

Known as "disqualifiers," these rules assure that benefits go only to workers discharged from their job with "good cause" and those who are "ready" for work (e.g. absence of personal conditions, such as illness or family obligations, preventing suitable employment). States initially defined "good cause" broadly enough to include personal reasons for leaving work. But the definition became more restrictive over time. In 1948, 1950, and 1954, when rising unemployment rates associated with the post-War demobilization and economic recessions caused insurance claims to surpass revenues, many states tightened their eligibility rules.[95] Once the definition of "good cause" was narrowed to mean "good cause attributable to the employer" or "good cause connected to work," the number of disqualifications increased dramatically, rising from 15.9 per 1,000 claimants in 1945 to 23.5 in 1964.[96] Many states still consider any quit that is not work-related ineligible for benefits.

These and other post-War changes, to be discussed below, made it more difficult for women and other less regularly employed workers to qualify for benefits. The restrictions paralleled post-War increases in female unemployment and the long-term rise in women's labor force participation. The doubly high jobless rates of women of color made their plight especially hard. Perhaps it was coincidental that as more women entered the labor force during the years following World War II, states tightened their eligibility rules, raised benefit amounts, and extended their duration. Although not the intent, a trade-off occurred in which restrictive eligibility—imposed on women of all races—helped pay for improved post-War benefits for white males. By not protecting women against wage loss after the War, government and industry conveyed the message that women's lost earnings did not need replacement. After all, government officials now wanted Rosie the Riveter to return to her home.

If the post-War treatment of jobless women was not totally successful in getting women to return to their homemaker roles, it did reinforce efforts to segregate them into "women's" jobs." At the end of the War, when employers laid off disproportionate numbers of women, those who refused new jobs at lower rates of pay failed to qualify for unemployment benefits. On May 4, 1945, the *Wall Street Journal* proclaimed "Laid-off Willow Run Workers 'Choosy' about New Jobs. Some Loafing. They Count on Unemployment Pay. Half the Women Through with War Work." The article went on to say that many workers interested in immediate employment had been "turning up their noses at jobs offered to them." Not noted was the role of pay differential in making workers "choosy" or that Willow Run made no effort to find jobs for its displaced female workers.[97]

Unemployment Insurance disqualifiers reflecting male labor force patterns fell heavily on the growing number of women workers. To the extent that voluntary and personal reasons for leaving jobs included marriage, relocation with a spouse, family obligations, and pregnancy, the program barred women in particular from qualifying for aid. In some states, such "domestic quit" rules deemed an applicant unavailable for work. Even where such personal factors were accepted as "good cause" for leaving a job, states treated "domestic quits" more severely than other "voluntary quits." Some actually limited domestic quit disqualifications to women workers. But even when they did not, rules which disqualify workers because of domestic reasons were an obvious disadvantage to women. According to one study, women make up 99 percent of those disqualified because of domestic quits.[98]

Until 1971 and the Equal Employment Opportunity Act, twenty-three states specifically ruled domestic quits ineligible for Unemployment Insurance. Today, only six states directly deny unemployment benefits to workers who have quit because of domestic obligations. Some states, however, simply use other provisions to accomplish the same end. For example, a rule that makes all non-work-connected quits ineligible for aid can automatically disqualify workers who leave a job for domestic causes. Where states accept child care, marriage, and emergency domestic obligations as grounds for quitting, a woman who leaves work to care for a sick husband, child, or relative would lose out not for "quitting without a good cause," but because family responsibilities made her "unavailable" for work during the period she was needed at home. Elsewhere, work-related quits with a domestic nature often become grounds for disqualification. For example, nearly all states deny benefits to workers who quit upon the denial of a transfer to accompany a spouse or to obtain child care. Ironically, men who leave work for domestic reasons may have an easier time receiving benefits. By definition they are viewed as permanently attached to the labor force and thus not in danger of dropping out, even if they voluntarily leave a specific job.[99]

Several states waive the domestic quit rule if a worker is the family's sole support. However, married women rarely qualify for the "major or sole support" exceptions because they are "secondary" earners. The language of the provisions suggests that in those states where the waiver rule was not limited to women on the basis of need, it was probably an attempt to avoid imposing the domestic quit disqualification on men.[100]

Originally, no state had a special pregnancy disqualification. Instead states deemed pregnant women "unavailable" for work or defined leaving work while pregnant as a "voluntary quit" and thus not work-related. Over the years, more states adopted special pregnancy rules. By 1968, thirty-eight states disqualified pregnant women for the entire period of their pregnancy or, if their unemployment (for whatever reasons) fell within a stated period, before and after childbirth. That is, few states distinguished between the unemployment of pregnant women due to the pregnancy and unemployment of pregnant women due to other factors.[101] A woman caught in a plant shut-down in her first month of pregnancy lost her benefits not only for the eight months prior to childbirth, but until she found another job, worked a stated period, and was laid off again. Meanwhile her former co-workers drew benefits to which she otherwise would be entitled except for the few weeks that her pregnancy left her unable to work.[102] The number of "voluntary quits" due to pregnancy and domestic obligations rose from 23.8 per 1,000 instances of insured unemployment in 1954 to 48.5 in 1964.[103]

Following the 1975 Supreme Court decision which struck down pregnancy disqualifications,[104] the 1976 Unemployment Compensation Amendments Act prohibited states from denying unemployment benefits solely on the basis of pregnancy or recentness of pregnancy. The new federal law entitled pregnant claimants to benefits if they were willing, able, and available for work and permitted women to receive Unemployment Insurance benefits when their employers violated the 1978 Pregnancy Discrimination Act and forced them to take maternity leave without pay. Many states skirt this law, however, by considering pregnant women to be claimants who leave work for health reasons not related to employment.[105] When the U.S. Supreme Court, in 1986, rejected mandatory unemployment benefits for pregnant women, it effectively upheld this interpretation of the law.

Benefits Based on Wages

Like Old Age Insurance, the Social Security Act tied unemployment benefits to wages. To control costs and to assure that jobless benefits did not exceed wages, states generally set weekly benefit amounts at a fraction of the individual's average weekly wage, up to a state-determined maximum and subject to a minimum. A 1946 Congressional report on Social Security programs explained, "If the system is to be effective...the proportion [of wage loss] replaced should certainly not be so small as to require any substantial proportion of beneficiaries to resort to relief while in benefit status, or unduly depress living standards. On the other hand, the proportion should not be so large as to make benefit status more attractive than work."[106]

The Unemployment Insurance payment replaces a proportion of a worker's pre-tax weekly wage for a specified period of time, usually twenty-six weeks (up from ten weeks in the 1940s) unless benefits are extended by special programs activated by unusually high unemployment rates. Although replacement rates vary widely by state, wages, and benefit levels, the official rate—about 50 percent of workers' former gross wages—typically exceeds the actual amount received. As early as 1939, average Unemployment Insurance payments equaled 42 percent of wages. By 1953, the replacement rate had fallen to 34 percent.[107] In 1985, a $124 average weekly benefit represented only 35 percent of the average weekly wage, down from 37 percent in 1983.[108] In nine out of thirteen years between 1970 and 1982, New York state's maximum benefit amounted to less than half the state's average weekly wage. In 1983, the state's average weekly benefit payment ranged from $63-153, but offset only one-third of jobless worker's lost earnings.[109]

Low replacement rates reflect the failure of benefits to keep up with inflation, but also the impact of the benefit ceiling, which lowers the absolute dollar amount received by higher paid workers. For example, in 1984, the benefits paid to jobless workers employed at minimum wage or part-time jobs replaced one-half of their former wage. As benefit payments reached the maximum level, they replaced an increasingly smaller portion of the wage-earner's lost income so that the top benefit replaced only 25 to 37 percent of the higher-paid worker's former wage.[110]

The work incentive features of Unemployment Insurance penalize women workers who are at the bottom of both job and pay ladders. Due to their low wages, many women qualify only for the minimum benefit which, in 1986, ranged from $5 in Hawaii to $62 in Alaska.[111] In 1982, only 3 percent of women claimants nationwide (compared to 22 percent of men) reached the highest benefit bracket of $175-199 a week.[112] Few earned enough to reach the maximum which went from a low of $90 in Indiana to a high of $310 in Massachusetts. To receive the top benefit, workers must earn $3,139 in Indiana, $17,250 in Massachusetts, and $22,500 in New Hampshire.[113]

In New York state, the $80 average weekly benefit paid to women in 1981-82, fell considerably below the $99 paid to men. Fifty-three percent of the state's eligible men, but only 19 percent of the women, received the state's maximum of $125 a week. In contrast, 36 percent of the women but only 13 percent of the men received the $70 a week minimum.[114] The unemployment benefits received by women fell below the poverty level for a single person while the average male benefit was above the poverty level for a family of two. Unemployment Insurance lifted 16 percent of female-headed households out of official poverty in 1982 compared to 29 percent of those headed by men.[115]

Unemployment rules contained traditional assumptions about women's work. Indeed, the legislative history of the Unemployment Insurance program is scattered with questions about the appropriateness of providing benefits to women supported by men. Married women were "suspect" as secondary workers. Families depended on their "supplemental" income, not for necessities, but "merely" to raise the family's standard of living. Reviews of program abuses often focused on cases of women "who pretend to be available for work when they are not."[116] As late as 1963, the President's Commission on the Status of Women received many questions "about the payment of unemployment benefits to unemployed wives or single female workers living at home if there is a male breadwinner in the home." In 1968, opponents of Unemployment Insurance for women argued that as "secondary workers" women were not interested in full-time, year-round work. One member of the House Ways and Means Committee went so far as to ask several witnesses if Unemployment Insurance benefits should therefore differentiate between male and female workers.[117] These questions arose even though 29.2 million women (or 41.6 percent of all women) were wage earners in 1968, comprising 37.1 percent of the civilian labor force.[118]

Assumptions about the economic dependence of women on men made it harder for jobless women than unemployed men to secure dependents' allowances. The few states[119] that offered supplemental allowances to members of jobless workers' families required workers' children or spouses to be wholly or mainly supported by the claimant. For example, a male claimant who had earned $170 a week and whose wife still earned $160 would receive an allowance for the family's only child. A female claimant who had earned $100 and whose husband was earning $110 would not be entitled to an allowance for any of the family's five children. Since married women rarely provide more than half of a dependent's support, relatively few qualify for this allowance. Until the mid-1970s, the law also assumed that the children and spouses of working men depended on them financially, while the dependency of a working woman's family on her income had to be proved.[120]

The presumption that all married women are loosely attached to the labor force, unavailable for work, and use their wages only to supply the household with extras echoes the family ethic. It never fully captured the reality of married women's post-World War II labor force participation, which rose steadily from 17 percent in 1940 to 55.5 percent in 1986.[121] The earnings of working wives have always contributed significantly to family income, bringing many households above the poverty line. Doubts about women's attachment to the labor force also ignored the fact that many women supported their families alone. The percentage of female-headed households has risen without interruption from 9.4 percent of all families in 1950 to 16 percent in 1987.[122] The labor force participation rate of never-married women and wives with an absent husband neared 50 percent in 1940 and has risen steadily since then.[123] More than three-fifths of the women maintaining families alone were in the labor force in 1984.[124] Despite their rising labor force participation rates, employed women rank high among the working poor, the underemployed, and the unemployed.

Recent and Future Trends

The current and future relationship between women and Unemployment Insurance will depend on the nature of employment opportunities that develop for women in the rapidly changing labor market and the character of Unemployment Insurance program reform. To date neither bodes well.

The Recent Labor Market Experience of Women

Employed women, who comprise nearly 45 percent of the entire labor force, remain highly vulnerable to unemployment, economic insecurity, and poverty. In addition to the male-female wage gap, women accounted for one-third of the workers who became unemployed due to the elimination of a job or a work shift or to a plant closing in the declining manufacturing industries.[125] The computerization of clerical occupations has left many other women, especially low-income women, without jobs.[126] Meanwhile, the conditions under which women work in the expanding service sector—low wages, high turnover, and part-time employment—increasingly correspond to those that historically made workers ineligible for Unemployment Insurance benefits.

The rapidly expanding service sector accounted for 86 percent of all new jobs in the private sector and absorbed most of the thirteen million women who entered the paid labor force from 1970 to 1980. Women, who comprised more than half the growth in each industrial sector of the economy, accounted for three-quarters of the increase in financial, real estate and insurance firms, and more than 60 percent in both the service-producing and retail food store industries. Thirty percent of women of color are service workers, nearly twice the proportion for white women.[127]

The sector's low wages mean that many jobless service workers receive only low Unemployment Insurance payments. The wage differential between service and manufacturing work, already large in 1959, widened dramatically between 1970 and 1980.[128] In 1986, service industries paid $270 weekly and retail trade paid $176 compared to $303 in the financial sector. Moreover, wages in the service sector have risen more slowly in recent years.[129] Its high turnover[130] and high rates of part-time employment[131] additionally prevent many women from receiving any unemployment benefits at all. Meanwhile, profits in the labor-intensive service industries depend on the presence of an ever-expanding number of low-paid, marginal workers who can be moved in and out of the market when needed. For every dollar invested, the service sector realized $1.92 in 1974, and $2.06 in 1981, compared to $1.50 and $1.60 respectively in manufacturing.[132]

The conditions conducive to high profits in the service sector—low-paid labor, irregular work patterns, and a so-called weak attachment to the labor force—create the very groups, now more and more female, that the Unemployment Insurance program sought to exclude. Thirty-nine percent of all unemployed workers received jobless benefits in 1983, compared to 24 percent of workers in personal service and entertainment, 26 percent in retail trade, 31 percent in professional service, and 33 percent in business and repair service. Workers in male-dominated manufacturing industries did better than the average: 67 percent of miners, 64 percent of manufacturing (durables) workers, and 51 percent of construction workers received benefits that year.[133]

The Congressional Budget Office (CBO) attributes the sharp decline in the number of all workers receiving jobless benefits that began in the early 1960s to the rising number of women workers and their inability to qualify for benefits. According to the CBO, the entry of more women (and youth) into the labor force reduced the number of insured jobless workers because they lack the strong work force attachment of older men and the requisite work histories needed to qualify for benefits.[134] The expansion of the service sector at the expense of manufacturing added to the decline because, as noted above, manufacturing tends to employ workers with the characteristics that enable them to qualify for Unemployment Insurance benefits, while the service sector does not. The CBO adds that coverage was extended to a new group of service workers (private household workers) in the 1970s many of whom do not claim benefits when unemployed.[135]

Changes in the Unemployment Insurance Program

Not until the women's movement agitated for change in the mid-1970s, did state Unemployment Insurance programs begin to take the needs of working women into account. The resulting reforms, however, have been few and far between. In the mid-1970s, new legislation banned Unemployment Insurance offices from discriminating against pregnant women and expanded coverage slightly to include a few more farm, private-household workers, and government (local and state) employees. The government appointed a National Commission on Unemployment Compensation in 1976 to assess the present system and make recommendations. Several recommendations pertaining to women in the July 1980 preliminary report focus on the troublesome disqualifications discussed above. The Commission recommended: (1) that states remove disqualifications if the voluntary quit was for good cause (including compelling family circumstances and sexual harassment on the job); (2) that states set no specific limitation which would automatically disqualify an individual who had a recent record of steady part-time employment, and that state policy not interpret job search or suitable work criteria in such a manner as to automatically require availability only for full-time work; and (3) that State Employment Service offices initiate services for displaced homemakers who register for work.[136]

However, the weakening of the economy in the mid-1970s, and the Reagan assault on the unemployment benefits along with most other domestic programs in the 1980s left little hope for reforming the Unemployment Insurance programs in the mid-1980s were distinguished by the absence of issues of concern to women. Instead of aiding the jobless, the Reagan administration worked to lower costs, increase work incentives and privatize features of the Unemployment Insurance program as part of its effort to diminish the federal government's social welfare role. These efforts continued into the 1990s as subsequent administrations encouraged the states to deny benefits, both the regular and the various extended benefit programs to workers. All of these plans accentuated the features of the program that adversely affected women, persons of color, and the poor.

In sum, Unemployment Insurance was enacted in 1935 as part of a package of benefits to workers that would enable them to remain viable while unemployed. The program also helped to assure that the working class' ability to reproduce and maintain the labor force did not deteriorate too far. Like other Social Security Act programs, the provisions of Unemployment Insurance enforced the family ethic, thus helping to regulate competing demands for women's home and market labor. The exclusion of many female occupations from coverage, the denial of benefits to part-time workers, and the disqualifications which fell especially hard on women effectively forced poor and husbandless women to take virtually any job regardless of its safety or security. Barriers to the receipt of Unemployment insurance benefits, their short duration, and low levels helped to keep women available to employers on a low-cost and as-needed basis and dependent on male breadwinners. Such rules placed women and others in need into a pool of workers whose ready availability and low wage rates helped to depress the wages and suppress the disssatisfaction of the growing number of regularly employed female, if not male, workers. The cuts in Unemployment Insurance benefits since 1981 (discussed in Chapter Eleven) have only strengthened the program's role in maintaining women as a reserve labor pool. By penalizing women who try to balance work and family roles, Unemployment Insurance has channeled many other women back into the home, enforced their economic dependence on men, and in general sustained patriarchal arrangements. It does so at a time when the rising economic insecurity of the middle class and the movement of even more married women into work outside the home once again posed a strong challenge to the reproduction of the labor force and patriarchal norms.

Notes to Chapter 9

1. Richard Sterner, *The Negro's Share* (New York: Harper & Brothers Publishers, 1943), p. 362; Raymond Wolters, *Negroes And the Great Depression* (Westport: Greenwood Publishing Corp., 1970), p. 92.

2. Roy Lubove, *The Struggle for Social Security, 1930-1935* (Cambridge: Harvard University Press, 1968), p. 14.

3. Abraham Epstein, *Insecurity: A Challenge to America* (New York: Harrison, Smith and Robert Haas, 1933), p. 191.

4. Epstein (1933) *op. cit.*, pp. 198-212.

5. *Ibid.*, p. 202, citing U.S. Senate, *Hearings on Unemployment Relief,* Before A Subcommittee of the Committee on Manufacturers, December 28, 1931-January 9, 1932, p. 75; California State Unemployment Commission, *Report and Recommendations,* November 1932, p. 116.

6. *Ibid.*, p. 204.

7. Cited by *Ibid.*, p. 199.

8. *Ibid.*, pp. 212-214.

9. Epstein (1933) *op. cit.*, p. 20.

10. Lubove (1968) *op. cit.*, p. 163.

11. *Ibid.*, pp. 347-348, citing U.S. Bureau of Labor Statistics, *Unemployment Benefit Plans in the United States,* Bulletin No. 544, July 1931, p. 19.

12. Irving Bernstein, *The Lean Years: A History of the American Worker, 1920-1933* (Boston: Houghton Mifflin, 1960), pp. 488-490.

13. Lubove (1933) *op. cit.*, pp. 144-174.

14. June Axinn and Herman Levin, *Social Welfare: A History of the American Response to Need* (New York: Harper & Row, 1975), p. 175.

15. United States, Federal Works Agency, *Final Report on the WPA Program, 1935-1943* (Washington, D.C.: Government Printing Office, 1946), p. 2.

16. Dorothy C. Kahn, *Unemployment and Its Treatment in the United States* (New York: American Association of Social Workers, 1937), p. 18.

17. Frances Fox Piven and Richard A. Cloward, *Regulating The Poor: The Functions of Public Welfare* (New York: Pantheon Books, 1971), pp. 66-72.

18. Frances Fox Piven and Richard A. Cloward, *Poor People's Movements* (New York: Vintage Books, 1979), p. 57.

19. *Ibid.*, pp. 41-95.

20. August Meier and Elliott Rudwick, *From Plantation to Ghetto* (New York: Hill and Wang, 1976), p. 261.

21. Jacqueline Jones, *Labor of Love, Labor of Sorrow: Black Women, Work, and the Family from Slavery to the Present* (New York: Basic Books, 1985), p. 229.

22. Wolters (1970) *op. cit.,* p. 301.

23. *Ibid.,* p. 26; Jones (1985) *op. cit.,* p. 203.

24. John Williams, "Struggles in the Thirties in the South," in Bernard Sternsher (ed.), *The Negro in Depression and War* (Chicago: Quadrangle Books, 1969), p. 167.

25. Bernstein (1960) *op. cit.,* pp. 351-355.

26. David Milton, *The Politics of U.S. Labor from the Great Depression to the New Deal* (New York: Monthly Review Press, 1982), p. 26; William E. Leuchtenburg, *Franklin D. Roosevelt and the New Deal 1932-1940* (New York: Harper and Row, 1963), pp. 188-189.

27. President's Committee on Economic Security, *Social Security In America: The Factual Background of the Social Security Act as Summarized from Staff Reports to the Committee on Economic Security,* (Washington, D.C.: Government Printing Office, 1937), pp.4, 91-92; Lubove (1968) *op. cit.,* pp. 144-174.

28. Susan Ware, *Holding Their Own: American Women in the 1930s* (Boston: Twayne Publishers, 1982); Bernstein (1960) *op. cit.,* p. 325.

29. Ware (1982) *op. cit.,* p. 92.

30. *Ibid.,* pp. 30-31.

31. Jones (1985) *op. cit.,* pp. 205-206.

32. Ware (1982) *op. cit.,* p. 30.

33. Jones (1985) *op. cit.,* pp. 196-213.

34. Meridel Le Sueur, "Woman Are Hungry," in *Ripening: Selected Works, 1927-1980* (Old Westbury, N.Y.: The Feminist Press, 1982), pp. 137-138.

35. *Ibid.,* pp. 140-141.

36. Susan Ware, *Beyond Suffrage: Women in the New Deal* (Cambridge: Harvard University Press, 1981), p. 106.

37. Donald S. Howard, *The WPA and Federal Relief Policy* (New York: Russell Sage Foundation, 1943), p. 280.

38. Jane Humphries, "Women: Scapegoats and Safety Valves in the Great Depression," *The Review of Radical Political Economics,* 8 (Spring 1976), p. 107.

39. Ware (1981) *op. cit.,* p. 108.

40. *Ibid.,* p. 105.

41. United States, Federal Works Agency (1946) *op. cit.,* p. 3.

42. Howard (1943) *op. cit.,* pp. 281, 283, 348.

43. Ware (1982) *op. cit.,* p. 40.

44. Howard (1943) *op. cit.,* p. 279.

45. *Ibid.,* pp. 341, 381.

46. *Ibid.,* pp. 281, 283, 348.

47. Winifred D. Wandersee, *Women's Work and Family Values 1920-1940* (Cambridge: Harvard University Press, 1981), p. 96; Ware (1982) op. cit, p. 40.

48. Wandersee (1981) *op. cit.,* pp. 96-97.

49. Ware (1982) *op. cit.,* p. 30.

50. United States, Federal Works Agency (1946) *op. cit.,* pp. 44-45.

51. Howard (1943) *op. cit.,* pp. 291-294, 390.

52. Robert S. McElvaine, *Down and Out in the Depression* (Chapel Hill: The University of North Carolina Press, 1983), p. 89.

53. Sterner (1943) *op. cit.,* p. 245.

54. Howard (1943) *op. cit.,* p. 294.

55. *Ibid.,* pp. 451-452.

56. Sterner (1943) *op. cit.,* p. 245.

57. Rosalyn Baxandall, Linda Gordon, and Susan Reverby, *America's Working Women* (New York: Vintage Books, 1976), pp. 249-251, citing letters from WPA files, Howard University, Washington, D.C., MSS W 89 Box 11.

58. *Ibid.*

59. Howard (1943) *op. cit.,* p. 282, n. 1.

60. Ware (1981) *op. cit.,* pp. 111-115.

61. Ware (1982) *op. cit.,* p. 38.

62. Wandersee (1981) *op. cit.,* pp. 95-96.

63. William H. Chafe, *The American Woman: Her Changing Social, Economic and Political Role, 1920-1970* (London: Oxford University Press, 1972), p. 82.

64. *Ibid.,* p. 85; Humphries (1976) *op. cit.,* p. 107.

65. Ware (1982) *op, cit.,* pp. 38-39.

66. Jones (1985) *op. cit.,* p. 210; Ware (1981) *op. cit.,* p. 91.

67. McElvaine (1983) *op. cit.,* p. 29.

68. John A. Salmond, "The Civilian Conservation Corps and the Negro," in Bernard Sternsher (ed.) (1969) *op. cit.,* pp. 78-92.

69. Sterner (1943) *op. cit.,* p. 214, see also pp. 218-238.

70. McElvaine (1983) *op. cit.,* p. 84.

71. Arthur Larson and Merrill G. Murray, "The Development of Unemployment Insurance in the United States," *Vanderbilt Law Review,* 8 (February 1955), pp. 184-185.

72. Paul H. Douglas, *Social Security in the United States* (New York: Whittlesey House, 1939), pp. 74-83.

73. Franklin D. Roosevelt, "Message To Congress on Social Security, January 17, 1935," in *The Report of the Committee on Economic Security of 1935 and Other Basic Documents Relating to the Development of the Social Security Act,*

50th. Anniversary Edition (Washington, D.C.: National Conference on Social Welfare, 1985), p. 141.

74. *Ibid.*

75. Almon R. Arnold, "Experience Rating," *The Yale Law Journal*, 55 (December 1945), p. 238.

76. U.S. Congress, Joint Economic Committee, *Hearings on the Economic Problems of Women*, Part 2, July 24-29, 1973, 93rd. Cong., 1st. sess. (Washington, D.C.: Government Printing Office, 1973), p. 408.

77. Larson and Murray (1955) *op. cit.*, p.211.

78. U.S. House of Representatives, Committee on Ways and Means, *Background Material And Data On Programs Within the Jurisdiction of the Committee on Ways and Means*, 1986 edition (Washington, D.C.: Government Printing Office, March 3, 1986), p. 305.

79. Center on Budget and Policy Priorities, *Left Out: The Plight of Jobless Workers in 1986* (Washington, D.C.: Center on Budget and Policy Priorities, March 1986).

80. John Bickerman, *Unemployed and Unprotected: A Report on the Status of Unemployment Insurance* (Washington, D.C.: Center on Budget and Policy Priorities, March 1985), pp. 3-5.

81. U.S. House of Representatives, Committee on Ways and Means (1986) *op. cit.*, p. 305.

82. Raymond Munts, *Policy Development in Unemployment Insurance,* Institute For Research on Poverty, Reprint Series, Reprint #237, 1977, p. 101.

83. Congressional Budget Office, *Promoting Employment and Maintaining Incomes with Unemployment Insurance* (Washington, D.C.: Government Printing Office, March 1985), p. 8, T. 1.

84. Congressional Budget Office, *Unemployment Insurance: Financial Condition and Options for Change* (Washington, D.C.: Government Printing Office, June 1983), p. 5.

85. W. E. Upjohn Institute for Employment Research, *Strengthening Unemployment Insurance: Program Improvement,* Kalazmazoo, MI, 1975, p.10.

86. U.S. Department of Labor, Women's Bureau, *Women Private Household Workers: A Statistical and Legislative Profile* (Washington, D.C.: Government Printing Office, 1978), pp. 8-9.

87. President's Committee on Economic Security (1937) *op. cit.*, p. 123.

88. Calculated from U.S. Department of Labor, Women's Bureau, *Time of Change: 1983 Handbook on Women Workers,* Bulletin 298, (Washington, D.C.: Government Printing Office, 1983) p. 42, T. 1-28.

89. Gladys Harrison, "Eligibility and Disqualification For Benefits," *The Yale Law Review,* 55 (December 1945), p. 120.

90. Earle V. Simrell, "Employer Fault vs. General Welfare as the Basis of Unemployment Compensation," *The Yale Law Review*, 55 (December 1945), p. 182.

91. Paul H. Douglas, *Standards of Unemployment Insurance* (Chicago: The University of Chicago Press, 1933), p. 50.

92. U.S. Department of Labor, Bureau of Labor Statistics, *Employment in Perspective: Women in the Labor Force*, Third Quarter 1986, Report 733, p. 1, T. A.

93. U.S. Women's Bureau (1983) *op. cit.*, pp. 36-37, T. 1-23.

94. Diana M. Pearce, "Toil and Trouble: Women Workers and Unemployment Compensation," *Signs: A Journal of Women in Culture and Society*, 10 (31) (Spring 1985), p. 456.

95. Larson and Murray (1955) *op. cit.*, pp. 211-212.

96. William Haber and Merrill G. Murray, *Unemployment Insurance in the American Economy* (Homewood, Illinois: Richard D. Irwin Co., 1966), p. 283.

97. Sheila Tobias and Lisa Anderson, "What Really Happened to Rosie the Riveter? Demobilization and the Female Labor Force, 1944-1947," in Linda K. Kerber and Jane DeHart Mathews, *Women's America: Refocusing the Past* (New York: Oxford University Press, 1982), p. 369.

98. Pearce (1985) *op. cit.*, p. 452.

99. *Ibid.*, pp. 452-453.

100. *Ibid.*, p. 453; Citizens Advisory Council on the Status of Women, *Report of the Task Force on Social Insurance and Taxes* (Washington, D.C.: Government Printing Office, April 1968) *op. cit.*, pp. 36-37.

101. Citizen's Advisory Council on the Status of Women (1968) *op. cit.*, pp. 22-31.

102. U.S. Department of Labor, Women's Bureau, *1975 Handbook on Women Workers*, (Washington, D.C.: Government Printing Office, 1975), pp. 341-342.

103. Haber and Murray (1966) *op. cit.*, p. 283.

104. *Turner v. Utah Department of Employment Security*, 435 U.S. 44 (1975).

105. "Denial of Unemployment Benefits to Otherwise Eligible Women on the Basis of Pregnancy: Section 3304(a)(12) of the Federal Unemployment Tax Act," *Michigan Law Review*, 82 (August 1984), pp. 1925-1957.

106. U.S. Congress, House of Representatives, *Issues in Social Security: A Report to the Committee on Ways and Means*, (Washington, D.C.: Government Printing Office, 1946), p. 388.

107. Larson and Murray (1955) *op. cit.*, pp. 213-214.

108. U.S. House of Representatives, Committee on Ways and Means (1986) *op. cit.*, pp. 311-312.

109. New York State, Department of Labor, *Unemployment Insurance Beneficiaries in New York State: Benefit Year Ending in 1982,* Labor Research Report 1984, No. 2, July 1984, p. 5.

110. Congressional Budget Office (1985) *op. cit.,* pp. 14-15.

111. *Ibid.,* U.S. Congress, House of Representatives, Committee on Ways and Means (1986) *op. cit.,* p. 312.

112. Pearce (1985) *op. cit.,* pp. 456-457.

113. *Ibid.,* pp. 305-307.

114. New York State, Department of Labor, *Unemployment Insurance Beneficiaries in New York State* (1984) *op. cit.,* p. 33.

115. Pearce (1985) *op. cit.,* pp. 456-457.

116. Haber and Murray (1966) *op. cit.,* p. 271.

117. Citizen's Advisory Council on the Status of Women (1968) *op. cit.,* p. 12.

118. U.S. Department of Labor, *1969 Handbook on Women Workers,* Bulletin 294 (Washington, D.C. Government Printing Office, 1969,) p. 10; U.S. Department of Labor, Bureau of Labor Statistics, *Employment in Perspective: Women in the Labor Force,* Third Quarter 1986, *op. cit.,* p. 2.

119. The 1935 Social Security Act permitted states to provide allowances for a jobless worker's family members but prior to 1945 only the District of Columbia offered this benefit. Three other states introduced it in 1945. Today, only eleven state Unemployment Insurance programs include supplementary funds for a worker's non-working spouse and children under eighteen.

120. Citizen's Advisory Council on the Status of Women, (1968) *op. cit.,* pp. 20-22.

121. U.S. Women's Bureau (1975) *op. cit.,* p. 18; U.S. Women's Bureau (1983) *op. cit.,* p. 16, T. 1-10.

122. U.S. Bureau of the Census, "Money Income and Poverty Status of Families and Persons in the United States: 1974," *Current Population Reports,* series P-60, no. 157, p. 32, T. 19.

123. U.S. Women's Bureau (1975) *op. cit.,* p. 18, T. 5.

124. U.S. Department of Labor, Women's Bureau, *Facts on U.S. Working Women,* Fact Sheet No. 85-1, July 1985.

125. U.S. Department of Labor, Bureau of Labor Statistics, *Employment in Perspective: Working Women,* Report #719, First Quarter, 1985.

126. Hilda Scott, *Working Your Way To The Bottom: The Feminization of Poverty* (London: Pandora Press, 1984), p. 34.

127. U.S. Department of Labor, Women's Bureau (1983) *op. cit.,* p. 65.

128. *Ibid.,* pp. 294-295.

129. "The New Service Economy," *Dollars and Sense,* 120 (October 1986), pp. 6-8.

130. *Ibid.*

131. Joan Smith, "The Paradox of Women's Poverty: Wage Earning Women and Economic Transformation," *Signs: A Journal of Women in Culture and Society,* 10 (Winter 1984), pp. 291-310.

132. *Ibid.*

133. Congressional Budget Office (1985) *op. cit.,* p. 8, T. 1.

134. *Ibid.,* pp. 9-12.

135. *Ibid.*

136. U.S. Women's Bureau (1983) *op. cit.,* pp. 155-156.

10

Aid to Families With Dependent Children

Single Mothers in the Twentieth Century

The 1935 Social Security Act, best known for bringing the idea of social insurance into the American welfare system, also included income-based or "means-tested" public assistance programs for aged and blind adults without means and poor children with absent fathers. The most controversial of these programs—Aid to Dependent Children (ADC)—known as Aid to Families with Dependent Children since 1962, provides financial assistance to indigent women raising children without a male breadwinner. Given the challenges husbandless mothers pose to the rules of both capitalism and patriarchy, the role of the family ethic in ADC was even stricter than in the other Social Security Act programs. To make this "deviant" family approximate the "normal" one, ADC substituted itself for the male breadwinner, judged female-headed households harshly, and subjected them to strict control. Johnnie Tillmon, a welfare mother and a leader of the National Welfare Rights Organization (NWRO) in the 1960s and early 1970s, described AFDC as

> ...a supersexist marriage. You trade in "a" man for "the" man. But you can't divorce him if he treats you bad. He can divorce you of course, cut you off anytime he wants. But in that case "he" keeps

313

the kids, not you. "The" Man runs everything. In ordinary marriage, sex is supposed to be for your husband. On AFDC you're
not supposed to have any sex at all. You give up control over your
body. It's a condition of aid..."The" man, the welfare system, con-
trols your money. He tell you what to buy and what not to buy,
where to buy it, and how much things cost. If things—rent, for instance—really costs more than he says they do, it's too bad for
you.[1]

With the passage of ADC, the state took direct responsibility for
reproduction in female-headed households. It assumed a permanent
role in assuring income and services to single mothers which, in turn,
enabled them to raise their children at home. Not only were poor
women who raised their children alone viewed as limited in their
reproductive ability, but they challenged patriarchal authority and its
prevailing norms. The program also mediated competition for women's
low-paid market and unpaid domestic labor by denying aid to "undeserving" women viewed as out of role.

Although AFDC's harsh regulations intervene in the daily life of
poor women on behalf of the *status quo,* the program also paradoxically contains the potential to counter social conditions on which
capitalism and patriarchy depend. Herein lies its threat to the haves and
its possibilities for the have-nots. Like Unemployment Insurance, AFDC
functions as a social wage, albeit a meager and punitive one, that supports women in times of distress. As an economic cushion, AFDC does
offer poor women some choice which, however limited, increases their
bargaining power at home and on the job. In general, even so small a
social wage may enable workers to take the economic risks involved
in resisting pressure to take any job at any pay or to engage in activities,
such as strikes, that might improve wages and working conditions. It
may also suggest the leverage that a larger social wage could provide.
For women in particular, the social wage offers additional protection
against entering into or remaining in marriages regardless of their safety
or security. These potentially positive outcomes of the AFDC program
lie beneath the harsh rules and regular attacks both the program and
its clients have suffered over the years. This chapter examines what
AFDC has meant to women. How has it punished and rewarded them?
How has it enforced the family ethic? How has it mediated the conflict
for women's low-paid labor in the market and their unpaid labor in the
home?

From Mothers' Pensions to
Aid to Dependent Children

The growth of female-headed households only deepened the sense of crisis within the family system during the Depression, intensifying feelings of instability and fears about the decline of familial or private patriarchy. The 1930 census reported 3.7 million female-headed households nationwide, 1.4 million with children under age twenty-one.[2] The rise in divorce and desertion rates promised to increase this pool of economically vulnerable women. Indeed, 10 percent of the two million jobless women in 1931 headed households and between 100,000 and 150,000 homeless women wandered the country.[3] But only 110,000 of the nation's 1.4 million female-headed families received Mothers' Aid in 1934. Another 358,000 households with over 700,000 children appeared on the federal emergency relief rolls.[4] The Committee on Economic Security (CES) figured that about 288,000 to 300,000 female-headed families might need economic assistance even in more normal times.[5]

Husbandless women and their children elicited a mixed response. Congress, for example, was tempered by "practical" politics, a negative attitude toward single mothers, and concerns about their fitness to reproduce the labor force. According to Edwin Witte, Executive Director of the CES from 1934 to 1935, "There was little interest in Congress in the Aid to Dependent Children."[6] The major impetus for ADC came from the Children's Bureau whose proposals, based on the Mothers' Pensions programs, CES accepted with little comment.[7] Tensions between the need to reproduce the labor force and to assure a supply of low-paid female labor along with general disregard for single mothers and racist attitudes shaped the ADC program from the start and help explain the program's stigma and low status.

The ADC program represented a more comprehensive version of the Mothers' Pension program. Like its forerunner, ADC was "designed to release from the wage-earning role the person whose natural function is to give her children the physical and affectionate guardianship necessary not alone to keep them from falling into social misfortune, but more affirmatively to make them citizens capable of contributing to society."[8] Thus the ADC program institutionalized the state's role in subsidizing the reproduction of the labor force and the maintenance of the non-working population by female family heads. It provided funds to the states, rather than counties or cities, to establish financial assistance programs for needy children. It expanded the program's coverage and in general increased women's access to relief funds. In contrast to Mothers' Pensions, where only one-half of the local units authorized to grant aid actually did so,[9] the Social Security Act required ADC programs to be implemented statewide. The Act also broadened both the definition of lack of parental support and the list of possible caretaking relatives.[10] Money payments could be made to a child under the age of sixteen who was deprived of parental support or care by reason of the death of a parent but also by reason of continued absence from the home owing to physical or mental incapacity. The range of possible caretakers included a father, mother, grandfather, grandmother, brother, sister, stepfather, stepmother, stepbrother, stepsister, uncle, or aunt.[11]

The mandate for statewide programming and expanded coverage was undercut, however, by more negative responses to the program. Most states delayed putting the ADC program into place. By November 1936, when forty-two states had an OAA program, ADC existed in only twenty-six. By early 1939, ten states still lacked the program for dependent children.[12] In addition to this slow start, Congress appropriated fewer funds and established lower matching and reimbursement rates for ADC than other public assistance programs. The $25 million initially recommended for ADC fell below the amount spent on such families by the "less desirable" Federal Emergency Relief Program, according to the CES.[13] Congress set a maximum federal ADC payment of $18 for the first child and $12 for the second and a federal reimbursement rate of one-third of state costs. In contrast, the OAA formula authorized a monthly grant of up to $30 and a reimbursement rate of 50 percent. Most startling, the initial ADC provisions included no aid for the dependent child's mother. A federal matching grant for the mother was added in 1950, fifteen years after the program's inception— only after states pressured the federal government to relieve them of the costs of aiding the ADC caretaker. Aid for the mother ceased, however, when her youngest child reached age sixteen, that is, once her reproductive and caretaking functions ended.

Some observers attribute the OAA-ADC differential to Congressman Vinson (D-KY) who reported that widows of veterans received $18 for the first child and $12 for each additional child. But Vinson failed to explain that the veteran's widow also received a $30 pension for herself. When the omission was discovered, it was criticized, but according to Witte, "there was so little interest on the part of any members in the Aid to Dependent Children that no one thereafter made a motion to strike out the restriction." When the CES later sought to remove it in the amendment process, the Senate Finance

Committee Chair suggested that it was "probably alright to start this aid at a very low figure, as subsequent Congresses easily could increase it." The motion made to strike the provision never came to a vote.[14] In the end, the CES did not challenge the reimbursement differential "lest we lose this aid altogether."[15]

As a result, by 1939, the average OAA and Aid to the Blind (AB) grants, hardly excessive, exceeded those paid to ADC families with states spending about four times as much for OAA as for ADC.[16] When Congress revised the public assistance matching formula that year, it raised the maximum for OAA and AB but not for ADC. The pattern of lower benefits for ADC relative to other public aid programs prevails to this day and reflects the ever-present tension between AFDC benefit levels and the prevailing market wage. In no state does the ADC grant raise a family above the national poverty level. Trying to keep benefits below current wages continues the poor law practice (known as "less eligibility") of lowering the social wage to assure that public aid does not become more attractive than the lowest paying job, and for women, more attractive than marriage and family life.

The ADC program remained limited to single-parent families despite several efforts over the years to extend it to two-parent households. The CES rejected the Social Security Advisory Council's 1935 efforts to include two-parent families fearing, once again, that if it asked too much for ADC it might undercut the entire Social Security Act. Arguing that their work in 1935 was only the first step in a broad strategy of income security, the CES told Roosevelt that "a piecemeal approach is dictated by practical considerations, but the broad objectives should never be forgotten."[17] A 1949 effort to extend the ADC program to two-parent families failed on the grounds that it undermined the work ethic.[18] Not until 1961 when Congress added coverage to a limited group of families with unemployed parents were any such families assisted by ADC and then only in the twenty-two states which eventually chose to adopt this program called ADC for unemployed parents or ADC-UP.

The ADC program also contained a compromise with racism. An early version of the Social Security bill included a national ADC benefit standard intended to discourage the states from capping payments below standards of minimum need which they commonly did. It made federal approval of state public assistance programs contingent upon the provision of "assistance at least great enough to provide, when added to the income of the family, a reasonable subsistence compatible with decency and health." Arguing that such a federal standard violated states' rights, southern opposition successfully struck the provision from both the ADC and the OAA programs.[19] But beneath the states' rights argument, southern states (which had also resisted establishing Mothers' Pension programs or limited them to white widows) feared that such a federal standard would require equal treatment of whites and blacks. This would, among many other things, confront the prevailing black-white wage differential.

Regulation by Exclusion

The ADC program perpetuated the Mothers' Pension philosophy that maternal employment negatively affected child development and that "deserving" women belonged in the home. Like its forerunner, ADC subsidized mothers to reproduce the labor force and maintain the non-working members of the population, but made receipt of a grant highly conditional upon compliance with the family ethic. Most state programs distinguished between women deserving and undeserving of ADC by continuing to use the "suitable home" policies developed under the Mothers' Pension program. The Social Security Act itself did not contain any "suitable home" or "fit parent" provisions. But the preliminary legislative debates, the Congressional Committee reports, and an early version of the bill implicitly granted states permission to evaluate ADC applicants' moral character. Most professional opinion at the time also supported the denial of aid to families with "unsuitable" homes.[20] The Federal Bureau of Public Assistance officially sanctioned the use of suitable home criteria after the 1939 Amendments to the Social Security Act removed many "deserving" widows from the ADC rolls to the Old Age Insurance program.[21]

Ambivalence about supporting female-headed households to reproduce the labor force was compounded by the need for low-paid female market labor. Along with suitable home criteria, some states also used "employable mother" rules which disqualified able-bodied women with school-age children, especially black women, from the ADC rolls on the grounds that they should work. In the late 1930s, one southern public assistance field supervisor reported that

> The number of Negro cases is few due to the unanimous feeling on the part of the staff and board that there are more work opportunities for Negro women and to their intense desire not to interfere with local labor conditions. The attitude that they have always gotten along, and that "all they'll do is have more children" is definite...There is hesitancy on the part of lay boards to advance

too rapidly over the thinking of their own communities, which see no reason why the employable Negro mother should not continue her usually sketchy seasonal labor or indefinite domestic service rather than receive a public assistance grant.[22]

A 1939 evaluation of the ADC program concluded that "the point of view embodied in the old restrictions still limited the granting of aid," and that "some states have been relatively slow in bringing into their new programs families who, though not eligible under their old Mothers' Pensions laws, might legally be aided under the more inclusive provisions now in effect."[23] Indeed, widows and orphans—that is, white widows and orphans—predominated on the ADC rolls, although the program technically admitted all "children deprived of parental support or care due to parental death, continued absence from the home, or physical or mental incapacity of a parent." In 1939, 61 percent of ADC mothers were widowed, compared to 25 percent who were deserted, divorced, or separated. Only 2 percent of the children accepted for aid lived with unmarried mothers.[24] While nearly 12 percent of all children in the twenty-nine states and District of Columbia with an operative ADC program were black, black women and children were underserved relative to their numbers among the poor.[25]

From 1935 to the end of World War II, the ADC program followed the pattern established by the Mothers' Pension program of aiding "deserving" women and denying help to those perceived as out of role and therefore "undeserving" of aid. The slow implementation of the ADC program, the lack of coverage for ADC mothers themselves until 1950, the highly selective suitable home rules and the program's low benefit levels left many other poor women with few options other than to enter unsafe and insecure jobs and/or marriages, to enter the labor force, or to apply for the even less generous local outdoor relief.

Under Attack: 1945-1962

The ADC program grew steadily from 372,000 families in 1940 to 803,000 in 1960, falling only temporarily during World War II and the Korean War.[26] During the same period, ADC costs also rose sharply, from $133 million to $994 million.[27] By mid-century, the ability of the ADC program to regulate the lives of poor women just by excluding those viewed as "undeserving" began to falter owing to the rapid expansion of the program, its rising costs, and a shift in the composition of the caseload from white widows to unwed mothers and women of color. Once women seen as out of role came to dominate the caseload, racism and sexism made it more difficult to distinguish among women as "deserving" and "undeserving" of aid based on their compliance with the family ethic. The massive attacks on ADC that accompanied these changes were not unlike earlier attacks on outdoor relief in the 1820s and 1870s. As before, the mid-twentieth-century assault reflected the program's declining ability to discipline work and family life according to the traditional rules, that is, to mediate the conflicting demand for women's home and market labor, to assure the reproduction and maintenance of the labor force, and to sustain patriarchal arrangements under new and more complex conditions. Additionally, the post-War attack also reflected widespread and systematic racism.

The changes in the ADC program that precipitated the attack reflected normal population growth, changing family structures, and labor market dislocations, not the behavior of mothers on ADC, as suggested by the program's critics. The natural growth of the population along with rising rates of divorce, desertion, fertility, and births outside of marriage enlarged the pool of women eligible for ADC from all demographic groups. After reaching a low point in 1935, the fertility rate of both black and white women began a steep rise, peaking in 1957, with black rates exceeding those of white. Black women were also much more likely than white women to be separated, divorced, or widowed. About equal proportions of previously married women of both races—four out of ten—headed households that included children."[28] The high fertility and marital disruption rates increased the number of black women in need of ADC. So did discrimination against black men and their persistently high jobless rates in the post-War years. The displacement of blacks from southern agriculture and their segregation in the lowest paying jobs created a pool of workers vulnerable to low wages, high unemployment, and isolation from the white working class.[29] In 1940, black unemployment exceeded that of whites by 20 percent. By 1955, the black rate was twice that of whites and has remained at or above that relative level ever since.[30] Among other things, such economic marginalization makes black men less available for marriage and family support.

Low pay and joblessness among women also led them to ADC. From 3.7 percent in 1947, women's unemployment rate rose to 6 percent in 1949 and remained high until the Korean War. During the next fifteen years, women's jobless rates, always higher than men's, fluctuated from a low of 4.8 percent to a high of 7.2 percent. Black women faced more frequent and longer periods of unemployment from 1955 to 1968, when their jobless rate ranged from 7.3 percent to 11.8 percent.[31] Due to racial discrimination, black women benefited considerably less than white women from expanded wartime employment, although they did break into some industrial jobs, typically the dirtiest and most dangerous one.[32] Black women tried very hard to avoid returning to domestic work, the one place they were in demand. White housewives who lowered their servants' pay right after the war found themselves without any help the next day. Even black women with expired unemployment benefits resisted the domestic labor market. The *Buffalo Courier Express,* called the result a "revolution—a quite bloodless one" that enabled domestic workers to set "their own hours and select…their own working conditions." The Women's Bureau, concerned about the post-War economic difficulties faced by black women *and* the anxieties of upper middle-class white women, developed training programs that tried to make domestic work an attractive option. But by 1950, lacking other alternatives, 60 percent of employed black women held private or institutional household service jobs, compared to 16 percent of their white counterparts.[33]

From 1948 to 1953, as widowhood declined as the primary source of female-headed households, the number of widowed ADC mothers dropped by 25 percent. Meanwhile, unwed mothers on ADC rose by nearly 58 percent. ADC families headed by deserted or separated wives increased 27.6 percent; those by divorced women rose 9.1 percent.[34] By 1961, widowed families comprised only 7.7 percent of the ADC caseload down from 43 percent in 1937.[35] The majority of ADC mothers were separated, divorced, or unwed.[36]

Blacks became overrepresented in the ADC caseload in the post-War years, although the absolute number of whites remained larger. According to one estimate, black families accounted for two-thirds of the increase in ADC rolls between 1948 and 1961,[37] rising from 31 percent of the caseload in 1950, to 48 percent in 1961. The addition of non-white Hispanics to the rolls produced a non-white majority in the sixties, although nearly 42 percent of the ADC recipients nationwide were white.[38]

Despite the many complicated reasons for the expansion of the ADC program, public opinion focused on rising costs, southern black migration, and out-of-wedlock births. The post-War attack on the program focused heavily on the personal characteristics of the ADC mother, criticizing her behavior and fitness. It seemed to warn against the consequences of marital disruption and unwed motherhood by punitively demonstrating what happens to women who live and raise children without men. ADC's harsh and moralistic policies also helped to discipline the female labor force to the extent that they channelled poor women into the low-wage sector of the market. Commenting on the attack's strong racial overtones, Greenleigh Associates noted that ADC has

> become one of the most controversial and misunderstood programs in the United States...the ADC families are considerably different than in the early years of the program; their problems are more complex, and the attitudes of the general public toward them are usually confused, accusing and hostile...there is much evidence that much of the criticism has grown out of racial tensions, a feeling that ADC families should behave in a manner not expected of others, and a lack of understanding of the ADC recipients and of the problems which they face which created their dependency.[39]

The major assault on ADC occurred at the state level, but federal policies also contributed. In 1950, Congress passed the Notification of Law Enforcement Officers (NOLEO) amendment to the Social Security Act which required public welfare departments to notify law enforcement officials whenever they granted aid to a deserted or abandoned child. This effort to secure support from absent fathers, not unreasonable in theory, paid little attention to prevailing research indicating that only 18 percent of the absent fathers contributed support, that half of the contributions fell below $50 a month, and three-fourths below $75.[40] The NOLEO rule subtly maligned the families on ADC. It reflected public disapproval of the "irresponsible" men who failed to provide for their families and of the ADC program for supposedly encouraging families to break up. But ADC mothers took the brunt of the blame. The new rule changed the principle of client confidentiality, made cooperation with NOLEO searches for absent fathers by the ADC mother a condition of eligibility, and deterred applications for aid. Despite subsequent court challenges to state interpretations of the NOLEO paternity and support provisions, many states still require mothers' cooperation as a condition of aid.[41]

The following year, Congress passed the Jenner Amendment as a rider to the 1951 Revenue Act. Responding to charges of welfare fraud, the Jenner Amendment allowed states to make names on the ADC rolls public provided that the information was not used for political or commercial purposes. Public scrutiny of the welfare rolls violated the confidentiality provision of the Social Security Act, put there to protect the welfare records from abuse in partisan politics and to protect parents and children from embarrassment.[42] Although numerous efforts to find evidence of fraud routinely produced negligible numbers,[43] about half the states adopted the Jenner Amendment, adding to the stigma and harassment of welfare mothers and to the idea that most did not need (read: deserve) economic aid.

These Congressional activities tacitly supported negative attitudes toward ADC, but the most direct attack took place at the state level. Many states, including Michigan (1949), Mississippi (1950-1952), and Florida (1951), reduced their financial support for the program. Others used a variety of administrative rules to discredit and shrink it. They investigated welfare departments for mismanagement and fraud, tightened eligibility rules, enforced residency requirements (often to prevent southern black migrants from qualifying for aid) and harassed clients in a variety of ways. The city of Newburgh, New York became symbolic of the overall trend. In 1961, Newburgh, facing deep economic trouble and a declining white population, announced a thirteen-point code of welfare regulations that combined many of the deterrent devices noted above. Although twice as many people collected Unemployment Insurance than welfare at the time, ADC became the focus of the attack which limited the time families could receive ADC grants, required all able-bodied men to work off their relief checks, threatened to remove children from "unsuitable" homes, and forced welfare families to pick up their checks at the police station. New York state eventually barred the Newburgh scheme which threatened the state's receipt of federal funds. But before the attack moved to the courts, it attracted wide press coverage and support.[44] Only later was it discovered that the majority of the town's relief recipients were white, that the city had spent only a tiny portion of allocated funds on the program, and that only one able-bodied chiseler was on the rolls.[45]

Meanwhile, the use of moral fitness standards rather than financial need to determine eligibility for ADC was becoming more widespread. Although fifteen states abolished their suitable home provisions after World War II, numerous others did not.[46] Instead, in the early fifties, various states enacted "suitable home," "man-in-the-house," and "substitute father" rules which disqualified large numbers of unwed mothers and women of color. The states also required ADC families to follow a variety of child care, guidance, and home management standards imposed by workers and agencies. By 1960, twenty-three states, many but not all in the South, had some type of suitable home policy on the books.[47] Some states unsuccessfully went beyond these criteria to try and enact laws that explicitly removed families from the roles if a child was born outside of marriage after the receipt of a welfare grant. The failure of these efforts did not, however, interfere with the continued use of traditional suitable home laws which produced similar results.

Using vaguely defined rules, state welfare departments denied aid to single mothers who took in male boarders, who co-habited with men, who refused to identify the fathers of out-of-wedlock children, or whose homes and behaviors simply did not look right to the investigating worker. They also threatened ADC mothers who applied for aid with child removal, informing them that a negative assessment might force the welfare department to press for the placement of their children in institutions or foster homes. If they withdrew their application, however, the agency's interest in the children would cease.[48]

Many states also enacted "substitute father" rules in the fifties. Broad interpretation of the provision that a child must be "deprived of parental support" and not living with two able-bodied adults allowed states to determine that any man in the ADC mother's life was a "substitute father." His presence immediately disqualified the entire family on the grounds that the children were no longer "deprived of parental support." To implement the policy, and because positive evidence of an ADC mother's relationship with a man was not easy to establish, states created special investigatory units to uncover resources the family had not admitted. In addition to credit checks and collateral contacts with relatives, friends, and neighbors, these units also conducted surveillance of the family home. Surprise "midnight raids" searched for a "man-in-the-house" who, if found, automatically became a "substitute parent."[49]

The surprise raids severely harassed welfare mothers. Welfare Departments authorized raids against recipients *en masse* and at all hours without regard to clients' privacy. Edward Sparer, a welfare rights attorney, reported that welfare departments instructed workers "to look in the bedroom, look in the closets, look behind the shower curtain, look in the drawers for articles of clothing."[50] The complaint of a Chicago woman against an investigator who arrived when she was taking a bath stated,

> He pushed past her nine year old daughter who answered the door, looked in the bedroom and the bathroom searching for a man or evidence of male company. He had no warrant. He did find a suit in a closet belonging to the mother's boyfriend who visited on weekends, and about whom the department had been fully informed. Nevertheless assistance was discontinued on the assumption that the man was living full-time with the family and that they could look to him for support—support which the part-time boyfriend could not provide.[51]

In another case, an investigator climbed into a tree at two o'clock in the morning to look into the window of a welfare family's apartment to see if a man was there.[52]

The use of moral fitness criteria to punish ADC mothers effectively shrunk the welfare rolls, making many women available for the paid labor force, particularly in the South. For many years, South Carolina ranked among the seven highest states in the nation for its proportion of unmarried ADC mothers. In 1950, it enacted a substitute parent law, denying aid to children whose mothers had even a casual, short-term relationship with a man, regardless of whether the man had an income, spent it on the children, or was in any way legally responsible for their support. The regulation, which equated a woman's relationship with a man to the availability of financial support from him, immediately disqualified 368 of 820 families in Charleston, South Carolina alone. This occurred even though the procedure violated the federal regulation that permitted children with legal stepfathers to receive ADC if the stepfather was unwilling or unable to pay and the family lived in a state that did not hold him legally responsible for the child. To avoid such harassment, many other poor women at work in low paid menial jobs simply decided not to apply for assistance. Eight years later in 1958, South Carolina ranked fifth from last in the proportion of unwed mothers it served.[53]

Georgia's 1952 moral fitness provision also reduced its rolls. It (1) required the mother to establish paternity and provide evidence of her efforts to secure child support from the father; (2) defined children as not deprived of parental support if they a had an able-bodied stepfather or substitute father in or around the house; (3) considered no family eligible for a grant unless the home was suitable; (4) suggested that the birth of an illegitimate child raised questions about the presence of a substitute father and the suitability of the home; and (5) forced able-bodied mothers with no children under twelve months to work (when work was available) by making their families ineligible for aid if they did not. Between 1950 and 1953, the state's ADC recipient rate dropped from 35 to 25 per 1,000 children under age eighteen, and the proportion of families headed by single mothers fell from 13.1 percent to 7.8 percent of the caseload. The policy also stayed the growth of black ADC families. Meanwhile, the average monthly benefit for the "deserving" families remaining on the rolls rose from $50.94 in 1952 to $82.90 in 1958.[54]

Similar moral fitness rules were adopted by other states throughout the country. The all-inclusive range of relationships caught up in these provisions and the methods the states used to detect them

suggest that the target of the policy was the ADC mother and her behavior, not the discovery of child neglect. Indeed, except in cases of
extreme anti-social behavior, states applied moral fitness standards almost exclusively to women. ADC regulations referring to "parent or
relative" appeared gender neutral on paper, but in practice they were
not. Men were not known to have illegitimate children nor was the
word "promiscuous" typically applied to male behavior.[55] In her clas-
sic book on ADC, Bell argues further that the states used suitable home
rules specifically to limit the coverage of black and illegitimate children
born outside of marriage.[56] The overrepresentation of black women
among husbandless females and their higher rates of fertility and illegitimacy left them uniquely vulnerable to suitable home rules based
on vague and discretionary definitions of moral fitness. The policy also
was an attempt to pressure black women into low-waged labor, especially domestic service, at a time when, as noted earlier, black women
released from wartime jobs resisted returning to this type of work.

Suitable home policies remained in force until a crisis in Louisiana
forced the issue. In July 1960, after the state introduced a severe suitable
home policy, 23,330 children immediately lost ADC eligibility. Children
born out of wedlock comprised 70 percent of those thrown off the rolls.
Although blacks comprised 66 percent of the overall caseload, 95 percent of the newly ineligible families were black. As was true in many
other states with similar policies, Louisiana made no alternative arrangements for the children whose families technically were disqualified
on the grounds of parental neglect. The American Civil Liberties Union
described the law as part of Louisiana's "parcel of segregation" bills
reflecting "the state's militant opposition to any attempt at desegrega-
tion."[57]

After much public outcry and considerable delay, Arthur Flemming, Secretary of the Department of Health, Education, and Welfare
officially ruled that states had to provide for the care of children
removed from the ADC rolls for reasons of neglect. He declared that,

> A state plan for aid to dependent children may not impose an
> eligibility condition that would deny assistance with respect to a
> needy child on the basis that the home conditions in which the
> child lives are unsuitable, while the child continues to reside in
> the home. Assistance will therefore be continued during the time
> efforts are being made either to improve the home conditions or
> to make arrangements for the child elsewhere.[58]

Given the decision's narrowness and its failure to address the
moral judgments involved, many states simply devised other means of

excluding women viewed as out of compliance with the family ethic. A binding policy against such actions did not appear until 1968, when the Supreme Court invalidated Alabama's (and nineteen other states') definition of a "man-in-the-house" and a substitute father. Between 1967 and 1971, 368,000 additional families nationwide headed by unwed mothers became eligible for welfare due, in part, to the change in the substitute father regulation.[59]

The Flemming ruling did not allow states to close cases on the grounds of unsuitable homes unless the child was removed from the home and provided with other adequate care. The next year Congress authorized the use of ADC funds to pay for the foster care of ADC children removed by court order from an unsuitable home.[60] By underscoring the right of the government to remove children from homes declared unfit by the courts, it offered children needed protection against child abuse and neglect. But this emphasis on child removal, necessary to protect children in some instances was not free of past bias. It also represented a departure from the original ADC intent to keep children in their homes and to prevent their institutionalization. Given prevailing practices, the threat and the reality of child removal became another way of punishing husbandless women and asserting state control over the reproduction and maintenance of families considered maladapted to the task.

The attack launched against ADC in the early fifties occurred in a prosperous but socially tense and conservative period characterized by McCarthyism and anti-unionism. The hostility to ADC may also have been an indirect backlash against the movements for women's rights and black civil rights that emerged after World War II. The wartime entry of women into traditional male jobs, the proposed equal pay bill, the Equal Rights Amendment, and the continued entry of women, especially white married women, into the labor force challenged patriarchal norms. Perhaps this is why post-War society blamed working women for the rise of family problems, encouraged middle-class, white women to return to the home, and justified excluding women of all races from the labor market or keeping them segregated in low paid "women's" jobs. The extreme cuts in welfare benefits also continued the harsh treatment historically meted out to poor women and women of color by public aid programs which forced them to work outside the home and routinely denied them the rights of womanhood under the terms of the family ethic.

The ADC backlash also represented an initial reaction to the emergence of the post-War civil rights struggle which radically challenged institutionalized racism.[61] A break in racial barriers opened up some jobs for skilled and semi-skilled black workers and caused black union membership to grow from 200,000 in 1940 to 1.25 million in 1945. During this same period, black workers won a ban against discrimination in defense production (1941), the elimination of the all-white primary (1944), and Truman's support for desegregating the military. In 1943, competition among whites and blacks for jobs and housing resulted in a wave of anti-black violence in Harlem, Detroit, and twenty-five other cities. White efforts to bar blacks from newly constructed public housing and anger at other racial barriers swelled the NAACP's membership from 50,000 to 450,000, contributed to the formation of the militant Congress of Racial Equality (CORE), and generated support for a young Baptist preacher named Martin Luther King, Jr. Dominated by southern Dixiecrats, Congress staunchly resisted most civil rights legislation. The Supreme Court's 1954 ban of segregated public schools sparked a violent racial struggle in the South in which black women played key leadership roles. The refusal by Rosa Parks to give her seat to a white bus passenger, for example, sparked the Montgomery bus boycott in which mostly female domestic and service workers refused to ride the Montgomery buses, throwing white households into disarray for 381 days. Between 1955 and 1965, many black women participated actively in mass demonstrations, acts of civil disobedience, and numerous voter registration drives.

The assault on ADC may also have reflected antagonism to the post-War consolidation of the welfare state. The significant expansion of the welfare state between 1945 and 1960 challenged laissez-faire doctrine, raised fears of "big government," and evoked cries of socialism. In this period of rising conservatism, Congress passed the Taft-Hartley Act to restrict the activities of strong and politically active trade unions and defeated efforts to enact national health insurance, federal aid to education, and numerous civil rights bills. But it also completed some unfinished New Deal business. The threat of post-War unemployment and the lingering influence of New Deal politicians and bureaucrats in Washington's halls of power, among other pressures, led Congress to enact the National School Lunch Program (1946), the National Mental Health Act (1946), the Hill-Burton Hospital Construction Act (1946), the Employment Act (1946), the Housing Act (1949), the School Milk Program (1954), and the Vocational Rehabilitation Act (1954). The 1950 amendments to the Social Security Act expanded coverage, raised public assistance benefits, provided federal aid for the medical expenses of ADC families, and established the fair hearing procedure. In 1956, Congress added Disability Insurance to the Social Security system and shortly thereafter farm workers and the self-employed, omitted from the original legislation, were brought into the social insurance program.

Strengthening Family Life: 1962-1967

The attack on the ADC program and its increasingly exclusionary policies failed to permanently lower the rolls or keep them free of unwed mothers and women of color. It was at this time that social service programs and work incentives were introduced into the ADC program. This shift from punitive exclusion to rehabilitative services for women viewed as "undeserving" meshed with the rediscovery of social problems, an increased demand for women workers in the newly expanding service sector of the economy, and the growing influence of the social work profession. The move from assault to reform may also have reflected the state's response to social movements in the late fifties, especially rising black consciousness, voting power, and civil rights.

Social Services

Social services became an important component of ADC in the sixties. Rising rates of unemployment, divorce, desertion, illegitimacy, juvenile delinquency, and mental illness in the late fifties and early sixties rekindled fears about the ability of all families, but especially the poor, to carry out the reproductive and maintenance tasks assigned to them and eventually resulted in more direct state intervention in family life. Between 1940 and 1960, for example, juvenile court cases rose from 10.5 to 39.2 per 100,000 population aged ten to seventeen; and in 1955 there were 558,000 psychiatric hospitalizations, 200,000 new admissions, and 300,000 clinic patients.[62] The ever-increasing employment of married women only aggravated these fears.[63] Analysts variously attributed the appearance of social problems to working mothers, industrialization,[64] the lack of legitimate opportunities,[65] and incipient social unrest.[66] John Ehrenreich suggests that the post-War emergence of social problems may have been an individual expression of social discontent which foreshadowed the massive social protests of the sixties.

The costs of rising illegitimacy, delinquency, and psychiatric admission rates focused official attention on the problems which no doubt had mounted unattended during the War. The overrepresentation of social problems among poor families on ADC soon became a major issue. As early as 1951, researchers concluded that a small proportion of the poor (whom they now called "hard-to-reach") absorbed a large part of the social welfare resources.[67]

States continued to contract the ADC program to save dollars and to punish women perceived as deviant. But federal officials, concerned about labor markets, family stability, and social control, responded differently and the provision of services to strengthen family life became a new ADC objective. Services, it was hoped, would both rehabilitate families and move them off the welfare rolls. The dual goals of reducing the welfare rolls by strengthening family life and facilitating self-support first appeared in the 1956 amendments to the Social Security Act. The Eisenhower administration urged counseling, guidance, and rehabilitation as "constructive services to enable families which have been threatened by family breakdown to rebuild the fiber of family living and provide for the children the kind of care which other children in the communities have."[68] The 1956 amendments authorized funds "to encourage the care of dependent children in their own homes...by enabling each state to furnish financial assistance and other services...to maintain and strengthen family life and to help such parents or relatives to attain the maximum of self-support and personal independence consistent with the maintenance of continuing parental care and protection."[69] Many professional social workers, especially those with a renewed interest in casework believed that financial aid should be supplemented with counseling service to help the poor adjust to single parenthood and urban life, learn to make friends, and develop self-esteem. They required housekeeping and budgetary instruction; above all they had to know how to secure and retain jobs.[70] This mixture of services, paternalism, and social control clearly was conditioned, at least in part, by the gender of the ADC population.

No services materialized from the 1956 law due to inadequate federal funding. But the proposed services marked a significant policy shift. They signaled the federal government's willingness to become involved in the direct provision of personal social services—services historically provided by the family itself. Until this time, federal involvement in reproductive activities consisted primarily of consultation and other non-financial support for child welfare services but not subsidies to ordinary families.[71]

The "rediscovery" of poverty in the early sixties fueled concerns about the reproductive capacity of poor families and put welfare reform on the public agenda. The development of a poverty index by the Social Security Administration in 1959, which provided an official count of the nation's poor, showed that the percentage of poor persons dropped only slightly from 22.4 in 1959 to 21 in 1962.[72] The publication of Michael Harrington's *The Other America* in 1962, the discussion of poverty in the 1964 *Economic Report to the President*, a series of recessions from 1948 to 1958, and the identification of depressed areas such as Appalachia placed poverty firmly on the national agenda.[73]

Picking up the service banner in 1960, Kennedy's Secretary of Health, Education and Welfare (HEW), Abraham Ribicoff, concluded that the United States must reorient "the whole approach to welfare from a straight cash hand-out operation to one in which the emphasis is on rehabilitation of those on relief and prevention ahead of time."[74] The service theme also appeared in the reports of two welfare reform commissions appointed in 1961. Designed to reinforce and support family life through rehabilitation, prevention, and protection, the commissions, which included many prominent social workers, recommended adequate financial assistance, efficient administration of public welfare programs, research into the causes of dependency and family breakdown, but first and foremost, the provision of rehabilitative services by professionally trained personnel.[75]

The 1962 amendments to the Social Security Act, often referred to as the Social Service Amendments, restated the twin goals of strengthening family life and self-support for ADC families. In the first presidential message devoted entirely to the subject of public welfare, President Kennedy hailed the amendments as "the most far reaching revision of public welfare" since 1935 because they stressed "services in addition to support, rehabilitation instead of relief, and training for useful work instead of prolonged dependency...to maintain family life where it is adequate and to restore it where it is deficient."[76]

Signaling the expanded family focus, the 1962 amendments renamed the ADC program Aid To *Families* With Dependent Children (AFDC). The Bureau of Public Assistance became the Bureau of *Family* Services. The amendments increased federal funding for services from 50 to 75 percent, and offered the new services to former and potential as well as current AFDC recipients. The AFDC-UP program, providing benefits to two-parent families with an unemployed parent, introduced as a temporary measure during the 1961 recession and left optional to the states, was extended for five years. The amendments also authorized federal funding for social worker training. Most states never fully implemented the 1962 service strategy due to the lack of staff and funds, weak federal incentives, and difficulties in defining and distinguishing mandated services.[77] Few who later blamed the service strategy for failing to rehabilitate families or to remove them from the welfare rolls recognized the narrowness of the programs' goals, its underfunding and overpromise, the difficulty of improving employability, or the underlying causes of the problems the services sought to address. Only later did it become known that two states, New York and California, absorbed most of the service dollars that the federal government made available to the states on a discretionary basis.

Work Incentives

At the same time that Congress adopted the service strategy, the question of the link between "work and welfare" entered the public debate at the national level. Congressional interest in the possibility of work for AFDC mothers first appeared in the mid-fifties, but remained overshadowed by official policy encouraging women to stay at home. In fact, federal policy defined AFDC recipients to be outside the labor force, prevented the use of public assistance funds to provide work, and eliminated any financial gain from employment by imposing a 100 percent tax on earned income. In 1954, however, a sub-committee investigation of Social Security heard approvingly of two state programs that encouraged ADC mothers and disabled fathers to work, "provided family life was not harmed." The 1957 amendments called for self-support and self-care. In stark contrast to past decisions, the 1962 amendments emphasized success in achieving financial independence for the first time. The new law contained an official work incentive for AFDC mothers, permitting state welfare departments to deduct some work expenses (including child care costs) when computing a family's welfare budget. The introduction of work incentives which also enhanced the value of the AFDC payment as a wage subsidy to industry conflicted with the idea that women belonged at home ensuring the well-being of children.

Contradictory policies reflected general ambivalence about women's changing roles, about the nature of reciprocal obligations between poor women and the state, and about the state's growing difficulty in reconciling the conflicting demand for women's home and market labor. At the hearings on the Amendments, a representative of the Association of Public Welfare declared that

> The crux of the matter is how and why the mother decides to work and what plans she is able to make for her children. Should mothers on ADC be forced to work because insufficient appropriations mean they cannot support their children in dignity and self-respect? Should social workers be pressured into forcing mothers

into the economy as proof of success or should mothers and social workers be free to plan jointly for the welfare of the family?[78]

Reflecting these tensions, the resulting rules continued to undercut the work incentive by subtracting one dollar from the welfare grant for every dollar earned. At the same time, AFDC's low payments and exclusionary eligibility rules still forced poor women to go to work. Welfare departments in southern and western states which used "employable mother" rules to deny aid to women made their work requirements more explicit.[79] As late as 1966, New Jersey sent a letter to AFDC recipients telling them that their grants would be cut because seasonal farm work was available.[80] As noted earlier, many states refused assistance to black women if their eligibility for AFDC interfered with local labor market demands.

The conflicting views about work by AFDC mothers initially meant that only men became subject to the ADC program's more stringent work criteria. When ADC became AFDC-UP, making certain groups of unemployed parents (mainly fathers) eligible for aid, the presence of men made the assumption that ADC recipients could not or should not work politically untenable. For the first time in 1962, federal law permitted states to require adult recipients to work in exchange for benefits. The Community Work and Training Programs (CWTP) established for this purpose required male participants (AFDC mothers could volunteer) to "work off" their public assistance grant for work performed in the community. A forerunner of "workfare" programs, the CWTP remained small at this time, drawing only 50 percent federal matching funds compared to 75 percent for social services. Only twelve states adopted the program by 1967. Most expanded their service programs instead since social service funds, capped in 1971, then had no lid.[81]

Given the limited work incentives and the virtual restriction of work relief to AFDC fathers, the 1962 amendments in effect relied most heavily on rehabilitative services to achieve their goals of strengthening family life and increasing the economic independence of AFDC mothers. A strong work policy for AFDC mothers still conflicted with the belief that women belonged at home and raised questions about the well-being of children. As late as 1968, Charles Schottland, president of the National Association of Social Workers (NASW) declared, "We cannot...accept compelling mothers with children to take jobs without due regard to the welfare of children and the limitations on AFDC families where the father is absent from the home. Forcing mothers with young children into a job goes against a universally held conviction that a mother's first responsibility is to her home and children."[82]

Work and Welfare Go Together: 1967-1980

By 1967, the more rapid expansion of the welfare rolls and the mounting number of unwed mothers receiving aid created what became known as a "welfare crisis." From 1961 to 1967, the welfare rolls grew from just over 3.5 million recipients to almost 5.0 million;[83] the family caseload jumped by 50 percent, reaching 1.3 million. The percentage of AFDC families headed by unwed mothers rose from 21.3 to 28.4 percent, accounting for 42.6 percent of the national net increase in AFDC during these years. The larger but slower growing group of AFDC families headed by divorced, separated, or deserted women increased from 40.5 to 45.3 percent.[84] By 1967, husbandless women headed 75 percent of all AFDC cases. The proportion of non-whites receiving AFDC peaked and stabilized at just below 50 percent.[85]

The sense of a crisis also existed because the program's cost soared from $994 million in 1960 to $2.2 billion in 1967, while the cost of Old Age Assistance and Aid to the Blind dropped somewhat.[86] Moreover, enrollment no longer rose and fell with the state of the economy. After 1953, AFDC rates ceased to drop with prosperity and climbed steadily throughout the Korean and Vietnam Wars.[87] The demand for AFDC increased during the various economic recessions from 1948 through the early sixties, but beginning in the sixties employment by AFDC mothers seemed to become less sensitive to improved market conditions.

Demographic and political forces also accounted for much of the "welfare explosion." Population growth, rising divorce and illegitimacy rates, a demographic excess of women relative to men, and other such trends simply increased the demand for assistance. So did grassroots pressure, the liberalization of the AFDC program, and the expansion of the welfare state. The intensification of the civil rights struggle in the South, the riots in northern ghettos, and the Democratic Party's fear that the lack of progress in civil rights might reduce its support among black voters resulted in, among other things, broadened AFDC rules primarily in the more wealthy northern states. Launched by a Democratic administration in 1964, the War on Poverty, especially its legal service arm, also made more people aware of their welfare entitlements, while greater federal matching funds enabled state and county welfare departments to accept more applicants. Under the combined pressure of the National Welfare Rights Organization (referred to by Guida West as the social protest of poor women[88]) and the civil rights movement, the Supreme Court removed major barriers to AFDC eligibility. It restricted home eligibility checks (1966), declared the residency requirements illegal (1967), outlawed midnight raids (1967), and abolished the man-in-the-house rule (1968). The elimination of the residency requirement alone added some 800,000 persons to AFDC rolls by 1970.[89] The net effect was a 35 percent expansion of the pool of people eligible for AFDC, three-fourths of which occurred in nine northern states. California and New York alone accounted for 40 percent.[90] The growth of AFDC occurred in the context of an overall expansion of the welfare state after 1960. The War on Poverty became more widespread, Congress enacted Medicaid and Medicare (1965), extended federal aid to elementary and secondary schools (1965), established the Model Cities urban renewal program (1966), and gave more support to low-income housing (1968).

Following the post-World War II pattern, demographic changes, the civil rights struggle, and the expansion of the welfare state provoked a backlash against AFDC and welfare mothers in the late sixties. A 1967 survey revealed that 42 percent of Americans thought poverty resulted from "lack of effort"; only 19 percent blamed "circumstances beyond control." Two years later, 58 percent of the respondents attributed poverty to the "lack of thrift and proper money management by poor people." A total of 84 percent agreed with the statement: "There are too many people receiving welfare who ought to be working"; and 71 percent said, "Many people getting welfare are not honest about their need." Only 34 percent agreed with the statement, "Generally speaking, we are spending too *little* money on welfare in this country."[91]

Politicians fueled anti-welfare sentiment. Ronald Reagan, then Governor of California, stated in his 1967 inaugural speech, "We are not going to perpetuate poverty by substituting a permanent dole for a paycheck." To Senator Russell Long of Louisiana, the welfare system was "being manipulated and abused by malingerers, cheaters, and outright frauds...There is no question in anybody's mind that the present welfare system is a mess."[92] When he referred to welfare mothers as "brood mares" who stay home to produce more children whom they raise in an atmosphere of dependency, Long articulated the prejudices against women underlying many of these polemics.[93]

Few people realized the deep deprivations associated with life on welfare. The 1966 average national payment for an AFDC family of four amounted to $144 a month or $1,728 year, well below the official poverty line of $3,355 for a non-farm family of four.[94] A 1967 survey of AFDC families by HEW revealed that 11 percent did not have private use of a kitchen; 24 percent lived in flats or shacks without running water; 30 percent lacked enough beds; 25 percent did not have sufficient furniture to sit down for meals; 17 percent had children who sometimes did not go to school because they had no decent clothing; and 46 percent had not had enough money to buy milk for their children at least once within the previous six months.[95]

Such conditions eventually led welfare mothers to organize and to engage in direct action. The first welfare rights group, formed in Los Angeles in 1963 to protest midnight raids, grew into an organization to help AFDC mothers win their rights from the welfare system. The organizer of Aid to Needy Children Mothers' Organization (ANCMO), Ms. Johnnie Tillmon, later emerged as a leader of the National Welfare Rights Organization (NWRO). New York's Committee on Welfare Families held its first meeting with city welfare officials in 1965, the first such encounter since the Workers' Alliance confronted public and officials during the Depression. The committee won an agreement for winter clothing and a formal grievance procedure. A ten-day march on the Ohio State capital for increased welfare benefits in June 1966 was the first major welfare rights action to receive national attention. On the same day that the marchers reached the Ohio capital, 2,000 sympathizers demonstrated outside New York's City Hall along with 2,500 more in fifteen cities from Boston to Los Angeles. The event, coordinated by the Poverty Rights Action Center in Washington, D.C. (a group headed by George Wiley of CORE), gave birth to the NWRO that year. NWRO adopted the strategy. proposed by Frances Fox Piven and Richard Cloward, to force change in welfare policy by "breaking the system" through a dramatic increase in applications from the pool of potential recipients. NWRO militantly opposed inequities in the welfare system until the mid-1970s when the strength of the national, but not necessarily all local groups, declined.[96]

The 1967 amendments to the Social Security Act were enacted in this conflict-ridden environment. With them, state policy for maintaining and reproducing the labor force and regulating the labor force participation of poor and husbandless women became more officially punitive. The 1966 Report of the Council of Public Welfare, *Having the Power, We Have the Duty,* recommended a continuation of the 1962 service strategy and urged that public aid be provided "as a matter of right." Ignoring this document of welfare state liberalism, the 1967 amendments turned regulations once reserved largely for "undeserving" female paupers into official policy for the entire AFDC caseload. The new rules restricted the number of children born out-of-wedlock on the AFDC rolls, strengthened the potential for child removal, and compelled AFDC mothers to work outside the home. Billed as promoting self-support and low welfare costs, the amendments can also be interpreted as penalizing the entire AFDC caseload, now largely composed of single mothers and families of color, for lack of compliance with the family ethic. Having failed to "normalize" the female-headed household by substituting itself for the missing breadwinner, the state instead began treating the entire caseload as "undeserving," redoubling its efforts to channel AFDC mothers into the labor market.

Punishing Out-of-Wedlock Births

The 1967 amendments imposed a freeze on federal aid to the states for AFDC cases arising from desertion or births outside of marriage. They continued, however, unlimited matching funds for cases attributable to a father's death or unemployment, and they included, for the first time, a birth control provision "for the purpose of preventing and reducing out-of-wedlock births." The law also clarified the responsibility of the states for apprehending deserting fathers under the 1950 NOLEO regulation, permitted the use of Social Security and Internal Revenue records to locate the absent father of an out-of-wedlock child, and created a special administrative unit to deal with obtaining child support.[97]

The freeze, applied solely to the AFDC program, sought to pressure states to cut assistance roles or face increased costs. It permitted the Federal government to deny matching funds to the states for any increase in the proportion of AFDC children whose mothers were divorced, deserted, separated, or unwed. Children of widows were exempt. Advocates of the freeze accepted the idea that the availability of AFDC *caused* the ongoing rise in desertion and illegitimacy rates even though these demographic trends predated the growth of the AFDC program itself. (Subsequent research has found no definitive link between the AFDC benefit and these demographic patterns.[98] Critics regarded the freeze as a means to punish helpless children and as a plot to reduce already inadequate benefits. They saw the freeze as another version of the suitable home policy that defined welfare eligibility in terms of the behavior of welfare mothers. The ensuing outrage and controversy led two presidents to delay imposition of the freeze. Although Congress finally repealed it in 1969, before it ever went into effect, its appearance on the legislative agenda and widespread support for it signaled interest, at least in some quarters, in a more repressive state role.

Child Removal

The 1967 amendments also strengthened the ability of welfare departments to remove children from the home. For the first time since the 1909 White House Conference on Children, Congress directly challenged the concept of the home as the best place for the child. The House of Representatives' Report concluded "that some children now receiving AFDC would be better off in foster homes or institutions than in their own homes...because of the poor environment for child upbringing in homes with low standards including multiple instances of illegitimacy."[99] The only characteristic of the "poor environment" mentioned in the Report was illegitimacy. Congress also required welfare agencies to "bring unsuitable home conditions of children to the attention of the courts or law enforcement officials." The vague definition of unsuitable homes as those where there "was neglect, abuse, or exploitation of a child"[100] established grounds for child removal that differed from those applied to non-welfare families. Although laws protecting children were needed in many cases, child removal had as much to do with punishing the mother as protecting the child.

Finally, the amendments expanded federal funding for foster and institutional care to cover eligible children not currently receiving assistance. This provision sought to facilitate needed placements and lower the costs of institutional care to states and localities. But restricted to poor and single-parent families, its punitive impact affected a largely oppressed and relatively powerless group.[101]

Mandatory Work

The 1967 amendments dramatically reversed years of the "mother-in-the-home" tradition, when the Work Incentive Program (WIN) transformed *official* AFDC policy from one that subsidized the reproductive and maintenance functions of "deserving" poor women at home to one that also directly subsidized the low paid employment of all AFDC mothers. The WIN program made AFDC's long-standing but largely unofficial work policy for women explicit. It shifted the strategy from simple exclusion of "undeserving" women from the rolls to a combination of the stick of coercive work requirements and the carrot of positive incentives such as job training and wage subsidization. Reflecting the new work orientation, Congress replaced the Bureau of Family Services established in 1962 with a new agency, the Social and Rehabilitation Service (SRS), and appointed the former commissioner of the Vocational Rehabilitation Administration as its head.

The controversial WIN rules made work mandatory for AFDC mothers. They required all employable AFDC recipients deemed "appropriate" by a welfare department to register for work, accept referrals for training and employment, and take any bona fide job offer. Only the aged, the ill, those living too far from a WIN project, and those needed to care for an ill relative were exempted from the new work requirement.[102] AFDC recipients who failed to comply were sanctioned with three-month grant denials or grant reductions. WIN also required the states to provide services aimed at achieving employment and self-sufficiency. To this end, the program replaced "soft" counseling services, associated with the 1962 amendments, with "hard" or concrete work-related services designed to upgrade the human capital of AFDC recipients. The "get tough" attitude produced an emphasis on job search, job placement, and on-the-job training, rather than rehabilitation and prevention. But a lack of job opportunities, the high cost of day care, and resistance within public welfare departments to enforcing employment by AFDC mothers meant that few job-related services latter were available to many WIN participants.

WIN also included a financial work incentive. Instead of continuing to tax earned income at 100 percent, AFDC recipients could now keep $30 and one-third of their remaining earnings before the grant was reduced, effectively lowering the tax to 66 percent. Work-related expenses such as the cost of child care, union dues, lunch, and transportation were deducted in addition before calculating the AFDC mother's welfare payment. To keep already employed women from applying for AFDC in response to the new incentives, they did not apply to new applicants or re-applicants off the rolls for more than four months. Limited to current AFDC recipients, these improvements provided genuine economic incentives even though the tax on earnings remained proportionately much higher than the income taxes paid by the average wage earner or the very rich.[103] During the 1960s and 1970s, similar work requirements and incentives became a central feature of welfare reform proposals including President Nixon's Family Assistance Plan and President Carter's Better Jobs and Income Program.

The strengthened work orientation marked a shift in the notion of mutual obligation between the ADC mother and the state. Until this time, in theory at least, the government supported mothers at home as an entitlement, so that they could raise their children to be productive citizens. The new stress on work conveyed the doctrine that recipients should be obligated to become self-sufficient in exchange for government assistance. The punitive character of the amendments derived from a perception of welfare mothers as unmotivated and unwilling to work. Wilbur Mills, Chair of the House Ways and Means Committee, proclaimed that mandatory work programs were imperative in view of the fact that welfare was becoming a way of life for too many people.[104] He asked, "What in the world is wrong with requiring these people to submit themselves, if they are to draw public funds, to a test of their ability to learn a job? Is not that the way we should go?...Is not that the way we should lead people from a condition that I am sure they do not want to be in—of need—into a position of independence and support?"[105] The Committee's report explained that "a proper evaluation [should] be made of the situation of all mothers to ascertain the extent to which appropriate child care arrangements should be made available so that mothers can go to work." The Committee recognized "that in some instances—where there are several small children, for example, the best plan for a family may be for the mother to stay home. But even these cases would be reviewed regularly to see if the situation had changed to the point where training or work is appropriate for the mothers."[106] The new work strategy, supported by HEW as well as Congress, implied that the children of welfare mothers were just as well off in day care centers as with their own mothers, a standard still not applied to non-AFDC families.

Some of those who accepted the work incentive, job training, and employment features of WIN opposed its more coercive character. Social workers argued that "Mothers must have the right of choice as to if and when it is appropriate and desirable for them to work outside the home, giving the care of their children to others."[107] They recommended a completely voluntary, individualized approach. Others opposed the selective focus on single and poor mothers. The National Association of Social Workers (NASW), the AFL-CIO, and other groups withdrew their support for the bill and urged the President to veto it, but it passed nonetheless. The growing demand for low cost female labor, evidenced in the increased labor force participation of all women, only made it easier to justify denying welfare mothers the choice of staying home with their children or going to work, a choice that poverty took away from many poor working women, but that still was available and considered reasonable for those in the middle and upper classes who also faced less exploitative jobs. Commenting a few years later on the double standard contained in the welfare work ethic, NWRO leader Johnnie Tillmon, declared, "It [the work ethic] applied to men and to women on welfare. It doesn't apply to all women. If you're a society lady from Scarsdale and you spend all your time sitting on your prosperity paring your nails, well that's ok."[108]

The shift to coercive work policies and economic incentives failed to be fully implemented owing to fiscal and labor market constraints. Limited funding, a lack of day care services, and an excess of AFDC recipients over WIN slots led numerous states to define mothers with pre-school children as "inappropriate" for job training or work and thus to exempt them from the work requirement. The sexist program priorities which favored fathers in the AFDC-UP program over AFDC mothers also "protected" women from a program that viewed them punitively. During the 1971 recession, for example, the AFDC-UP program doubled and the female proportion of WIN enrollees dropped to 62 percent and again to 53 percent in 1972.[109] Thirty-eight percent of all WIN enrollees were male, in 1971; 56 percent were white far exceeding their proportions in the AFDC program.[110] Finally, the labor market did not welcome the welfare mother with decent jobs or adequate wages. Indeed, only small numbers of WIN participants of either gender found permanent jobs and left the welfare rolls forever. Even when WIN managed to place women, it was usually in sex-segregated training and job slots with wages below the poverty line. Indeed, WIN participants could be required to work in jobs that paid as little as 75 percent of the minimum wage.

That funding and market constraints exempted many AFDC mothers from WIN's rules and limited the program's punitive impact should not belie the program's underlying purpose or goals: to channel poor women into the low paid labor market or "proper" family life. Stricter enforcement of sanctions, the selection of more employable volunteers, and a declining unemployment rate subsequently combined to improve WIN's short-term results. But WIN produced neither permanent jobs for many women nor smaller welfare caseloads. The AFDC rolls jumped from 5.3 million recipients in 1967 to 11 million in 1972 and peaked at 11.3 million in 1976, after which the growth leveled off. Between 1976 and 1986, the number of AFDC recipients fluctuated only slightly, moving between 10.3 million and 11.3 million in any one year.[111] Meanwhile, the real purchasing power of AFDC benefits fell sharply. The value of the median state's benefit slid by nearly 30 percent from 1970 to 1980.

In sum, AFDC, like its predecessor, The Mothers' Pension Program, substituted itself for the male breadwinner to make the "deviant" husbandless family approximate the "normal" one. In so doing, the state assumed more direct responsibility for reproduction in female-headed households and continued to punish women viewed as out of role. But by the seventies, a variety of social, economic, and political forces weakened the ability of AFDC to carry out these reproductive and maintenance functions.

Chapter Eleven suggests that the thrust of welfare reform in the 1980s and 1990s has been to restore the faltering functions of the welfare state. As the wages and the standard of living sank, this required an intensification of the program's work requirements. The benefits cuts, more extensive workfare programs and proposals to place a five year, lifetime, limit on eligibility for AFDC all represented a more forceful attempt to mediate the competing demands for women's home and market work. At the same time, the spread of single motherhood and non-maritieal births to women from all walks of life was accompanied by new proposals (reminiscent of the 1950 and early 1960s) to deny aid to children born welfare. The intensified regulation of social reproduction by poor women stigmatized single motherhood, enforced the belief that women living without men (if not any women raising children on their own) are improperly equipped to carry out the reproductive and maintenance tasks assigned to the family, and sent a message to all women about what happens to those who do not "play by the rules."

Notes to Chapter 10

1. Johnnie Tillmon, "Welfare is a Women's Issue," in Rosalyn Baxandall, Linda Gordon and Susan Reverby (eds.), *America's Working Women: A Documentary History—1600 to the Present* (New York: Vintage Books, 1976) p. 356.

2. Committee on Economic Security, *Social Security in America, The Factual Background of the Social Security Act as Summarized from Staff Reports to the Committee on Economic Security* (Washington, D.C.: Government Printing Office, 1937), pp. 239-240.

3. Susan Ware, *Holding Their Own: American Women in the 1930s* (Boston: Twayne Publishers, 1982), p. 33.

4. Committee on Economic Security (1937) *op. cit.,* p. 243.

5. *Ibid.,* p. 248.

6. Edwin E. Witte, *The Development of the Social Security Act* (Madison: The University of Wisconsin Press, 1963), p. 164.

7. Jean Taft Douglas Bandler, *Family Issues in Social Policy: An Analysis of Social Security,* unpublished dissertation, Columbia University School of Social Work, New York, 1975, p. 197.

8. "The Report of the Committee on Economic Security," reprinted in *50th Anniversary Issue, The Report of the Committee on Economic Security of 1935 and Other Basic Documents Relating to the Social Security Act* (Washington, D.C.: National Conference on Social Welfare, 1985), pp. 5-6, 35-36.

9. Committee on Economic Security (1937) *op. cit.,* p. 233.

10. A similar argument was made on behalf of excluding comprehensive health insurance from the Social Security Act.

11. Social Security Act, Title IV, sec. 406(a).

12. June Axinn and Herman Levin, *Social Welfare: A History of the American Response To Need* (New York: Harper and Row, 1975), p. 189; James T. Patterson, *America's Struggle Against Poverty, 1900-1980* (Cambridge: Harvard University Press, 1981), p. 69.

13. "The Report of the Committee on Economic Security" (1935/1985) *op. cit.,* p. 56.

14. Witte (1963) *op. cit.,* p. 165.

15. *Ibid.,* pp. 164-165.

16. White House Conference on Children in a Democracy, *Final Report, January 18-20, 1940* (Washington, D.C.: Government Printing Office, 1941), pp. 126-127.

17. "The Report of the Committee on Economic Security" (1935/1985) *op. cit.*, p. 23.

18. Bandler (1975) *op. cit.*, pp. 213-215.

19. Grace Abbott, *The Child and the State,* Vol.II (Chicago: The University of Chicago Press, 1938), p. 240; Winifred Bell, *Aid To Dependent Children* (New York: Columbia University Press, 1965), pp. 28-29.

20. Jane M. Hoey, "Aid to Families with Dependent Children," *The Annals of the American Academy of Political and Social Sciences,* CCII (March 1939), pp. 17-19, cited in Robert H. Bremner (ed.), *Children and Youth In America: A Documentary History,* Volume III, 1933-1973, Parts 1-4, (Cambridge: Harvard University Press, 1974), p. 539; Bell (1965) *op. cit.,* pp. 29-30.

21. Bell (1965) *op. cit.,* pp. 35-36, citing Federal Security Agency, Social Security Board, Bureau of Public Assistance, "Bureau Circular No. 9," May 1, 1940, sec. 209, p. 1.

22. Bell (1965) *op. cit.,* p. 35, citing Mary S. Larabee, "Unmarried Parenthood Under The Social Security Act," *Proceedings of the National Conference of Social Work,* 1939 (New York: Columbia University Press, 1939), pp. 447-449.

23. Hoey (1939) *op. cit.,* p. 539.

24. *Ibid.,* pp. 538-541.

25. Richard Sterner, *The Negro's Share* (New York: Harper & Brothers Publishers, 1943), p. 281.

26. U.S. Congress, Joint Economic Committee, Subcommittee on Fiscal Policy, *Studies in Public Welfare Paper No.20, Handbook of Public Income Transfer Programs: 1975* (Washington, D.C.: Government Printing Office, December 31, 1974), p. 169, T. 9.

27. *Ibid.,* p. 170, T. 10.

28. Jacqueline Jones, *Labor of Love, Labor of Sorrow: Black Women, Work and The Family From Slavery to the Present* (New York: Basic Books, 1985), pp. 262-263.

29. John Ehrenreich, *The Altruistic Imagination: A History of Social Work and Social Policy in the United States* (Ithaca: Cornell University Press, 1985), p. 149.

30. *Ibid.*

31. U.S. Women's Bureau, *1969 Handbook on Women Workers,* Bulletin 294, (Washington, D.C.: Government Printing Office, 1969), pp. 67-76; *Time of Change: 1983 Handbook on Women Workers,* Bulletin 298 (Washington, D.C.: Government Printing Office, 1983), p. 44.

32. Jones (1985) *op. cit.,* p. 234.

33. Cited in *Ibid.,* p. 258.

34. Maurine McKeany, *The Absent Father and Public Policy in The Program of Aid to Dependent Children,* (Berkeley: University of California Press, 1960) p. 2.

35. U.S. Advisory Council on Social Security, *1938 Final Report,* pp. 17-19, in Bremner (1974) *op. cit.,* p. 535.

36. Gilbert Y. Steiner, *The State of Welfare* (Washington, D.C.: The Brookings Institution, 1971), p. 42.

37. Daniel Patrick Moynihan, "Employment, Income and the Ordeal of the Negro Family," *Dedalus: Journal of the American Academy of Arts and Sciences,* 94 (4) (Fall 1965), p. 766.

38. U.S. Congress, House Ways and Means Committee, *Background Material and Data on Programs Within the Jurisdiction of the Committee on Ways and Means, 1986 Edition,* (Washington, D.C.: Government Printing Office, 1986), p. 392.

39. Quoted in Bell (1965) *op. cit.,* p. 75.

40. Bandler (1975) *op. cit.,* p. 321; McKeany (1960) *op. cit.,* np.

41. Bandler (1975) *op. cit.,* p. 326.

42. McKeany (1960) *op. cit.,* p. 36.

43. Lucy Komisar, *Down and Out in the USA* (New York: New Viewpoints, 1974), p. 88.

44. Axinn and Levin (1975) *op. cit.,* p. 236; Bell (1965) *op. cit.,* p. 211; Patterson (1981) *op. cit.,* pp. 107-108.

45. Komisar (1974) *op. cit.,* pp. 85-86; Patterson (1981) *op. cit.,* pp. 107-108.

46. *King v. Smith,* 392 U.S. 309, in Bremner (1974) *op. cit.,* p. 593.

47. Bell (1965) *op. cit.,* p. 29.

48. *Ibid.,* pp. 124-136.

49. Judith Levin and Patricia Vergata, "Welfare Law and Women: An Analysis of Federal Sexism," May 1971, unpublished paper, Center For Social Welfare Policy and Law, 25 West 43rd. St., New York, NY, pp. 76-92.

50. Edward Sparer, "Legal Entitlement Assurance Program," Address Before the Suffolk County Public Welfare Staff (New York: Center for Social Welfare Policy and Law, October 19, 1965), cited in Komisar (1974) *op. cit.,* p. 82.

51. Komisar (1974) *op. cit.,* p. 81, citing Ben B. Seligman, *Poverty as a Public Issue* (New York: The Free Press, 1965), p. 222.

52. *Ibid.*

53. *Ibid., pp. 76-80.*

54. *Ibid.,* pp. 82-84.

55. Levin and Vergata (1971) *op. cit.,* pp. 14-15.

56. Bell (1965) *op. cit.,* pp. 93-110, 111-123.

57. *Ibid.,* p. 138; "The 'Suitable Home' Requirement," *The Social Service Review,* XXXV (1961), pp. 2-3, 214, in Bremner (1974) *op. cit.,* p. 579.

58. Bandler (1975) *op. cit.,* pp. 353-354, citing State Letter No. 452 (U.S. Bureau of Public Assistance, January 17, 1971).

59. *Ibid.*, p. 296.

60. Bell (1965) *op. cit.*, p. 149.

61. This section draws from Jones (1985) *op. cit.*, pp. 232-301; and Susan Hartman, *The Home Front and Beyond: American Women in the 1940s* (Boston: Twayne Publishers, 1982), pp. 5-7.

62. Ehrenreich (1985) *op. cit.*, p. 153; Patterson (1981), pp. 99-105.

63. U.S. Women's Bureau (1969) *op. cit.*, pp. 23-27.

64. Harold L. Wilenksky and Charles N. Lebeaux, *Industrial Society and Social Welfare* (New York: The Free Press, 1965).

65. Richard A. Cloward and Lloyd E. Ohlin, *Delinquency and Opportunity: A Theory of Delinquent Gangs* (New York: Free Press, 1960).

66. Ehrenreich (1985) *op. cit.*, pp. 149-151.

67. Mildred Rein, *Dilemmas of Welfare Policy: Why Work Strategies Haven't Worked* (New York: Praeger Publishers, 1982), pp. 15-16.

68. Bandler (1975) *op. cit.*, p. 51, citing Jay Rooney, Director of Bureau of Public Assistance, House Committee on Ways and Means, Social Security Hearings, 1956, p. 21.

69. Bandler (1975) *op. cit.*, p. 352, citing Senate Committee on Finance, *Senate Report 84-2311*, 1956, p. 28.

70. Walter I. Trattner, *From Poor Law to Welfare State* (New York: The Free Press, 1984), p. 300.

71. Willard C. Richan, *Social Service Politics in the United States and Britain*, (Philadelphia: Temple University Press, 1981), p. 154.

72. James T. Patterson, *America's Struggle Against Poverty 1900-1980* (Cambridge: Harvard University Press, 1981) *op. cit.*, p. 105.

73. Michael Harrington, *The Other America: Poverty in the United States* (New York: Macmillan Co., 1962); Council of Economic Advisors, *Economic Report of the President, 1964* (Washington, D.C.: Government Printing Office, 1964), pp. 55-83.

74. Patterson (1981) *op. cit.*, p. 131.

75. George K. Wyman, *A Report for the Secretary of Health, Education, and Welfare*, August 1961; *Report of the Ad Hoc Committee on Public Welfare to the Secretary of Health, Education, and Welfare*, September 1961. Both reports can be found in U.S. Congress, House Committee on Ways and Means, *Hearings on H.R. 10032, Public Welfare Amendments of 1962*, 87th Congress, 2nd sess., February 7, 9, and 13, 1962.

76. Bandler (1975) *op. cit.*, p. 380.

77. Rein (1982) *op. cit.*, p. 18.

78. Bandler (1985) *op. cit.*, p. 383.

79. *Ibid.*, pp. 47-48.

80. Komisar (1983) *op. cit.*, p. 83.

81. The Work Experience Program (WET), part of the Economic Opportunity Act that launched the "war on poverty" in 1964, gave further impetus to workfare programs. Also directed to AFDC-UP fathers, WET enrolled 133,000 recipients, 60 percent of whom were white and over 50 percent were male. Of these only 22,000 found jobs, 70,000 remained in training. See Sar A. Levitan, *Anti-Poverty Work and Training Efforts: Goals and Realities* (Washington, D.C.: University of Michigan Institute of Labor Relations and the National Manpower Policy Task Force, January 1970), pp. 76-80; Steiner (1971) *op. cit.*, p. 44; Levitan, Rein, and Marwick, *Work and Welfare Go Together* (Baltimore: The Johns Hopkins University Press, 1972), p. 72.

82. "The Year in Congress," *NASW News* (February 1968), pp. 8-9, in Bremner (1974) *op. cit.*, pp. 565-566.

83. Rein (1982) *op. cit.*, p. 18.

84. *Ibid.*, p. 18; Steiner (1971) *op. cit.*, p. 84.

85. Steiner (1971) *op. cit.*, p. 42.

86. U.S. Congress, Joint Economic Committee, Subcommittee on Fiscal Policy (1974) *op. cit.*

87. Rein (1982) *op. cit.*, pp. 4-5.

88. Guida West, *The National Welfare Rights Movement: The Social Protest of Poor Women* (New York: Praeger Publishers, 1981).

89. Sar A. Levitan, Garth L. Mangum, Ray Marshall, *Human Resources and Labor Markets* (New York: Harper and Row Publishers, 1972), p. 403.

90. Francis Fox Piven and Richard Cloward, *Regulating the Poor, The Functions of Public Welfare* (New York: Pantheon Books, 1971), pp. 192-194.

91. Patterson (1981) *op. cit.*, p. 172.

92. *Ibid.*, pp. 172-173.

93. Steiner (1971) *op. cit.*, p. 53.

94. Patterson (1981) *op. cit.*, p. 163.

95. *Ibid.*, p. 106, citing President's Commission on Income Maintenance Programs, *Poverty Amid Plenty: The American Paradox* (Washington, D.C.: Government Printing Office, 1969), pp. 87, 220.

96. Komisar (1974) *op. cit.*, pp. 105-124. For a more detailed discussion of the National Welfare Rights Organization see, Susan Handley Hertz, *The Welfare Mothers' Movement: A Decade of Change for Poor Women?* (Washington.D.C.: University Press of America, 1981); Frances Fox Piven and Richard A. Cloward, *Poor People's Movements* (New York: Vintage Books, 1979), pp. 264-363; and West (1981) *op. cit.*

97. *Doe v. Shapiro,* 301 F. Supp. 760-768; Meyers and McIntyre, "Welfare Policy and Its Consequences for the Recipient Population: A Study of the AFDC Program, pp. 7-9, both cited in Bremner (1974) *op. cit.*, pp. 597, 567.

98. Heather L. Ross and Isabel V. Sawhill, *Time of Transition: The Growth of Families Headed by Women* (Washington, D.C.: The Urban Institute, 1975), pp. 93-128.

99. Bandler (1975) *op. cit.*, p. 362, citing House Committee on Ways and Means, *House Report 90-544,* 1967, p. 100.

100. *Ibid.*

101. *Ibid.*, p. 364.

102. Bandler (1975) *op. cit.*, p. 396.

103. *Ibid.*, p. 49.

104. Levin and Vergata (1971) *op. cit.*, p. 20.

105. Quoted in Bandler (1975) *op. cit.*, p. 385.

106. Steiner (1971) *op. cit.*, p. 43.

107. Bandler (1975) *op. cit.*, p. 390, citing testimony of Mr. McCoy, Family Service Society of America, *1967 Social Security Hearings,* p. 2037.

108. U.S. Congress, Joint Economic Committee, *Hearings on Economic Problems of Women,* Part 2, July 24, 25, 26, and 30, 1973, 93rd. Cong., 1st. Sess. (Washington, D.C.: Government Printing Office, 1973), p. 392.

109. Rein (1982) *op. cit.*, p. 70.

110. Levitan, Rein, and Marwick (1972) *op. cit.*, pp. 79, 97-99.

111. U.S. Congress, House Ways and Means Committee, *Background Material and Data on Program 1986* (1986) *op. cit.*, p. 391.

11

Restoring the Family Ethic

The Assault on Women and the Welfare State in the 1980s and 1990s

The U.S. welfare system established by the 1935 Social Security Act came under open attack again in the 1980s and 1990s. The retrenchment of the Aid to Families with Dependent Children (AFDC), the Old Age Pension, and the Unemployment Insurance programs beginning in the 1980s marked the end of the post-World War II expansion of the U.S. welfare state. Along with the subsequent attacks during the 1990s on all the entitlement programs and on the role of the federal government in social welfare, the assault can be best understood as part of the economic recovery strategy designed to restore the workings of both capitalism and patriarchy.

Launched in the early 1980s, the strategy called for redistributing income upwards, cheapening the cost of labor, shrinking social welfare programs, and weakening the political influence of popular movements. Called supply-side economics, Reaganomics, or deficit reduction—it emerged after international competition, cheap foreign labor, and the loss of U.S. dominance in the world economy cut into the profits of U.S. corporations. The pressure to lower the costs of production led the nation's leaders to downsize corporations, export production to low-wage countries, and depress market wages at

349

home. The latter, in turn, relied on holding down the minimum wage; increasing the supply of low-cost workers; and limiting the enforcement of labor, anti-discrimination, and environmental regulations.

Since welfare benefits provided an alternative to the market wage, any plan to push wages down had to include reducing the value of social benefits so that stagnating paychecks would not cause workers to choose government assistance over low-paid market work. During the post-World War II years, corporate leaders had, however reluctantly, supported social welfare spending because the resulting cash assistance, education, training and social service programs increased consumer purchasing power; created healthy, educated, and properly socialized workers; and promoted political stability. This support receded in the mid-1970s. Changes in the domestic and global economies led business and government to denounce the welfare state for interfering with private investment, for providing workers with an alternative wage which increased their leverage at the workplace, and for empowering popular movements. Since the 1930s, these popular movements had politicized the process of income distribution carried out through collective bargaining and government tax and spending programs. By the 1980s, business and government no longer desired to meet these continued demands. Instead, they disinvested in social welfare and acted to weaken the influence of organized labor, civil rights, and women's groups who might object to these changes.[1]

During the same time that the economy stalled, changes in family strucure challenged the foundations of patriarchal arrangements. This gave rise to efforts to restore traditional gender roles and the family ethic.

The declining marriage rate, combined with more single motherhood, non-marital births, and gay and lesbian parenting, produced near hysteria about the need to restore "family values." Searching for explanations, the White House Working Group on the Family appointed by President Reagan issued a report in 1986 that blamed government programs. *The Family: Preserving America's Future* maintained that the expansion of the welfare state and the social revolutions of the 1960s forced the traditional American family to cede "too much of its authority to courts and rule-writers, too much of its voice in education and social policy, too much of its resources to public officials at all levels." The "abrasive experiments of two liberal decades," it concluded, have "frayed the fabric of family life." The Working Group added, "Neither the modern family nor the free enterprise system would long survive without the other." As the "seedbed of economic skills, money, habits, attitudes toward work, and the art of financial independence," it is families that teach that "effort results in gains and prepares skilled and energetic workers who are the engine of democratic capitalism."[2] The White House group and its supporters hoped that shrinking social welfare benefits would help to restore the two-parent, male-headed heterosexual family. Deprived of cash assistance, women would be less likely to turn to public aid as an alternative to work or as an alternative to marriage and economic dependence on men.

In sum, the welfare state came under assault in the 1980s because its programs no longer supported the work or family ethics and, as such, appeared to undermine both the economic recovery strategy and the patriarchal family structures. From the perspective of business and government, AFDC, Social Security, and Unemployment Insurance no longer worked. Once changes in the political economy and family life had limited the regulatory powers of the welfare state, weakened its capacity to carry out its labor market and family maintenance functions in the old ways, and exposed its subversive potential, its programs had to be "reformed."

Aid to Families with Dependent Children

The weakening of the welfare state's regulatory functions first became apparent in the AFDC program. AFDC seemed increasingly unable to delegitimize single motherhood or to reconcile the competing demands for women's home and market labor. By the mid-1970s, the welfare critics had concluded that too few women on AFDC entered the labor market despite the availability of jobs increasingly dependent on cheap female labor, and too many lived outside of marriage. From their vantage point AFDC's low benefits and strict work rules had failed to discourage poor women from choosing public assistance over wedlock or work. Although many women on AFDC worked, to opponents the program appeared to help poor women avoid both low-paid jobs *and* unhappy or unsafe marriages, and to consider social welfare benefits as a right. Welfare reform began to reverse these potentially "subversive" trends in the early 1980s, first by making it harder for poor women to qualify for AFDC and then by forcing them to work or change their family life choices as a condition of receiving aid. By the 1990s, the conservatives' anti-government rhetoric and the liberals' failure to adamantly oppose increasingly punitive welfare reforms had paved the way for the Contract with

America,[3] which both endorsed harsher welfare requirements and took aim at nearly all entitlement programs serving the middle class and the poor.

AFDC and the Work Ethic

The original goal of AFDC was to provide for the care of children by enabling their mothers to remain at home. But Chapter Ten has shown that the program has always contained an implied, and by the late 1960s, an explicit work ethic for the women it served. The program's exclusionary eligibility rules, financial work incentives, and increasingly coercive work requirements disabused poor women of the idea that they, too, were entitled to a "place in the home" and undercut the program's subversive potential: to empower women by enabling them to resist exploitation on the job and at home. Contrary to popular opinion, the perception of critics of welfare programs, and the imperatives of the family ethic, AFDC program statistics showed that many women on welfare already worked, actively sought a job, or became enrolled in an educational or training program. In any one month, the number of women on welfare who were either working full-time or part-time or looking for work rose from about 14.3 percent in 1961 to 16.1 percent in 1975. During the same time the number of women actively seeking work or enrolled in school or training rose from 5 percent in 1961 to 13.8 percent in 1977. Thus, by the mid-1970s, nearly 40 percent of the AFDC caseload was either working, looking for work, or in school. In 1979, of the rest, nearly 6.6 percent were incapacitated, and 39.8 percent were at home caring for young children or disabled family members.[4]

Nonetheless, by the mid-1970s, changes in wider society—the employment of more and more mothers, the ideas of the women's liberation movement, the growing demand for low-paid women workers, and the belief that women on welfare avoided work—led many to conclude that too few AFDC mothers went to work. The tension grew as well because, while the employability of AFDC mothers rose in the mid-1970s, the labor market became less welcoming. Between 1960 and the mid-1970s, following national trends, the average AFDC family became smaller, thus freeing women for employment. In addition, some 75 percent of the women on welfare had previous work experience, with two-thirds in white-collar jobs or service industries. There were also more AFDC mothers with high school diplomas or some college, the number increasing from 15 percent in 1961 to 27 percent in 1975.[5]

However, by the mid-1970s, fewer AFDC mothers had jobs. One reason was that more and more workers became unemployed as the economy sagged and as poor women with limited education faced greater competition from more skilled, but downsized workers. Second, deindustrialization and international competition created pressure to lay off workers. Finally, due to the downward pressure on wages in some local labor markets, wages fell below the AFDC grant. In 1974, 61 percent of all AFDC recipients lived in the twenty-eight states where the AFDC payment for a family of four exceeded the net pay from a minimum wage job by $211 a month; with Food Stamps the monthly difference grew to $304.[6]

This differential made it economically more rational for poor women to choose welfare over work, especially since most poor women lacked access to child care and most of the jobs available to them lacked health insurance coverage.

By the 1980s, as more poor women received welfare instead of working for wages, critics of welfare argued that AFDC—not low wages—undercut the work ethic. Although the growth of the AFDC rolls leveled off in the mid-1970s, the policymakers worked hard to restore its past regulatory role, which channeled welfare mothers into the labor force. Improving the work ethic of women on welfare became a major objective of welfare "reform." The debate strengthened negative attitudes toward AFDC, and helped to deflect attention from the underlying failure of the market economy to provide jobs for all those ready and willing to work.

AFDC and the Family Ethic

Welfare reform also sought to restore the family ethic. A restrictive and paternalistic provider during the postwar years, AFDC nonetheless failed to adequately recreate the patriarchal norms it originally had sought. The expansion of AFDC, especially the integration of more and more "unworthy" (that is, never-married) women into the caseload, made it more difficult to distinguish between "deserving" and "undeserving" poor women based on their marital status. Thus, researchers found that the program assisted women *even as they were violating the rules of patriarchy.*

> [I]ncome opportunities and social supports outside the tradi-
> tional family arrangements do enable women and children to
> exist in units of their own during at least transitional periods
> should they choose or be required to do so. The availability of
> those income support opportunities, notably women's own earn-
> ings and social welfare benefits...relieves the constraints which
> used to bind families together, happily or not, for utilitarian
> reasons.[7]

In spite of itself, AFDC had helped to legitimize single motherhood. Instead of upholding the family ethic, AFDC increasingly gave
single women the wherewithal, however meager, to establish independent households. The 1986 *Report of the White House Working
Group on the Family* suggested that welfare "provides valuable
temporary help to a family, yet that same help in effect replaces the
breadwinner," "enables mothers to raise children without the help of
a father or a job"; and "deprives men of their traditional role as
providers, severing them from family responsibilities."[8] Upset by
greater female autonomy, the Domestic Policy Council implied that
the welfare recipient who described AFDC as "the invisible husband"
who "gives you food, housing, medical protection, pays your bills and
lets you stay home and take care of children,"opposed these supports.[9]

The hostility toward AFDC as a program that let women live
apart from men also reflected deep concerns about children being
raised by women alone without a male to socialize them. Conservatives warned that,

> Raised in an environment in which fathers don't provide for
> their young and [in which] dependency on the government is
> assumed, few children will develop the skills of self-sufficiency
> or even the concept of personal responsibility. Young men will
> not strive to be good providers and young women will not expect
> it of their men. Family breakdown becomes cyclical, out-of-
> wedlock births become cyclical, and poverty and dependency
> become cyclical. [10]

Blaming AFDC for changing family structures ignored the
wider social reasons why women might not be able to marry or might
reject the nuclear family model, and sent a message to all women
about what happens to those who depart from prescribed wife-and-
mother roles.

Restoring the Regulatory Functions of AFDC: From Cutbacks to the Contract with America

AFDC's faltering regulatory functions created strong pressure for its "reform." In the 1970s policymakers used work incentives, social services or intensified stigma to steer women from welfare into work thereby upping the ante in the 1980s. The Reagan administration resorted to cutbacks and greater coercion to enforce the work and family ethics. Its first major initiative, the Omnibus Budget Reconciliation Act of 1981 (OBRA), retrenched AFDC and many other social programs for the poor. The second major initiative, the 1988 Family Support Act, used government dollars to leverage change in work behavior of poor women on welfare. The third round of welfare reform, begun in the early 1990s, sought to modify the marital, childbearing, childrearing, and work choices of AFDC mothers. The last two initiatives fueled the even more fundamental drive—symbolized by the Contract with America, to destroy the idea of entitlement to social benefits and to delegitimize the entire welfare state.

Harsh Cutbacks: The Omnibus Budget Reconciliation Act (OBRA) of 1981

OBRA fed into the administration's economic recovery plan by making it much more difficult for women to qualify for AFDC benefits. Entitlement programs such as AFDC are guaranteed federal funding. By law the states must pay benefits to all eligible applicants, and unlike discretionary programs, the entitlements cannot be cut back simply by reducing authorizations or capping federal funds. Instead, the program's rules must be tightened. Thus, OBRA limited AFDC eligibility to families with a gross income of 150 percent of a state's need standard (raised by Congress to 185 percent in 1984), required welfare departments to count previously excluded moneys as income when determining eligibility and setting benefit levels, restricted AFDC to the last trimester of a first pregnancy, and denied aid to families of strikers.[11]

Between 1981 and 1983, over 400,000 working welfare mothers lost their AFDC grant. In 1970, 80 percent of all poor families with children under eighteen had received AFDC benefits, but by 1982 only 49 percent did. The proportion rose slowly to 60 percent in 1990, but never returned to its pre-OBRA level.[12] The changes also added to the downward pressure on the value of AFDC, causing it to fall 31 percent between 1970 and 1983. That year, the combined value of AFDC and Food Stamps failed to lift a three-person family above the poverty line and in half of the states it provided no more than 75 percent of this official threshold.[13] Unlike other social welfare benefits, AFDC is not tied to the Consumer Price Index.

OBRA also replaced AFDC's work incentives with more coercive work requirements. Prior to OBRA, AFDC encouraged women to work by allowing them to keep the first $30 of earned income and one-third of the remainder, in addition to their AFDC check, and allowed for work-related expenses such as clothes, transportation, and child care. OBRA reduced all these supports and, although Congress restored them somewhat in 1984, the number of women benefiting from the "$30 and one-third" plan fell from 12.5 percent of the AFDC caseload in 1979 to 1.8 percent in 1983. Those able to claim child care and other work expenses dropped from 15.3 to 5.4 percent over the same period.[14] Finally, OBRA introduced stricter work rules for AFDC mothers. It cut Work Incentive Progam (WIN) training funds from $200 million in 1979 to $100 million in 1984, encouraged the states to re-introduce the controversial mandatory workfare program, and offered a wage subsidy to employers who hired AFDC recipients. By January 1987, forty-two states were operating one or more of the new optional work programs.[15]

OBRA saved the federal and state governments about $1.1 billion in 1983, but further impoverished many women and children. In 1980, 49 percent of the people living in poverty were on AFDC compared to 40 percent in 1982, and on average each family lost $1555 in benefits per year. The AFDC rolls rose slightly during the 1980s, but did not reach pre-OBRA levels until mid-1991, in the midst of a recession.[16] According to the government's own evaluations, OBRA sent thousands of women into soup kitchens as well as into dangerous welfare hotels, drug-plagued streets, and unsafe personal relationships.[17] Forcing women to work supported the administration's economic recovery plan. Crowding the already sex-segregated labor market with more workers helped to fill the increasing demand for low-paid, female labor and to hold wages down. The combination of reduced wages, a smaller welfare grant, and more people seeking low-paid jobs reduced workers' leverage and increased the ability of employers to discipline labor.[18] Coercive OBRA policies also foreshadowed the intensification of work mandates in the next round of "welfare reform."

Mandated Work: The 1988 Family Support Act

In 1987, welfare "reform" suddenly reappeared on the national agenda. Armed with advisors and new White House reports that blamed social welfare programs for everything from family break-up to crime in the streets to the deepening deficit, the Reagan administration launched a drive to reform welfare. Instead of the straightforward and cold-hearted budget cuts found in OBRA, welfare reform now called for more coercive programs that modified the work behavior of poor women.

The 1988 Family Support Act (FSA), which finalized the transformation of AFDC from a program that helped single mothers to stay home with their children into a mandatory work program, had considerable bi-partisan support in Congress. Introduced by Senator Daniel Patrick Moynihan (D-NY), the legislation articulated a new social contract between women on welfare and the state. "Just as society has a moral obligation to help its most needy citizens," declared President Reagan's Domestic Policy Council, so, "those who are able-bodied and receive assistance have an obligation to make some contribution to their local community in return."[19]

Welfare reform had captured the support of many liberals because it initially promised changes favorable to poor women: a national minimum benefit, child care and Medicaid coverage, voluntary work programs, increased social services, an extension of AFDC to two-parent families, and child-support enforcement. The debate recognized that work for welfare mothers, like other women, is virtually impossible without support for their child-care and health insurance expenses as well as for their education and training. However, little of the liberal agenda remained in the final legislation. Instead, the FSA became another step on the slippery slope toward increasingly punitive "reforms," fueling the efforts of those seeking to dismantle the entire welfare state.

The FSA went beyond the OBRA cuts to specifically target the work behavior of poor women on welfare. Mirroring business concerns about high wages, the proposals to institute a national minimum AFDC grant and to increase benefits levels were the first to disappear from the welfare reform bill. Congress dropped the idea of a minimum grant even though the real value of the AFDC grant had declined and the costs of the AFDC program had leveled off in the mid-1970s. The wide and inequitable variation in AFDC payments among the states (above and beyond differences in the cost of living) and the fact that the combined costs of AFDC, Food Stamps, and Supplemental Security Income accounted for only about 3.2 percent of the federal budget held no sway among those who wanted to ensure that no woman choose welfare over work.[20]

Voluntary work programs gave way to the need to reduce labor shortages. The National Alliance of Business (NAB) feared major labor market "shocks" during the next ten to fifteen years, including the slowed growth of the pool of young workers age sixteen to twenty-four, which would reduce the number of workers willing to take the low-wage service jobs.[21]

Thus the FSA replaced the already strict Work Incentive Program (WIN) with the more coercive Job Opportunities and Basic Skills Program (JOBS). The "reformers" rationalized the new program by billing AFDC recipients as lazy and unmotivated women who needed the strong arm of the state to make them go to work.

JOBS, the centerpiece of the FSA, also reflected business concerns about the quality of the labor force. In addition to labor shortages, the NAB projected a pervasive mismatch between workplace needs and workforce capabilities. Corporate executives worried that a serious imbalance was developing between a workforce increasingly dominated by "the less well-educated segments of the population that have been the least prepared for work [and] the growth of entry level jobs requiring, at minimum, basic analytical and interpersonal skills." To maintain our position in the world, including our economic preeminence and military strength, the Department of Labor concluded that "we must find ways to better employ the disadvantaged, immigrants, and women who have not been able to contribute fully to our economy."[22]

JOBS required women on welfare with children under age three (or age one in some states) to find work or enroll in a work or training program. In turn, the state welfare departments had to provide basic employment, education, and training programs; one year of transitional child care and Medicaid payments; and enriched social services. Women who refused to participate in the new JOBS program faced a reduction in, if not the loss of, their benefits. No sanctions seemed to apply if state welfare departments failed to carry out their end of the bargain, although states that did not meet their JOBS enrollment quotas risked the loss of federal matching funds. FSA also left it to the states to decide which work programs to provide. Of the wide range of programs covered by the act, only the least costly job search, basic education, and workfare programs were mandated. In the end, only the states that could afford to do so offered women on welfare the education and training services that built skills.

Although forcing AFDC mothers to work is hardly a new practice, client advocates continued to oppose making participation in JOBS a condition of receiving aid because it would flood the labor market with more workers, increase the competition for jobs, and push wages down. They argued that strict work requirements wrongly implied that women on welfare had to be forced to work, failed to account for different levels of employability among women on AFDC, and showed an unsavory preference for the stick over the carrot.

The opponents also pointed out that strict work programs defied prevailing research findings which showed that 70 percent of women on welfare left the rolls for work or marriage within two years, with only 7 percent staying on AFDC for more than eight years. Those who returned to welfare did so because of failed personal relationships or because they lacked adequate child care services, could not find jobs with health insurance coverage, and could not survive on the $3.35 federal minimum wage which in 1988 fell far below the poverty line for a family of three. Moreover, most of the returnees used welfare as a short-term economic back-up during such crises. As in the 1970s, the small number of women needing AFDC for more than eight years tended to be single mothers who had dropped out of school and had young children, had little work experience, or who were too ill or disabled to work.[23] They needed supportive services, not punitive reforms. By this time, the initial evaluations of the welfare-to-work experiments conducted by the Manpower Demonstration Research Corporation (MDRC), the U.S. Government Accounting Office (GAO), and other researchers had also found that work programs cost a lot but did not yield significant employment for AFDC mothers or reductions in the AFDC rolls.[24] However, the "reforms" left women poor: of the forty-five programs studied by the GAO, about half reported an average wage of less than $4.14 an hour.

The liberal legislators, policymakers, and advocates of the poor argued that the economic limits of part-time, minimum-wage jobs and the poor quality of underfunded day care programs made staying home the most reasonable choice for many poor women and their children. They also maintained that employment outcomes reflected the health of the local economy so that programs in states with high economic growth and low unemployment placed dramatically more participants in jobs. Finally, the supporters of less coercive changes wondered why only the poor have a "reciprocal obligation" to work off their government benefits. Did the government make homeowners work off the housing benefit contained in the mortgage interest tax deduction or insist that corporations work off their government subsidies and tax breaks?

The only liberal proposal that survived the welfare reform debate was the plan to make the then optional Aid to Families with Dependent Children for Unemployed Parents (AFDC-UP) mandatory in all the states. However, a legislative compromise restricted the already limited program for two-parent households in new ways. It permitted the states to impose a workfare requirement on AFDC-UP families (who comprised about 236,000 families out of a total welfare caseload of 3.8 million families [25]) and allowed the states to confine aid to six months in any twelve-month period. (Such time limits would become a major issue during the welfare reform debate in the early 1990s.)

Unlike subsequent welfare reform legislation, which targeted both the work *and* the family choices of poor women, the 1988 FSA focused largely on work issues. It did not take up the question of women's marital, childbearing, or parenting behavior in any major way, although its strengthened paternity and child support enforcement provisions focused on absent fathers. The FSA demanded that women on welfare provide the state with more information to help locate the fathers of AFDC children and that the states withhold payments from the absent fathers' wages immediately rather than after they fell into arrears.

The Reagan administration was committed to shrinking the federal government, beginning with the welfare state. The FSA began what turned into a lengthy process of chipping away at the structure and philosophy of social programs by delegitimizing the liberal tenets of entitlement, self-determination, and federal responsibility, and promoting more conservative notions of contract, compulsion, and states' rights. Reagan weakened the concept of entitlement (flawed though it may have been) by replacing its rights-based underpinnings with the market-based concept of exchange. This turned AFDC into an employment program based on an contractual obligation between two extremely unequal parties—the welfare mother and the state instead of entitlement based on need.

The democratic principles of self-determination and free choice were undermined by mandatory features of the FSA, including forced work for welfare mothers and automatic wage garnishment for welfare fathers. Using the stick rather than the carrot makes it nearly impossible for poor women to decide for themselves whether staying home or going to work is best for them and their children, a choice still granted to many women in the middle class. Finally, the Reagan administration undermined federal responsibility for social welfare by turning more control over to the states. His administration waived federal regulations so that selected states could experiment with alternatives to AFDC. By 1987, forty-two states operated one or more of the new optional work programs.[26] The even broader waiver policy built into the FSA further increased state control over welfare policy.

The effort to shift responsibility for AFDC from the national government to the states contrasted sharply with long-standing efforts by liberals to federalize the program in order to make it less vulnerable to local discretion and to the pressures of racism, sexism, and anti-welfarism. The 1988 Family Support Act did not strip AFDC of its entitlement status. However, the new social contract it promulgated paved the way for the mean-spirited welfare reform debate that surfaced in the early 1990s and that opened the door to the 1995 Contract with America, whose supporters were waiting in the wings to reduce federal responsibility for the entire welfare state.

Welfare Reform in the 1990s

The 1988 Family Support Act was heralded as the first major welfare reform in twenty years. Therefore, it took many people by surprise when Clinton announced in 1992 that if elected president, he would "end welfare as we know it."[27] Although the FSA remained in its infancy, Clinton decided to establish his conservative credentials by being tough on the poor. Since the Family Support Act already required women on welfare to work in order to receive benefits, Clinton had to up the ante. When Clinton's "Work and Responsibility Act" of 1994 finally appeared, it proposed to turn JOBS into a *transitional* and *temporary* work program by placing a two-year lifetime limit on the receipt of welfare. To help women find work, Clinton promised to continue the education, job training, and child care assistance provided by JOBS. He spoke of job guarantees and promised to double federal spending for work-related activities available to women, before the time limit expired. But he would place those unable to find work after twenty-four months on AFDC into a "work-

fare" program—euphemistically called community service jobs—
where they would be required to "work off" their AFDC benefit in
some kind of menial job such as cleaning parks, office buildings, or
toilets. In the majority of instances, the resulting wage-equivalent
would fall far below the minimum wage.[28]

Instead of encouraging business to attract workers by increasing wages and offering health benefits, once again officialdom used
harsh welfare rules to push more poor women into low-wage jobs—a
more difficult prospect at this time since the recession of 1989 had
forced unemployment to record heights in some of the nation's cities
which housed the poorest of the poor.[29] Meanwhile, the combination
of AFDC and Food Stamps approximated the income of minimum-
wage workers (although both groups lived below the poverty line),
and welfare entitled poor women to Medicaid, which, unlike low-paid
jobs, covered their health costs.[30] Placing a lifetime limit on AFDC
would make welfare less attractive—and altogether less available—
than work.

While developing his formal welfare plan, Clinton continued
Reagan's and Bush's practice of increasing state influence over AFDC
so that the states, without waiting for Congress to act, reformed
welfare on their own. By November 1995, the Department of Health
and Human Services had granted twenty-two states—nearly all that
had applied—permission to experiment with time limits and workfare programs with more waivers in the pipeline. Congress and the
states continued to push time limits and workfare despite persistent
corporate downsizing, the export of jobs abroad, and new research
findings that showed, once again, that despite the odds, many women
on welfare already work. According to the Institute for Women's
Policy Research (IWPR), the average AFDC mother works about 950
hours a year, approximately the same as all mothers in the workforce;
over 40 percent of women on welfare "package" AFDC income with
wages, either simultaneously or sequentially; and an additional 30
percent spend substantial time looking for work, although they do
not find it. The IWPR also reported that many working welfare
mothers can only find sporadic full-time jobs rather than steady
part-time ones, the majority of which are in low-wage "women's"
occupations; that the ability of poor women to work depends primarily
on local labor market conditions; and that even those who do find jobs
do not earn enough to make ends meet.[31]

The Economic Policy Institute estimated that swelling the labor
pool through time limits and workfare could press the wages of
low-paid workers down by more than 10 percent—more in states with
larger welfare populations, such as New York (17.1 percent) and

California (17.8 percent). In five states, wages would end up below the federal minimum.[32]

Workfare programs also lower wages by taking jobs away from someone who must then apply for AFDC. Unions, especially those representing public employees, have been especially concerned about this consequence of workfare, but effective guarantees against displacement appeared in few, if any, welfare reform bills.

By the mid-1990s, the welfare reform agenda had shifted further to the right: the November 1994 Republican congressional victory and the Contract with America moved shrinking the role of the federal government to the top of the political agenda. Clinton's first federal welfare reform proposal never became law. But his mean-spirited, racially-tinged rhetoric about welfare as a "way of life" and the need for women on welfare to behave "responsibly" by going to work and limiting their families opened the door to even more draconian proposals. The Contract with America supported severe time limits and workfare but dropped all the surrounding education and training programs. However, the most dramatic change occurred when the Republicans shifted the focus of welfare reform from work issues to "family values." By this time they had decided that "illegitimacy" was the nation's number one social problem—"more important than crime, drugs, poverty, illiteracy, welfare, or homelessness because it drives everything else."[33] They called for ending welfare altogether because it rewarded non-marital births and failed to adequately penalize single motherhood.

With this, both the House and the Senate welfare reformers began to target women's marital, childbearing, and parenting behavior, as well as their work behavior. The proposed reforms appeared in various degrees of severity and effectively punished single mothers in at least three different ways. First, the highly controversial child exclusion (also called the family cap) denied AFDC forever to children born while their mothers are receiving AFDC and to unmarried teen mothers and their children. If women insist on becoming pregnant, say the lawmakers, they should turn to relatives, apply for charity, or place their children in orphanages—ignoring the fact that these cost an average of $36,500 per child per year. The 1995 federal welfare reform proposals also stiffened the paternity penalties put into place by the 1988 FSA. Most bills required the states to withhold benefits from mothers who refused to provide information that would identify the child's father as well as from mothers who cooperated with the authorities but failed to establish paternity due to bureaucratic red tape or the father's ability to conceal his whereabouts. One 1995 estimate suggested that enforcement of such a strict paternity rule would throw nearly 30 percent of children off the AFDC rolls.[34] Finally, the reformers included an "illegitimacy" bonus—extra federal money for states that lower their non-marital birth rate without increasing the number of abortions.[35]

Just as he did with time limits, Clinton also encouraged the states to develop programs that controlled women's reproductive choice without waiting for federal welfare reform. As of November 1995, the Department of Health and Human Services had authorized thirteen child exclusion experiments, with several more on the way.[36] In addition, Florida and Ohio have proposed cash bonuses for mothers who agree to use Norplant (the long-lasting but controversial contraceptive implant) along with a separate plan to reward fathers who have a vasectomy, while Colorado has considered penalizing women on welfare who refuse family planning counseling. Meanwhile, the Utah legislature has considered a Republican plan to pay $3000 to unwed pregnant women who carry their babies to term *and* put them up for adoption.[37]

These proposals may sound reasonable, but when they are imposed as a *condition* of aid, they take advantage of a woman's dire financial situation, leaving her with little choice but to trade her health, as well as her contraceptive and religious preferences, for the AFDC check. This type of economic coercion also strips women of their privacy and mandates medical intervention that may be unwanted or counter-indicated. It presumes that poor women lack the capacity to make their own reproductive decisions and therefore must be subject to the strong arm of the government. According to the American Civil Liberties Union, to the extent that a federal welfare reform bill requires or permits the states to condition the receipt of public assistance on childbearing decisions, it "infringes upon the constitutional right of reproductive choice."[38]

The effort to control women's reproductive choices implies that women on welfare have large families. But the average welfare family includes two children, the same as the national average. Forty-three percent of families receiving AFDC have one child and 30 percent have two. Since a woman must have at least one child to qualify for AFDC in the first place, and since most women have only one more child while on the rolls, welfare can hardly be considered to *cause* large families; rather, the figures mirror national trends.

In 1992, just over half the children on AFDC were born outside of marriage, a slight drop from 1990, reversing a long *upward* trend. Non-marital births in the wider U.S. population rose from 26 per 1000 live births in 1970 to 44 per 1000 in 1990, after which the rate began to drop, just like the AFDC rate.[39] The rate is higher for African

Americans than for whites, but the majority of non-marital births in the U.S. (60 percent in 1993) are to white women, and their rate is rising fastest. Moreover, *many* women at all income levels have unintended pregnancies, suggesting the futility of bonuses and penalties.[40]

The rhetoric also claims that women on welfare have kids for money, but in 1994, seventy-nine scholars well-known for their research on poverty, labor markets, and family structures issued a press release stating that no evidence existed for a link between the availability of welfare and a woman's childbearing decisions.[41] Not only does the average state provide about $60 a month for each additional child, barely enough to pay for milk and diapers, but the states with more stringent welfare systems do *not* have fewer non-marital pregnancies. Instead, some states with the lowest benefits have very high non-marital birth rates. Moreover, during the 1970s, while the value of the AFDC grant fell by 36 percent due to inflation and benefit cuts, the non-marital birth rate soared. The preliminary evaluation of New Jersey's two-year-old child exclusion policy found no drop in the state's out-of-wedlock births. But the number of abortions rose by 4 percent and 8000 babies and their mothers faced even greater deprivation.[42]

To support their plan, the child exclusion advocates argued that workers' wages do not automatically rise when they have children. But, in fact, workers do receive an additional tax exemption for each new dependent, and some may still count on an annual pay raise when planning to expand their families. While fearing that AFDC benefits invite women to have children, the child exclusion supporters never suggest that working- and middle-class families have kids "for money" in response to the income tax exemption for dependents, the Earned Income Tax Credit for families with children, and the proposed $500 tax credit per child.

It is also a myth that AFDC breaks up marriages and invites the creation of single motherhood. AFDC *is* comprised of single mothers, but the program does not create this type of family structure. To begin with, except for the restricted AFDC-UP program, AFDC will not serve women who are married and living with their husbands. Second, rates of marriage have fallen nationwide because people are getting married later, divorcing and separating more, and remarrying less than they did in earlier periods. In 1993, half of *all* women in the United States between the ages of fifteen and forty-four were not married. Meanwhile, single motherhood has risen throughout society and shows up among women in all walks of life. Single parents headed 27 percent of all families with children in 1993, up from only 12.8 percent in 1970, and more than half the children born today will be raised by only one parent during a part of their lifetimes. While single motherhood is more prevalent in the black community than in the white, those who hold welfare responsible rarely note that two-thirds of all single parents are white.[43] Aside from these numbers, research, psychological knowledge, and plain common sense suggest that even poor people marry and divorce for a host of reasons that have nothing whatsoever to do with the availability of an AFDC check.

While single motherhood has a long history in the United States, the reason why women become single mothers has changed. Fewer and fewer mother-only families are headed by widows—the most socially acceptable basis for a mother-only family—and more and more single mothers have *never* been married—the group that poses the greatest challenge to patriarchal family norms. Most importantly, these changes have arisen among *both* AFDC recipients *and* women at large. Until 1980, divorced and separated women headed most mother-only families in both groups. Then never-married single mothers took the lead. From 1976 to 1992, the number of never-married single mothers on AFDC more than doubled, from 21 percent to 52 percent, following the rise of never-married single mothers in wider society, which surged from 7 percent of all single mothers to 36 percent. Contrary to popular stereotypes, it is the white community that has experienced the sharpest rise in households headed by women who have never married.[44]

Welfare reform also targets the parenting behavior of poor women and men. The welfare reform debate displays a deep *distrust* of parenting by poor women, even though many of the reformers hire poor women to care for their own children. From the belief, heard years ago, that poor children needed Headstart to correct for the improper socialization provided by their parents to the most recent discussions suggesting that the children of welfare mothers might be better off in group homes and orphanages, the reformers seem all too willing to remove poor children from their mothers' care. The recent round of welfare reform penalizes parenting by AFDC mothers through "Learnfare" and "Healthfare," which dock the family's grant if children are too truant or do not get their immunization shots on time. Where parental guidance is needed—as it is in some cases—positive outreach would work much better than threats of punishment by the state. Stricter child support enforcement also clamps down on the parenting by so-called "dead-beat dads." While men should be expected to support their children, welfare reform ignores the fact that most welfare fathers are poor and unemployed, that some are already involved with their children, or that too aggressive a pursuit of child support could expose women to male violence.

These efforts to enforce parental responsibility actually make it harder for mothers on welfare to parent effectively. The welfare critics seem oblivious to the fact that women still have primary responsibility for children, that poor single mothers do the work of two parents with fewer resources, and that women turn to AFDC to provide better care for their children. Instead, welfare reform forces mothers to work, which makes it harder for them to properly supervise their children, a task that requires even more time for single mothers living in neighborhoods plagued by poor schools, lack of health care, substandard housing, and in some cases drugs, crime, and violence. A Wisconsin welfare mother avoided attending a job search program while going to school so she would have time to see her kids. When her caseworker challenged her decision, the mother replied, "But who would my kids be eating dinner with? Who would put them to bed if I were to work nights and go to school during the day? Even AFDC recipients' kids need their moms."[45]

Poverty undermines effective parenting, yet most of the current reforms—time limits, benefit cuts, child exclusion, Learnfare, and Healthfare—deepen the poverty of AFDC families. The "reforms" also defy the research that shows that the deprivations of poverty, not the receipt of a welfare check, impair children's development on all fronts. Although the combined value of AFDC and Food Stamps falls below the poverty line in all fifty states, the welfare reformers are silent on raising the grant and ending poverty "as we know it."

The Social Security Retirement Program

The traditional regulatory functions encoded in the 1935 Social Security Retirement program also began to falter in the mid-1970s as more women went to work outside the home and as divorce became more widespread. These trends helped to weaken the ability of the Old Age Pension program to uphold the family ethic. Instead of excluding women from coverage, aiding them primarily as dependents of men, and penalizing them for becoming employed, the Social Security Retirement program of the 1980s began to show signs of favoring working women over homemakers and unmarried women over wives.

By 1981, 52 percent of all adult women worked in the paid labor force, up from 38 percent in 1960. In twenty-one years, they rose from 33 to 43 percent of the total civilian labor force. As working women started to retire, they began to receive benefits on their own work records rather than as dependents. From 1960 to 1983, the number of female Social Security beneficiaries aged sixty-two or older rose 167 percent and those receiving Social Security benefits on their own earnings record increased 258 percent. During this same period, the number of women entitled on their husband's record also increased, but more slowly, at a rate of 97 percent. Owing to these changes and contrary to the prior pattern of enforcing the family ethic, the proportion of all female Social Security beneficiaries entitled as dependents fell to 43 percent of the total, while those entitled on their own record rose to 57 percent from 1960-1983 and continued to rise.[46]

A 1982 Social Security Administration study of the status of new beneficiaries confirmed the above trends. It showed that, contrary to earlier patterns, whether they were married, widowed, divorced, or single, the program "rewarded" large numbers of women for their economic independence. Seventy-three percent of divorced women, 65 percent of married women, and 44 percent of widowed recipients received benefits based on their own earnings, either exclusively or as dually entitled recipients. Of the married women, 27 percent qualified for a higher benefit as a worker than as a wife. Sixty-five percent of divorced women, 40 percent of wives, and 30 percent of widows earned a pension entirely on their own records, while 18 percent of divorced women, 15 percent of wives, and 14 percent of widows supplemented their own pension with a partial spousal benefit.[47] Projections at that time suggested that by the year 2030, the majority of wives (53 percent) would qualify for their own retirement benefits rather than as a spouse and that 40 percent would be dually entitled. Only 7 percent of married women would receive "wife-only" benefits fifty years from the date of the study. Not only did many fewer female Social Security recipients secure benefits solely as dependents, but a comparison of benefits received by husbandless women from 1980-1981 revealed a decline in the value of having been married: single women received larger benefits ($450) than widowed ($432) or divorced ($385) female retirees.[48]

The long-standing pattern of favoring one-earner over two-earner couples also began to change in this decade. The 1982 survey of beneficiaries noted above found that, in some cases, two-earner couples reported greater benefits than one-earner couples in which the wife did not work and that dually entitled couples received higher benefits. This reversal of a traditional pattern also appeared among blacks, although their benefits continued to be less than those of whites due to their lower wages.[49] Likewise, women's benefit amounts still fell below those of men due to their low wages and movement in and out of the labor force to bear and raise children.[50]

These trends suggest that the capacity of the Social Security Retirement program to mediate the conflicting demands for women's home and market work according to the terms of the family ethic began to change. The program's rules seemed to be rewarding, if not encouraging, work by women—including married middle-class women—rather than penalizing employed women, traditionally viewed as departing from prescribed wife and mother roles. As if to restore the traditional regulatory role of Social Security, both OBRA and the1983 Social Security amendments made changes that seemed to enforce the family ethic.

Beginning in 1981, OBRA phased in reductions for future retirees through a variety of highly technical changes made in the calculation of future benefits. Other benefits, such as the $122 minimum grant received by low-income and sporadically employed Social Security recipients since 1975, ceased to exist in January 1982. Without this guaranteed minimum cushion, benefits once again were based solely on a worker's wages during employment. As a result, some of the lowest-paid workers received no benefits at all.

These changes adversely affected women, especially women newly entitled to benefits on their own work record. Three-quarters of the three million current and future beneficiaries who lost the basic minimum benefit were females: widowed homemakers and low-paid women workers.[51] While women with means might absorb these losses, many female Social Security recipients living far below the poverty line could not, in part because they lacked a private pension. Forty-three percent of men aged 65 or older, but only 20 percent of the women of this age, received private pension income at this time. The median monthly amount for the pensioned women was $233, compared to $484 for men.[52] One woman told *The Wall Street Journal* that the $388 monthly Social Security check meant "food on the table, light, heat, the telephone and the great bulk of her income, but that she had never planned to live that way."[53]

The Reagan administration, whose long-range goals included transforming Social Security from an entitlement program serving all the elderly to a welfare program just for the elderly poor, argued that the "truly needy" would not suffer because they could still apply for Supplemental Security Income (SSI). However, before the cuts, 50 percent of potential recipients chose not to apply for SSI, often because of the program's stigma as "welfare." In 1982, Tish Sommers, leader of the 5000-member Older Women's League (OWL), announced a protest in which 200 older women pushing grocery carts would be chained together in front of the Baltimore Social Security office. The carts contained the amount of food older women could buy with their Social Security checks.[54]

The Social Security cuts also worsened the "widow's gap" by ceasing payments to mothers (or fathers) when their youngest child reached age sixteen instead of eighteen. Lowering the child's age lengthened the time that widows under age sixty must be without Social Security. By 1982, some 200,000 previously entitled persons were deprived of this benefit. Some of these middle-aged women had other means of support, but those with the fewest resources were forced into the labor market regardless of their work background, health status, or the availability of jobs. The change had a strong impact on families of color, particularly blacks, who are overrepresented among the younger Social Security beneficiaries with children.[55]

Phasing out student benefits for eighteen- to twenty-two-year-old children of retired, disabled, or deceased workers also affected many younger widows. In 1981, approximately 700,000 students received this benefit, and another 500,000 would have received it in 1982 had it not been eliminated. Almost two-thirds of all student benefits went to families with incomes below $15,000 and 22 percent to people of color. Especially burdened were the high proportion of elderly black women who raise and educate their grandchildren. Families turning to other government programs aiding college students discovered that they too had been cut by OBRA.[56]

The 1983 amendments to the Social Security Act, based largely on the recommendations of the Social Security Reform Commission appointed by President Reagan to address the issue of the solvency of the Social Security Trust Fund, contained still other benefit reductions harmful to women.[57] The amendments lowered benefits over the long run by phasing in a postponement of the retirement age from sixty-five to sixty-seven over a period of years and dropping the benefit payments for early retirees from 80 to 70 percent of the full-benefit amount. Women workers and wives of workers were heavily overrepresented among early retirees, many of whom could not modify their retirement decisions to accommodate the new law: 75 percent of those who retired early did so because of health or employment problems. The lowered benefits were particularly problematic for displaced homemakers, who often just get by while waiting for their eligibility to begin.[58]

The amendments also placed the cost-of-living adjustment (COLA) on a calendar year, which led to a six-month postponement (from June 1983 to January 1984) and a permanent benefit cut of 2 percent over the average beneficiary's lifetime. They also imposed a tax of 50 percent on benefits for individuals with adjusted gross income of $25,000 or more ($32,000 for couples). Basing the COLA on average wage increases when the Trust Fund falls below 15 percent of annual benefit payments instead of price increases (e.g., the Consumer Price Index) would also lower benefits, depending on the future relationship between the two indicators. Unmarried women were the hardest hit by these changes, followed by unmarried men. The least affected would be married couples.[59]

Although the list of Social Security reforms designed to help women have been most notable by their absence since the mid-1960s,[60] the 1983 amendments did improve the program for women in a few ways. To expand the Social Security tax base, the amendments mandated coverage of employees of federal, state, and local governments, as well as of non-profit organizations. Until 1983, these groups entered the system on an optional basis or not at all. This change, which brought many white women and women (and men) of color into Social Security for the first time, improved their pension coverage.

Divorced widows and divorced women with living husbands secured some redress under the 1983 amendments. Prior to this, widows of deceased workers who remarried after age sixty received benefits, but not disabled or divorced widows between the ages of fifty and fifty-nine. By 1982, about 200,000 previously entitled persons were deprived of this benefit. The 1983 act redressed this inequity. By changing the wage calculation to reflect more recent pay rates, the law also improved payments for widows who became eligible many years after the death of their husbands. The new law also enhanced the ability of some divorced women with living husbands to collect their retirement benefit. After January 1985, benefits became available to divorced women without having to wait until their ex-husbands retired. Although women still must be divorced for at least two years before they can collect these more accessible benefits, the change was especially helpful to women older than their ex-husbands or whose ex-husbands continued to work. Finally, the amendments formally eliminated gender-based distinctions changed by the courts over the years and already in effect on an administrative basis.

Despite these marginal improvements for women, most of the 1983 changes put women at a further disadvantage. To begin with, the loss of income support generally shifted costs of reproducing the labor force and maintaining the non-working poor—that is, caretaking from the federal government back to older individuals and their families and intensified the demand for women's labor in the home. In addition, the new rules conveyed to women a message about the dangers of economic independence, especially to married and middle-class women who increasingly received benefits on their own work record. Moreover, the efforts to reform Social Security in ways that would accommodate the changes in women's roles and grant women greater independence in retirement made no headway at all.

The 1983 amendments had authorized a feasibility study for the reform known as earnings sharing, an idea first proposed by the 1979 Advisory Council on Social Security.[61] Earnings sharing offered women, including full-time homemakers, income protection upon retirement by defining marriage as an economic partnership and permitting a married couple to share equally any earnings credited for Social Security purposes during the years of their marriage. The proposal would have provided women with a "portable earnings record" as homemakers *and* as paid workers, offering better protection to divorced and widowed spouses. It received a mixed to unfavorable response from Reagan's Social Security Administration, which critics claimed was biased against the idea of earnings sharing from the start.[62] Nonetheless, supporters introduced several full-scale earnings sharing plans into Congress, but none was enacted. Among other obstacles, such a plan would have reversed the Social Security tradition of enforcing women's economic dependence on men and their role in the home.

Other structural reforms considered in the 1970s and early 1980s would also have enhanced female autonomy. The homemaker credits for the non-employed spouses of covered workers would have provided payments to women in their own right, as would the provision of caregiving credits for a specified time to account for the need to care for young children and elderly relatives. Another proposal was the double-decker or two-tiered system comprised of a wage-based benefit paid out of Social Security taxes and a second grant drawn from general funds and payable to everyone (who met certain requirements) regardless of their earnings.

The debate about the Social Security program engendered by the radical changes in women's roles—the increased labor force participation by women, the decline in full-time homemakers—fell silent in the mid-1980s, leaving women underrepresented among the insured and overrepresented among both senior citizens and the poor. By the late 1980s, most of the reform energy was focused on the program's fiscal side. Given Social Security's historical lack of special safeguards for women, the ongoing effort to retrench and privatize the program promises to bring women little good and much harm.

By successfully tampering with Social Security benefits during the 1980s, the Reagan administration broke the political barrier against doing so and opened the door to long-standing but, at the time, failed attempts to privatize the program. Barry Goldwater's assault on the long-range workability of Social Security in 1964 was widely given as a reason for his defeat at the hands of President Johnson. Ronald Reagan also tripped over Social Security in his 1976 presidential bid by merely suggesting that the program was in actuarial trouble. However, after winning the presidency, Reagan gave serious consideration to a 1982 recommendation by the Heritage Foundation to privatize Social Security.[63] Advocates of privatization have proposed to means test Social Security benefits, to make participation partly or fully voluntary, and to allow workers to make their contributions to a personal individual retirement account rather than to the Social Security Trust Fund. In 1987, The Cato Institute, another Washington, D.C.-based, conservative research organization, argued for privatization, and now the Concord Group, led by Paul Tsongas and Peter Peterson, is promoting the same idea on the highly disputed grounds that Social Security, once a good retirement investment, will not serve the baby-boom generation very well.[64]

While the bi-partisan Commission on Entitlement and Tax Reform appointed by President Clinton in 1994 could not reach consensus on how to constrict Social Security, the 1995 Republican Contract with America forged straight ahead with proposals that could undercut the entire program. The short-run gains it offered to beneficiaries could threaten the program's economic base in the long run by draining too many dollars from the Social Security Trust Fund. For example, the Contract proposed to allow recipients to earn up to $30,000 per year before losing any benefits, up from the current limit of $11,289, after which earnings would be indexed to the cost of living for a loss of $7 billion over five years.[65] It also promised to repeal the 1993 budget agreement provision that raised the proportion of Social Security benefits treated as taxable income for the most affluent recipients to 85 percent and reset it back to 50 percent by the year 2000. However, this tax cut would deprive the Social Security Trust Fund of an estimated $15 billion in the first five years and $33.5 billion in the second five years instead of sustaining the current surplus needed to cover the costs of pensions for the baby-boom generation.[66] In addition, the Contract created a new more generous type of Individual Retirement Account (IRA) for taxpayers at all income levels. While not directly using Social Security contributions, this could undermine support for the public pension system which provides some income to fully 92 percent of those over age sixty-five, 90 percent or more for 25 percent of the beneficiaries, and 50 percent or more for 60 percent. Only 25 percent of those over the age of sixty-five have a private pension.[67] While both parties put off direct cuts in Social Security for political reasons, the pressure to balance the budget, if continued unabated, will inevitably lead to greater long-term reductions in Social Security than would otherwise be the case. In 1995 the Congressional Budget Office had already proposed ways to lower the Social Security costs, including the elimination of benefits for unmarried children of retirees age sixty-two to sixty-four, instead of age sixty-five, which would fall heavily on women.[68]

Unemployment Insurance

Changes in the Unemployment Insurance (UI) program made since the 1970s also seemed to restore the faltering family ethic. As their new work patterns made even more women eligible for UI, Congress shrank the program. Although more than 50 percent of all women were in the labor force by 1980, representing over 40 percent of all workers, the Reagan administration's discussions about insurance for the jobless were especially distinguished by the absence of attention to issues of concern to women. Instead, women, persons of color, and the poor were adversely affected by efforts to lower the costs, increase work incentives, and privatize the Unemployment Insurance system.

The UI program, which has provided cash benefits for over half a century to involuntarily unemployed workers, includes two basic parts. The regular state-funded benefits for a maximum of twenty-six weeks began in 1935. Congress later established an "extended" benefits program (EB) funded by the federal government and the states to provide an additional thirteen weeks of assistance to workers who have exhausted their regular benefits and are still looking for work. The extended benefits kick in when a state's unemployment rate rises above a specified level and during periods of especially high unemployment, when it takes longer to find a job.[69] In the early seventies, as the economy began to sag, Congress introduced a third program of temporary benefits for the jobless in response to economic downturns. The Temporary Compensation (1972), Federal Supplemental Benefits (1975-1978), and Federal Supplemental Compensation (1982-1985) programs made federally financed assistance available for those exhausting all other UI benefits.[70]

By the 1990s, UI covered more people than ever before—90 percent of all workers—but the protection it offered had dwindled. Benefits that had once replaced more than 59 percent of their wages now accounted for only 37 percent.[71] Moreover, the number of eligible unemployed persons who actually received benefits dropped off. Between 1955 and 1979, this number ranged from a high of 75.5 percent (1975) to a low of 39 percent (1966), and during the 1970s averaged over 40 percent. In 1981, the Reagan administration, which sought to cheapen the cost of labor by retrenching social programs, changed the system in ways that further reduced these recipiency rates. The cutbacks harmed all workers, but especially women, youth, and people of color, whose labor force participation was rising but who, as described in Chapter Nine, were already disadvantaged by the structure of the program.

Despite high unemployment rates, Congress changed the UI program in ways that encouraged the states to deny benefits to jobless workers. Among other revisions, for the first time the government began to charge interest of up to 10 percent on federal loans to fiscally strapped states. In addition to making it harder for states to assist the unemployed, Congress discouraged workers from using the program by subjecting more of their UI check to federal income taxes. In 1982 Congress reduced the income level at which UI benefits were taxed from $20,000 to $12,000 for single taxpayers and from $25,000 to $18,000 for married couples filing jointly. However, this gain was eroded by the 1986 Tax Reform Act, which raised the taxable portion of the UI benefit from 50 to 100 percent.[72] Congress also considered restricting aid to those with the strongest work experiences, and extending the pre-benefit waiting period from one to two weeks; strengthening the experience rating provision to encourage employers not to hire workers who could become financial liabilities.[73] In addition, Congress discussed the privatization of UI benefits. One plan would offer a loan to workers who exhausted their regular twenty-six weeks of unemployment benefits, which they would repay with interest upon re-employment. Another would permit long-term recipients to cash their benefits into vouchers payable to new employers who would redeem them for a portion of the worker's wages.[74]

The 1981 OBRA also made changes that significantly reduced extended benefits. The Department of Labor explained that restrictions were necessary in order to assure that unemployed workers using extended benefits did not avoid taking any available job regardless of its pay and skill level: "We are saying that if you haven't found a job in twenty-six weeks maybe you ought to look for something that is obtainable. If a school teacher cannot find another job teaching maybe she should take a job in a department store instead of being automatically entitled to unemployment compensation."[75] To accomplish this, the legislators raised the unemployment rate that triggered extended benefits in the individual states from 4 to 5 percent, eliminated the lower national trigger which would have activated extended benefits in all the states simultaneously, and required recipients to have worked for twenty weeks in the base period to be eligible for them. During the Reagan years, the number of states with an activated EB program dropped sharply, and in other states the program simply shut down despite persistently high levels of unemployment.[76] By allowing Federal Supplemental Compensation (FSC) to expire in 1985, Congress ended supplemental assistance for some 325,000 workers—all without jobs for more than six months and still searching for work—even though the unemployment rate stayed stuck at over 7 percent, the longest stretch at this level since the 1930s. Without the FSC program, virtually all states had no choice but to limit benefits to twenty-six weeks, although 1.3 million of the five million workers fell into the category of long-term unemployed. Rarely, between 1949 and 1985, had the economy produced so much long-term joblessness.[77] Despite the lack of work due to the export of production to low-wage nations, OBRA decimated the Trade Adjustment Assistance (TAA) program, which assisted workers who had lost their jobs due to federal policies that encouraged competition from imports. The program's cash grants, re-training, job search, and employment services had helped thousands of workers facing dislocation in the ailing auto industry as well as apparel, footwear, and textile workers, which included large numbers of women.The number of TAA recipients peaked at 532,000 in 1980 but dropped to 16,000 in 1984; and outlays fell from $1,622 million to $35 million.[78]

In the mid-1980s and early 1990s, record low numbers of jobless workers received regular and extended unemployment insurance benefits. The national unemployment rate stayed at or above 7 percent from 1980 to 1986, the longest stretch at this level since the 1930s, with much higher rates for youth and persons of color. However, the share of unemployed women and men receiving benefits fell sharply, from 40 percent in the 1970s to a new low of 26 percent in October 1987—half the number aided in 1980, despite comparable unemployment rates in both years. In 1989, only one in three of all jobless workers and one in five unemployed minority workers received benefits. The numbers of unemployed stayed in the cellar until pushed up by the recession of 1991,[79] when the largest number of workers in any month since 1950—perhaps in the history of the UI program—had exhausted their benefits. Since no states offered extended benefits in 1990 and only six small states and Puerto Rico met the requirements that activated the EB program in 1991, just 16,000 of the 334,000 jobless workers with expired benefits lived in areas where they could qualify for aid.[80]

Faced with historically high rates of long-term joblessness and low levels of government protection, in 1991 President Bush vetoed legislation authorizing emergency benefits to the long-term unemployed. Nonetheless, later that year Congress passed the Emergency Unemployment Compensation Act (EUC) and made the regular EB program more responsive to high unemployment in the states. By February 1992, Congress had extended EUC and states were paying from twenty-six to thirty-three weeks of benefits for upwards of half the unemployed—a substantial increase from 41.6 percent of the jobless receiving assistance in 1991. Without EUC, the recipiency rate would have been only 35 percent. After the program was allowed to expire in April 1994, this rate plummeted from 42.5 percent (April 1994) to 32.5 percent (December 1994). Meanwhile, nearly a quarter million jobless workers were exhausting their regular UI benefits each month.[81]

The cutbacks in Unemployment Insurance during the past 15 years affected many women, youth, and men of color, whose jobs became especially vulnerable once unemployment soared. At the same time, policymakers regularly blamed working women for high unemployment rates.[82] Trying to minimize the 1982 recession, Reagan once stated, "Part of the [reason for] unemployment is not as much recession as it is the great increase in people going into the job market, and ladies, I'm not picking on anyone, but [it is] because of the increase in women who are working today and the two-earner families and so forth."[83] Similar arguments were made about youth employment. If nothing else, this kind of rhetoric masked the reality that the restructuring of the economy created more unemployment for women and that the expansion of low-paid, part-time jobs in the expanding service sector reduced the likelihood of women collecting benefits.

It also hid the reality that the Unemployment Insurance system remained unresponsive to women's special work patterns. The Institute for Women's Policy Research (IWPR) found that 80 percent of the unemployed women they studied in 1988-1990 did not meet the eligibility criteria for Unemployment Insurance, compared to 74 percent of the unemployed men. Likewise, part-time workers were almost four times less likely than full-time workers to receive UI benefits—90 percent of part-time workers did not qualify. Due to their caretaking responsibilities at home, women were more likely than men to lose out because they could not meet the length-of-employment rule, which in many states disqualified part-time workers, and the monetary eligibility rules, which denied benefits to those who earn too little.[84] However, since the mid-1970s, the labor force has been characterized by low wages and rising part-time and contingent work, the very conditions that leave workers, especially women workers, ineligible for UI.

Since length-of-employment and monetary requirements disqualify so many women from UI benefits, the IWPR has recommended reforms that would make the UI system "more accessible to workers with low earnings and more sporadic work patterns and expand the definition of 'good cause' reasons [for leaving a job] to acknowledge the reality of the relationship between women's labor force participation and their family care responsibilities."[85] To increase women's UI benefits would also acknowledge them as permanent members of the workforce and to provide them with an alternative to depending on men or the lowest-paid job for income. That this would undermine rather than restore the family ethic may help to explain long-standing lack of attention to such reforms.

Welfare State Hiring Practices

Paradoxically, the welfare state's hiring practices also helped to undermine its regulatory role. Instead of channeling middle-class and married women into the home, the government's own demand for labor and the implementation of affirmative action policies drew many white women and women of color, including many wives, into public sector employment. Indeed, starting in the early sixties, employment of women by the federal, state, and local governments grew much faster than that of men. Twenty percent of all employed women, but only 16 percent of all men, worked in a federal, state, or local government office in 1981.[86]

In 1981, when the cuts began, women comprised 48 percent of *all* government workers, up from 45 percent in 1974, 39 percent in 1964, and 27 percent in 1947. Although they remained concentrated in the lower civil service jobs, in 1981 women comprised 32 percent of all federal employees, 46 percent of all state, and 54 percent of all local employees, up from 29 percent of all federal, 42 percent of all state, and 49 percent of all local government workers in 1973. During the 1970s, the federal government employed twice as many women of color than in earlier periods, with women in each racial-ethnic group experiencing substantial employment gains. By 1980, of all women in federal white-collar jobs, black women made up nearly 30 percent; Latina women, 4 percent; American Indian and Asian American, 2 percent each.[87] Some of the major advances for women occurred in the professional grades. The number of women in these jobs rose nearly 57 percent between 1974-1983, compared to a 21 percent rise in the number of male professionals, a 14 percent increase among non-professional women, and an 18 percent expansion in the female white-collar labor force.[88]

Many female public employees work in the expanding human service sector. Between 1960 and 1980, the social welfare industry generated jobs for two out of every five women compared with only one out of five men. In 1980, women held fully 70 percent of the 17.3 million social service jobs in all levels of government, including education. This accounted for a quarter of all female employment and for half of all the professional jobs held by women. Between 1964 and 1990, for every job added in government social services that were held by a man, two were added that were held by women. By 1986, the goverment employed more women than men.[89] The large number of female professionals at work in government agencies or federally subsidized programs, no doubt, contributed to the neo-conservative critique of human service workers as a "new class" of employees selfishly benefiting from the expansion of the welfare state.[90]

But by the 1980s, social program cuts and the attack on affirmative action rules cost many women their jobs. Indeed, Reagan laid off nearly 12,000 federal workers in 1981 alone. Women administrators lost their jobs at a rate 150 percent higher than men. Black and Hispanic administrators of both sexes were laid off at a rate about 220 percent higher than white administrators in similar positions. In 1981, the Office of Management and Budget projected that cutbacks for fiscal years 1981-1984 would trim the federal non-defense payroll by 8 percent, or 150,000 workers.[91] Another 700,000 state and city federal human service workers lost their jobs in 1982 due to federal social service retrenchments. Likewise for the large numbers of human service workers in the private health and social welfare sector, which also depended heavily on public funding and which employs one half of the nation's eleven million female human service workers.[92] The employment cuts continued through the decade into the 1990s. In March 1986, the Government Accounting Office reported that the Social Security administration planned to reduce its employment, this time by some 17,000 full-time equivalent positions, from fiscal year 1985 through 1990.[93] Meanwhile, the concurrent increase in military spending did not benefit women very much. Military contracts employ only 0.5 percent of the entire female workforce. According to Employment Research Associates, with each one-billion-dollar increase in the military budget, some 9,500 jobs were lost to women in the social welfare or private sectors. Due to these and other cuts, instead of continuing to grow, public employment remained stable—at about 15.5 percent of all total employment. The proportion of women fell from 45 percent in 1981 to the low forties during the rest of the 1980s. In 1991, women represented 41.8 percent of government workers.[94]

In the mid-1980s, the federal government initiated the "bulge program," designed to save money through a reduction of its higher-paid personnel. Over a four-year period, the program cut 40,000 grade-eleven to fifteen federal positions.[95] The number of female federal employees in grades nine to twelve had nearly doubled between 1974 and 1983, and those in grades thirteen to fifteen had more than doubled. The cuts could only slow the upward mobility of women who in recent years had made rapid employment advances in the upper grades and who as the last hired would be the first to be fired. As of 1990, women and minorities made up the majority of federal workforce grades two to eleven, but only 30 percent of grade thirteen and just 17 percent of Senior Executive Services.[96]

The federal government also saved money by slowing down the rate of wage increases. In August 1983, after first calling for a 5 percent salary reduction, Reagan recommended a wage freeze for all federal employees other than postal and military workers.[97] The three-month deferral of 1983 and 1984 pay increases amounted to a wage cut. Beginning in 1978, the pay adjustment rate recommended by the president for white-collar workers in government service has lagged behind that needed to keep federal wage scales comparable with those in the private sector, but the gap has intensified considerably since 1981, the year the cutbacks began.[98] By 1990, on average federal public employees made 30 percent less in salaries than did their private sector counterparts: the wages of public employees at every level did not keep pace with changes in the economy.[99]

Despite many references to strengthening family life and preserving traditional family values, with the exception of the Family and Medical Leave Act providing unpaid leave to care for new or ill family members, Presidents Reagan, Bush, and Clinton have made few, if any, affirmative proposals to help families. Rather, the government's "family policy" has struck deeply at the social welfare programs that support the economic security and independence of women, including those that have provided some social, psychological, and economic relief to families in an increasingly troubled economy.

The assault on the welfare state that began in the 1980s was a major component of the economic recovery program designed by business and the state. Stimulated by the current transformation of the economy and implemented to address the wider economic crisis, the cutbacks also mitigated the regulatory crisis of the welfare state by restoring the family and work ethics encoded in the Social Security Act of 1935. To the extent that the rules and regulations of social welfare programs increasingly supported behaviors that undercut these imperatives, the programs had begun to contradict the workings of patriarchy and capitalism. The cutbacks, therefore, helped to revive the system's old patterns and rewards. Tightening public assistance eligibility, imposing time limits, and intensifying workfare requirements re-created the practice of punishing single mothers, increasing the flow of women into the service sector, and exerting the desired downward pressure on wages. The effort to modify the marital, childbearing, and parenting behavior of poor women that began in the mid-1980s eased the moral panic based on false fears that the changing family structure heralded its demise. The attack on welfare also scapegoated poor women in order to deflect the attention of the increasingly economically insecure middle class from the structural sources of the nation's social, economic, and political woes. [100]

Meanwhile, just as Social Security began to benefit women on their own work record and as the program showed signs of "rewarding" women's economic independence, it was cut back. Likewise, at the moment when more than 50 percent of all women worked outside the home, Unemployment Insurance was severely retrenched. Finally, the domestic program cuts reversed the employment gains made by women employed in the public sector. These changes effectively helped to revive the pattern whereby the welfare state mediated the conflicting demand for women's home and market labor by channeling women viewed as deviating from prescribed wife and mother roles into low-paid employment and encouraging those who complied with these roles to remain at home, where they reproduce the labor force and maintain the non-working poor.

Notes to Chapter 11

1. Thomas Weisskopf, "The Current Economic Crisis in Historical Perspective," *Socialist Review* 11(3) (May-June 1981); Edward Cowan, "Debate Over Blame for Recession Blurs Reagan's Economic Record," *The New York Times,* January 21, 1982.

2. The White House Working Group on the Family, *The Family: Preserving America's Future,* November 13, 1986, pp. 5, 12, 15.

3. The Contract with America is the set of proposals prepared by the Republican Party prior to the 1995 congressional elections. It reflected their proposed political agenda, including welfare reform. The Republicans failed to pass all these items during the first 100 days of the 1996 Congress as desired, but the Contract nonetheless exerted a significant influence on the overall political climate.

4. Sar Levitan, Martin Rein, and David Marwick, *Work and Welfare Go Together* (Baltimore: Johns Hopkins University Press, 1972), p. 60; U.S. House of Representatives, Committee on Ways and Means, *Overview of Entitlement Programs (1992 Green Book)* (Washington, D.C.; U.S. Government Printing Office, May 15, 1992), p. 670. (These reports are issued annually. Hereafter, they will be referred to as the *Green Book* by year).

5. Greg Duncan, *Years of Poverty, Years of Plenty: The Changing Economic Fortunes of American Workers and Families* (Ann Arbor, Institute for Social Research, University of Michigan, 1984), pp. 71-94; Levitan, Rein, and Marwick, *op. cit.* p. 60; Mildred Rein, *Dilemmas of Welfare Policy: Why Work Strategies Haven't Worked* (New York: Praeger, 1982), pp. 148-150; *1992 Green Book, op. cit.,* p. 699.

6. U.S. Congress, Joint Economic Committee, Studies in Public Welfare, Paper #14, *Public Welfare and Work Incentives: Theory and Practice* (April 15, 1974) (Washington, D.C.: U.S. Government Printing Office, 1974), p.13.

7. Heather Ross and Isabel Sawhill, *Time of Transition: The Growth of Families Headed by Women* (Washington, D.C.: The Urban Institute, 1975), p. 5.

8. The White House Working Group on the Family (1986), *op. cit.,* p. 32.

9. Domestic Policy Council, Low Income Opportunity Working Group, *Up From Dependency: A New National Public Assistance Strategy* (Washington, D.C.: December 1986), pp. 47, 55.

10. The White House Working Group on the Family (1986), *op. cit.,* p. 32.

11. *1983 Green Book,* pp. 444-449.

12. *1992 Green Book,* p. 663.

13. *1983 Green Book,* p. 257.

14. *1986 Green Book*, p. 398.

15. Congressional Budget Office, *Work Related Programs for Welfare Recipients* (Washington, D.C.: U.S. Government Printing Office, 1987), pp. 24-25.

16. *1994 Green Book,* p. 399.

17. Congressional Budget Office,*Work Related Programs for Welfare Recipients* (1987) *op. cit.,* pp. 24-25.

18. Sameul Bowles and Herbert Gintis, "The Crisis of Liberal Democratic Capitalism: The Case of the United States," *Politics and Society* 11(1) (1982), pp. 53, 84.

19. Domestic Policy Council, *Up From Dependency* (1986), *op. cit.*

20. *1992 Green Book,* p. 1759.

21. National Alliance of Business, *Employment Policies: Looking to the Year 2000* (Washington, D.C.: February 1986), p. 1.

22. *Ibid.*; U.S. Department of Labor, *WorkForce 2000* (Government Printing Office:Washington, D.C.: 1987), p. 5.

23. LaDonna Pavetti, "The Dynamics of Welfare and Work: Exploring the Process By Which Young Women Work Their Way Off Welfare," cited in *1994 Green Book*, pp. 441-442.

24. See, for example, U.S. Government Accutting Office, *Work and Welfare: Current AFDC Work Programs and Implications for Federal Policy* (Washington, D.C.: U.S. Government Printing Office, January 1987); Barbara Goldman, Daniel Friedlander, and David Long, *Final Report on the San Diego Job Search and Work Experience Demonstration* (New York: Manpower Demonstration Research Corporation, 1986); Judith M. Gueron, "Work for People On Welfare," *Public Welfare* 44 (Winter 1986), pp. 7-12.

25. Julie Rovner, "Welfare Reform: The Issue That Bubbled Up From the States to Capitol Hill," *Governing* (December 1988), p. 18.

26. Congessional Budget Office, *Work Related Programs for Welfare Recipients* (1987), *op. cit.*, pp. 24-25.

27. Katherine S. Newman, "What Inner City Jobs For Welfare Moms?" *The New York Times,* May 20, 1995, p. 23.

28. Lawrence Mishel and John Schmitt, *Cutting Wages By Cutting Welfare: The Impact of Reform on the Low-Wage Labor Market* (Washington, D.C.: The Economic Policy Institute, 1995).

29. Jodie Levin-Epstein, "Clinton Welfare Options Under Consideration," *States Update: A CLASP Report on State Welfare Reform Developments*

(Washington, D.C.: Center For Law and Social Policy, December 23, 1993), pp. 1-2.

30. Government Accounting Office, *Low Income Families: Comparison of AFDC and Working Poor Families* (Washington, D.C.: U.S. Government Printing Office, January 25, 1995).

31. Roberta Spalter Roth, Beverly Burr, Heidi Hartmann, and Lois Shaw, *Welfare That Works: The Working Lives of AFDC Recipients* (Washington, D.C.: Institute for Women's Policy Research, March 20, 1995, pp.40,43.

32. Mishel and Schmitt, *Cutting Wages by Cutting Welfare: The Impact of Reform on the Low-Wage Labor Market* (1995), *op. cit.*

33. Charles Murray, "The Emerging White Underclass and How to Save It," *The Philadelphia Inquirer,* November 15, 1993, p. A15.

34. U.S. Department of Health and Human Services, *Characteristics and Financial Circumstances of AFDC Recipients* (Washington, D.C.: U.S. Government Printing Office, 1992), p. 34, Table 16.

35. Because anti-abortion groups feared that the child exclusion would lead pregnant women to seek abortions, they insisted that the bonus be based on non-marital births *and* abortions as a percentage of births to all women in the state instead of just within the AFDC caseload. This links the control of reproduction among AFDC women to the control of all women in the state.

36. Center on Social Welfare Policy and Law, "State Welfare Reform Continues With Federal Waivers," *Welfare News*, November 28, 1994, pp. 9-10.

37. Timothy Egan,"Take This Bribe, Please, For Values To Be Received," *The New York Times*, November 12, 1995, p. E 5.

38. Reproductive Rights Update, A Quarterly Report of Policy and Analysis, American Civil Liberties Union, December 1995, p,6.

39. Center On Hunger, Poverty and Nutriton Policy, *Statement on Key Welfare Reform Issues: The Empirical Evidence,* Medford, MA, 1995, p. 3.

40. Data from the 1988 National Survey of Family Growth indicate that 88 percent of the pregnancies experienced by never-married women, 69 percent of the pregnancies of previously married women, and 40 percent of the pregnancies of married women were unintended. U.S. Department of Health and Human Services, *Report to Congress on Out-Of-Wedlock Childbearing* (Executive Summary), West Hyattsville, MD, September 1995, pp. 2-3, 6, 8.

41. "Researchers Dispute Contention That Welfare Is a Major Cause of Out of Wedlock Births," press release issued June 23, 1994 by Sheldon Danziger, Director, Research and Training Program on Poverty, the Underclass and Public Policy, School of Social Work, University of Michigan, Ann Arbor, MI.

42. *NASW News,* "Welfare Bill Said Flawed; Defeat Urged," September 1995, pp. 1, 12.

43. U.S. Department of Health and Human Services, *Report to Congress on Out-of-Wedlock Childbearing* (1995), *op. cit.,* pp. 2-3; *1994 Green Book,* p. 1111; U.S. Bureau of the Census, Studies in Marriage and the Family, *Singleness in America,* Current Population Reports, Series P-23, No. 162, Washington, D.C.: U.S. Government Printing Office, 1990) p. 6.

44. *1994 Green Book,* pp. 401, 1111; U.S. Government Accounting Office, *Families on Welfare: Teenage Mothers Least Likely to Become Self Sufficient* (Washington, D.C.: U.S. Government Printing Office, May 1994), pp. 16-17.

45. Ruth Coniff, "Big Bad Welfare," *The Progressive* (August 1994), p. 21.

46. "Women Social Security Beneficiaries, Aged 62 or Older, 1960-1983," *Social Security Bulletin,* 48(2) (February 1985), p. 27, T. 1; p. 28, T. 2; p. 29, T. 3 (calculation by author); Karen Holden,"Women's Economic Status in Old Age and Widowhood," in Martha N Ozawa, (ed.), *Women's Life Cycle and Economic Insecurity* (New York: Praeger, 1989), p. 152.

47. *Ibid,* pp. 19-24.

48. Virginia Reno and Anne Dee Rader, "Benefits for Individual Retired Workers and Couples Now Approaching Retirement Ages," *Social Security Bulletin,* 45 (February 1982), pp. 25-31; Barbara A. Lingg, "Social Security Benefits of Female Retired Workers and Two-Worker Couples," *Social Security Bulletin,* 45 (February 1982), pp. 3-24.

49. "Women Social Security Beneficiaries, Aged 62 or Older, 1960-1983" (1985), *op. cit.,* p. 31.

50. Lynn Hecht Schafran, "Women: A Decade of Progress," in Alan Gartner, Colin Greer, and Frank Reissman (eds.), *What Reagan Is Doing to Us* (New York: Harper and Row, 1982), p. 178.

51. *Ibid.*

52. Older Women's League, *Report on the Status of Midlife and Older Women in America,* Mother's Day Report, 1986, p. 3.

53. John J. Fialka, "Older Americans: What Social Security Means to The Retired and About to Be," *The Wall Street Journal,* February 2, 1983, p. 1.

54. U.S. Congress, House of Representatives, Select Committee on Aging, *Report of the Impact of Administration's Social Security Proposals on Present and Future Beneficiaries,* 97th Congress, 1st Sess., July 1981 [Committee Publication No. 97-280], pp. 26, 27; Judy Klemesrud, "Older Women: Their League Gains Strength," *The New York Times,* November 22, 1981.

55. U.S. House of Representatives, Select Committee on Aging (1981) *op. cit.,* pp. 27-28; Barbara Nash, "Social Security is a Women's Issue," *WEAL Facts,*

November 1982; Jean Bandler, "Social Security for Children and Families," Study Group on Social Security," *Fact Sheet #7,* July 1980, p. 3.

56. U.S. House of Representatives, Select Committee on Aging (1981) *op. cit.,* pp. 27-28; Nash (1982), *op. cit.;* Women's Equity Action League, "Social Security and Minority Women," *WEAL Facts,* Fact Sheet #2, June 1983.

57. See U.S. Congress, House of Representatives, Committee on Ways and Means, *Social Security Act Amendments of 1983, Report on H.R. 1900* (Washington, D.C.: U.S. Government Printing Office, March 4, 1983); Lori Hansen, Social Security Study Group, "Social Security Rescue Plan Enacted," *Update #25,* April 20, 1983; Jules H. Berman, "The Social Security Act Amendments of 1983," *Washington Social Legislation Bulletin,* 28(8), April 25, 1983; Child Welfare League of America, Nash (1982), *op. cit.;* Women's Equity Action League (June 1983) *op.cit.,* Women's Equity Action League (April 1983), *op. cit;* Women's Equity Action League, Social Security Fact Sheet #4 (no date), *op. cit.*

58. Dorothy Miller, "The Feminization of Poverty: Women and Proposed Social Security Cuts," *Washington Social Legislation Bulletin,* 27(16) (August 24, 1981).

59. Sheila Zedlewski, "The Increasing Fiscal Burden on the Elderly," in John R. Gist (ed.) *Social Security and Economic Well-Being Across Generations* (Washington, D.C.: American Association of Retired Persons, 1988), pp. 146-149.

60. For earlier discussions, see, Citizens' Advisory Council on the Status of Women, *Report of the Task Force on Social Insurance and Taxes* (Washington, D.C.: U.S. Government Printing Office, April 1968); U.S. Department of Health, Education and Welfare, *Social Security and the Changing Roles of Men and Women,* February 1979; National Commission on Social Security, *Social Security in America's Future, Final Report,* March 1981, Chs. 11, 20 (Appendix D); *Report of the 1979 Advisory Council on Social Security,* reprinted by the House Committee on Ways and Means, WMCP:96-45, 96th Congress, 1st. Sess., January 2, 1980.

61. *Report of the 1979 Advisory Council on Social Security* (1980), *op. cit.* p. 85.

62. Robert Pear, "Study Challenges Pension Proposal," *The New York Times,* December 12, 1984, p. A1. See also U.S. Social Security Administration, Office of Legislative and Regulatory Policy, "Report on the Earnings Sharing Implementation Study," *Social Security Bulletin,* 48(3) (March 1985), pp. 31-41.

63. Wayne King, "Alternative to Social Security Urged," *The New York Times,* November 24, 1987, p. 18; Peter J. Ferrara, *Social Security Reform: The Family Security Plan* (Washington, D.C.: Heritage Foundation, 1982); G. Norquist, *IRA and Social Security: The Family Security Plan,* The Heritage

Lecture No. 18; *Rebuilding Social Security* (Washington, D.C.: Heritage Foundation, 1982); Robert Pear, "Voluntary Social Security Plan is Studied," *The New York Times,* October 4, 1984, p. 32.

64. David Boaz, "Privatize Social Security," *The New York Times,* March 21, 1990.

65. National Academy of Social Insurance, *Newsletter*, February 1995, No. 39, pp. 4, 5.

66. *Ibid*; Center on Budget and Policy Priorities, *The New Fiscal Agenda: What Will it Mean and How Will it be Accomplished?*, January 1995, pp. 15, 18.

67. Marianne Ferber, "Women's Employment and the Social Security System," *Social Security Bulletin,* 56(3), Fall 1993, p. 42.

68. Congressional Budget Office, *Reducing the Deficit: Spending and Revenue Options* (Washington, D.C.: U.S. Government Printing Office, February 1995), pp. 309-312.

69. The 1935 Report of Committee on Economic Security, which designed the Social Security Act, had recommended that Unemployment Insurance be followed by employment in public service jobs for those who exhausted their benefits. Congressional Budget Office, *Family Incomes of Unemployment Insurance Recipients and the Implications for Extending Benefits* (Washington, D.C.: U.S. Government Printing Office, February 1990), p. 45.

70. *Ibid.*, p. 11.

71. *Ibid,* p. 275.

72. *1994 Green Book,* pp. 273-74.

73. Congressional Budget Office, *Promoting Employment and Maintaining Incomes with Unemployment Insurance* (Washington, D.C.: U.S. Government Printing Office, March 1985), pp. 47-54.

74. Congressional Budget Office, *Reducing the Deficit: Spending and Revenue Options: A Report to the Senate and House Committees on the Budget Part II* (Washington, D.C.: U.S. Government Printing Office, February 1985). p. 144; Robert Pear, "Vouchers, Emerging as a Theme, Provoke Debate," *The New York Times*, February 8, 1983.

75. Phillip Shabecoff, "Reagan Seeks Tighter Work Test for Those on Extra Unemployment Benefits," *The New York Times*, September 8, 1981, p. A22.

76. Congressional Budget Office, *Family Incomes of Unemployment Insurance Recipients and the Implications for Extending Benefits* (1990) *op. cit.*, p. 11; Pamela Fessler, "Congress Accepts Reagan's Proposal to Curtail Extended Unemployment Benefits," *Congressional Quarterly Weekly Report* 39(33) (August 16, 1981), p. 1469; *1986 Green Book, op. cit.*, pp. 314-315.

77. John Bickerman, *Unemployed and Unprotected: A Report on the Status of Unemployment Insurance* (Washington, D.C.: Center on Budget and Policy Priorities, March 1985), p. 2.

78. *1986 Green Book, op. cit.*, pp. 289-295; Pamela Fassler (1981), *op cit.*, pp. 1468-1469.

79. *1994 Green Book*, p. 267.

80. Isaac Shapiro and Marion E. Nichols, *Unprotected: Unemployment Insurance and Jobless Workers in 1988* (Washington, D.C.: Center on Budget and Policy Priorities, August 1989), p. 4.

81. Marion Nichols and Isaac Shapiro, *Unemployment Insurance Protection in 1994* (Washington D.C.: Center on Budget and Policy Priorities, May 15, 1995), p. 5.

82. Mimi Abramovitz, "Blaming Women for High Unemployment: Refuting a Myth," *Social Casework* 65(9) (November 1984), pp. 547-553.

83. Irwin Molotsky, "Jobless Rate Tied To Big Work Force," *The New York Times,* April 18, 1982.

84.Young-Hee Yoon, Roberta Spalter Roth, and Marc Baldwin, *Unemployment Insurance: Barriers to Access for Women and Part-Time Workers: A Report to the National Commission for Employment Policy* (Washington, D.C.: Institute for Women's Policy Research, 1995), pp. 1-4.

85. *Ibid.*

86. U.S. Department of Labor, Women's Bureau, *Time of Change: 1983 Handbook on Women Workers,* Bulletin 298 (Washington, D.C.: U.S. Government Printing Office, 1983), pp. 68-74.

87. *Ibid.* U.S. Department of Labor, Women's Bureau, *1975 Handbook on Women Workers,* Bulletin 297 (Washington, D.C.: U.S. Government Printing Office, 1975), p. 114.

88. U.S. General Accounting Office, *Distribution of Male and Female Employees in Four Federal Classification Systems* (GAO/GGD 85-20) (Washington, D.C.: U.S. Government Printing Office, November 27, 1984), p. 37, T. 5.

89. Harold Brackman and Steven P. Erie, "The Future of the Gender Gap," *Social Policy* 16(3) (Winter 1986), p. 7; Barbara Ehrenreich and Frances Fox Piven, "The Feminization of Poverty: When the Family Wage System Breaks Down," *Dissent* 31(4) (Spring 1984), p. 165; U.S Women's Bureau, *1993 Handbook on Women Workers: Trends and Issues* (Washington, D.C.: U.S. Government Printing Office, 1994, pp. 21, 111-115, 137.

90. Peter Steinfels, "What The Neo-Conservatives Believe," *Social Policy* 11 (May/June 1979), pp. 4-14.

91. Augustus F. Hawkins, "Minorities and Employment," in Alan Gartner, Colin Greer, and Frank Reissman (eds.), *What Reagan Is Doing to Us* (New York: Harper and Row, Publishers, 1982), p. 134.

92. Brackman and Erie (1986) *op. cit.*, p. 7.

93. U.S. Government Accounting Office, *Social Security: Actions and Plans to Reduce Agency Staff* (GAO/HRD 86-76 Br) (Washington, D.C.: U.S. Government Accounting Office, March 17, 1986).

94. Ehrenreich and Piven (1984), *op. cit.,* p. 165; Public Employee Department, AFL-CIO, *Public Employees: Facts at a Glance* (Washington, D.C.: AFL-CIO, 1995), p. 34; U.S. Department of Labor, Women's Bureau (1993) *op. cit.*, p. 21.

95. U.S. General Accounting Office, *Federal Workforce: How Certain Agencies Are Implementing the Grade Reduction Program* (GAO/GGD 86-33) (Washington, D.C.: Government Printing Office, January 1986), p. 1.

96. U.S. General Accounting Office (1984), *op. cit.*, p. 33, T. 1.

97. Bernard Weinraub, "Reagan Proposes a Freeze on Pay of Civil Servants," *The New York Times,* August 30, 1985, p. A1.

98. U.S. General Accounting Office, *Comparison of Federal and Private Sector Pay and Benefits* (Washington, D.C.: U.S. Government Printing Office, September 4, 1985), pp. 8-11.

99. AFl-CIO, Public Employee Department(1995), *op. cit.*, p. 38.

100. Mimi Abramovitz, *Under Attack, Fighting Back: Women and Welfare in the United States* (New York: Monthly Review Press, 1996).

Conclusion
Dare to Struggle, Dare to Win

The critical analysis contained in this book suggests several broad steps necessary to modify and ultimately reverse the negative effects of the institutionalization of the family ethic within the welfare state. First, we must be aware of its presence and power within the social welfare system. Second, we must continue ongoing efforts to strengthen the features of those programs that benefit women of all races and classes and eliminate those that discriminate against them. Third, we must develop policies within and outside the welfare state that enhance the autonomy and independence of women, thereby undercutting one of patriarchy's main props. Fourth, we must replace the current family ethic with a more positive one that recognizes different family structures, promotes equal rights and responsibilities within the family, and satisfactorily meets the needs of all family members. Fifth, we must continually create and support political struggles that envision a society which structures equality into the political economy rather than one that leaves the achievement of this critical social goal to shifting political winds, the ravages of the market economy, or the imperatives of patriarchal capitalism. At the very least, we need to fight to restore the domestic cuts made during the past fifteen years and strenuously oppose the most recent attempts of business and the state to strip social programs of their entitlement status, to shift federal responsibility for social welfare from the federal government to the states, and to undo the right to basic social benefits that it took sixty years to develop.

In the first edition of this book, published in 1988, I suggested some short-range changes that would make the Aid to Families with Dependent Children, Social Security, and Unemployment Insurance programs more beneficial to women and other recipients. Beginning with AFDC, I argued for simplifying the application process, removing its deterrent features, and placing the program under a single *federal* administration. I suggested that the benefit level needed to be raised, tied to the Consumer Price Index, and standardized nationally, taking into account family size and regional differences in the cost of living. Such a national minimum benefit should not leave any family living below the official poverty line. I also called for

391

broadening AFDC eligibility to include two-parent as well as single-parent families, and creating a service-enriched but voluntary work program that gave AFDC mothers a choice about whether or not to work outside the home. Furthermore, child-support enforcement programs should not disrupt the AFDC mother's life or jeopardize her welfare grant.

The Social Security Retirement program, I concluded, would better serve women by restoring the minimum benefit amount that had been removed in the 1981 budget cuts and eliminating the remaining gender inequities. I urged acceleration of the prevailing debate over reform proposals that would recognize women's unique labor force patterns and would support a plan that would credit women's work in the home when calculating benefits; end the preference for wives and full-time homemakers at the expense of single, divorced, and employed women; close the "widow's gap," which deprived widows below sixty with no children at home of survivors' benefits; assist disabled widows before age fifty; and bring the remaining uncovered occupations containing large numbers of women and persons of color into the program.

The Unemployment Insurance program would also be improved by tying benefits to the cost of living, restoring extended benefits, and making sure that more of the jobless workers qualified for assistance. In addition, the programs needed to be revamped to give equal recognition to female and male work patterns and to remove those provisions that implicitly or explicitly discriminated against women, including disqualifiers that deny benefits to persons who leave employment due to family obligations or to relocate with a spouse.

By 1988, support for this long-standing liberal agenda lost ground to punitive welfare measures, retrenchment of the Social Security and Unemployment Insurance programs, and a push toward privatization. Just as the Republicans used their down time in the 1960s and 1970s to build leadership, create an agenda, and mobilize a base, so liberals and radicals must use this period to both defend social programs and to envision alternatives.

Beyond the short-term recommendations listed above, more far-reaching reforms are needed to enhance the economic security and autonomy of women who receive their income from men, markets, or the state. To escape destitution, women must marry well, find a good job, or turn to the income support programs discussed in this book. Many women do marry, but some do not, and not all marriages last. Few women "marry up," and men in both the working and middle class are losing their jobs or facing stagnant wages. Only a small number of husbandless mothers can count on child support. The fragility of marriage as a route to economic security means that women must also find jobs—ones that lift them above the poverty line—or rely on government programs for their support.

A labor market policy that assured employment, training, or retraining for all those able to work; that set the minimum wage to automatically keep pace with changes in the standard of living; and that tolerated neither unemployment as a means to check inflation nor discrimination of any kind would go far toward assuring that women (and men) could work and be economically secure. Such labor market changes depend heavily on corporate decisions. Instead of simply allowing big business to downsize companies, export production, depress wages, and undermine unions, some politicians have reached the conclusion that corporations must become more socially responsible. By early 1996, President Clinton had proposed raising the minimum wage, protecting pensions, and making health insurance portable from job to job. Going somewhat further, the congressional Democrats recommended tax breaks for corporations that provide their workers with such protections as pensions, education and training, health insurance, and profit sharing or stock purchases. To get the tax break, companies would also have to pay their bosses no more than 50 times as much as their lowest-paid workers, put at least half of their new investments into research and development, keep 90 percent of their new plant investments in the United States, and maintain above-average or improving safety and environmental records. If the Democrats can call for this progressives must demand even greater "responsibility" from corporations.

Given business and industry's heavy reliance on women workers, including many immigrant women, activists should also encourage employers to open all male-dominated and white-dominated jobs to women; eliminate the male/female and white/non-white wage gaps; enforce anti-discrimination and affirmative action laws; and recognize the value of both paid and unpaid labor. Women also need flexible work hours, affordable and quality day care, high-quality health insurance coverage, and other services that accommodate the needs of working mothers. In the final analysis, achieving greater social and economic justice through the labor market will require a full-employment policy with good wages that does not accommodate gender- or race-segregated labor markets.

Given the fragility of today's marriages and labor markets, women also need more comprehensive income support programs: universal cash grants that provide both a decent standard of living for those who cannot work and economic support for those who work in the growing number of jobs that pay below poverty-level wages.

The benefits in such a system would never fall below the official poverty line. Instead, they would be 40 to 50 percent of the median income and tied to the Consumer Price Index. Every step would be taken to avoid the current two-tiered, class-based social welfare system that penalizes and stigmatizes the poor, including making benefits available to women regardless of their marital status or family composition, and empowering them to resist exploitation on the job and at home. That such expanded cash assistance programs have existed for many years in Canada, Western Europe, and Scandinavia indicates that they can readily be accomodated without challenging the foundations of patriarchy and capitalism. In the final analysis, ending poverty will require a guaranteed income for those whose labor the economy cannot absorb and for women seeking to establish autonomous households free of economic dependence on men.

For women who must balance work and family responsibilities, access to male, market, or state income is no longer enough. Both the public and the private sector must also facilitate caretaking work, which is still largely assigned to women, even when they work outside the home. Caretaking work would be enhanced by a national day care program, pre- and post-natal health care, expanded after-school programs, and *paid* family and medical leave, as well as the universal cash grants (as noted above) for women who cannot work or earn too little. This must be accompanied by a universal national health program, an adequate supply of low- and moderate-income housing, equal access to quality education and training, safe workplaces, and a clean environment. Activists should also work for a greater allocation of societal resources to the caretaking role, regardless of who carries it out—mother, father, day care center, or school—and ultimately for the eradication of the gender division of labor.

The history of the trade union, civil rights, women's liberation, and other social movements shows that profound changes such as these are not handed down from above. Rather, they emerge from the organization and mobilization of people seeking to improve their lives. During the 1980s and 1990s, many liberal Democrats and some grassroots advocates concluded that their agenda was best served by toning down their demands, echoing the centrist analysis of social welfare problems and policies, or in some cases accepting it outright. The changed political climate, the desire to retain access to the halls of power, and simple weariness after years of struggle contributed to this rightward shift. But hindsight reveals that this strategy of catering to the right failed. Instead of protecting the liberal agenda against the conservative assault, the silence of many liberals and the absence of a strong alternative voice opened the door to the extremely regressive and repressive agenda which culminated in the Contract with America and Pat Buchanan's fear-mongering campaign for the Republican Party's presidential nomination in 1996. The Republican Party has not been able to turn all of its proposals into programs. But its Contract, followed by the Buchanan campaign, has shifted the political debate around domestic issues even further to the right.

The media, which devoted endless pages to the intricacies of mainstream politics, covered very little of the considerable opposition to the conservative social welfare agenda that arose during the 1980s and 1990s. The elderly and their organizations, such as the American Association of Retired People (AARP), the National Council of Senior Citizens (NCSC), Senior PAC, The Gray Panthers, and the Older Women's League (OWL), regularly flooded Congress and the White House with letters, phone calls, faxes, e-mail, and lobbyists and held many protest demonstrations to fight the government's efforts to shrink Social Security. Calling Reagan's proposed cuts an "abdication of responsibility to the elderly," the AARP vowed to "fight anything we don't like to the bitter end," "to move to something more drastic than letter writing," "to pull out all the stops." Back in 1983, the seventy-seven-year-old leader of the Gray Panthers, Margaret Kuhn, insisted that the Gray Panthers "were tough," "had people of all ages," and would "take to the streets." Since then, the senior lobby has helped to stall major assaults on Social Security and Medicare, and with the Contract "on" America, they are fighting for their lives.

The renewed attack on AFDC recipients has also reinvigorated welfare rights activism both nationally and locally. On June 30, 1987, the twenty-first anniversary of the founding of the National Welfare Rights Organization (NWRO), welfare mothers and organizers formed the National Welfare Rights Union (NWRU), which "rededicated [itself] to the pursuit of social justice for all members of our society, particularly those who have been excluded from the benefits of this nation." The NWRU, with chapters in several states, regularly holds national meetings that draw one to two hundred women (and men) on welfare as well as their supporters from around the country. In the late 1980s, they launched the Up and Out of Poverty Now! campaign. Led by people in poverty, the campaign continues to fight punitive welfare reforms as well as hunger and homelessness, using legislative, court-based, and street-based strategies.

In addition to the NWRU, local welfare rights groups exist in many cities and states around the country, and in some cases they have staved off some of the worst "reforms." This growing activist network includes long-standing welfare rights groups in Massachusetts, New Hampshire, Wisconsin, New York, Missouri, Illinois, and Vermont as well as groups that surfaced in the early 1980s, such as the Welfare Warriors in Schenectady New York; the JEDI Women (Justic, Economic Dignity and Independence for Women) in Salt Lake City, Utah; and the Women's Economic Agenda Project (WEAP) in Oakland, California. Welfare reform activism has cropped up additionally on many college campuses now that local, state, and national welfare reforms are making it nearly impossible for the many thousands, perhaps millions, of welfare recipients in college to stay in school. On February 14, 1994, welfare rights groups in seventy-seven cities and thirty-eight states participated in a national day of action protesting the war on the poor. Since then, this fledgling but growing coalition has played a major role in lobbying state legislatures and successfully urged President Clinton to veto the first welfare reform bill that emanated from Congress. Their work and that of all welfare rights activists is regularly reported by *Survival News* in Boston and the *Welfare Mothers Voice* in Milwaukee—newspapers that are published by and for welfare mothers—as well as by many smaller organizational newsletters.

This time around, middle-class women from feminist organizations, human service coalitions, and the universities have begun to see that welfare is an issue for all women. In varying degrees, they have joined the fight against punitive welfare reforms by working directly with the NWRU and local groups of welfare mothers as well as by lobbying legislators, taking out ads in major newspapers and news magazines, organizing and attending local and national demonstrations, providing resources and technical assistance to welfare rights groups, writing letters to the editor and op-eds, and otherwise adding their voice to the opposition. In addition to the important bridges built to the welfare rights movement by the National Organization of Women (NOW) and the NOW Legal Defense and Education Fund, the Institute for Women's Policy Research, Wider Opportunities for Women, the Center for Reproductive Law and Policy, the National Black Women's Health Project, the American Civil Liberties Union Reproductive Rights Project, the Committee of 100 Women, and the Council of Presidents (of major women's organizations), among other groups, have concluded, in the words from one of their ads, that "A War Against Poor Women is a War Against All Women!" Women's organizations' opposition to punitive welfare reform is now higher on their agenda than ever before. This sort of cross-class and -race solidarity is a first step toward a better tomorrow.

The many paradoxical features of the welfare state make it a productive site for these struggles. While serving the interests of patriarchal capitalism, social welfare policy can also contradict them. On the one hand, social welfare benefits keep capital by increasing purchasing power while lowering the cost of reproducing and maintaining the labor force, mediating the conflicting demand for women's home and market labor, and securing the social peace. At the same time, the benefits cushion the blows of poverty, mediate economic inequality and provide an economic backup to marriage and the labor market. As such, social welfare programs contain the potential to strengthen the political and economic power of women, persons of color, workers, and the poor. They make it financially more possible for women (and men) to survive in a market economy, but also to disrupt it by enabling them to leave unsafe and insecure jobs as well as unsafe and insecure marriages. Perhaps this is why social movements have always struggled to secure welfare state protections against the abuses their constituencies face living and working in a patriarchal, capitalist, and racist society.

The outcomes of these struggles within the welfare state reflect, of course, the contending parties' relative power—a complex equation—at any one moment in time. But victories, however small, can bring significant change. As a system that has the potential to help women and pose a threat to the status quo, fighting to improve it, to democratize it, and to shift its costs from labor to capital makes immediate good sense. In the long run, a movement for women's economic justice must join forces with organizations of similarly underrepresented groups to form a movement that fights for social, economic, and political justice for all.

Notes to the Conclusion

1. Adam Clymer, "Clinton Is Cool to Democrats' Ideas on Shielding U.S. Workers," *The New York Times*, February 29, 1996, p. A17.

2. See, for example, Jennifer G. Schirmer, *The Limits of Reform: Women, Capital and Welfare* (Cambridge: Schenkman Publishing Company, Inc. 1982), which examines the impact of the Danish national program for social equality on the lives of women; and Nancy Fraser, "After the Family Wage: What Do Women Want in Social Welfare?," in *Women and Welfare Reform: A Policy Conference*, Washington D.C., October 23, 1993, co-sponsored by the Institute for Women's Policy Research, Washington, D.C.

3. "The Social Security Crisis," *Newsweek*, January 24, 1982, p. 23; Ben Bedell, "Reagan Ups the Ante, Hits Social Security," *The Guardian*, May 20, 1981, p. 3.

4. Testimony of Marian Kramer, President, National Welfare Rights Union, before the Subcommittee on Human Resources, Government Operations Committee, Washington, D.C., March 10, 1994. p. 1.

Index

About the Author

Mimi Abramovitz is a Professor at the Hunter College School of Social Work in New York City. She has written extensively about the issues of women, poverty, and social welfare policy. In addition to appearing in all the major journals of her profession, Dr. Abramovitz's work has been published in the popular press (including *The New York Times, The Nation, The Washington Post, The San Francisco Examiner, Christian Science Monitor*, and in the grassroots publication *Survival News*, the newspaper of the the welfare rights movement. Dr. Abramovitz, a frequent keynote speaker at local, national, and international conferences, is also interviewed regularly by the print and broadcast media. She received the 1994 annual award for significant contributions to Social Services and Political Activism from New York City Chapter of the National Association of Social Workers. Dr. Abramovitz's is presently researching a book on the history of activism among poor and working class women in the United States during the twentieth century.

About South End Press

South End Press is a nonprofit, collectively-run book publisher with over 200 titles in print. Since our founding in 1977, we have tried to meet the needs of readers who are exploring, or are already committed to, the politics of radical social change.

Our goal is to publish books that encourage critical thinking and constructive action on the key political, cultural, social, economic, and ecological issues shaping life in the United States and in the world. In this way, we hope to give expression to a wide diversity of democratic social movements and to provide an alternative to the products of corporate publishing.

Through the Institute for Social and Cultural Change, South End Press works with other political media projects—*Z Magazine;* Speak Out!, a speakers bureau; and the Publishers Support Project—to expand access to information and critical analysis. If you would like a free catalog of South End Press books, please write to us at: South End Press, 7 Brookline St., Cambridge MA 02139.

Visit South End Press, *Z Magazine*, Z Media Institute, Left On-Line University, and the Chomsky Archive on Z Net at http://www.lbbs.org/sep.

Other Titles Of Interest

For Crying Out Loud: Women's Poverty in the United States
by Diane Dujon and Ann Withorn
$22.00 paper; $40 cloth

Glass Ceilings and Bottomless Pits
Women's Work, Women's Poverty
by Randy Albelda and Chris Tilly
$18.00 paper; $40.00 cloth

Race, Gender, and Work
A Multi-cultural Economic History of Women in the United States
(Revised edition, 1996)
by Teresa Amott and Julie Matthaei
$21.00 paper; $40.00 cloth

Women in the Global Factory
by Annette Fuentes and Barbara Ehrenreich
$6.00 paper

WITHDRAWN

Chaos or Community?
Seeking Solutions, Not Scapegoats, to Bad Economics
by Holly Sklar
$15.00 paper; $35.00 cloth

Sisterhood and Solidarity
Feminism and Labor in Modern Times
by Diane Balser
$10.00 paper; $35.00 cloth

Power on the Job
The Legal Rights of Working People
by Michael Yates
$16.00 pap; $30.00 cloth

Mink Coats Don't Trickle Down
The Economic Attack on Women and People of Color
by Randy Albelda, Elaine McCrate, Edwin Melendez, and June Lapidus
$5.00 paper

Thinking Class
Sketches from a Cultural Worker
by Joanna Kadi
$14.00 paper; $40.00 cloth

How Capitalism Underdeveloped Black America
by Manning Marable
$15.00 paper; $30.00 cloth

Another America
The Politics of Race and Blame
by Kofi Buenor Hadjor
$15.00 paper; $40.00 cloth

When ordering, please include $3.50 postage and handling for the first book
and 50 cents for each additional book. To order by credit card,
call 1-800-533-8478.